Globalisation and Eurasia

Globalisation and Eurasia

Editors
Prof Ajay Patnaik
Prof Tulsiram

KNOWLEDGE WORLD
KW Publishers Pvt Ltd
New Delhi

KNOWLEDGE WORLD

KW Publishers Pvt Ltd

NEW DELHI: 4676/21, First Floor, Ansari Road, Daryaganj, New Delhi 110002
Email: mail@kwpub.in / knowledgeworld@vsnl.net Tel.: +91.11.23263498 / 43528107
MUMBAI: 15 Jay Kay Industrial Estate, Linking Road Extn., Santacruz (W), Mumbai 400054
email: mumbai@kwpub.in Tel.: +91.22.26614110 / 26613505

www.kwpub.in

ISBN 10: 81-87966-82-3
ISBN 13: 978-81-87966-82-1

Published by Kalpana Shukla, KW Publishers Pvt Ltd
4676/21, First Floor, Ansari Road, Daryaganj, New Delhi 110002

Printed and bound in India

Contents

List of Contributors

Peter Rutland teaches at Government Department, Wesleyan University, Middletown, USA.

R. G. Gidadhubli is Professor (Retd.) and former Director, Centre for Central Eurasian Studies, University of Mumbai.

P. L. Dash is Professor and former Director, Centre for Central Eurasian Studies, University of Mumbai.

Arun Mohanty is Associate Professor, Centre for Russian & Central Asian Studies, School of International Studies (SIS), JNU.

Kuldip Singh is Professor, Department of Political Science, Guru Nanak Dev University, Amritsar.

Preeti D. Das is Assistant Professor, Centre for Russian & Central Asian Studies, SIS, JNU.

Phool Badan is Assistant Professor, Centre for Russian & Central Asian Studies, SIS, JNU.

Nandini Bhattacharya is Senior Lecturer, Department of History, Calcutta Girl's College, Kolkata.

Tursunay Usubalieva-Oktai is at the International University of Kyrgyzstan, Bishkek.

Marfua Tokhtakhodjaeva is with "Sharkh and Tavsia"sociological center. Tashkent, Uzbekistan.

Najam Abbas is with Central Asian Studies Unit, Institute of Ismaili Studies, London.

Dilafruz Buranova is a Research fellow at the Institute for the Study of Civil Society, Tashkent, Uzbekistan.

Abel Polese is a Marie Curie Research Fellow, Hannah Arendt Institute, Dresden, Germany.

M. Kaw is Professor, Centre for Central Asian Studies, University of Kashmir, J&K.

Sofia Kasymova is with Gender Education Center, Dushanbe, Tajikistan

Beibit Shangirbayeva is at the Eurasian National University named after L. Gumilev, Astana, Kazakhstan.

Marufjon Usmanov is the Director, Institute for the Study of Civil Society (ISCS), Tashkent, Uzbekistan.

Mirhamdam Abdullayev is the Chief, International Relations Department, ISCS, Tashkent.

Jamaliddin Khakimov is the Director, Public Fund for Support and Development Independent Printed Press and News Agencies of Uzbekistan, Tashkent.

Nirmal Kumar Azad is an Indian Police Service Officer and was Former Private Secretary, Minister of State, Ministry of Human Resource Development, Government of India, Delhi.

Sally Daultrey is Programme Manager, Cambridge Centre for Energy Studies & Central Asia Forum, University of Cambridge, U.K.

Doel Mukherjee has worked with UNDP and other International Organisations.

Vikas Jha is Project Coordinator, NGO PRIA, New Delhi.

Lessya Karatayeva is Associated Professor, Al-Farabi National University, Almaty, Kazakhstan.

Ajay Patnaik is Professor and current Director of the Russian and Central Asian Area Studies Programme, SIS, JNU.

Viachaslau Ivanovich Menkouski is a Professor, Department of History, Belarusian State University, Minsk.

Alexey Dundich is a research scholar at the Moscow State Institute of International Relations (MGIMO), Russia.

Nursin A. Guney is Professor, Yildiz Technical University, Istanbul, Turkey.

Visne Korkmaz is a Lecturer at Yildiz Technical University, Istanbul, Turkey.

Anita Sengupta is a Fellow, Maulana Abul Kalam Azad Institute of Asian Studies, Kolkata.

Bek-Ali Yerzhan is a Lecturer in the Faculty of International Relations, Al-Farabi Kazakh National University, Almaty.

Nalin Kumar Mahapatra is Assistant Professor, Centre for Russian & Central Asian Studies, SIS, JNU.

Enayatollah Yazdani is Assistant Professor, Department of Political Science, Faculty of Administrative Sciences and Economics, University of Isfahan, Isfahan, Iran.

Selcuk Colakoglu is Associate Professor, Adnan Menderes University, Department of International Relations, Nazilli, Turkey.

Adil Kaukenov is Director, Center for Chinese Studies, IWEP under the Kazakhstan's First President Foundation.

Introduction

Consisting of former Soviet Republics, the Eurasian region has drawn international attention due to its geopolitical significance and hydrocarbon resources. The region is a potential major exporter of oil and natural gas and this has prompted the US and other external powers like China, Turkey, Iran, the European Union and India to actively engage themselves in the region. Russia is once again emerging as a central player in the region as it moves towards stabilising its economy and political system. At the same time, given the pluralities within the region, there are multiple conflicts based on ethnic, religious and geopolitical discontents, making the region susceptible to rivalries and conflicts.

The region being vital to India's long term interests, it is essential for Indian scholars and policy makers as well as entrepreneurs to understand the developments happening in Eurasia since Soviet disintegration. The book would help in that process. The articles are by scholars from a wide range of countries including the CIS, India, the US, Turkey, Iran and Europe. This underlines that competing and complementing perspectives have been covered in the book. An informed analysis will help arriving at better understanding and conclusion.

The Eurasian countries liberalised around the same time as India did. The experiences were somewhat similar—central planning and state's role in allocation of resources. It would be interesting for Indian scholars to look at the experience of former Soviet republics. The positives and negatives of globalisation on these societies should not be lost on other countries following similar policies. Post-Socialist economic reforms in Eurasia have several facets. Of particular relevance are those aspects of reforms that have direct bearing on state capabilities and distributive policies. Transition from a centrally planned economy to a market-oriented one has so far been complex. The consequent policy and institutional reforms have been wide-ranging and affect output, income and employment in different ways. The impact on the social sector and the living standard of the population in general needs to be studied.

Globalisation is not about economic processes alone. The political and socio-cultural aspects are as important. Some scholars have linked the rise of social inequality, radical religious and nationalist movements, inter-ethnic strife and rise in sub-national identities in the post-Soviet era to globalisation. The link between globalisation and conflict can ultimately be posited only in the context of the empirical case studies and their findings. One of the issues focused in this book is if and how globalisation has caused or exacerbated social disharmony and conflict by transforming the spatial organisation of social relations and transactions.

Social and cultural dimensions of post-Socialist changes have been discussed in the context of a range of economic and political transformations, economic development, democratisation, role of the state and ruling elite and human security to name but a few. The proposition that links changing alignment of state with society in the context of globalisation to human security/insecurity and social harmony/disharmony has been scrutinised in this book.

Eurasia is also a region where many external powers are seeking to intensify their geopolitical influence, control of resources and their transportation routes. This region, which lies in the extended neighbourhood of India, has had longstanding ties with the subcontinent in the past. The developments in the region have immense security implications for India. In view of India's rapidly increasing energy requirements, the region could be an alternative source of energy. This region's strategic importance for India includes (a) ensuring access to energy and other resources in its neighbourhood (b) containing and eliminating international terrorism emanating from the region (c) strengthening its influence in a region that can deny strategic depth to its potential adversaries. To achieve these objectives, India has to carefully calibrate its strategy of involvement in the region. This book discusses the strategic environment in Eurasia and issues related to security, stability and inter-state relations in Eurasia. The involvement of external powers and their relations with different Eurasian countries is an important theme of the book.

This book is a product of the seminar organised between 9–12 November 2008 by the Centre for Russian and Central Asian Studies, School of International Studies, Jawaharlal Nehru University, New Delhi. It is structured around four sections which are: *Globalisation: Political, Economic and Cultural Dimensions; Sustainable Development, Social Welfare and Human Resources; Civil Society, Informal Networks and Local Governance;* and, *Globalisation: Security and Strategic Dimensions.*

The first section of the book, ***Globalisation: Political, Economic and Cultural Dimensions***, has nine articles dealing with various opportunities and challenges faced by Eurasian states in political, economic and cultural spheres. The onset of globalisation, as Peter Rutland argues in his article *Post-socialist states and the evolution of a new development model*: *Russia and China*, coincided with the shift from autarkic central planning to trade-driven market economies in Russia and China. During the 1990s it was widely assumed that globalisation was more a threat than an opportunity for Russia, since the onset of globalisation seemed causally connected to the collapse of the Soviet state. However, the picture has changed over the past decade, as Russia has regained political stability and experienced rapid and sustained economic growth. Both Russia and China have emerged from the transition to global capitalism without fully embracing the liberal values and institutions of the Washington Consensus. The Russian and Chinese domestic development model combines an acceptance of market forces and global integration with a rejection of liberal democracy and the reaffirmation of nationalism and sovereignty. This, Rutland argues, opens the door to a phase of global development in which the rules of the game are not dictated by the established Western powers. Russia and China want to be rule-makers and not just rule-takers on the international stage.

There are three articles that dwell upon different dimensions of Russian economy. Both Gidadhubli and Dash argue in their articles that Russia is no longer a country of Yeltsin years in chaos. According to P.L. Dash, the Putin years steered the country clear of lethargy. From a debt trapped nation, it has now looked forward to prosperity by liquidating all its western debt that attests deft handling of the country's resources and finance. The country has a sustained economic growth of 6.5 percent over the past few years and hopes to maintain that tempo over foreseeable future. The ruble, once sagging and devalued in 1998 has largely stabilised, gaining strength and appreciating against a declining dollar and has become fully convertible. All these positive tendencies in Russia's economic performances, Dash underlines, are largely due to Russia emerging as a major energy and metal superpower.

Gidadhubli has given exhaustive statistics to show how Russian economy recorded major achievements in its economic development during the last about 8 years and has become the sixth largest economy in the world. At the same time, Russian economy suffers from many shortcomings and challenges—high inflation rates ranging between 8–12 percent per annum; rising inequality in income and opportunities; growing regional economic disparities; unsatisfactory conditions of infrastructure, public health and educational system and so on. The prevalence of these shortcomings indicates that the country faces major challenges in economic development—the need for diversification and modernisation of the economy and reducing the dependence on energy and defence sectors; enhancing economic competitiveness of the country in the global market; promotion of small and medium industries; overcoming the problem of crime and corruption in the country; improving investment climate; reducing state regulation and making Russian economy conducive for creating a genuine market economy and so on, argues Gidadhubli.

The other article on Russian economy by Arun Mohanty focuses on a new dimension in Russian economic policy—strategic planning, which was missing in the first decade after Soviet disintegration. 'Long term planning', which became almost a slang and a hate word in the post-Soviet Russia for long, has finally staged a come back to the discourse on Russia's socio-economic development and economic thought, argues Mohanty. It should be noted that for the first time in almost two decades, the Russian government has adopted a long term development strategy which would guide the country's development up to the year 2020. Implementation of this strategy, approved by the state council, is based on the concept of socio-economic development of the country drafted by the government. This article analyses the salient features of this strategy and highlights its difference from the earlier neo-liberal model executed in Russia.

This section has three other articles dealing with Central Asia. In the recent years, Central Asian countries, prominent among them being Kazakhstan and Kyrgystan, have been trying to model their economies on free-market economy basis, the process which is likely to be halted under the prevailing circumstances, argues Kuldip Singh in his article *Globalising Central Asia in Changing Times: A Critical Note*. The Central Asian countries have been in the transitional phase throughout 1990s and they entered 21st century in the same mode. The impact of present recession would also be felt in the Central Asian countries where already Kazakhstan, which has been the most vocal supporter of economic reforms, has responded to the global crisis by bringing state structures to the rescue of market. The search for self-reliance, the model that the former Soviet Union practiced for a long time and to which Central Asian countries are no strangers, may become more pronounced, underlines Singh.

Preeti Das, in her article *Globalisation: Socio-cultural conflicts and their implications*, identifies some of the major conflicts of socio-cultural nature which have acquired a new and important historical significance due to the influence of globalisation. Identification of conflicts due to the influence of globalisation poses a few basic questions like: how globalisation influences cultural diversity and what are the changes taking place in the nature of socio-cultural conflicts? The author studies Russian society in three phases: pre-Soviet, Soviet and post-Soviet. In search of their identity, the cultures are looking back as to who they were and are trying to bring back some elements of their past. However, through the ages, various collisions between different cultures have given a different shape to those traditions. For example: Russians are no more the same people who were there in pre-Soviet period. Their contact with different communities over the past years in different socio-political conditions, at peaceful times or war time, has changed them drastically without their knowledge of it, concludes Preeti Das.

The next article is *State and democracy in Central Asia* by Phool Badan, who has attempted to study the political system of the Central Asian republics in different phases. The article deals with the steps which have been taken by the leaders and the governments of the Central Asian states to democratise the political system in their respective countries in the post-Soviet period. The leaders of the region have introduced liberal measures in their economic sectors and democratic values in political systems. In this regard, the author would like to conclude that the leaders of the region have adopted the gradual and evolutionary method rather than the revolutionary method to establish democracy in Central Asia.

The pressure of globalisation in the economic sphere was unavoidable for these weak and immature states and they had to a large extent accept a number of demands put forth by the global market dynamics. But how far they succumbed to the ideological and cultural forces of globalisation remains a curious puzzle, says Nandini Bhattacharya in her article *New challenges towards Nation States in Central Asia with the advent of Globalisation*. Globalisation as an all pervasive force has endangered the national ethno-cultural entities and weakened the ideological strength of many nation-states in general. But in Central Asia the advent of globalisation nearly coincided with the rebuilding of nationalism on a broken platform of socialist experiment. The challenges in the reshaping of nationalism are, therefore, manifold of which globalisation is the toughest. How Central Asian states had taken up these challenges with caution, while participating in the forces of globalisation, is a matter of serious academic investigation. In this article Bhattacharya analyses how the processes of globalisation are encountered in these states and societies without sacrificing their national entities.

Tursunay Usubalieva-Oktai in her article, *International trade development of the Kyrgyz Republic within the Central Asian region*, analyses the dynamics of international tradė development of the Kyrgyz Republic with other four countries of the Central Asia (Kazakhstan, Tajikistan, Turkmenistan and Uzbekistan). Nowadays, these countries are faced with challenges and achievements to expand market-based trade with both neighbouring and foreign countries, integrating into the global economy. The article also seeks to show how these above mentioned countries can increase the gains from participation in international trade through regional cooperation in trade policy.

The second section of the book deals with ***Sustainable Development, Social Welfare and Human Resources*** and has eight articles. The first article, *Trafficking of Women: the Case of Uzbekistan* by Marfua Tokhtakhodjaeva, discusses the issue of trafficking in women from the former post-Soviet countries, especially Uzbekistan. There is information about trafficking some women and men to Russia and China for forced labour in cotton and tobacco industries and in construction. In 2005, International Organisation for Migration (IOM) estimated that more than 500 000 Uzbeks were trafficked annually. According to IOM experts, poverty and unemployment are major reasons that many Uzbeks to look for jobs abroad. Other reason is weak information about job opportunities abroad, about legislation and status of illegal migrants and absence of understanding of life in alien countries. According to Tokhtakohdjaeva, trafficking of women is linked with high level of corruption in the country and high level of domestic and cultural violence in Uzbekistani society. The article includes evaluation of reasons of trafficking of women from Uzbekistan.

Najam Abbas's article on *How Globalisation Impacts Tajikistan's Youth: Exploring the Human Development Aspect* examines to what extent an interface with globalisation allows the youth to make constructive contribution to the society, generate social capital vital for a civil society, through creativity in the education phase and connectivity in their practical life. A principal aim of this article is to understand how the process of globalisation influences Central Asia's youth in achieving their aspirations. This article also explores if there is any impact on youth's education and career when globalisation visits their isolated mountain region. This helps to cast a close look at the challenges faced by Tajikistan's youth coping with ensuing changes.

The issue of youth is also discussed in the article of Dilafruz Buranova on *Youth of Uzbekistan in Conditions of Globalisation*. The process of reforming in Uzbekistan has touched all spheres of life: economy, social relations, political system, the state building, agriculture, sphere of national interests, ideology and others. One of the central and key questions in reforming a society at all times is the problems of young generation. Uzbekistan is a country where the basic segment of the population consists of youth. More than third of labouring population are the young people. Besides, every third voter belongs to the youth. Thus, the youth makes the most socially significant part of the population. The views, expectations and decisions of young people influence the development of the state and society. Therefore, underlines Dilafruz, the Uzbek state carries out a special policy directed to the youth which is systematic and progressive, which includes all possibilities for getting education, work and housing.

The impact of globalisation on Central Asia is discussed in the article, *Profiling the Impact of Globalisation in Central Asia: A Perspective,* by Mustaq Kaw in which he argues that globalisation represents a coin with two faces: one symbol of economic prosperity and another social conflicts and contradictions in Central Asian context. No doubt it is exposing the peoples of the region to the new trends of scientific and technological temperament and improving their quality of life and social sustainability. But such benefits are, more or less, specific to particular strata of the society whereas the larger segments, especially in villages, are devoid of them. This is why the villages do not indicate a worthwhile improvement and they relatively wear a medieval look despite the enforcement of numerous schemes of economic restructuring as warranted under the norms of globalisation. In addition, globalisation is contributing to environmental and ecological disaster as huge firms, factories, business houses, occupy the spaces that were actually meant for agriculture operation. In view of this, there is a great need of preserving the Central Asian culture from the onslaught of globalisation, argues Kaw.

Sofia Kasymova's article in this section, *Globalisation of the Labour Market and the status of women in post-Soviet Tajikistan,* looks at the impact of globalisation on gender relations that could be illustrated by the changes in traditional status of Tajik women, majority of whom are living in rural areas and under the strict control of family and rural community. Economic crisis together with the reduction of social policy of the Tajik government provoked an increase of women's employment outside of the home. Tajik women in many cases took on their shoulders the role of the bread-winner that was not peculiar to them before. Tajik women's labour migration is a new phenomena and it is not studied yet in the context of globalisation of the labour market. That is why it is not only academically but also practically important to study problems of women labour migration, she argues

Beibit Shangirbayeva's article, *Aspects of providing security in international law-making of Kazakhstan*, discusses the international law-making activity of the contemporary Kazakhstan, which aims at ensuring long-term national interests such as self-preservation (security) and development of the country, including building domestic economic capacity. This in turn promotes integration into the world economy and world community based on principles of partnership. The article argues how the well-balanced and multi-vector foreign policy of the Republic of Kazakhstan is reflected in its international law-making.

The third section of the book is on ***Civil Society, Informal Networks and Local Governance*** and contains eight articles. M.Usmanov's article, *Forming a civil society: The Uzbek experience*, focuses on the traditional customs and institutions that are shaping the Uzbek civil society. A closer look at the development of civil society in Uzbekistan shows that Tashkent is adopting a pragmatic policy in implementing the policy through a stage by stage approach where civil society can co-exist with larger democratic political structure. Usmanov points to the Uzbek *Mahalla*, a unique traditional system of self-governing institution of citizens, that is playing a more and more important role in the structure of civil society.

The other article on Uzbekistan's civil society, *Globalisation and role of state in forming a civil society*, by another Uzbek scholar, M.Abdullayev, underlines the necessity of maintaining social harmony in a transitional social system. A strong society is the backbone of a transitional social system. This is due to the fact that unless and until a strong society comes into being it is very difficult to transfer important functions to civil society groups. At the same time, Abdullayev argues that since these civil society networks are in a nascent form they need the state structures for implementing programmes and policies.

Jamaliddin Khakimov's article on *Role of mass media in the formation of information society in Uzbekistan* looks at the role of mass media in Uzbekistan as an efficient instrument for forming a new way of thinking and understanding among the population. For this purpose mass media should become free and objective voice of the people's views and will and active protectors of their interests. At the same time he cautions that in market conditions it is necessary to pay serious attention to professional ethics of journalists. In information society, ethics of a journalist as a separate author and ethics of journalism as a social institution can contradict each other. In general, Khakimov concludes that ethical approach of Uzbek journalists in the process of civil society building is divided into the following stages: ethics of searching for and selecting theme; ethics of communicating with people during the collection of information; ethics of evaluating the facts; ethics of proving their view and argument; ethics of mutual relations with the audience; ethics of mutual relations with colleagues.

There are three articles by Indian scholars analysing different aspects of civil society in India. Nirmal Kumar Azad in his article, *Policing and the Role of Civil Society*, argues that though the role of civil society in policing in India is promising; it is still at nascent stage. Many organisations have been working to reform the system though multiple efforts. The democratisation process of the system is worked through advocacy, training, sensitisation and partnership. It needs improved interaction, commitment and hard work to bring accountability in the system. Efforts are on by both the civil society and the government to improve things and make the system user friendly. At present it is felt that the civil society could help police as being a watchdog for keeping checks and balance in the system. Also, it can support police through research and training module in different areas of policing. Public opinion documented by civil society should also be fed to the police on regular basis to evaluate their performance. And above all, concludes Azad, civil society should become a genuine partner in making policing more democratic, equitable and accountable to the people.

The article by Doel Mukherjee on *Civil Society in India: A partner in democracy* examines the progression of civil society from pre-independence to the present period and argues whether civil society has been a partner in democracy building or has it slowed the process with unrealistic arguments which are contrary to fast development. Also the paper questions whether civil society matters in a democracy. NGOs still have a long way to go before they can substantively influence the political process and make a huge impact in governance and democracy. There are numerous gaps left by the government, sometimes by intention, lack of funds and lack of awareness. These are the gaps that many NGOs have tried to fulfill. Mukherjee concludes that government and civil society partnership can remain edgy and it should be so, because the idea is not to get co-opted to the existing systems and create cliques, but to deliberate and constantly find alternatives to government policies. The state can only think along a certain line, but someone has to think out of the box for all those who don't fit into the regular schemes, and no one can do it better than activists, practitioners, experts, field workers, journalists, trade unionists and all those who can voice a concern for a better India.

Vikas Jha looks at the local self-government in India in his article, *Panchayati Raj System in India and the Role of Civil Society*. The enactment of the 73rd and 74th Constitutional Amendments in 1992 was a defining moment in the history of democratic evolution in India. These amendments provided the constitutional framework for establishing local self-government institutions in rural and urban areas. It turned the nearly fifty years of centralised model of development on its head and paved way for democratic decentralisation where emphasis was on bottom-up and participative planning, access of community to control over natural and human resources and implementation of development programmes. This article elaborates how and why democratic decentralisation has not realised its real potential and it suffers from some deficits.

It is difficult to estimate interdependence of the transnational terrorism and globalisation without precise definition. The article by Lessya Karatayeva on *Transnational Terrorism in the Information Space of Kazakhstan* discusses the threat of terrorism, proceeding from the premise that this threat is always constructed. Karatayeva draws attention to the information space of Kazakhstan, which borders on the countries that have undergone terrorist attacks though no terrorist act has been registered officially in Kazakhstan. The article discusses the features of the articulation of the transnational terrorist threats in various segments of Kazakhstan's information space. Karatayeva concludes that the population of Kazakhstan as a whole shares the official discourse of the transnational terrorism, however, in a passive mode.

The final article in this section is by Sally Daultrey on *Dynamics of societal responses to environmental change in Jammu and Kashmir*. Rapid environmental change in the Jammu and Kashmir region, within the broader dynamics of climate change across the western Himalayas, is impacting the quality and availability of natural resources with implications for the livelihoods of its people. Population migration in the region places further stress on the already fragile environment and limited natural resources, and displacement of people leads to loss of indigenous knowledge about survival and resource management (especially of its limited water resources and arable lands) in the challenging environment of the Himalayas and Karakoram. Population migration and instability is not directly linked to the impact of environmental change, however the effects of climate change are compounding the stresses placed on the region's fragile environment and the observed societal responses, suggests Daultry.

The fourth and final section of the book ***Globalistation: Security and Strategic Dimensions*** contains eleven articles. Energy has emerged as the most important factor that is shaping the geopolitics of Eurasia. Ajay Patnaik in his article The *Geopolitics of Energy in Eurasia* argues that significance of energy is not just for its value as a commodity in short supply in most parts of the world, but due to its role as an instrument to advance the strategic goals of global and regional powers in the Eurasian space. Such has been the game that those who cannot play it in strategic terms and merely look to the region as a source of oil and gas are bound to become marginal beneficiaries of the energy wealth of Eurasia. Energy is part of a larger strategic competition between the two main players—Russia and the USA—with some regional powers playing second fiddle in the process. Energy has been the legitimising factor that hides the real strategic games. The seeming gains to the energy producing and transit countries of Eurasia are a charade. These states are being used as pawns and the benefits from being on either side of the super-power, concludes Patnaik.

Viachaslau Ivanovich Menkouski's article on *Republic of Belarus between the West and the East in the Context of Globalisation* discusses how the specific geopolitical features of Belarus are connected with its location on the boundary of East-Slavic and West-European civilisations. The Byelorussians themselves do not consider the boundary position as a problem. Instead, they look at it as natural advantage for a variety of cultural and economic relations with neighbours. Belarus essentially defends the idea of good-neighbourhood and does not consider any state as a potential opponent. As a result, underlines Menkouski, the Belarusian state, considering its geopolitical as well as social and cultural realities, adopted the multi-vector foreign policy directed at mutually advantageous relations with the West and the East.

Since the very beginning of the collapse of the USSR, the United States of America became a politically and economically important actor in the Central Asia region. The only superpower in the world, which has been having sustainable interests in the region, has gained a big influence in the region during 1990s and has gradually fulfilled a big part of post soviet vacuum, according to Alexey Dundich in his article *Global Stability with 'American face': problem or solution for Central Asia?*. A lot of American researchers and analysts see this influence as positive. However, in post-Soviet states many specialists have the opposite opinion. This article of Dundich analyses the research works of both American and post-Soviet researchers in the context of global stability and discusses the strengths and weaknesses of American presence in Central Asia.

The recent row between the West and Tehran government has created an impact not only in the Middle East but also beyond. And it is widely expected that the repercussions of the crises will be felt in Eurasia. That is why unless this important issue is solved, all the actors in the region (Russia, India, China, Central Asian states, etc.) are expected to be influenced negatively—particularly in the field of arm race, argues Nursin A. Guney in the article *Nuclear Crises in the Realm of Eurasian Security: The Iranian Crises and Future of NPT*. Therefore, the author underlines, Iranian crises and its possible impacts on the region would point out once again the importance of arms control regimes and credibility of the NPT agreement. Discussing the Western approach and the conditions of stability in Eurasia together, this article tries to examine possible policies to cope with nuclear issue in the Eurasian region.

The article of Visne Korkmaz is on *The Nexus of Globalisation and Regionalism within the Eurasian Security: Shanghai Cooperation Organisation*. It is still too early to reach a conclusion regarding the successes and/or failures of regional cooperation in Eurasia via the SCO. However, both the solution of border conflicts in the region and the maintaining of (relative) peace, which is apparently the case at the moment even though there are number of instability sources alive, points to the importance of regional security issues for actors facing the difficulty of nation-building and region-building processes simultaneously. Unfortunately, the unilateralism in security policies and globalisation, which brings new threats on the scene, cannot ease the adaptation to the new security environment for either the old or new states of the region. Therefore, regional instruments, such as the SCO, become important variables which make balancing and bandwagoning possible, concludes Korkmaz.

Anita Sengupta's article deals with *Globalisation and Eurasian geopolitical discourses* particularly in the context of Eurasia. At the end of the Cold War, anti-geopolitics dominated the understanding of global politics. It was assumed that globalisation and a free flow of goods, money, ideas and people would make traditional geopolitical assumptions defunct. However, expectations that globalisation would transform international politics did not work out. As a consequence, focus on the relationship between geopolitics, geography and strategy again assumed significance. The return of geopolitics was followed by the revival of certain geopolitical concepts and models that had become largely defunct in the recent past. Since 1990s, the use of the term and concept of the 'new' great game and the 'heartland' overshadowed the analysis of events in Central Asia and the Transcaucasus. Most of these had geopolitical references or allude to them as significant. This paper examines the resurgence of interest in geopolitics in Eurasia in the context of a vastly changed global situation. It will also bring into focus a 'civilisational' dialogue that has emerged as an alternative to this realist understanding and its significance in Eurasian discourses.

The other five articles in this section deal with countries in the neighbourhood like India, China, Iran and Turkey. Bek-Ali Yerzhan in his article *Central and South Asia in the globalized world* draws attention to the huge opportunities for mutual cooperation between Central Asia and South Asia. Advancing regional and cross-regional cooperation in the globalised world requires strong political commitment by the participating countries. There is need to ensure the right balance between improving hard and soft infrastructure. Improving regional and cross-regional physical (or 'hard') infrastructure,

such as roads and bridges, and physical customs facilities, is important to facilitate cross-border movements of goods and people. However, policy and procedural reforms of 'soft' infrastructure, such as harmonisation of standards, liberalisation of transit barriers and streamlining of customs procedures, are just as important if benefits of regional and cross-regional cooperation are to be realised. Therefore, underlines Yerzhan, interaction and the building of synergies between hard and soft infrastructure need to be enhanced in regional and cross regional cooperation activities in the globalised world.

Nalin Mohapatra's article *India's energy diplomacy in CIS* critically examines India's energy interest in the Eurasian region. Mohapatra foresees that energy resources of CIS states will play a catalytic role in sustaining India's economy as it is an energy deficient country. In this regard he thinks that India's energy policy towards this region is a part of broader Indian diplomacy in this region. Mohapatra argues for developing alternative pipeline routes, rather than simply focusing on the proposed Iran-Pakistan-India (IPI) or the Turkmenistan-Afghanistan-Pakistan-India (TAPI) pipelines to secure oil and gas from the CIS states.

Enayatollah Yazdani discusses Iran's relations with Central Asia in his article, *The Importance of Central Asia for the International Powers: A case study of Iran-Central Asia relations*. This article explores the importance of Central Asia for the international powers in the age of globalisation. It addresses the factors which have made the region important to those powers. Yazdani argues that with the opening up of Central Asia, those interested actors have become engaged in the region for different combinations of geopolitical, economic, security, cultural and religious reasons. Iran has similarly sought to improve its ties with the region.

Turkey's role in the region has been discussed in the article, *The Turkic Brotherhood Policy and Its Effects on Globalisation Process in Central Asia,* by Selcuk Colakoglu. The end of the Cold War was a historical turning point not only for international system, but also for Central Asia and Turkey. The collapse of the Soviet Union has created 15 newly independent states, and five of them have common cultural, ethnic and religious links with Turkey. Therefore, declaring independence of Azerbaijan, Kazakhstan, Kyrgyzstan, Uzbekistan and Turkmenistan in 1991 was also an emotional development for Turkey and Turkic Republics. Newly emerging Turkic states, which have great deal of economic and strategic potentials, offered new opportunities for Turkey's foreign policy. The article focuses on Turkey's facilitator role toward Turkic Republics to integrate them to international community. It also analyses whether the 'Turkish Model' was helpful to the Central Asian and Caucasian states in the process of globalisation.

Adil Kaukenov in his article, *Chinese policy in the Central Asia*, discusses different steps taken by China to strengthen its position in the region. Strong presence of China and Chinese capital in the strategically important economic sectors of the Central Asian countries, presence of a transport-communication infrastructure connecting Central Asia with PRC etc. create conditions in which no change of events (a leadership change, dominant influence of another power etc.) would make the Chinese factor less significant.

Ajay Patnaik **Tulsiram**

Section I

Globalisation: Political, Economic and Cultural Dimensions

Post-socialist States and the Evolution of a New Development Model: Comparing Russia and China

Peter Rutland

Introduction

The onset of globalisation in the 1980s-90s coincided with the shift of China and Russia from autarkic central planning to trade-driven market economies. The Chinese leadership consciously embraced globalisation and saw it as an opportunity rather than a threat. The reaction in Russia has been quite different, since during the 1990s Russia seemed to be suffering from the impact of globalisation. Some observers even argue that globalisation was in fact one of the causes behind the collapse of the Soviet state. However, the picture has changed over the past decade as Russia has regained political stability and experienced rapid and sustained economic growth, while continuing a policy of greater integration with the global economy.

Both Russia and China have emerged from the transition to global capitalism as stronger and more stable states. Yet neither of them has fully embraced the values and institutions of the 'Washington Consensus'—the belief that the best economic policy is one of free trade, freely floating currencies, the lifting of government regulation and the privatisation of state-owned industries. Nor do they conform with the 'Washington Hypothesis'—the idea that globalisation promotes democratisation[1]. The Russian and Chinese development model combines an acceptance of market forces and global integration with a rejection of neoliberal economics and liberal democracy, and the reaffirmation of nationalism and sovereignty.

The first section of this article compares and contrasts the evolution of the Chinese and the Russian economic systems over the past two decades.

We find some sharp differences and a few points of similarity. One important debate is the extent to which it was the initial conditions or the leadership choices which determined the outcome of the transition. A third factor, the external economic environment, must also be taken into account. The final section of the article summarises the common features that have emerged in 2008 and speculates whether this convergence amounts to the emergence of a new development model—one that could even contribute to the evolution of a new type of international economic order.

A Tale of Two Transitions

Russia and China are large autonomous countries with strong state traditions. They both turned their backs to the global capitalist system in the 20th century and adopted communist systems. Prior to that, they had emerged historically as land empires in the centre of Eurasia. This left them with a legacy of a strong central state with a distinct identity and legitimacy. Correspondingly, they had weak traditions of civil society. The state acted as a gatekeeper for their interactions with the outside world, which was seen as hostile and threatening. Both had been subjected to military defeats in the 19th-20th centuries and subsequent loss of territory, and had then emerged bloodied but victorious from World War Two. Both Russia and China have distinct cultures, tracing their roots and maintaining their identities outside of European culture. However, Russia's interactions with Europe were much more intense, so Russia is a hybrid with strong European elements unlike China. Both countries' elites currently see themselves—and have long seen themselves—as economically backward compared to the West (since the early 19th century in the case of China, since the 16th century in the case of Russia). 'Modernisation' is a term that Chinese and Russian leaders still use when discussing their goals.

Under communist rule, their state-owned, centrally-planned economies had many common features and stood in stark contrast to the Western model of democratic capitalism. But in the 1990s, both countries abandoned many elements of their model. At first, they seemed to be headed in opposite directions: Russia towards Western integration and market democracy, while China strove to preserve its authoritarian rule alongside limited opening to foreign trade and investment. Russia experienced rapid political liberalisation under the General Secretary Mikhail Gorbachev, followed by *system collapse* and the break-up of the Soviet Union. China embarked on a *managed transition* that involved the step-by-step introduction of elements of capitalism while the Chinese Communist Party (CCP) retained a monopoly of political power. The

Tiananmen Square crackdown in 1989 led some to believe that Communist China was experiencing the same profound contradictions that were sundering the Soviet system. However, the Chinese political system to this day remains intact, and expectations that the introduction of capitalism must inevitably lead to the introduction of democracy have eroded[2].

Table 1: Development Indicators, 2006

	China	Russia
Life expectancy (years)	72	66
Fertility (births per woman)	1.8	1.3
Infant mortality (per 1000 births)	24	16
GNI per capita (Atlas, $)	2,010	5,800
GNI per capita (PPP, $)	4,700	12,810
Agriculture as % of GDP	12	5
Inflation (%)	3.3	15.7
Gross Domestic Capital formation as % of GNI	44	21
Phone subscribers (per 100 people)	63	137
Internet users (per 100 people)	10.4	18.0
High tech as % of manufacturing exports	30	9
Merchandise trade as % of GNI	66	47
Government revenue as % of GDP	9.6	28.7
Foreign direct investment (net inflow, $ bn)	78	12.5
Exports as % of GNI	40	34

Source: World Development Indicators, www.worldbank.org, accessed 20 October 2008

China's transition from state socialism is generally considered a success, while Russia's is generally considered a failure. China has doubled its GDP every decade, and has lifted 400 million people out of absolute poverty—perhaps the largest single increase in human welfare in world history. In key development indicators such as phone lines, internet usage, life expectancy and high-tech exports, it has closed the gap with Russia. These economic achievements have translated into a substantial rise in China's global status, a process symbolised by the success of the 2008 Olympic Games. In contrast, the Soviet state lost half its territory and population, and the Russian Federation has struggled to maintain its status as a great power. Although the implosion of the Soviet Union was shocking enough to Chinese leaders, equally disturbing was the collapse of the Russian society that occurred after 1991—economic recession, an upsurge in crime and lawlessness, a falling birth rate and a rising death rate, and the war in Chechnya. The Chinese leadership tried to learn from

Moscow's mistakes. They scrutinised the developments in the Soviet Union very closely and adjusted their policies accordingly[3]. They concluded that not only they must be willing to use repression, but also that reforms were needed to increase the state's capacity to rule and to bolster the regime's legitimacy in the eyes of the people. In contrast, there is little evidence of Russian leaders making any serious effort to draw lessons from China's success.

Initial Conditions

The initial conditions at the onset of transition in Russia and China were very different. Moreover, the political leadership of the two countries pursued radically different transition strategies. Despite starting in different places and heading in different directions, the two countries are now converging on a similar model of state-led development in the face of common global challenges and opportunities.

By the late 1980s, Russia was a mature industrial economy with an educated urban labour force. It was a military superpower equal to the United States which saw itself as a world leader in science and technology. At the onset of its transition in the late 1970s, China was still overwhelmingly agricultural (80 percent peasants compared to 15 percent in Russia), with a small and uncompetitive industrial base and minimal scientific capacity. China struggled with the problem of excess population relative to the available land, but at least this meant it had a pool of cheap labour. Russia faced a declining population and chronic labour shortage but was resource rich, while China was relatively resource poor.

Not only were the economic conditions quite different, but the political evolution of the two countries prior to 1980 was also very distinct, although both Chinese and Russian elites saw the need for reform. The CCP was rebuilding in the wake of the Cultural Revolution (1966-76) which had seriously damaged its organised coherence, governing capacity and popular legitimacy. The Soviet Union had experienced 20 years of stability under the General Secretary Leonid Brezhnev, but this period had produced rising corruption, bureaucratic ossification, economic stagnation and a number of costly foreign policy adventures (notably, the invasion of Afghanistan and a renewed arms race with the US).

An obvious difference is that while China was ethnically homogenous (90 percent Han), the Soviet Union was ethnically diverse. Ethnic Russians made up only 53 percent of the Soviet population and 80 percent of the Russian Federation. It might be argued that this ethnic homogeneity should have made it easier for Beijing to introduce democracy but Chinese leaders had other reasons to fear democratic contestation—strong regional differences in the vast country and a huge pool of desperately poor peasants.

Different Paths

Not only were the initial conditions different in the two countries, but also the respective national leaderships chose divergent development strategies. It is often said that the key difference between Russia and China was the *sequencing* of reform. The argument goes that Gorbachev's big mistake was to opt for political liberalisation first and economic reform later. Clearly, the Chinese leadership cannot be accused of committing that error. In Gorbachev's defence, however, it can be argued that economic reform without political reform had been tried by a succession of Soviet leaders since the 1950s and was attempted again by Gorbachev in 1985-87. It was the failure of these earlier economic reforms in the face of bureaucratic intransigence that forced Gorbachev to embrace political reform.

Western scholars had predicted that political liberalisation would cause problems for economic reform in the socialist bloc. Subsequent events proved them right but they got the political mechanism wrong. In an influential 1991 book, Adam Przeworksi argued that democratisation in Eastern Europe would empower the workers, who would mobilise to protect their state-guaranteed jobs[4]. Thus political reform would enable the interest groups created by the socialist economy to block radical economic reform.

As it turned out, this did not happen. It was nationalism and not worker unrest that sealed the fate of the Communist states in Europe. In Poland, the workers were swept up in the nationalist project of getting out from under Soviet influence by joining the West, which meant embracing capitalism. In Russia, the political turmoil that the country experienced in 1989-93 was so severe that the workers were politically neutralised and were unable to prevent President Boris Yeltsin's embrace of liberal market reforms. What happened next was equally unexpected: the emergence as if from nowhere of a small group of powerful oligarchs, who helped to keep Yeltsin in power while blocking the second wave of reforms that liberals had hoped for.

Second, there is the contrast in *pace* of reform. The conventional wisdom is that China followed a gradual path while Russia embraced shock therapy in 1992. The Chinese were burned by a century of failed efforts at radical change and were thus philosophically committed to incrementalism[5]. In contrast, Moscow had grown tired of decades of incremental change and the crisis conditions of early 1992 seemed to leave Yeltsin with no option but to embrace radical reform.[6] It also reflected his advisors' conviction that the only way to break with central planning was to enforce hard budget constraints and market-clearing prices as part of an integrated package. The reformers also made a Przeworksi-type argument, about a political window of opportunity, which said that Yeltsin had to capitalise on his power in early 1992 before the anti-reform forces rallied and used the democratic process to unseat him. Freed from the threat of a democratic turnover of power to reactionaries, the CCP leadership could afford to take a more gradual reform path.

The Politics of Transition

In retrospect, it was neither the sequencing nor the pace of reform that was the crux of the problem. The key question is more basic—the need to maintain political power and state capacity. Putting economic reform first allowed the Chinese state to maintain the political capacity to manage the process, correcting for mistakes and imbalances as they arose. In a more negative light, Minxin Pei argues that it gave the political elite the resources they needed to maintain their repressive system of rule[7]. In contrast, Gorbachev threw out the very tools with which he hoped to promote economic reform. Gorbachev's reforms disrupted the organisational cohesion of the Communist Party apparatus and directly undermined its ideological legitimacy[8]. His reforms first destroyed the party and then the Soviet state itself. In their struggle to hold onto power, both Gorbachev and Yeltsin used divide-and-rule strategies that split the elite and fragmented political institutions.

Chinese leaders seem to have managed to avoid such divisions, despite—or perhaps because of—the fact that the CCP leadership was historically much more ridden by factionalism than its Soviet counterpart. The Chinese learned their lesson from the Cultural Revolution and the Soviet break-up. Despite deep disagreements over policy (such as over Tiananmen[9]), they have managed to preserve a united front in the public arena. They have also undergone two relatively smooth transitions in the top leader position (from Deng Xiaoping to Jiang Zemin in 1997, and then to Hu Jintao in 2002) without experiencing a political crisis.[10] This is something Russia has not been able to manage. Yeltsin's nomination of Putin as his successor in December 1999 was a fairly smooth transition, though it was accompanied by the second war in Chechnya. The transition from Putin to Dmitry Medvedev is not yet a clean break.

Looking back, one sees a surprising pattern. In both Russia and China, the highest level of democratic debate occurred in the late 1980s, during the early experimental period when various reform paths were being debated by the national leadership. Over time, as the economic reforms eventually took over, the scope for political dissent actually shrank. This is the opposite of what one would expect from modernisation theory, which expects socio-economic development to produce new constituencies (workers, the middle class and businessmen) that demand a say in decision-making.[11]

In the wake of the Tiananmen crackdown in China, oppositionists were jailed or driven from the country; reformists were purged from the CCP leadership and intellectuals lost their faith in the possibility of the 'fifth modernisation'—democracy. Nevertheless, Deng Xiaoping in his 1992 tour of the south made the historic decision to accelerate economic reform in a bid to build a new basis for CCP legitimacy and thereby prevent a repeat of 1989. This danger was magnified by the dramatic implosion of the Soviet state at the end of 1991. The failure of the August 1991 coup attempt by Soviet hardliners was a blow to CCP leftists who thought that repression was a sufficient basis for rule. Subsequent political reforms in China have been limited to the spread of electoral competition at village level, introduced in 1988; a strengthening of the oversight role of national and local legislatures and steps to bolster the rule of law and fight corruption[12]. None of these measures have been allowed to infringe on the authority of the CCP. The CCP has undergone some organisational reforms to maintain its effectiveness post-Mao: most notably, the 2002 decision to allow private entrepreneurs to become CCP members.[13]

Ironically, the quality of Russian democracy arguably peaked in 1990-91, the last year of the Soviet Union. In 1992-96, politics settled down into an ugly standoff between a reformist president and an opposition-dominated parliament and after 1996, the level of competition steadily eroded from election to election.

The most well-known democracy index is that compiled by Freedom House, grading the level of Political Rights (PR) and Civil Liberties (CL) on a 1-7 scale, with 1-2 being 'free' and 6-7 as 'unfree'. Freedom House regarded the new Russian Republic as 'partly free', ranking it 3 for PR and 4 for CL from 1993 through 1997. Russia's grade slipped to 4/5 in 1999 and 5/5 in 2000-2003. In 2004, Russia was relegated to the 'unfree' category, with a 6 for PR and 5 for CL, which has stayed its rating through 2008.[14]

There has been much less variation in the political climate in China, especially since 1989. Freedom House scored China a 7/7 from 1972 through 1977, when it jumped to 6/6. In 1989, it slipped back to 7/7 and stayed there until 1998, when it rose to 6 for CL and 7 for PR. Freedom House has kept that score for China through 2008.

In both countries, the traditions of one-party rule have created a culture inimical to pluralism, in which politics is seen as a 'winner takes all' game. The key liberal argument for pluralism is that you cannot always be sure of being a winner, so it is better to share power and grant rights to all political actors. But in neither country has the political elite accepted this idea. Both countries have preserved one-party systems based on clientilistic networks in which particularism rather than pluralism is the structuring principle of political life.

The Economics of Transition

There are many differences between the Russian and Chinese economic reform strategies. Russia's government unleashed a hastily assembled package of radical reforms in 1992. Beijing's reforms were middle-up rather than top-down—the centre encouraged and tolerated initiative from below, and local entrepreneurs and politicians responded to the challenge. The operative metaphor in China was 'feeling the stones as you cross the river'[15] while in Russia, one of the reformers' favourite sayings was that 'you cannot cross a chasm in two jumps'[16]. Crucially, the CCP preserved the capacity to monitor the implementation of the reforms and adjust them when necessary. While the Chinese talked about 'growing out of the plan', Russia was effectively 'falling out of the plan'[17].

Russia launched the 'shock therapy' in 1992 but the government was unable to control monetary and fiscal deficits, which meant that high inflation and macroeconomic instability prevailed until stabilisation was finally achieved in 1999. The privatisation programme was hijacked by a small group of well-connected insiders, leaving the Russian public feeling cheated and the state treasury empty. Foreign investors were largely shut out from the 'crown jewels' of the economy—oil, gas and metals. Although the basic structures of a market economy had emerged by 1999, yet free entry was limited, oligopolistic rents were high and the incentives to efficiency and investment were low. By 2001, the country's 23 largest firms accounted for 30 percent of Russia's GDP and these were effectively controlled by a mere 37 individuals[18]. In addition to the national oligarchs, many regional markets were controlled by local monopolists.

After Putin was elected president in March 2000, he started an energetic campaign to strip the oligarchs of their political influence. Putin both consolidated and rolled back the market reforms. On the one hand, he created a more robust legal infrastructure, increased taxation and oversaw eight years of economic growth, averaging 6 percent a year, while on the other hand, he strengthened state control over key industries, and a new system of state corporatism took shape. The post-Soviet state bureaucracy, spearheaded by a team of ex-KGB officials, had asserted its dominance over the newly-minted capitalist oligarchs.

China started off in 1978 by freeing peasant farmers from plan controls through the Household Responsibility System. This boosted output and also started releasing labour for factory work. Then local state authorities were allowed to set up profit-seeking Town and Village Enterprises (TVEs). State Owned enterprises (SOEs) were likewise freed to become more entrepreneurial. The seventh five year plan that began in 1986 encouraged coastal regions to engage in manufacturing assembly for foreign markets. Between 1978 and 2003, China recorded an annual growth rate of 9.4 percent, while per capita income rose from $150 in 1978 to $1,700 in 2005. China maintained the state industry sector with its social guarantees, initially through budget subsidies and then through soft credits via the four state-controlled banks. The rapid growth of the private sector meant that the state sector's share of the industrial labour force fell from 80 percent in 1978 to 29 percent in 2000[19]. Small and medium SOEs began to be privatised in 1994, though the government avoided using this term and instead talked of restructuring and asset transfers. In 1997, a major programme of restructuring SOEs was launched, leading to wage arrears and layoffs. The government softened the blow by introducing severance pay at 60 percent of the previous wage for three years. Overall, the state planners showed caution and flexibility in introducing these reforms. For example, price controls on grain were lifted in 1993 but restored in 1995 after the move triggered shortages and price gouging. In 2001, controls were once again eased in grain consuming regions.[20]

While agriculture was the initial driver of the Chinese, in Russia the organisation of farm production was largely untouched by the reforms. There was a divergence in the pace of change in the opposite direction in the case of banking. The Chinese state kept firm control over the banking system, while in Russia the lifting of controls led to the sprouting of 1,500 private banks, many of which collapsed in the financial crisis of August 1998. Russia's mass privatisation programme converted state firms into legally independent corporations, in line with Western theory stressing the importance of creating clear property rights in a rule of law system. China pursued a very different path: no mass privatisation, but the evolution of a hybrid model of SOEs and TVEs behaving as profit-seeking entities with unclear property rights. These Chinese enterprises were also deeply embedded in strong local and even family networks[21]. One important step was the 1998 decision ordering the CCP and army to divest themselves of businesses. In practice, the Russian approach failed to generate the transparent and secure property rights that the reformers claimed as their goal. There were hundreds of cases of organised crime groups seizing control of enterprises by force, and dozens of cases of state officials seizing firms through manipulation of tax arrears and other instruments. Putin's expropriation of the leading private oil company Yukos in 2003-05 and Shell's forced sale of its majority stake in Sakhalin II in December 2006 are two striking examples of the political contingency of property rights.

So at the end of the day, the weakness of property rights is something that unites, rather than divides, the Russian and Chinese cases. And in neither Russia nor China has the state given up control over key strategic sectors such as telecommunications or power generation.[22] Small steps have been taken in both countries to promote competition in these sectors and create a modern regulatory framework, but in practice political dirigisme is still decisive. Another similarity is that in both countries, the tax-gathering capacity of the central state shrank and then recovered in the course of reforms. In China, central government revenues fell from 31 percent of GDP in 1978 to 10.7 percent in 1995, rebounding to 17.1 percent in 2001.[23] Similarly, Russian federal revenues fell to 9.2 percent of GDP in 1998, recovering to 17.1 percent in 2001.[24] But after 2001 the two countries drew apart, with China's state revenues shrinking to 10 percent while Russia's grew to 28 percent, thanks to the oil boom.

Regional and social inequalities sharply increased in both countries as a result of the reforms. In Russia, the Gini coefficient rose from 0.29 in 1992 to 0.40 in 1997, where it stayed through 2008, while in China it went from 0.28 in 1978 to around 0.45 in 2000.[25] In Russia, there was a more extreme concentration of wealth in the hands of the new oligarchs than in China. This was a result of the more uncontrolled nature of the privatisation, the weakness of law enforcement agencies and the resource-based character of the economy. By 2006, *Forbes* magazine was reporting 33 dollar billionaires in Russia, but 'only' eight in China.[26] Their ranks had risen to 87 by 2008, putting Russia in second place after the US. In contrast to the Russian oligarchs, who were in effective control of the political system between 1993 and 2000, Chinese tycoons stayed in the political shadows, colluding with regional political bosses but avoiding anything like a direct challenge to the national state[27].

Corruption is a debilitating problem for both countries; a drag on efficiency and a turn-off for foreign investors.[28] Its practice is so commonplace at both high and low levels that bribery and clientilism seem to be the glue holding the political system together.[29] The character of corruption in China shifted after 1992 as marketisation took root and the role of 'connections' (*guanxi*) diminished.[30] Leaders in both Moscow and Beijing claim that battling corruption is a top priority, but their actions have barely made a dent in the problem. China has seen the arrest of thousands of top officials, even including a Beijing mayor and two governors.[31] Russia has been less decisive: Putin's anti-corruption campaigns have taken down a few top private businessmen and some police generals, but it was not until 2006 that a sitting governor was arrested.

External Integration

Both countries relied on external integration as a key driver of their economic transition. But here, again, their experiences diverged. China's trade tripled in every decade, raising its share in world trade from 0.8 percent in 1978 to 7.7 percent in 2005. Because of the 1990s slump and the breakdown of the Comecon trading bloc, Russia's share of world trade fell from 3.4 percent in 1990 to 1.5 percent in 2000, recovering slightly to 1.8 percent in 2005.[32] China's economic regeneration was led by an explosion of manufacturing assembly plants in coastal locations, importing components and raw materials and exporting manufactured goods to foreign markets, and tapping into its seemingly limitless supply of cheap labour[33]. Russia did not have the labour reserves, ports close to global shipping routes, entrepreneurial spirit and the political will to embrace this kind of export manufacturing-led growth path.

Unlike Russia, the Chinese relied on an influx of Foreign Direct Investment (FDI) while keeping portfolio investors at arm's length. China attracted an annual average of $12 billion FDI during 1985-95, rising to $78 billion in 2006.[34] Russia averaged only $1.3 billion FDI per year during 1985-95 and $12.5 billion in 2006 while experiencing an annual outflow of capital far in excess of those figures. By 2006, China had accumulated a net stock of $207 billion FDI (15 percent of all capital), while Russia had only $17 billion[35]. To facilitate this inflow of capital, China created Special Economic Zones with favourable tax and regulatory conditions. This process was greatly facilitated by the existence of Chinese capitalist exclaves in Hong Kong and Taiwan, part of the 50 million-strong Chinese diaspora[36]. Though foreign investors were encouraged, they were typically forced into joint ventures with their own stake capped at 50 percent.

China preserved tight controls on capital flows. The renminbi is convertible on current account but not on capital account, and was pegged to the dollar after 1995, at a rate equal to about 25 percent of Purchasing Power Parity (PPP). (In July 2005 the peg was switched to a basket of currencies). Thanks to these controls, China has maintained its cheap labour advantage, and has prevented the speculative capital inflows and outflows that have devastated other developing economies. They rode out the 1997 Asian financial crisis largely unscathed.

In contrast, Russian reformers largely followed Western advice to pursue external liberalisation—in part because IMF credits were conditional on such policies[37]. Russia lifted many capital controls in 1992-94 and dollars flooded in, forming a parallel currency for most of the 1990s. Approximately, $40 billion of speculative capital entered the country—mainly to cover the government's yawning fiscal deficit. This reckless borrowing led to the August 1998 financial crash, which was triggered by the slump in the price of oil following the 1997 Asian crisis. August 1998 saw a 75 percent devaluation of the ruble, a default on foreign loans and the destruction of the assets of most of the financial oligarchs. The crisis ironically cleared the decks for an economic recovery by making Russian food and manufactures more competitive with imports. More importantly, it enabled a renaissance of state power by fatally weakening the oligarchs, financially and politically.

Future Prospects: Stability or Instability?

According to conventional Western assumptions about the congruence of political and economic liberalism, the current situation in Russia and China is unsustainable. In both countries, the economic system is significantly more market-driven and hence pluralist as compared to the political system. "The market's irresistible force is meeting the party's immovable object. At some point, one of them must surely give"[38]. Liberals assume that a breakthrough to democracy is still possible and necessary in both countries. Pessimists expect the state to take more steps to rein in the market—jailing businessmen, nationalising private companies, erecting protectionist barriers.

Moves by the CCP to broaden the political elite to include businessmen have exposed the contradictions within a regime that embraces capitalism while maintaining Marxism-Leninism as its official creed. The dismantling of the Maoist-era social safety nets and the never-ending battles with corruption also raise doubts about the long-term viability of the Chinese model. The country is highly vulnerable to cyclical and exogenous shocks—the bursting of the property bubble; the collapse of the pyramid of bad loans to loss-making SOEs; a slump in demand for China's manufacturing exports; health crises and ecological disasters.[39] This all leads Pei to conclude that without democratic reforms, economic growth will stagnate and regime will face a series of mounting internal challenges,[40] though his pessimism is not shared by all China watchers.[41] The international climate that was so favourable for China's export-led growth cannot continue indefinitely: the 2008 global financial crisis may well mean the end of growth driven by US consumers with money borrowed from China, Japan and the petro-states.

But in a world replete with failed and failing states, the Chinese state still looks fairly effective. It is still able to identity problems and deal with them, to complete massive projects such as the Three River Gorges Dam or the building of pipelines from Kazakhstan. Even their ability to create a system to effectively censor the Internet is something of a technological and political achievement.[42] On the other hand, the dismal failure of regulatory agencies to prevent the tainted milk scandal in 2008, thousands of protests each year surrounding illicit land seizures are persisting challenges to state capacity.

There are also plausible crisis scenarios in Russia's near future. Russia gained little from its political and economic opening in the 1990s. Not until the commodities boom, which saw the oil price rise from $12 a barrel in 1997 to $60 in 2005, did Russia enjoy a clear benefit from global integration. During the years 2000-08, oil and gas alone were accounting for 60 percent of export earnings and one-third of government revenues. The bursting of the financial bubble and global economic slowdown in 2008 caused the world oil price to fall from a peak of $147 in July to below $80 in October, which bodes ill for Russia's future growth prospects.

The 'Regulated Market' Consensus

The differing trajectories of Russia and China underline the point that the impact of globalisation on individual states is unpredictable. Despite the common pressures brought by global economic competition, leadership choices and the contingencies of historical evolution still matter. Both China and Russia present a common lesson for theorists of globalisation: the world is not 'flat' and strong states can find a niche role in the new global economic order.

Both countries now seem to be converging on a regulated market model in which elements of market pluralism are embedded in post-communist, authoritarian institutions and practices.[43] (This is sometimes called the 'Beijing consensus'[44]). What are the elements of this new 'regulated market' model?

- The leaders are committed to preserving the integrity of **state sovereignty and national identity**. This means preventing foreign leaders and institutions from forcing political or economic decisions on the government of Russia or China. Participation in international economic integration must not require a trade-off of national sovereignty. Critics argue that this insistence on sovereignty is merely a façade to justify the leaders' grip on power. Defenders would say it is a principled stance, based on a concern for the welfare of their people, whose histories have shown the dire consequences of allowing foreigners to infringe on the country's territory.
  Nationalism is part of the leaders' rhetoric, but they do not want to allow it to get out of control, lest it ignite a destabilising mass movement, and/or threaten relations with important trading partners.[45] Still, it seems clear that nationalism has been strengthened in both Russia and China as they opened up to international market forces, contrary to the argument that globalisation necessarily produces "the continuing fragmentation of identities and institutions".[46]
- The leaders are focused on **economic growth** as a major goal—something that is good for national security and good for boosting the popular legitimacy of the regime—at a time when other ideological justifications are eroding. Growth also expands the opportunities for personal enrichment by political cadres while regrettably taking their attention away from human development issues.
- The **market mechanism** is the most effective tool for economic growth, both domestically and internationally. International trade is a win-win situation for all participants.[47] The country must find the most appropriate place in the international division of labour by accepting the logic of comparative advantage. In China, that means exploiting the country's pool of cheap labour through export-oriented manufacturing. In Russia, it means selling off the country's mineral resources. But in each case, the leaders want to move up the food chain by developing more capital and technology-intensive industries. China has outpaced Russia in accepting the logic of globalisation. Beijing is even more committed to lowering trade barriers than the old US ally Japan.[48]

- As already mentioned, the **market has its limits** which must be policed by the state. Market forces that erode state legitimacy and capacity, and unleash uncontrollable social protests must be corrected. The state must step in to provide public goods, right from investment in infrastructure to compensation for the reform losers and creation of a regulatory framework. The political elites are uncomfortable with the idea of economic actors beyond their control. So the political economy that emerges is the one characterised by the hybridity of political and economic power. This may be less efficient than a separation of politics from economics, but it has the advantage (for the leaders) of ensuring the indispensability of the political class.
- **Liberal democracy is inappropriate** or unnecessary, and open public contestation between rival members of the ruling political elite is to be kept to a minimum. The Chinese leadership unequivocally rejects the liberal-democratic paradigm. As Andrew Nathan puts it, "The argument that democratization, freedom, and human rights would lead to a truer kind of stability—as convincing as it may be to the democrats of the world—holds no appeal for these men".[49] They even have the audacity to issue a report critical of human rights in the US in response to the State Department's report on China's human rights record.[50] The Russian position is more nuanced: the leadership officially embraces democratic values, and they are enshrined in the 1993 Constitution. But Russian practice diverges markedly from democratic theory. In partial recognition of this, Kremlin ideologists have floated notions of 'managed democracy' and 'sovereign democracy' to try to bridge the gap between Russian practice and Western ideas.[51]
- The **new middle class** that the economic boom has produced serves as a social basis for the regulated market regimes. This is contrary to the expectations of Western liberals, who traditionally saw the middle class as the trusted standard bearers for democracy. Fewsmith writes that the basis of the post-1989 social contract in China is "economic prosperity in exchange for political quiescence". (p. 103) Ed Freidman argues that "The new middle class in urban China tends to imagine democracy as a system that would empower the majority who are the rural poor"[52]. The Chinese middle class were also frightened by the chaos that followed the Soviet collapse and were thus more willing to support a technocratic authoritarian leadership[53].

  In Russia, professionals were traumatised by the economic shocks of the 1990s and welcomed the stability brought by Putin's firm hand, as is evidenced by opinion surveys and election results. In both countries the middle classes have embraced consumerism and 'bourgeois individualism' with a vengeance, fusing it with politics in what Wang Hui has called 'consumer nationalism'.[54]

Conclusion

Does this 'regulated market' approach really amount to a coherent paradigm, intellectually and practically? Or is it a contradictory mixture of ideas and policies, a temporary coincidence of diverse trends that will pull apart within a few years?

The previous wave of authoritarian developmentalism of the 1960s-80s, from Brazil to East Asia, fell apart in the 1990s. The context of that previous wave was quite different. There was a real anti-capitalist threat, both internationally (global communism) and domestically (powerful labour unions). So the state needed to defend the market from its adversaries. When those adversaries were weakened by the end of the Cold War, the rationale for authoritarianism dissolved. But the regulated market model is rooted in a different world order, that of globalisation, which is not likely to vanish any time soon. The state's role is seen as providing the political stability for market forces to do their work, and the regulatory interventions needed to ensure that international trade and investment benefits the host countries and not just its foreign partners. The regulated market seems to represent a viable organisational response to the exigencies of life in the post-Cold War world for these two large, ex-socialist powers.

This phenomenon opens the door to a new phase of global development in which the rules of the game may not be dictated by the established Western powers. Russia and China want to be rule-makers and not just rule-takers on the international stage. But is the development path of the two respective countries sustainable? And if so, will they be able to forge a consensus with the other leading powers on a new set of values, different from those currently in force, which will shape the global political and economic institutions of the next decade? Countries such as Brazil, India, South Africa, Mexico and Indonesia are also experiencing rapid growth having embraced international integration—but unlike Russia and China, they are robust democracies. So, the globalised world is not 'flat': there is a broad and diverse range of viable models that have emerged in response to its challenges.

Figure 1: Contrasting Reform Paths

	Sequence	*Pace*	*Initiative*	*Spirit*	*Western advice*
Russia	Politics First	Rapid	Top-down	Shock therapy	Strong influence
China	Economy first	Gradual	Middle-up	Controlled transition	No influence

Notes

1. Nita Rudra, "Globalization and the Strengthening of Democracy in the Developing World", *American Journal of Political Science*, vol. 49, no. 4, October 2005, pp. 704-730
2. Andrew Nathan, "Authoritarian Resilience", *Journal of Democracy*, vol. 14, no. 1, 2003, pp. 6-17.
3. Christopher Marsh, *Unparalleled Reforms. China's Rise, Russia's Fall and the Interdependence of Transition* (Lexington Books, 2005).
4. Adam Przeworksi, *Democracy and the Market: Political and Economic Reforms in Eastern Europe and Latin America* (Cambridge University Press, 1991).
5. Joseph Fewsmith, *China since Tiananmen. The Politics of Transition* (Cambridge University Press, 2001), pp. 80-83.
6. Yegor Gaidar, *Days of Defeat and Victory* (University of Washington Press, 1999).
7. Minxin Pei, *China's Trapped Transition* (Harvard University Press, 2006), pp. 19.
8. Shiping Hua, "The Deng reforms and the Gorbachev Reforms Revisited", *Problems in Post-Communist Politics*, vol. 53, no. 3, May 2006, pp. 3-16.
9. Liang Zhang, Andrew Nathan and Perry Link (eds.), *The Tiananmen Papers* (Public Affairs, 2001).
10. Nathan 2003, *op. cit.*
11. Minxin Pei, "China: Can Economic Growth Continue without Political Reform?", *Strategic Asia 2006*, (National Bureau for Asian Research, 2006), pp. 303-332.
12. Pei, *ibid.*, ch. 2; Fewsmith, *ibid.* Even so, the Standing Committee of the National People's Congress only rejected government-proposed bills three times in 28 years. A more positive statistic is that 21% of lawsuits filed against government officials succeeded in 2002. Pei, *ibid.*, 60, 67.
13. Bruce Dickinson, "Threats to Party Supremacy", *Journal of Democracy*, vol. 14, no. 1, 2003, pp. 25-35. 20% of entrepreneurs are members, but the CCP has branches in less than 1% of the 1.5 million private enterprises.
14. Robert W. Orttung, "Russia", *Nations in Transit 2005* (Freedom House, 2005), at http://www.freedomhouse.org. That puts Russia's political system *below* that of Afghanistan, Bahrain or Burkina Faso.

15. Fewsmith, *op. cit.,* 83.
16. George Taber, "Rx for Russia: Shock Therapy", *Time Magazine*, 27 January 1992. Taber writes that the well-known advisor Jeffrey Sachs "frequently cites the old Russian maxim that you cannot cross a chasm in two jumps."
17. Barry Naughton, *Growing Out of the Plan: Chinese Economic Reform, 1978-1993* (Cambridge University Press, 1995).
18. World Bank, *From Transition to Development*, April 2004, www.worldbank.org.ru.
19. Pei, *op. cit*, 2006, 3. SOE share of industrial output fell from 78% to 41%.
20. Pei, *op. cit*, 2006, pp. 97-102.
21. Shu-Yun Ma, "Understanding China's Reform", *World Politics,* vol. 52, no. 4, 2000, pp. 586-603.
22. Margaret Pearson, "Institutions and Norms of the Emerging Regulatory State. The Business of Governing Business in China", *World Politics*, vol. 57, no. 2, 2005, pp. 296-322.
23. Dali Yang, "State Capacity on the Rebound", *Journal of Democracy*, vol. 14, no. 1, 2003, pp. 43-50.
24. OECD, *Economic Survey: Russian Federation 2004* (OECD, 2004).
25. Rosstat, www.gks.ru; Pei, *op. cit*, 2006.
26. India was listed with 23 billionaires. *Forbes*, April 2006, at http://www.forbes.com/billionaires/
27. For example they are absent from the national legislature, in contrast to the Russian case – Margaret Pearson, *China's New Business Elite: The Political Consequences of Economic Reform* (University of California Press, 1997), 111; Bruce Dickson, *Red Capitalists in China: The Party, Private Entrepreneurs, and Prospects for Political Change* (Cambridge University Press, 2003)
28. Transparency International's Corruption Perceptions Index, based on surveys of international businessmen, rates Russia 126th out of 159 countries surveyed in 2005, with a score of 2.4 out of 10, while China is seen as less corrupt, ranked 78th with 3.2. The situation is unchanged since 1998, when Russia ranked 52nd (out of 85) with 2.4, and China 76th with 3.5. www.transparency.org
29. Pei, *Transitions, op cit.*, 2006, ch. 4; Yan Sun, *Corruption and Market in Contemporary China* (Cornell University Press, 2004.
30. Sun, *ibid.* Sun's data suggest that the number of cases did not substantially increase in the 1990s, although the author herself does not highlight this point. Table 1.2 shows the number of economic crimes fell from 65,000 in 1992 to 35,000 in 1999, and Table 1.8 shows the number officials investigated rose from 150,000 1992 to 175,000 2001.
31. Yan Sun provides a list of 21 such officials 1986-2004 – *ibid*, 49.

32. Martin Wolf, "China should risk bolder trials", *Financial Times*, 6 June 2006; Giorgio Navaretti, "Patterns of Trade and Protection", World Bank, May 2004; WTO, "World Trade 2005", 11 April 2006.
33. Shang-jin Wei, ed., *The Globalization of the Chinese Economy* (Edward Elgar, 2002); Peter Nolan, *Transforming China: Globalization, Transition, and Development* (Cambridge University Press, 2004); Nicholas Lardy, *Integrating China into the Global Economy* (Brookings Institution, 2001). By 2007 wage costs were rising, providing a constraint on growth in the coastal region.
34. UNCTAD, *World Investment Report 2005* www.unctad.org
35. Yasheng Huang, *Selling China: Foreign Direct Investment During the Reform Era* (Cambridge UP 2003).
36. Brunson McKinley, "Migration is Here to Stay, so Get Used to it," *International Herald Tribune*, 24 June 2005.
37. Randall Stone, *Lending Credibility* (Cornell University Press, 2004).
38. Martin Wolf, "An Autocracy of Bureaucrats can only Crush China's Growth", *Financial Times*, 31 May 2006.
39. Gordon Change, *The Coming Collapse of China* (Random House, 2001).
40. Pei, *op cit,* forthcoming 2006.
41. Andrew Nathan, "Present at the Stagnation", review in *Foreign Affairs*, vol. 85, no. 4, July 2006, pp. 177-82.
42. Pei, *op. cit.*, 2006, pp. 84-88.
43. See Wei-Wei Zhang, "The Allure of the Chinese Model", *International Herald Tribune*, 1 November 2006; and the debate between Professor Wu Shuqing and Cheng Enfu, "Washington Consensus and Beijing Consensus", *People's Daily*, 18 June 2005 (online). Harley Balzer uses a more neutral term,"managed pluralism," to describe the Russian-Chinese convergence, "China in comparative perspective", ch. 12 in Peter Hays Gries and Stanley Rosen (eds.), *State and Society in 21st-century* China (Routledge, 2004).
44. The term "Beijing consensus" was coined by Goldman Sachs advisor Joshua Cooper Ramo, in his article "The Beijing Consensus", Foreign Policy Center, UK, May 2004. http://fpc.org.uk/fsblob/244.pdf Ramo focuses on China's embrace of the neo-liberal paradigm, and he arguably overlooks the distinctive political features of China's policies which are outlined in this section.
45. Peter Hays Gries, "Popular Nationalism and State Legitimation in China", in Gries and Rosen, *ibid.,* ch. 9.
46. Philip G. Cerny, "Globalization and the Erosion of Democracy", *European Journal of Political Research*, 1999, vol. 36, no. 5, pp. 1-26, 20.
47. *China's Peaceful Development Road*, State Council Information Office, 22 December

2005. http://www.chinadaily.com.cn/english/doc/2005-12/22/content_505678.htm
48. William H. Overholt, RAND Corporation, "China and Globalization", testimony to the U.S.-China Economic and Security Review Commission, 19 May 2005. http://www.rand.org/pubs/testimonies/CT244/
49. Nathan, 2003, *op. cit*, 16.
50. "The Human Rights Record of the United States in 2004", issued by the State Council of the People's Republic of China, *People's* Daily, 3 March 2005. http://english.people.com.cn/200503/03/eng20050303_175406.html
51. Vladislav Surkov, "Nationalization of the Future", *Ekspert*, 20 November 2006.
52. Ed Friedman, *The Rise of China and its Impact on the World*, International Political Science Association, Fukouka Japan, July 2006.
53. Gongqin Xiao, "The Rise of the Technocrats", *Journal of* Democracy, vol. 14, no. 1, 2003, pp. 60-65.
54. Wang Hui, *China's New Order* (Harvard 2006).

Russia's Economic Development and Challenges

R. G. Gidadhubli

Overview of the Economy

Being a part of the world economic system, Russia has also been affected by the current global financial crisis. However, efforts are being made by the leadership of Russia to reduce the impact of the crisis on the economic development of the country. Looking back, in June 2008, the Russian Deputy Prime Minister Igor Shuvalov had stated that Russia was on the verge of becoming the sixth largest economy in the world and that its economic growth during the last seven-eight years had been quite impressive.

Incidentally, this almost coincided with Vladimir Putin's presidency of Russia. As Putin passed on the presidency of the country in the middle of 2008 to Dmitri Medvedev, there were reports that the Russian economy was witnessing a boom in sharp contrast to the economic crisis and negative growth rates that prevailed for most of the period in the 1990s. There was stability in the economy and the major economic indicators did support this argument. During the last seven years, Russia maintained a reasonably consistent and high GDP annual growth rate of six-eight percent which enabled the country to register an increase of about 67 percent in the GDP. According to the World Bank Report of 2007, the Russian economic performance remained robust with a GDP growth rate of over seven percent. In 2008, GDP per capita had risen to above $9,075. The foreign exchange reserves of the country exceeded $480 billion by July 2008 and there was appreciation in the exchange rate of ruble against the US dollar. Russia recorded a surplus budget of six percent in 2007 and the country's foreign trade performance had been quite impressive. This is evident from the fact that Russia's exports increased by three times between 1995 and 2005, when it was about $268 billion. In comparison to this, total imports only doubled during this period reaching $165 billion.

Subsequently, the country also consistently maintained a surplus balance on trade account. This helped in bringing down the external debt of the Federal Government from $130 billion in 1999 to $41 billion in July 2008. The Paris Club Debt also declined from $39 billion in 1999 to $1.5 billion in July 2008. In 2007 itself, the Russian Government had declared the policy decision to wipe out these debts. With this impressive performance, the country was able to build up on the hard currency reserves, which amounted to $420 billion, an increase of 35 times over the last decade. Moreover, the country had a Stabilisation Fund of over 3.4 trillion rubles by the end of 2007, the highest recorded amount so far. Hence, the Russian Economic Development Minister Elvira Nabiullina had stated that with such a strong growth in the economy, Russia's foreign exchange and gold reserves exceeded 500 billion dollars, the Foreign Direct Investment was expected to grow at 33.3 percent year-on-year in 2008.

But Russia's international reserves which stood at $581.6 billion on September 1, 2008 have gone down by $14.3 billion because of the global financial crisis, as reported by the Central Bank of Russia. At the same time, Russian economy faces several problems such as high inflation, corruption, bureaucratic controls, overdependence on energy and raw materials for economic development, disparities in income among the population and regions in the country and so on. In fact, it is opined that the windfall of petrodollars, which have flooded Russia in the last decade, seemed to have given a feeling of false security and stability. Hence, several questions arise: What factors have contributed to Russia's economic achievement? What policy measures have been adopted by the leadership of the country? Will Russia be able to sustain its economic development? What is the likely impact of the global financial crisis on the Russian economy? What are the challenges that the country faces with regard to its economic development?

An effort has been made in this paper to examine some of the issues concerning development and challenges in the Russian economy.

Growth Performance

In the background of what has been stated above, it may be worthwhile to examine factors contributing to the growth performance of the country. Firstly, under the leadership of Putin, Russia has concentrated mainly on two sectors, namely energy and defence, having realised their immense scope and potentiality for exports and thus earn the much needed hard currency. Being rich in hydrocarbon resources, Russia has been able to achieve nearly a two-fold increase in the production of oil and natural gas, which was stagnant in the 1990s, in the last about five years. Equally significant has been the unprecedented rise in oil and gas prices from about $40 per barrel in 2002 to over $140 per barrel in July 2008 in the global market. It has brought rich dividends for Russia. Subsequently, oil prices have declined to below $50 per barrel. This huge inflow of petrodollars has made a qualitative difference to the financial position of the Russian economy, a major portion of which is again invested in the energy and defence sectors. It is important to note that in order to make Russia an energy superpower, Putin has succeeded in forging close economic and political ties with energy rich but landlocked Central Asian States in which Russia's energy giants Gazprom and Lukoil have been actively involved (producing their oil and gas and exporting them to world markets through the Russian pipelines). With a control of about 18-20 percent in oil and 30 percent in natural gas, the Russian state and energy companies have been working in tandem to achieve their target in the global energy market. This strategy has become more effective as Russia's energy firms, Gazprom, Lukoil, Rosneft, with the support from the Russian government have used immense reserves of petrodollars to acquire assets in energy related objects including energy infrastructure in several countries such as Kazakhstan, Turkmenistan, Uzbekistan, Belarus, Moldova, Armenia, Hungary, Algeria, Iraq, Venezuela, etc. More significantly, Russia has used the network of pipelines to assert its geo-economic role in the global energy market. As far as the defence sector is concerned, Russia's military exports were expected to exceed $8.5 billion in 2008, as stated by a senior government official in October 2008. Russia has doubled annual arms exports since 2000 to $7 billion last year, becoming the world's second-largest exporter of conventional arms after the United States.

Secondly, Russia under Putin's presidency pursued a policy under which the economy has been partially renationalised and brought under the control of the state. President Medevdev has stated that this policy will be continued. This is particularly the case with regard to 'strategic sectors' such as energy, raw materials and minerals in which the state has to play a critical role and hence the role of private sector is restricted. Control over strategic sectors has enabled Russia to promote its geo-economic and geo-political interests. As a matter of policy, during the last few years, the Russian government has also reduced the share of foreign companies and that of several international oil giants in the strategic sectors, which had made their presence in the Russian oil sector under the presidency of Boris Yeltsin. At the same time, with enormous petrodollars at the disposal of the state, the Russian government has acquired the shares of foreign companies operating in Russia including that of TNK-BP to reduce them to minority shareholders. While this is done as a matter of strategy to serve Russia's national interest, it has raised genuine concerns in the West about the investment climate in Russia. As opined by some analysts, since the European Union countries have adopted a market-liberalisation approach even in the case of oil industry, this total state domination of the energy sector in Russia has increased energy-related tensions (according to a recent study carried out by energy experts in Paris).

Thirdly, an important policy measure relates to the merging of state controlled enterprises to create mega corporations, which are expected to play a dominant role in the Russian economy. For instance, defence sector enterprises play an important role in Russia's economic growth. They are the major exporters of defence equipments and hence hard currency earners for the country. In May 2007, the Russian government created 'United Aviation Corporation' which combines civil and military aircraft producers such as MiG, Sukhoi, Tupolev, etc. Similarly, in July 2007, 'United Shipbuilding Company' was formed which combines Russia's civil and naval ship builders. This company is headed by Sergei Naryshkin who is close to the top leadership in Kremlin. This measure has been taken to strengthen the hold of the Russian state on these corporations and also to enhance the bargaining power of Russia, particularly in dealing with foreign countries and companies. This will also help Russia to enhance its status in the world defence market by giving it a political edge vis-à-vis the USA. India being one of the major importers of Russian defence equipments may also have to deal with this new development. Unlike during the Soviet era when the State was the sole organisation, Russia may selectively intervene and allow the market element to play its role so long as the national interest of the country is served. At the same time, being aware of the fact that military technology of Russia lags behind the West, Putins's objective is to improve the quality of defence production.

Fourthly, economic growth has been driven by high and rising domestic demand and household consumption, and rapidly growing business investment. While manufacturing sector's growth was solid, service sector was showing a high growth as well. As stated earlier, energy sector continued to remain the main source of exports and large capital inflows. In 2008, the increase in GDP has been mostly spurred by strong investment and consumer spending. For instance, in the first four months of 2008, the domestic fixed investment increased by 20.3 percent year-on-year and retail sales saw a rise of 15.6 percent. The Russian president Medvedev wants to emphasize on 3

'I's— Investment, Infrastructure and Innovation—for the development of the economy. One bright spot of the economic growth has been the sharp rise in foreign trade turnover, which grew up to 48.4 percent during the first half of 2008 from the earlier year, to 235.2 billion U.S. dollars, exports up by 51.8 percent, to 150.3 billion dollars, and imports up by 42.8 percent, to 84.9 billion dollars. The structure of foreign trade is similar to that of the past. During the first four months of 2008, exports of energy jumped to 65.7 percent and reached $102.9 billion, while imports of machinery and vehicles grew by 63.8 percent and became $41.3 billion.

Fifthly, analysis of growth rates of the major sectors of economy during the last few years reveals an interesting picture. It may be noted that the service sector and retail trade have registered fairly high growth rates of 9-12 percent per annum, which also seem to have contributed to the overall growth performance of the economy. On the other hand, in the case of industrial sector, annual growth rates were just about 4-7 percent. Agricultural sector growth performance was the poorest with less than 1.6 percent per annum up to 2004 and subsequently, there has been a moderate increase to about 2.6 per cent. Transport sector recorded a rather modest annual growth rate of 6-7 percent during the period 2000-2004 and has subsequently declined.

Problems Affecting the Russian Economy

One problem facing Russia is the high rate of inflation. According to Rosstat, the official Russian source, Consumer Price Index (CPI) was in double digits ranging between 11 to 18 percent between 2001 and 2006. In 2007 and 2008, the inflation rate continued to be in the range of 10-12 percent. In fact, the Russian government raised its 2008 inflation forecast to 0.5 percent from the initial projection of 7-8.5 percent. The first Deputy President of the Central Bank Gennady Melikyan admitted that the country's inflation rate was likely to reach 12 percent in 2008. Some western analysts contend that the actual inflation rate is much higher than what is claimed by the official sources. As opined by economists of the World Bank and the IMF, inflation in 2007 was over 15 percent and that it would be about 14 percent in 2008. In their analysis, the Russian economy was overheating with the domestic demand outpacing the overall economic growth and real wages which were growing faster than the labour productivity. Thus there are several factors which have contributed to this high rate of inflation. Firstly, on the financial side, apart from the huge inflow of petrodollars, there was an increase in the money supply. Hence, the money supply growth was more rapid than the overall economic growth. Secondly, large capital inflows in 2007 pushed the balance of payment surplus to record highs, becoming an important source of reserve accumulation ($450 billion.). Thirdly, the fact that the average monthly wages shot up from $179 in 2003 to over $497 in 2007, a rise of about 2.8 times in five years, also contributed to this high rate. In fact, wages were rising faster than the labour productivity due to shortages of man-power in the labour market. As a cumulative effect of all these factors, there has been a growing demand for consumer goods, pushing the inflation rate in the country. On the supply side, there was a decline in agricultural production, particularly with regard to vegetables, milk and bread, leading to shortages of these essential food products and giving rise to a sharp increase in their prices by over 20 to 30 percent in 2008. In fact, the surge in inflation was also partly explained by the rising world food prices. Medevedev has admitted that the country has been facing the problem of inflation and hence has proposed to deal with it on priority basis. According to Arkady Dvorkovich, economic adviser to Medvedev, the best way to fight inflation is to increase competition and raise investment. Expressing a similar view, the Russian Deputy Prime Minister and Finance Minister Alexei Kudrin has opined that the government would take a series of measures, including establishment of inflation target mechanism, to bring the inflation rate down to 6 percent before 2011.

Small and medium industrial units have been coming up on a large scale during the last decade. But many of them are facing an acute problem of not being able to get credit due to the financial crisis which the country has been facing. In addition, getting credit has become more costly. For instance, Zvyagin who has a small scale unit has opined that inflation has already driven up production costs—metals prices have risen by 25 percent this year—and will soon begin eating away his profits. This is becoming increasingly common in Russia as small and medium-sized businesses struggle to survive amid declining demand and tightening credit. The present financial crisis has also affected many Russian big business companies. This is evident from the fact that on 3 October 2008, Russian billionaire Oleg Deripaska had to sell his 20 percent stake in the Canadian car-parts makers to the creditors.

Corruption, excessive state control and interference, relatively poor infrastructure including that of transport, income disparities are some of the major problems affecting the Russian economy. This is amply evident from the views expressed by some Russian economists and political leaders, including a few former ministers, who are critical of Putin's policies. For instance, former Deputy Prime Minister Anatoly Chubais, who played an important role in the economic reforms under Yeltsin and was till recently the chief of Unified Energy System, considers that the increasing role of the state in business has been a tactical mistake which might affect economic growth in the long run. Similarly, the former Prime Minister Mikhail Kasyanov has also opined that excessive government interference in the economy and increasingly servile judiciary will adversely affect the economy. Andrei Illarionov, economic advisor to Putin for many years, resigned from his position in 2005 because of strong differences with the economic policies pursued by the Russian government. Some western analysts have opined that the 'Siloviki' clan who are part of Putins's inner circle have seized control of commanding heights of Russia's economy. Echoing similar views, Russia's Alfa Bank President Pytor Aven stated at a economic forum in London in 2006 'In our country, the State Apparatus is growing at a gigantic speed. It poses a serious question about how effectively economic problems can be tackled in this situation'. In view of this, some economic experts contend that what has emerged in Russia after the Soviet breakup is state capitalism and not a competitive market economy.

On its part, the Russian government is also critical of the policies and methods used by some big Russian companies that affect the development of economy. Thus Russia's antimonopoly regulator, the FAS, has initiated proceedings against several companies including Evraz Holding (cooking coal company), Mechel (mining company) etc, which are being criticised by the government for their unfair trading practices of charging high prices by using their monopoly position in the Russian coal market.

Economic disparities have widened in Russia during the last nearly two decades between the superrich 'Novie Russkie' and economically disadvantaged population, particularly the pensioners and older generation of Russians. As opined by some analysts, about a dozen Russian billionaires control more than 60 percent of the economy. At the same time according to some Russian analysts, despite several achievements in the economy, about 20-25 percent of the population is still below subsistence minimum, whose living conditions have worsened due to persisting high inflation in the country. There were demonstrations on this issue in various parts of Russia during the last couple of years. Only then did the Russian government and the Duma take cognizance of the problem. To alleviate the problems of the pensioners in October 2007, the Duma, after having done three readings of the Bill, raised pensions by about 300 rubles (about 12 dollars) which was still inadequate. Hence as reported by Rossiskaya Gazeta of October 19, 2007, the Deputy Speaker Oleg Morozov conceded that the condition of the pensioners was far from satisfactory and that the amount of pension should be raised to ensure them a worthy standard of living.

Global Financial Crisis and its Impact on the Russian Economy

Russian economy has become integrated with the world economy, which has brought both the positive and negative consequences of global economy. This is evident from the fact that during the last decade, Russia has attracted substantial investment from the western financial institutions. They are motivated by prospects of earning high profits considering Russia's huge resource potentialities and sustained economic growth. It is important to note that as opined by Russian economist Oleg Mityayev, even Russian banks have become somewhat dependent upon western credits. Also, the government was aware that the Russian banks had taken numerous loans from abroad, for themselves and for the Russian companies, in the past few years to attract investors to the rapidly growing economy.

In view of this, the present world financial crisis has affected the Russian financial sector. This is clearly evident from the fact that Russia's domestic stock market has suffered from the volatility of global financial and banking crisis. In fact Mikhail Delyagin, the Director of the Moscow-based Institute for Globalization Studies, had rightly stated that it won't be long before the global financial crisis trickled down to the Russian financial sector. In September 2008, the bankruptcy of Lehman Brothers, one of the biggest US banks, and the crumbling of the insurance giant American International Group (AIG) resulted in a large number of western banks withdrawing from the Russian financial market. It was reported that many foreign investors were selling Russian bonds at stock exchanges for rubles, and were then buying dollars for rubles at the currency exchange to transfer them abroad. With that, the Russian stock market went into a deep dive. The Russian Economics Minister Elvira Nabiullina stated that in the third week of September 2008, the share prices plummeted to their lowest levels in nearly three years amid worsening global financial troubles. Efforts were being made by the Russian government and the Central Bank of Russia to prevent the fall of the ruble against the dollar by injecting dollars from its reserves into the market. According to official information, the Central Bank spent almost nine billion dollars for this purpose in the first week of September 2008. Subsequently, to bail out the banking sector, which was being affected by the financial crisis, the Russian government pumped in $120 billion into the economy in the middle of September 2008. Again on 6 October 2008, seeing the panic as the Russian stocks went into a freefall, Medvedev announced up to $36 billion in credit to bolster the country's banks. It is noteworthy that despite facing its own problems, Russia was also lending it $5.4 billion to Iceland to help the island's efforts to prevent national bankruptcy. Moreover, as reported by Russian Finance Analyst Anatoly Medetsky, the Russian Prime Minister Vladimir Putin unveiled a new $14.6 billion policy measure in November 2008 which was aimed at helping Russia's businesses to withstand the current economic downturn.

The acuteness of the problem lies in the fact that as per some expert estimates, in September-October 2008, the Russian banks and companies had to pay about $10 billion to their foreign creditors and about $45 billion of refinance loans at a higher interest rate in the fourth quarter of 2008. But considering the credit crisis in the West, the Russian banks are in a critical financial condition. The Central Bank and the Finance Ministry have been doing all they can to inject liquidity into the banking system and resolve this problem. To tide over the problems, it was reported that Sberbank, Vnesh Torg Bank and Gazprom Bank, the backbone of the Russian banking sector, were to be offered up to 1,126.6 trillion rubles from the federal budget for a term of three months or longer. The Central Bank of Russia was to give them another two trillion rubles for up to six months. Hence the Russian Prime Minister Vladimir Putin was confident in saying that the Russian economy was strong enough to overcome the global crisis. There is considerable credibility to such contention since at the Investment Forum held in Sochi in the third week of September 2008, Nabiullina said that 114 contracts and memorandums were being signed, worth a total of 14.42 billion euros ($21 billion) and which included one-third coming from foreign investors.

In the opinion of some Russian economic experts, the financial crisis might necessitate the Russian leaders to push ahead the much-needed economic reforms, since the oil-fuelled boom had made them indifferent to the reform process. The government became less vigilant and overconfident and believed that the economy was shock-resistant. The global financial crisis has taken the government bodies by surprise. Fyodor Prokopov, Executive Vice President of the Russian Union of Industrialists and Entrepreneurs, has opined that Russia's labour legislation was unable to take the blow because it had been drawn up in a completely different economic situation. Analysts like Yelena Malkova, faculty at the Russian Academy of National Economy, admit that dismissals of workers from factories and layoffs are inevitable but at the same time it is important to note that the impact of the current global financial crisis on the citizens as a whole in Russia might not be as severe as in the case of some western countries. This is because so far the financial sector in Russia is not as integrated into the society as it is in most western countries. For instance, mortgages as a percentage of GDP in Russia are only around 4 percent compared to around 130 percent in the U.S. and even higher in places like the U.K. So the chances of negative equity resulting from this crisis are relatively less on the average Russian.

On the other hand, some experts predict a different scenario, assuming that the country's economy doesn't go to pieces. Vladimir Gimpelson, Ph.D., Director of the Center for Labor Market Studies at the Higher School of Economics in Moscow, said that employers facing plummeting demand for their products would naturally try to cut costs, but not by firing people, rather by slashing the salaries, bonuses and other benefits of the employees. They won't resort to dismissals, not out of compassion, but, because they are constrained by legal restrictions. Some will stick to the old 'socialist tradition' and some will be pressurised by the administrative measures taken by local officials to avoid heightening social tensions.

Challenges

In view of what is stated above, the Russian economy faces several challenges in its development. Firstly, it is over dependent upon two sectors namely energy and defence. They account for over half of the hard currency earning of the country. Hence, decline in the international prices of oil and natural gas during the last few months together with the global financial crisis has adversely affected the Russian economy. Therefore, reducing this overdependence on only two sectors is a major challenge for the Russian policy makers. There is an urgent need for the diversification of the economy, with due focus on engineering industry, production of a wide range of consumer goods, agro-processing and so on. In June 2008, Medvedev highlighted the financial policy for the period 2009-2011 in which there was focus on the anti-inflation drive. He said that it was imperative for Russia to slow down the price growth since inflation was both a macroeconomic and a social problem.

Secondly, in the opinion of Russian Economic Expert Former Minister Aven, who now leads Alfa Bank, even as there is a huge inflow of petrodollars, the country's economic growth during the last decade has been driven by consumption rather than judicious investment to develop a broad based competitive economy. He was candid in his observation at an international forum held recently, saying that in non-energy sectors, the international competitiveness of Russian manufacturing industries has "stayed more or less on the same level as in the Soviet Union". In his opinion, the growth paradigm should shift from consumption to investment.

Thirdly, there has been a felt need in the country that administrators of the government and enterprises must change their bureaucratic approach and adapt their ideas to market economy. Ensuring efficiency and transparency of state institutions is a major challenge for the present leadership of Russia. In fact reducing state interference in the management of the economy is essential to make Russia economically efficient, competitive and dynamic. There was a frank admission of this fact at the St. Petersburg Economic Forum held in June 2008, attended by a large number of Russian and foreign businessmen, when the Deputy Prime Minister Igor Shuvalov stated that there was need for reducing state interference in the economy and protect the property rights of the citizens. Considering the fact that he occupies an important position as a coordinator between the prime minister and the president, the Russian government might initiate policies to promote market reforms in the economy.

Fourthly, it is a major challenge for the leadership to deal with the problems of corruption and the high level of inflation. For instance, the former minister of Economic Development and Trade German Gref frankly admitted the prevalence of this problem when he said that everyone knew about the corruption in the Russian Taxation Service. While it was reported that tax evasion was rampant in Russia, raids on business companies by men carrying machine guns as was shown on televisions indicated a heavy-handed approach to collect taxes, which is not conducive to building trust among the business community. However, as opined by some Russian analysts, how soon and how far the policies of the Russian government will get implemented into reality would be an important factor since there are vested interests in the state apparatus. In this context, it is important to note the report in Moscow News on 26 June 2008 in which the financial policy for the period 2009-2011 was outlined by the president, who gave priority to fighting inflation and improving the planning system in the country

Fifthly, improvement and modernisation of the infrastructure facilities in Russia has been a major challenge for the Russian authorities. There was a realisation that any neglect of infrastructure would severely affect the economy. To remedy the situation, certain policy decisions were taken by the Russian leadership in 2007. For instance, in September 2007, speaking at an investment forum in Russia's southern city of Sochi, acting First

Deputy Prime Minister Sergei Ivanov said that Russia aimed to invest $1 trillion in infrastructure over the next 10 years. In fact, the former President Vladimir Putin stated that private investors, including foreigners, would have a major role in this programme planned to modernise Russian industry and infrastructure. To improve road transport conditions, Russia also planned to build 4,000 kms of new roads annually by 2010 and to invest one trillion rubles ($437.9 billion) in its rail network by 2030. Similarly, investment in the country's airport network would reach $30 billion by 2020. The Russian leaders have also called upon state monopolies such as Gazprom, Unified Energy System and the Russian Railways to invest billions of dollars in the next 8-10 years to upgrade Soviet-era machinery and equipment to modernise the economy and increase the production capacity in general. As stated above, Medvedev wants to give emphasis on increasing investment in the economy. The development of power and transport infrastructure is a key to the economic development of Russia in the years to come. While these are policy decisions, it will be a challenge to implement the 'national projects' in reality. Sixthly, even as Russia needs foreign investment and technology, improvement of the investment climate is a major challenge for the leadership of Russia. This is because apart from the global financial crisis, what might be worrying the western investors is the manner in which Yukos was liquidated and TNK-BP (Russian-British Petroleum joint venture) has been targeted and raided by 14 different government authorities for alleged tax evasion and so on. Some western analysts opine that both the state and Russian companies have a common interest in reducing the share of BP substantially in the joint venture.

To conclude, it may be stated that notwithstanding the prevailing global financial crisis, the Russian economy is fairly stable, strong and prosperous. Economic development under the former presidency of Vladimir Putin during the last decade has been quite impressive. However, the growth has been contributed by only two sectors, energy and defence, which have brought in huge petrodollars to the country. But, the role of the state has increased in the economy through its policies of re-nationalisation, resource nationalism, acquisition of shares of foreign companies, merging of state controlled enterprises to form mega corporations and so on.

Despite major achievements, Russian economy faces several problems such as high level of inflation, lack of efficient infrastructure, bureaucratic interference, wide income disparities, corruption and so on. The global financial crisis has also affected the Russian economy since it has become largely integrated with the world economy. Efforts are being made by the Russian government and the Central Bank of Russia to reduce the impact of the crisis by taking timely policy measures and injecting liquidity into the economy. At the same time, there is also a growing concern and realisation among the academics as to whether the windfall of petrodollars which have flooded Russia in the last decade has given a feeling of false security and stability. Hence Russia faces many challenges to make the economy efficient and competitive—reducing overdependence on energy and defence sectors by diversification of the economy; reducing state interference in the economy; modernisation of the economy and improving investment climate for attracting foreign capital and technology and so on.

References

Vasily Zubkov, 'Consumer Boom Russian Reality', New Theme On Russian-Indian Affairs, New Delhi, July-August 2006, pp. 12-13

V. Krushin, 'Gosudarstvennone Regulirovanie Economiki', Ekonomist Monthly Journal, Moscow, no. 11, November 2007, pp. 3-12

R.G.Gidadhubli, 'Putin's Economic Formula For Russia',the Economic and Political Weekly, Mumbai 2007

Arun Mohanty, 'Emerging Trends in Russian Economy', World Focus, New Delhi, August 2008, pp. 202-296

Nikolay Komelv, 'Building a Favorable Business Environment', New Theme on Russian and Indian Affairs, New Delhi, November –December 2006, pp. 13-15

Anatoly Medetsky, 'Putin Unveils $14.6 billion tax cut', RIA Novosti, Moscow, 21 November 2008.

Robert Coalson, 'Unified Russia Congress Promises Stability Despite Financial Crisis', Radio-Free Europe: Daily Report, November 2008

Victor Yasman, 'Law and Property, Kremlin-Style', RFERL: Daily Report, 6 August 2008

Vremya Novostei, Gazprom Continues Buying Foreign Assets, Russian Paper: Moscow, 14 July 2008

'President Outlines Budget Priorities', Moscow News, 26 June 2008

Russia in the Process of Globalisation

P. L. Dash

Introducing Russia to Globalisation

Karl Marx was the true apostle of globalisation when he wrote in the very first sentence of the Communist Manifesto "Workers of all countries unite, you have nothing to lose, but a world to gain". Marx was indeed detailing the forces of labour that have flattened the world.[1] As the proponents of private ownership of property are turning to the government for bailout, Marx's popularity has soared in this era of globalisation. The world has been passing through an incredible phase of development. In the past twenty years, we have witnessed how bad politics failed the Soviet Union. Throughout the economic downturn in the capitalist world, we have been witnessing in recent years how bad economics has wrought havoc to the capitalist system, pushing it to the precipice collapse, when bailouts by the governments seem imminent. Long before the new millennium dawned, anterior and posterior to Perestroika, the socialist world was passing through a systemic crisis, primarily engineered by the world capitalist system and wrecked from within by excessive centralisation, and the former Soviet President Mikhail Gorbachev was handicapped by the plaguing crisis in the Soviet economy. His was a country largely isolated from the mainstream capitalist world. An asymmetric development with a lopsided leviathan of the military industrial complex was discernible in sharp contrast to the low development in other economic sectors. This was a time when symptoms of Dutch disease were setting in. In a country of 285 million people, nearly 18 million communists, who were Communist Party of Soviet Union (CPSU) cardholders, were not the same stoic stock of patriots who had built the Soviet system, fought the Second World War and believed in prospects of socialism. The country also had a different breed of communists like Mikhail Gorbachev and Boris Yeltsin who believed in the winds of change but certainly did not know how to bring it about. The two leaders, both from the professional party cadre, were unanimous on this issue up to the launch of Perestroika and Glasnost. This was the inception of Russia's globalisation process. In the late 1980s, differences arose about the pace of Soviet reforms: Gorbachev believing in gradual and therapeutic approach, while Yeltsin favouring radical and surgical 'shock therapy' method of reforms. In their personal traits, both Russian leaders differed vastly.

Gorbachev was sophisticated and urbane, young and dynamic, ambitious and forward looking, while Yeltsin was as rough as a husbandman and blunt in his approach to issues and problems. He was impatient, intolerant and wanted to be the numero uno leader of Russia. Gorbachev's dilemma was neither the country, nor the party, nor a handful of people in the upper echelon of the ruling elite, but two more segments of leadership: Yeltsin and his cronies and the hard core communists, handpicked by Gorbachev himself, who staged the August coup d'etat in 1991 headed by Gennady Yanayev. Gorbachev clearly failed to balance out the genuine interest of the country with the selfish interests of these two vying groups. He was at the centre of the storm where the rigidly centralised Soviet system did not allow him to neither ventilate further democratisation, nor undertake reforms as per his desire. By then the divide among these three groups—Gorbachev at the centre, Yanaev thrown out after the coup and now in political doldrums and Yeltsin still aspiring to rise by fishing in troubled waters—was too discernible for anyone to ignore. The country began to disintegrate under its own weight, while these three groups were fighting one another. One could hark back to the debate in the Ukrainian Rada, when the members chastised their own representatives of the Soviet era in the Kremlin, saying that they were sitting in a foreign parliament. Russia's isolation from Ukraine was visible; let alone from the world.

When cracks began appearing on the body polity of the Soviet system, patriotism vanished like a bubble. The allurement of the west overwhelmed Yeltsin, rather than the specifics of the Soviet past and the sacrifice his countrymen had made. He was the representative of the era in a sense that he and his followers were the true capitalist disciples of Karl Marx. He measured the success of capitalism differently from his predecessors and overtly hinted at hugging the mainstream of world capitalism that was peeking at globalisation. If Gorbachev's economic advisors were Zaslavskaya and Shmelov, Yeltsin chose Jeffry Shacks and company. He even gave them a place in the Kremlin. Sachs and socialism were not on compatible terms, and the result was quick dismantling of the Soviet economic system without having a well-thought-out reform plan; and hence the resultant chaos. The political superstructure was quickly demolished. The communist party crumbled. Its spineless members were not even asking where the money they had paid throughout their life as membership fee every month had vanished. On the ruins of socialism, the Russian neo-rich grabbed state property. Even Gorbachev had grabbed the then Communist Party School to set up Gorbachev Foundation in that very premise. The oligarchs closeted Yeltsin and pioneered reforms to fulfil their own greed rather than the need of Russia. Yeltsin's daughter Tatyana Dyachenko, her husband and their oligarch cronies were the real demons at work to destroy Russia. Berezovsky was the Kremlin kingmaker. The facade was to introduce capitalism in Russia and integrate the country into the capitalist mainstream of emerging globalisation. Yeltsin was too drunk with power and vodka to pay any attention to what was happening across Russia.

However, Russia was not to be destroyed so soon. Russia's tryst with destiny began when the reforms were still faltering. Capitalism was on war path with remnants of socialism and the tug of war continued. The society was unable to digest the sudden shock of the transformations that the leaders in Russia had brought about. Yeltsin's 'shock therapy' reforms failed to alleviate their miserable predicament. The reforms indeed pauperised them when their life-long savings were washed away by soaring inflation. A couple of years after the Soviet break up, their saving bank accounts were frozen by the state for a few days. By the time the state allowed people to draw their money, the currency had been devalued a thousand times. Money had no worth. Workers did not get their pay, pensioners their pensions and students their stipends. Thousands of unwed mothers were passing through a phase of misery. The voucher privatisation had sapped off common Russians like nothing else. Their hopes were shattered and the promised participatory democracy was never introduced. And precisely around this time, billions of roubles were siphoned off Russia to the western banks. The west got enriched by Russian money and offered financial help to reconstruct a broken Russia. Russia outlived the pangs of these reforms with valour and vamp; and a few years later refused western loan under Putin.

But there were many mute spectators from the army, the KGB, the police and the bureaucracy. Putin, a political novice, a KGB colonel, was reticent in reading the minds of the oligarchs, the economic downslide of his country for which these oligarchs were responsible and pondering over the ways how to stem the rot and arrest further degradation. He was also concerned with the loss of Russia's international prestige. From the vantage point of his Kremlin position as Yeltsin's programme manager, he could see the real Russian drama unfolding each day with new nuances. He could identify the responsible men and the affected areas. Much as he wished to pinpoint the lacuna, he was afraid that the time was not so opportune to do so and the people around him were not so naive to digest criticism so easily. As an inherited verity bequeathed from yesteryears, the entire nation was afraid to speak up the truth to Yeltsin. Even introspection was forbidden. But esoteric studies were allowed and an opportune moment was awaited that arrived when Putin was nominated as the Russian Premier by none other than Yeltsin himself. The moment of triumph ogled at Russia when Putin was chosen the interim president and Russia's glance riveted on him when people elected this commoner as their country's president. Had an oligarch been chosen as Russia's president in place of Putin, Russian history of the past nine plus years could have taken a different course than what it has taken thus far; maybe far closer to globalisation than where Russia is today.

Once in power, Putin focused on two things: bridle the influence of oligarchs on Kremlin affairs and arrest the economic sledge of Russia to the abyss. Both these actions were an introspective quest away from globalisation. His auxiliary objective encompassed the indictment of the culprit and induction of efficient and loyal cadres to ensure the rule of law that would provide the legitimate base for using the wealth of the country to meet the aspirations of the Russians. He was initially a darling of the west because he was handpicked by Yeltsin. But as time passed by and issues cropped up, the west began to realise why they liked Yeltsin the way they could never like Putin. His first major step was to insulate the Kremlin from Yeltsin and his coterie. While Yeltsin signed a tacit deal with Putin to obtain immunity from law for his family and himself, his oligarch friends could not stomach the independent way of Putin running the country, and yelled aloud about the rape of democracy and did everything to undermine the power of the state and the president. Russia's reform from above that had unleashed the stream of misery across the country for a decade began to look at the grassroots for support and the people stood by what Putin did. Willy-nilly, the oligarchy had to wake up to throw their support to Putin because far too long they were tranquilised by the shocks of reforms year after year under Yeltsin.[2]

Climbing the ladder of power from a city manager in his native St. Petersburg through the KGB hierarchy in Berlin, Putin was in the know-how of what was wrecking his country. With absolute power as president and commander-in-chief of Russia, he presided over the country at a time when no one could have coveted his position. He had inherited an empire without an umpire; and his intentions were to turn his challenges into opportunities by every stroke of his decision. He reposed immense faith on the Russian people to salvage the country from the sunken predicament they had slid to. Putin quickly realised that what has been destroyed so far in Russia was just the political superstructure and not the economic base. Should Russia revive its strong hand politics to protect the economic base, the situation could be remedied and remodelled effectively. Oligarchs and the neo-rich were at their bewildering low after the exit of patron-in-chief Yeltsin. They had collectively taken inceptive steps to proliferate into the strong economic base of Russia and there was an urgent need to forbid their audacious entry into the Kremlin. This was Russia's crucible that changed the course forever.

Thus began the process of deftly handling the economy without any interference of the oligarchs. Politics and economy were twin issues which the oligarchs were told not to intermingle. The moment they vented their political aspirations, they were reminded by Putin about their economic responsibilities to a Russia in crisis. This was the most unpalatable truth the oligarchs would have liked to listen from the Kremlin, where they were the real masters throughout Yeltsin reforms. From the jungle rule of self-styled free capitalism (where they were never questioned by anyone) to the rule of governance through a legitimate tax payment system; the oligarchs had passed through a long way. This man called Putin summoned them to sermon on tax, rules and regulations, governance, corporate responsibility and social obligations. They abhorred the way Putin treated them, but there was no way he could have otherwise done to save Russia.[3] The facade of Russian democracy underwent a change. Berezovsky, Gussinsky, Deripaska, Abramovich and their ilk, who questioned Putin found their way tumultuous and left Russia, perhaps forever. Those who persisted in questioning the Kremlin like Khadorkovsky were in turn asked to explain the way they had amassed their huge fortune and the tax details of their past, which they failed to provide. Such oligarchs were shown their way to the prison. The pro-oligarch Kremlin became suddenly anti-oligarch, although it could not be called entirely pro-people. This was a point of departure from the past. As the gap between Putin and the oligarchs widened, the western world revealed why they did like Yeltsin and began to dislike Putin.

Glory and Globalisation

Then began the forward march of repositioning Russia on the world map, integrating it to the process of globalisation. Regaining the lost glory was a tough task. Positing a decadent socialist system against advanced capitalism was no less easy. Globalisation posed a challenge to Russian isolationism. Right from Gorbachev, all successive leaders have strongly felt the yearning to globalise Russia, but were severely handicapped by the country's peculiar self-confinement to isolation. As Russia began to rise from the rubble, those who had written off this country from their calculations frowned at a feeble Russia limping back with minus four percent economic growth and slowly marching toward prosperity, thanks to the oil boom. However, the spike in oil price helped Russia not only in overcoming the negative growth, but also allowed it to marshal its strength to cushion a consolidation fund of billions of dollars—to be exact 256 billion in 2007-2008. Oil was a globalising commodity and Russia was quickly back to the basics of it. Soon the oil boom brought prosperity to the economy and the outcome of this prosperity was reflected on the social spheres. Simply speaking, Russians began to live better, spend better and looked to their future with optimism. Their crimson hopes about a new Russia revisited them, and they rated Putin high, all through his reign of eight years as president. This however did not mean that Russia had overcome all her problems. But it certainly put its weight as well as a part of the oil money to bolster its international prestige that has surged in recent years. This has made the rivals of Russia more fearful, who looked at Russia's renewed strength gingerly. Zoltan Barany, a professor at the University of Texas, wrote: "in 2007 alone Russia resumed regular, long range bomber missions after a 16 year hiatus, conducted a military exercise with the People's Republic of China and other members of the Shanghai Cooperation Organization (the 'Dictator's Club') that included 6500 troops and over 100 aircrafts, increased defence spending by more than 30 percent, announced a new rearmament programme and began planning the reclamation of the old Soviet naval base at Tartus in Syria in order to establish a Mediterranean naval presence".[4] The second globalising means was thus Russia's weapons' industry, which was back with a bang under Putin.

While these efforts to regain past imperial glory continued relentlessly, the changing regional context along the southern fringes of the erstwhile Soviet Union precipitated two scenarios for the leadership to handle. The first postulate advocated that the Cold War was over. Hence the conduct of international relations, based on Cold War principles, could not logically follow on the Cold war paradigm, more so if Russia wished to integrate into the world of globalisation. In the relations among nations, there has to be a restructuring of bilateral and multilateral ties based on post Cold War equations that should presumably be based not on antagonism of two rival social systems; but on the three concurrent parameters renting the air everywhere such as globalisation of the international system, marketisation of the economy and democratisation of the polity. Once this sympathy to the globalisation system was in place, there has to be a restructuring of the energy supply system. Secondly, the existing energy supply system is lopsided and geared to cater to the demands of the western countries and their markets. The Asian demand component of recent years after the emergence of China and India as major energy consumers has been totally ignored in the existing energy supply and energy security system. Therefore, there is a need to restructure the supply channels, taking into account emergent demands for energy coming from countries like India, China, Japan, South Korea and other Asian nations. The demand for energy is huge in the orient and an eastward pipeline, rather many lines, is imperative in these changing times.

The post-Soviet years since the emergence of new Russia have thrown open several challenging scenarios. Russia is no longer a country of Yeltsin years in chaos. The Putin years have steered the country clear of lethargy. From a debt trapped nation, it has now looked forward to prosperity by liquidating all its western debt that attests deft handling of the country's resources and finance. The country has a sustained economic growth of 6.5 percent over the past few years and hopes to maintain this tempo over foreseeable future. The rouble, once sagging and devalued in 1998 by lopping off three zeros, has largely stabilised, gaining strength, month by month, appreciating against a declining dollar and has become fully convertible. All these positive tendencies in Russia's economic performance are largely due to Russia emerging as a major energy and metal superpower. A dollar rise in world oil market pushed up Russia's GDP by half percent and similar fall in oil prices caused corresponding decline. Russia as one of the countries with large oil and gas reserves expected the tendency in oil prices to continue; so does its economic growth. However, this notion may be trammelled by the country's own slugging industrial and agricultural growth, and a plummeting oil price worldwide subsequently that has put Russian leadership in the fuzzy zone of taking risks. After all, spikes and slide in energy prices were dependent on a series of reasons over which Russia has no control.

Such a notion is corroborated by other side of the story in Russia's negative developments. It is admittedly one of the most corrupt countries in the world and ranked among the top ten in world corruption index in 2007. On her way to democracy, Putin is accused of excessive centralisation, muzzling the press, hounding the tycoons, abhorring the oligarchs and demonstrating a strong hand. The very way a non-party president sided with United Russia to ensure its victory in the Duma elections on December 2, 2007 was itself not very democratic. On the Russian television, while all political parties were debating their election agendas, the United Russia was not visible anywhere. However, everywhere on the street side one could discern placards of president Putin as the Russian hero, the national flag of Russia hoisted side by side with the flag of United Russia, implying thereby that Putin, Russia and United Russia were synonymous. No other political party has had the financial wherewithal to put such a demonstrative show of electoral strength and propaganda as did United Russia in the pre-election phase. No other political party had synonymous views with United Russia although many of them worked in tandem in a plaint Duma without confronting United Russia all through the Putin years. Did election divide them and post-election politics unite them? This was the moot question Russians ought to ask themselves about their opportunist politicians. In terms of democracy, Russia has everything: an electoral, multi-party system, a bi-cameral Duma elected at regular intervals, a constitution, a flexible press different from Soviet yesteryears, an elected president et al. But all these do not necessarily ensure Russia a place among the world democracies because the whole process of electioneering is opaque and sometimes flawed.

The flag of Russia is flying high today. Seldom did Russia inspire so much awe in the western world as it did in the aftermath of testing a new thermobaric bomb, known as the father of all bombs. In a befitting response to the most powerful non-nuclear bomb that the US had called the mother of all bombs, Russia came out exactly four years later with a lethal weapon. 'The Russian bomb is four times more powerful; yet it uses fewer explosives. It carries 7.1 tonnes of explosive load against 8.2 tonnes carried by mother of all bombs and generates a blast equivalent to that generated by 44 tonnes of TNT compared with 11 tonnes of TNT in the US device.'[5] The bomb coupled with Russia's rearmament programme for upcoming ten years has generated fear in the minds of all, who have thought post-Soviet Russia insignificant. Russia after Putin is a reality for all to reckon with, a fact to face and deal with, a country to live with and a proud nation whose deserving place in the process of globalisation it ought to get.

Beyond Potato Globalism

Russia's Eurasian content was amply evident in the efforts of Peter the Great to modernise his motherland, Europeanise it and in a sense take Russia out of isolation to face the process of globalisation. A telling example is the introduction of potato to the Russian farmers to grow. Russia had no potato before Peter. When he brought that from England to grow in Russia, the farmers experimented with the crop enthusiastically. However, within a few months farmers were disillusioned with no crop. Potato crop was still standing in the field. The plant had not yet dried up. They tasted the stems and flowers that were not sweet. The farmers went on a countrywide strike known in Russian history as the famous 'Potato Strike'. When the matter reached the emperor, he benignly admonished them to wait until the plant dried up, then harvest the root and try it. The farmers' strike was called off. Potato thus became the staple of Russian dining table then and since. Can anyone imagine today a Russian home, whether in village or city, without potato in their daily menu? The famous 'Potato Strike' is just a single instance of the Russian way of globalising itself to a new agricultural crop.

Peter also had introduced the process of urbanisation in big cities such as St. Petersburg and Moscow. The process has not picked up well over the centuries. The formation of middle ages cities across Russia was significantly slow because of the fundamental clash between emerging urban industrial culture and decaying feudal ethos in the countryside. Four hundred years after the reign of Peter, we find Russia hesitant to globalise. It has fewer cities than many of its numerous neighbours: just 13 cities with more than a million people. It is not the question of the number of cities, but the very proclivity inherent in Russians to value what is national and avoid what is alien. The Russians do not abhor what is alien, but endear and prefer native to non-native things to do in isolation as compared to the rest of the world. One reason why proclivity to nativity prevails over other considerations is the shattered and expansive character of the landmass and its populace. Obsessed with their nativity, in the far eastern flanks of the country, there are people such as the Chukchi, the Eskimos and Khanti Mansi, who have never heard of Peter the Great, they cannot grow potato; they live in their own world away from the process of globalisation. Has the process of globalisation devised the modus operandi of incorporating the Chukchi or Eskimos to the mainstream of development from their looped periphery of inaccessible Siberia? Certainly not.

However, what remains certain is that Moscow is not Russia; nor Khabarovsk. They are integral part of the microcosm called Russianness because they are territorially akin to the name of a country. That has spawned awe in others. They are part of a country where nativity, nationality and identity are different categories never to be confused with universality; let alone globalisation. The essence of globalisation is lost in the very process of its identification. Take the example of Russian oil and gas industry. Russian oil industry is inherently national, while the oil and gas pipelines are visibly international. Russia has been selling and exporting energy to the world market for centuries now. It was the Nobel family who set up their oil wells in Tsarist Azerbaijan. At the beginning of the twentieth century, Tsarist Russia's finance

Minister, Sergei Witte, had decreed to sell kerosene to India. Was Russia not globalised then when it was selling oil to England in the West and kerosene to British India in the East? Similar was the case with China. Long before the pipelines became modes of convenience for energy transportation in the second half of the twentieth century, Russia was deeply entrenched in energy business and it continues to do so even today. As the demand for energy in the world grows, the pipelines assume cross-country character. In the context of cross-country demands, Russia has been only fulfilling its mission of an energy giant: it has been trying to bridge the schism between what is inherently national and what is visibly international and global.

The case of the arms industry is significantly not different. Russia is one of the biggest manufacturers of armaments and it sells its arms to its clientele across the world. The Russian arms industry is thus globally integrated to the world market, but with a lot of difference. The Russian arms and weaponry industry is purely national. There is nothing notionally alien in it. From Kalashnikov rifles to Mikoyan and Gurevich fighter aircrafts, the Russian weapon industry is too indigenised to accommodate foreign collaboration. With advanced fighters such as Sukhoi and various other frigates, naval vessels and submarines, they are inherently national and notionally international. But they have world appeal for their efficacy as time tested weapons; hence their worldwide marketability. No army in the world can afford to ignore Kalashnikov rifles. Post-Soviet Russia has been trying to integrate itself to international arms trade with a clear motive of retaining its national manufacturing brand. It will be futile to expect Russia to eschew what is nationally Russian and accommodate multinationals to venture into the turf of arms competition. Russia will hence globalise on its own terms: keeping up what is national, and embracing what is notional without the encumbrances of sacrificing its interests.

Strength and Weakness

Why can't resurgent Russia be considered among the booming economies of the world? Sheer politics has excluded Russia from its legitimate position of a booming economy. Although Russia figures among the fastest growing economies in the world that constitute BRIC (Brazil, Russia, India and China), the three other countries are often talked of while Russia is deliberately slighted. Russia is awe-inspiring; its prowess is abhorred by the capitalist west. But the west is forgetting the truism that many bourgeois disciples of Marx and Lenin have endeavoured to ensure that for straight ten years through the past decade, Russia has maintained an impressive economic growth of 9-10 percent per annum in contrast to US and Europe that have faltered to maintain 0-1 percent growth during this time. The fear of the bear is therefore real, and its bouncing capabilities are more a concern for those who design to write Russia off the map of globalisation. Russia is no longer in the economic doldrums of the Soviet aftermath. It is no longer a state in chaos. Anarchy of the oligarchs is passé. It has been assiduously building a political system under Putin to overcome the lag in progress although in terms of real democracy, it lags far behind. It has more billionaires than any other country in the world. Like Joan of Arc turning the tide of an entire war before she turned 18 years old, Putin has turned a ravaged Russia from poverty to prosperity before he completed his eight years in presidency. And more importantly, before he demitted office in May 2008, he put Russia in a unique power sharing arrangement with his crony turned president, Dmitri Medvedev and himself assuming premiership where he could really call the shots. No other Russian political party but United Russia provided him with the platform to do this political summersault from presidency to premiership.

How can one ignore an energy superpower in these days of rising energy demands? Russia outpaced Saudi Arabia in oil production at the beginning of 2008. International Energy Agency reported that in the first quarter of 2008, while Russia produced 9.5 million barrels of oil per day, Saudi Arabia's output was pegged at 9.2 MBPD.[6] These two countries were followed by the USA, Iran and China with 5.1, 4 and 3.8 MBPD respectively. Russia has all attributes of being considered a power to reckon with; yet it is sidestepped perennially decade after decade. The Cold War yesteryears were different. That type of intense, systemic antagonism has evaporated. Russia of the twenty first century is a different country, confidently marching ahead with nearly eight percent sustained average economic growth for the past eight years in a row. But Russians have a different set of challenges to face and altogether different problems to solve. They are more eponymous in nature than the problems of globalisation.

For instance, inflation has remained the government's biggest worry. Inflation occurs when too much money chases too few goods in the market. But Russia is flush with money due to high oil prices year after year that are still growing as well as the massive inflow of FDI. It also has too many goods in the market; so much so that urban Russians have had no such imagination in the Soviet or immediate post-Soviet years. How long and how far the government will strike a balance between foreign capital inflow and sterilise the economy from inflation is a worrisome matter to watch. Foreign money circulating in the hands of Russians to buy foreign goods available in the Russian market does neither help in boosting indigenous production nor enhancing labour productivity: the two major worries that would finally tell on the health of Russian economy. Russians at the grassroots do not know much about where the economy is heading as long as they get to eat, drink and live well. Putin has ensured all three elements of social well-being during his tenure that has unquestionably distracted the Russians from the real challenges facing the country. The problem is that there will be fewer Russians to manage the economy because the population has been falling fast enough to man the affairs of a huge country. Russia figures nowhere near the sustainable demographic parameters of having a minimum of 2.1 births per couple across the country. Instead, it has just 1.2 births per couple that has pushed the country to the cliff of disaster. Thus a sustainable economic growth with an unsustainable demographic growth is likely to push the country into the red light zone of catastrophe sooner or later, away from the process of globalisation.

Lack of Multiculturalism

Globalisation and multicultural ethos are complementary categories essential for the success of Russia's integration to the world. The Russian concept of multiculturalism has been largely confined to her interaction with multiple ethnos and nationalities populating the vast landmass of the Russian Federation and beyond in the near abroad periphery. In this predominantly Russian space, Russia is the big brother in reality, whereas other peoples and their cultures have distinct identity encouraged by the Russians. While this policy of preserving the national identities of 100 odd nationalities within the Russian Federation has remained a kind gesture on the part of big brother, it is not helpful in the ongoing context of globalisation because Russia is too vast a country to be too easily accessed. Its resources are mostly located in far flung national areas some of whom are claiming ownership and sovereign rights over their resources from the Federal government. This is just the tip of the iceberg. Several other factors, particularly their cultural isolation from the mainstream Russianness, are responsible for creating obstacles in the process of integrating these regions to globalisation. While these national regions are seemingly well-integrated with Russia politically, they are economically resource-rich but technologically alienated and remain backward. To overcome their technological lag, globalisation may be the way out but the federal government is recalcitrant for integrating the regions to the process of globalisation. Some Russian scholars in the Siberian branch of the Russian Academy of Sciences consider the far flung regions as Russian colonies, awaiting their freedom some day.

This rift between the regions and the centre is an anomaly bequeathed from the Soviet years. The exigencies of globalisation require that Russia must carry its resource rich regions with globalisation savvy legislations to integrate itself to the world economy. The efforts of the G-8, WTO, IMF and World Bank are evident of such an integrative process. However, membership in these august bodies will not necessarily imply that Russia has multiculturalism to embrace any alien culture. Succinctly, it also does not imply to have well-integrated regions, whose independent economies can gain access to the world markets sovereign of the Kremlin. Neither the old Soviet laws nor many of the new laws are conducive to the globalisation process; hence the impediments to interact freely with multinationals and other developed capitalist countries. The centre is still inclined to exercise legislative control over the activities of foreign companies participating in joint ventures in the periphery. The periphery does not have the independence to enter into joint economic activities with foreign entities without the Kremlin approval, and this is the major roadblock to integrating Russia to the process of globalization.

The indictment of foreign oil companies participating in the exploration of oil in the Far East under the pretext of violation of environmental regulations is a telling tale of how the Kremlin was determined to bridle any foreign entity any time it wants. The Kremlin has the right to fire the warning salvo to send a message to others not to play truant and fall in line with the Russian legislations, which are more pro-centre than pro-region. The crux of the problem is that a work culture to undertake joint economic activities with foreign entities is almost absent and slowly emerging under the influence of nascent capitalist relations taking roots through the post-Soviet years. The international character of labour is grossly misconstrued and workers in the Russian periphery do not have a 'world to gain'; they have everything to lose if they do not pay heed to Kremlin. It would take years before multicultural economic ethos becomes a reality across Russia. The Russian understanding of cross-cultural activities does not permit peripheral entities or foreign entities to work out projects bypassing the Kremlin. As a result, vast swathe of Russian periphery is out of bound to Foreign Direct Investment, let alone to globalisation.

A Russian worker in Irkutsk or Ufa or Khakasia or Primorskyi Krai or Krasnodarskyi Krai is acutely unaware of the multicultural work ethos. He is linguistically alienated from the rest of the world because he does not know any other language but Russian, religiously alienated due to his orthodoxy and ethno-nationally alienated even from genuine, supra-national Russianness because of his own ethnic and national identity in the far flung regions. Russia is thus a difficult country to introduce any uniformity across its vast space. Therefore, the absence of multicultural features and varied differing salience despite unifying Russianness will not easily imply economic integration to the globalisation process. Even territorial integration is infeasible. While meeting with Italian Prime Minister Romano Prodi in Moscow in January, 2007, Putin succinctly defined the ongoing process thus: "As Russia's economic, political and military capabilities grow in the world, it is emerging as a competitor that has already been written off. The West wants to put Russia in some pre-defined place, but Russia will find its place all by itself".[7]

Winds of Change

We are living in changing times. A few years back what was unimaginable is now possible. Countries which were regarded as backwaters of development, centres of demographic implosions and incremental chaos are now powers to be reckoned with. Russia that was written off in the aftermath of the Soviet collapse has been bouncing back to the world arena in a big way to reassert its lost glory. In fact, two things that had fundamentally altered and largely impacted the conduct of international relations in recent memory were the demise of communism in Soviet Union and Eastern Europe and the 9/11 terrorist attack on the World Trade Centre. The former ended the cold war between the west and the east and the latter led to another war—war on international terrorism. The second war that has started at the dawn of this millennium is characterised by altogether different and unconventional parameters. It is a war against an invisible enemy, home grown or alien enemy, who can wreck havoc from within and from outside. On the basis of religious hostility and related linguistic, ethnic and territorial divides, it generates a potential fear in the minds of people everywhere, thereby joining issues of territorial and national security with human security in every society. This war has also created a distinct dichotomy between the imperatives of globalisation that demand more and freer interactions among nations and jihadi culture of freedom that demands distinction of a religious community living pervasively across the world on the basis of loyalty to a religion whose name itself implies peace.

While the overall dichotomy of what Samuel P. Huntington called 'Islam versus the West and Islam versus the rest' holds largely good in the context of war against terror, there are too many impeccable economic developments in China and India to ignore. These two counties —one with predominant Hindu population and the other with Confucian/Buddhist population —are too large in size and demography. Every second person out of six world citizens is either Chinese or Indian. These two countries have a large young population in contrast to the ageing population in Russia and Europe. Their impact on the world is obviously felt. But what is visibly felt is that too much of their economic prosperity has been too quickly achieved. Their sustained economic growth is another discernible factor, a matter of great debate and incalculable surmises. This brings us to count upon the weighty political and diplomatic role these two emerging Asian powers can play in world affairs in the years to come to integrate their regions to the western world in the process of globalisation with all its nuances. Can Russia be left far behind? Russia's challenges in this regard are similar. With orthodox Christianity as its professed religion and with a sizeable Muslim population, Russia is a vast dichotomy in itself. But it has great integrative potential for a globalising world.[8] And that ought not be ignored.

References

Thomas L. Friedman, *The World is Flat, The Globalised World in the Twenty-first Century* (London: Penguin Books), pp. 235-236. Also refer to the sub-chapter "From Russia with Love" in the same book at pp. 227-229.

Vladimir Radyuhin, "Why the West loved Yeltsin and hates Putin", *The Hindu*, 20 March 2008, p.14.

Kathryn Stoner-Weiss, "Russia: Authoritarianism without Authority", *Journal of Democracy*, vol.17, no.1, 2006, pp. 104-117.

Zoltan Barany, "Resurgent Russia? A Still Faltering Military", *Policy Review*, February-March 2008, p. 147.

Vladimir Radyuhin, "Matching Response", *Frontline*, October 2007, p.51.

The Times of India, 12 June 2008, p.21.

"Vstrecha v Kremle", *Rossiskaya Gazeta*, 25 January 2007.

Joseph Stilitz, *Globalisation and its Discontents* (New Delhi: Penguin Books, 2002), v.

Russia's Socio-Economic Development Strategy Up to the Year 2020 —An Analysis

Arun Mohanty

'Long-term planning' which became almost a slang and a hate word in the post-Soviet Russia for long has finally staged a come back to the discourse on Russia's socio-economic development and economic thought. It should be noted that for the first time in almost two decades, the Russian government has adopted a long-term development strategy to guide country's development up to the year 2020. Implementation of this strategy, approved by the state council and drafted by the government, is based on the concept of socio-economic development of the country. This paper makes an attempt to analyse the salient features of this strategy and highlights its difference from the earlier neo-liberal model executed in Russia.

President Putin had once said that Russia's national idea should be to make the Russian economy competitive in the world stage. The central objective of the current development strategy approved by the state council is to raise the competitiveness of Russian economy at the global level. While disastrous neo-liberal reforms formed the bedrock of Gaidar's 'shock therapy' and Gref and Yasin's neo-liberal model implemented in 1990s , the current strategy sets the objective to accelerating economic growth and raising effectiveness of the economy on the basis of scientific-technological progress and strengthen the social orientation of the economy. For the first time in post-Soviet Russia, there is a hope that the government is serious about transferring the economy to the rails of innovative methods of development.

The concept of long-term socio-economic development of Russia has been drafted on the basis of the decree issued by President Putin following a decision taken in the state council meeting on 21 July 2006. The objective of the concept is to determine the ways and methods for a steady rise in the living standards of Russian citizens, strengthening national security and dynamic development of the economy with a long-term perspective (2008-2020) and strengthening the Russian position in the international community.

The major goals of the long-term development strategy up to 2020 are to make Russia one of the technological leaders of the world, raise the labour productivity by four times in the major sectors of the economy, increase the share of middle class in country's population up to 60-70%, decrease the death rate by one and half times and increase the average life expectancy to 75 years. The strategy emphasises on concentrating efforts for finding the solution to three key tasks: creation of equal opportunities for people, encourage motivation for innovation-based development and significantly raise the effectiveness of the economy, primarily, on the basis of growth of labour productivity.

While the previous strategies crafted and implemented by Gaidar, Gref and Yasin emphasised that the market magic would solve all the problems, the current strategy has a realistic assessment of the complicated situation of the economy that is fast loosing its competitive edge and is receding to the raw material periphery of the global economy, destroying the internal potential for self-development.

Debate on Development Strategy

Soviet Union plunged into an intense debate on economic reforms ever since its leader Gorbachev's acceleration (Uskoreniye) strategy failed to achieve desirable result. This was followed by a debate on fundamental issues like ownership and market which occupied the centre stage towards the end of 1980s. Market and private ownership were considered incompatible with the socialist system of USSR from an ideological standpoint. Thanks to an in-depth debate on these issues, USSR got rid of its ideological dogmas, accepting market as a tool for economic development. It was only then that the Soviet leadership talked about market-based economic reforms. The country's academic community was split on the issue of methods and means for converting the state-controlled economy into a market-based economy. A group of economists headed by academician Leonid Abalkin, who was appointed as the deputy prime minister in charge of economic reforms in USSR, drafted a comprehensive programme that advocated a gradualist approach for reforming the economy without heaping much hardship on the population. However, his programme was challenged by the so called '500 days programme' drafted by academicians Shatalin and Grigory Yavlinsky. The '500 days programme' was an ill-conceived plan to transform the centrally-planned socialist economy into a booming capitalist economy in 500 days, which was absolutely absurd. While Abalkin's programme was made on the basis of deep analyses and forecasts, the '500 days programme' was full of intentions and guidelines without having any analysis. The major differences between the two programmes were the speed, tenure and sequence of reform. As Gorbachev's arch rival, maverick Yeltsin, extended support to the '500 days programme'; the country got split on the crucial reform agenda. Attempts were made to formulate a compromise reform programme through an active involvement of economists from both sides of the barricade. In the process, the country witnessed 11 economic reform programmes that aimed at transferring the centrally-controlled economy to the rails of capitalist economy (Mohanty, 2001). It should be however noted that the battle on these reforms was largely political in nature.

However, when USSR broke up into 15 separate states, and the Russian Federation emerged as an independent and sovereign country as a result of the Belovezhski conspiracy in 1991, the situation changed radically in Russia with Yeltsin enjoying monopoly and extraordinary constitutional powers to implement his own reform agenda. In the completely new situation, Gaidar was appointed as the acting prime minister by President Yeltsin to execute the reforms. Gaidar's economic agenda, popularly known as 'shock therapy' reform, was a reproduction of the '500 days programme' in many ways. The programme dictated by the IMF stood on four pillars: price liberalisation, radical privatisation, elimination of state monopoly over domestic and foreign trade and macro-economic stabilisation. As a result of the implementation of 'shock therapy' reform under Yeltsin and Gaidar, Russia's industrial production declined by almost 60%, agricultural production by 45% while some of the industrial branches got completely wiped out and the country lost almost half of its GDP. Gaidar's neo-liberal programme was based on the dogma that state should have no role in the economy and that the market would resolve all problems. As a result of this model, significant part of the economy came under the control of criminal structures (Putin's speech-Feb 2008). Real income of the population dropped to 40% of the 1991 level while one-third of the population lived below poverty line.

The 'shock therapy' model met its logical end when Russia faced unprecedented financial meltdown and was declared a sovereign bankrupt country in August 1998.

The 10-months old Primakov-Maslyukov government that came to power in the aftermath of the financial meltdown reinforced state's role in regulating the economy and created conditions for a fast economic growth. As a result of this, Russia's economy went through a trajectory of positive growth. Primakov's government was sacked in May 1999 when President Yeltsin perceived him as a threat on seeing his enormous popularity.

Putin's Economic Agenda

When Vladimir Putin became Russian President in the year 2000, he never openly declared his economic agenda. During the presidential elections of spring 2000, he never revealed his economic agenda and later set up two commissions for drafting it after he was sworn in as the president. The first programme was drafted by the commission headed by eminent economist Sergei Glaziyev and Khavarovsk's Governor Vladimir Isayev, while the second programme was prepared by the strategic centre headed by German Gref. The programme drafted by Gref was a continuation of the neo-liberal programme implemented by Gaidar and subsequently by the Economic Development Minister Evgeny Yasin, whereas the programme drafted by Glaziyev and Isayev was fundamentally different, stipulating a strong role for state in the economic management of the country. Putin never declared his support to either of these programmes publicly, but silently executed the programme drafted by Gref.

However, Putin's economic agenda took a sharp turn from 2003 when he started bringing the strategic resources and assets of the country under state control. Formation of State Corporation that controlled strategic assets of the country became the hallmark of Putin's second presidency heightening the role of state in the economy.

It must be noted that Russia witnessed a robust annual growth of nearly 7% in the course of eight years of Putin's presidency. Thanks to this, the objective of doubling the country's GDP in ten years looks quite feasible. Russian economy has become the seventh largest economy in the world with a GDP worth 2 trillion dollars on the basis of Purchasing Power Parity (PPP). This is important in the back drop of President Putin's declaration in his millennium speech in 2000 that it would take 20 years for Russia to catch up with Portugal, Europe's poorest country, if it develops at the then growth rate. The GDP during eight years of Putin's presidency grew by 70%, industrial production by 75% while investment increased by 125%. Russia's GDP in 2007 reached the 1990 level, which means the country has overcome the consequences of the economic crisis that devastated it in the 1990s.

During the eight years of Putin's leadership, accumulated foreign investment grew by seven times while foreign investment in Russian economy reached 82.3 million USD in 2007 alone. Capitalisation of the stock market grew by 22 times as compared to 1999. While capitalisation of the Russian stock market was a mere 60 billion USD in 1999, it reached 1 trillion 330 billion USD in 2007. Russia's trade turnover with foreign countries grew by five times during this period. Russia's foreign debt constitutes 3% of the GDP which is one of the lowest in the world while foreign currency reserves touched more than 500 billion USD in 2008. The real income of the population during the period grew by 2.5 times while people living below poverty line dropped to 13%[1].

Presently, the country faces the daunting task of making a transition to an innovation-driven economy.

Debate over New Long-term Development Strategy

While in the initial years of the 21st century, some economists were stressing that the growth which Russia enjoyed in the beginning of the century was merely a recovery growth, Russia sprang a surprise by maintaining the high growth rate for the ninth year in a row. However, almost all economists are unanimous in their opinion that Russia will not be able to maintain this growth rate any more unless it diversifies its economy, highly dependent on energy and raw-material. One of the major achievements of President Vladimir Putin was that under his leadership, Russia attained political as well as economic stability. The country's leadership since then has been repeatedly emphasising that its next move is 'diversification from stability'. In spite of repeated calls for 'diversification from stability', precious little has been done in practical terms. The country once again found itself in intense debate regarding the strategy for achieving diversification of the economy and high economic growth.

Leonid Grigoriyev , one of Russia's leading economists believe that there are only four possible development strategies before Russia – rent centered strategy , mobilization strategy , inertia –based strategy and modernization strategy.[2]

Rent-based Strategy

The essence of this strategy lies in the fact that the source for development would be rent collected from natural resources. Active support would be provided to poor people and poor regions under the strategy. The strong side of the strategy is rise in the domestic demand and reduction of poverty while the weak side lies in dependence on unreliable, unpredictable and non-sustainable sources of financing.

Different groups of the society happily support this strategy because federal authorities continue to distribute the resources. In such a scenario, modernisation does not find itself at the centre of the problem. On the other hand, resources may not be enough for the entire society. In case of decline in energy and raw-material price, the risk of conflict based on redistribution is fairly high under this strategy.

Mobilisation-based Strategy

This strategy is based on concentration of resources in state sector and its redistribution for the development of priority sectors like energy, infrastructure etc.

The coalition that supports this strategy includes bureaucrats and players of 'breakthrough' sectors. This strategy stipulates significant participation of the state budget, state companies and institutes of development, and to some extent coercive public-private partnership. The strong point of the strategy is that it facilitates accelerated modernisation of branches named as 'breakthrough sectors' while the weak point is low effectiveness of the extremely large state and lack of sustainability of financing.

Inertia-based Strategy

This strategy stipulates tactical manoeuvring between various groups of interests to find solution of the problem as it gets acute. The strategy envisages consistent manoeuvring between populism with subsidy given by the state and partial mobilisation, and also the attempt to reform market institutions in order to satisfy the interests of different groups while resolving most important tactical issues. It does not provide fair chance for long-term strategic success but helps in meeting the requirements of strong coalitions or remove immediate threats. The elite part of the population, satisfied with the status-quo, lend support to this strategy. This scenario is also convenient for the ruling elite. The strong side of the strategy is the absence of radical change in the situation of all the groups and layers of population which favour status-quo, since bitter memories of radical change are still very fresh in their minds. The weak point is the lack of systematic approach toward modernisation and growth which is lagging behind other countries falling in the same category.

Modernisation Strategy

This is a complex institutional modernisation of the society, business and state. In principle, this strategy does not have opponents, but everybody has his own vision and understanding of the strategy. The strong point of the strategy is the positive long-term outcome in the sphere of socio-economic development while the weak point lies in excessive time required for bringing about the modernisation, limits to the realisation of the interests of groups and necessity to form broad coalition to support the strategy. At present, this strategy is the most complex one for all participants and the probability of its execution is paradoxically low.

The strategy requires a significant sacrifice from some of the actors and would take a long time to produce result. Thus this strategy needs patience, both from the citizens and the ruling elite. Modernisation is not possible without some sort of consensus in the society and strengthening of civil society, joint progress of institutions of market and state, rise of effectiveness of the business society. Since a whole generation has to wait for this strategy to be executed, there is a need for building a broad-based coalition that would function in the course of long run. Emergence of such a coalition would form a reliable basis for modernisation.

Experts estimate the probability of execution of the above-mentioned strategies as follows: rent strategy-20%, mobilization strategy-20%, inertia strategy-50% and modernisation strategy-10%.[3]

The first three scenarios would lead the country to an impasse and moreover, each of the three scenarios has its own risks. Though these strategies do not create an immediate threat for the country, yet they do not resolve the main problem—modernisation of the economy and entry into a new level of development. Neither the state, nor the business, nor the civil society on its own can ensure modernisation of the economy. These three forces can take the country on the modernisation path only through their joint efforts.

In spite the fact that the Russian economy maintained an average annual growth of 6.5 to 7 %, facilitating to achieve the objective to double the GDP in ten years, the new strategy highlights the fact that the inertia-based development would lead the country to a dead-end by converting Russia into a raw-material appendage of the world economy. In contrast to the previous strategies, the new long-term development strategy gives priority to investment in human capital, improving the quality of education, science, health care, building of national innovation system, modernisation of the economy taking advantage of natural advantages, development of new competitive sectors in high-tech areas of the knowledge economy, reconstruction and expansion of production, social and financial structure .

In order to transfer the economy to the rails of innovation, the strategy sets the tasks for raising the innovative and investment activeness, take the level of accumulation to 30% of the GDP, achieve the standards of developed countries in the sphere of budget policy . This means the level of financing the education has to reach 7% of the GDP, health care to 6%, science to 3%. In other words, state expenditure for these sectors has to be doubled.

For the first time in the post-Soviet Russia, the state decided to keep the strategic initiative under its control. So far this initiative was in the hands of international financial organisations, raw-material exporters, transnational corporations, natural monopolies, etc. Each of these organisations imposed its own strategy over the country as a result of which the economy passed through degradation. The country's development in the near past took place on the basis of inertia of these strategies. Whatever positive development took place, it was achieved not as a result of government policy rather in defiance of it.

Even today, the Russian government policy is largely formulated on the principles of Washington Consensus. The attempt to bolster the institutes of development, stimulate investment and innovation activities and resolve acute social problems is not adequate.

Long-term Development Strategy of the Government

In order to implement the development strategy adopted by the state council, the government has to bring radical changes in its policy. The central thrust of the development strategy up to 2020 is to transfer the economy from the rails of raw-material export to innovation-based development.

It should be noted that the Russian economy remains excessively dependent on energy exports while the global economy is becoming increasingly competitive , driven by a shifting balance of financial power to developing countries, regional economic integration and technological innovation. Heavy dependence, predominantly, on revenues from energy and raw material resources leaves Russia in an unstable and unenviable economic situation. If Russia wants to be a global economic power, it must move towards innovation-based development. The strategy highlights using Russia's current competitive advantage in energy, transport and agriculture; creating a scientific and technological complex to enable specialisation in high technology; diversifying the structure of the economy; creating economic and social conditions that support development of the best human capital and developing democracy and the protection of rights and freedom.[4]

While assuming identical external economic conditions, the strategy offers three alternative scenarios: 1) inertia-based development, 2) energy and raw material based development through increasing investment in energy and raw material sector, 3) innovation-based development. The forecasts for the stipulated period up to 2020 differ from scenario to scenario. Though both energy and raw material based strategy and innovation-based strategy ensure doubling of GDP during the stipulated period, the GDP increase in case of innovation-based strategy is 21% more than that in the energy and raw material based strategy. Moreover, the volume of investment in innovation-based scenario would be 59% more than that in the energy and raw material based scenario.

The authors of the development strategy up to 2020 have planned four fold increases in investment during the stipulated period. This confirms the assessment that Russia is not fully utilising its investment potential as a result of 50% reduction in accumulation rate compared to savings rate and massive capital flight, estimated to be one trillion US dollars during the reform period. Along with massive investment, the strategy envisages a sharp rise in innovative activities. The strategy stipulates that the share of industrial enterprises executing technological innovation would increase to 40-50% (In 2005 it was 9.3%), share of innovative products in total industrial production would rise up to 25-35%(In 2005 it was 2.5%).[5]

The first but the least desirable case is the inertia scenario, which is basically a continuation of resource-export based model of development, even as energy production gradually decreases. Innovation and competitiveness of Russian products will decline while income disparities in the country will increase and regional integration process would stagnate under the scenario. The GDP growth will fall to around 3 to 3.5% by 2015 and between 2008-2020, GDP will grow only by 1.6 times. As a result of such slow growth, Russian government will be unable to implement its plans for social development, national security and strengthening Russia's position in the world.[6]

The second scenario offers a moderately better outcome than the first one. In this case, Russia would succeed in maximising productivity and growth in the energy sector, with impressive improvements in the efficiency of extracting techniques and power generation. The country would manage both—diversification of its export destinations and modernisation of the transportation infrastructure. Innovation under the scenario is confined to the energy sector, which means that the country would remain uncompetitive in the sphere of manufactured goods and below the potential in terms of human capital. GDP growth in this scenario is slightly better, declining gradually to 5.5 % by 2015, then to 4.5% to 5.5% by 2020, though this is too low to achieve government's objectives for social development and national security. Likewise, Russia's global leadership is confined to the energy sphere and the economy would remain dependent on imported technology and fluctuating energy prices.

Innovation-based development model is the optimal scenario stipulated in the strategy. Under the scenario, Russia would be able to expand its competitive advantage beyond the sphere of energy and natural resources, and become a leader in technology as well. Consequently, this would help in successfully integrating Russian economy with global market as well as with the former Soviet space. Besides, Russia will be able to significantly reduce the gap in its living standards with developed nations, with per capita GDP increasing to 21000 USD by 2015 and 30000 USD by 2020. Russia's share in global GDP will rise from 2.6% in 2006 to 3% by 2015 and then to 3.4% by 2020.[7]

In each of the three scenarios of development, the effectiveness of the economy would rise in different degrees. Under the innovation–based strategy, the energy intensity and electric intensity of the GDP would be reduced by 39% and 27% respectively, and the labour productivity would rise by 138% .The innovation–based strategy differs from the other two scenarios in terms of volume of investment as the former ensures a much higher volume. Here it is noteworthy that the indicators of effectiveness of the economy and GDP increase would significantly lag behind the increment in GDP, which makes experts believe that the strategy aims at production rise on the basis of extensive rise in fixed capital. Thus it is clear, inertia also plays a significant role in innovation-based strategy. That is why the rate of growth under innovation strategy is not significantly higher than that under inertia-based strategy. The authors of the strategy have clearly underestimated the potential of innovation-based strategy linked to the break-through in technologies.

According to Sergei Glaziyev, this is the first methodological error committed in the strategy. The second methodological error in the strategy, according to him, is linked to the hypothesis about the overtaking growth of import and reduction in positive trade balance up to negative balance from the middle of the stipulated period under all three scenarios. Under the innovation scenario, the import is almost doubled whereas export increases by only 60%.

It is expected that the deficit in trade balance would be covered by foreign investments, whose inflow would rise from 50 billion USD in 2010 to 180 billion USD in 2020 as a result of improvement in investment climate.[8]

The third methodological error of the strategy is linked to the traditional transfer of the effect of innovation-based development to the second half of stipulated period. This can be explained by the fact that there is always a time gap between the application of the new technology and emergence of its economic effect. However, the government has already increased the expenditure in this sphere during the last three years and has the right to expect positive return. Secondly, according to the strategy, domestic expenditure on research and development should rise up to 3.5-4% of the GDP (In 2006 it was 1% of the GDP) as a result of which GDP increment should constitute more than 2% of the GDP. If research and development expenditures are not wasteful expenditures and are aimed at producing effect in the form of rise in effectiveness and volume of production, then the GDP increment should be to the tune of 3%.[9]

The above mentioned methodological errors explain the decline in the rate of growth in innovation scenario from 6.7% to 6.1% of GDP increase in the first half of the stipulated period. Though the rate of growth goes up to 6.6% in the subsequent period in the course of the stipulated period, it is still less than the growth rate during the two preceding years when the economy grew in the quasi-inertia and energy and raw-material based scenario. Resultantly, in the subsequent five years, difference in the rates of growth under innovation-based and energy raw material based strategy would be insignificant to the tune of 0.1% of GDP increment. Only towards the end of the stipulated period, the rate of growth under innovation scenario would be 1.7% more than the rate of growth under energy and raw-material based scenario. A similar situation is likely to occur in the rate of growth in labour productivity under both the scenarios. What is deplorable is that the real income of the population would decline under all three scenarios.

Objectives

The ultimate goal of the strategy is to make Russia one of the top five economies of the world. Along with this, it aims at establishing Russia as a leader in technological innovation and global energy infrastructure, its emergence as a major international financial centre. By establishing itself as a leading economic power, Russia plans to raise the living standards of its people to the level of developed countries and safeguard its national security.

The broad objectives of the strategy are to increase the GDP to a level that would ensure twenty-one thousand USD per capita income by 2020, bring 60-70% of the population to the category of middle class and reduce poverty to the level of developed countries.

Transition to innovation-based development stipulates significant change in the mechanism and structure of the economic growth and the scientific-technical progress would be its main source .

Under the innovation-based strategy, the share of the industrial enterprises implementing technological innovation would rise to 40-50% (In 2007 it was 8.5%), the share of innovation-based products in the total industrial production will rise up to 25-35% (In 2007 it was 5.5%), the share of high-tech sector and knowledge economy in GDP would be 17-20% (In 2007 it was 10-11%).[10]

The strategy aims at making innovation the leading factor of economic growth in all sectors of the economy, raising labour productivity by 3-5 times in leading sectors that determine the national competitiveness and reducing energy-intensity by 1.6-1.8 times on an average. In order to achieve this, budget allocation for research and development would increase to 2.5-3% of the GDP which was 1.1% in 2007.

In order to transfer the economy to the rails of innovation, the strategy emphasises on the development of human capital. The expenditure for education from both public and private funding would constitute 6.5-7% of the GDP in 2020 while this spending constituted 4.2% of the GDP in 2007.

The sectoral structure of the economy would undergo a significant change as a result of the implementation of innovation-based strategy. The share of high- tech sector in the added value would increase two fold from the current 10% to 20% under the innovation strategy , while the share of energy sector would decline from 20% to 12%. The share of raw material would decrease marginally from 8.4% to 6.8% while the share of trade would sharply decline from 17.7% to 12.2%.[11]

The strategy stresses that the new technological wave on the basis of Nano, bio-technology, IT and dynamic growth of international market for high-tech products and services opens new avenues before Russia for achieving technological breakthrough. Russian export of these high-tech products would grow by 15-20% annually and the total export value of such products would reach 80-100 billion USD by 2020, which would be 1% of the world market compared to the current 0.2%. [12]

The peculiarity of the innovation-based strategy lies in the fact that Russia has to fulfill the tasks of both 'catching up' and 'passing ahead' development strategies. In conditions of global competition and open economy, it is not possible to catch up with the developed countries in the sphere of living standards as well as effectiveness of the economy unless a breakthrough development is ensured in those sectors of Russian economy which determine its specialisation in the world economy and permit to use the national competitive advantage to the maximum extent .

The innovation-based growth strategy outlined above involves two very distinct processes: modernisation and innovation. While the first process involves transfer and adoption of the technological advancements of the West through trade and investment policies, the second process involves moving beyond the simply adoption of current technologies to developing qualitatively new ones.

Transition from raw material and energy export based development model to innovation-based growth model is linked to formation of a new model of social development. One of the inherent contradictions of the current model lies in the fact that significant GDP growth, rise in income and living standards of the population are largely dependent on collection of rent—high volume income from energy and raw material export . Such rise in living standards is accompanied by an increasing polarisation of the population in terms of income and violation of principles of social justice which are very important for the Russian society. Solution of this contradiction requires formation of new mechanisms of social development corresponding to the resources of the economy and its innovative effectiveness. The foundation for this kind of harmony can be formed on the basis of a combination of enterprise freedom, social justice and national competitiveness.

The strategy stresses several directions for the transfer of Russian economy to innovation-based growth model:

The first direction is the development of human potential. This means ensuring favourable conditions for the development of capabilities of each citizen, improvement in living standards of population, rise in competitiveness of human capital and development of social sectors of the economy that form the key components for innovation-driven growth.

The second direction is the creation of highly competitive institutional environment, stimulating entrepreneurship and attraction of capital into the economy.

The third direction is the structural diversification of the economy on the basis of innovation-led technological development.

The fourth direction is the reinforcement and expansion of Russia's competitive advantage in traditional spheres (energy, transport, agricultural sector, processing of natural resources).

The fifth direction is the expansion and strengthening of external economic position of Russia, raising effectiveness of its participation in global division of labour.

The sixth direction is transition to a new model of territorial development of Russian economy. This stipulates formation of new centres of socio-economic development, based on development of energy and transport infrastructure and creation of a network of territorial-production clusters, realising the competitive potential of the given territory. This direction also aims at reducing the gap in living standards of the population inhabiting on the territory with the help of prudent social and regional policies.

Stages of Innovation-led Development

Innovation–driven growth strategy along with the traditional competitive advantage in the energy-material sector stipulates creation and stimulation of new factors of economic growth that would meet the challenges of long-term development period. This includes breakthrough in raising the effectiveness of human capital and creation of comfortable social conditions, liberalisation of economic institutes and strengthening the competitiveness of business climate, accelerating the use of new technologies in the economy and development of high-tech production, and stimulation of external economic policy. The combined effect of all these factors would ensure the transfer of Russian economy to the trajectory of long-term sustainable growth with an average annual growth rate of 6.4-6.5%.

Innovation–driven development of Russian economy in the course of 2008-2020 would pass through two stages, distinct from each other in terms of conditions, factors and risks of socio-economic development and priorities of the government policy.

First Stage (2008-2012)

The first stage is based on realisation of expansion of those globally competitive advantages that Russian economy enjoys in traditional sectors like energy, transport, agrarian sector, extraction of natural resources. Along with this, institutional conditions and technological components ensuring systemic transfer of Russian economy to innovation-led regime would be created.

This stage would witness an adaptation of the economy to negative tendencies of the world financial markets, contraction of possibilities of accelerated growth of energy and raw-material export, adaptation of the economy to deterioration of external economic environment and reduction of world price of oil and raw-material, and also proliferation of world financial and economic crisis, reduction in labour forces of the country caused by population decline, aggravation of deficit in professional cadres, negative influence of limitation in energy and transport infrastructure, change in the macro-economic situation and the end of strengthening of ruble as a result of reduction in foreign trade balance.

The major priorities of the socio-economic development during this period would incorporate the following:

In the sphere of development of human capital ,urgent steps would be taken in areas of demography and health care in order to stabilise the demographic situation in the country and fix the minimum salary at the subsistence level.

In the sphere of highly competitive institutional environment, measures would include development of competitive markets of products and services, capital, work force, creation of infrastructure for international financial centre in Moscow; liberalisation of the economic sphere, reduction of investment and enterprise risks, establishment of institutes of public-private partnership; building effective state, reduction of corruption level; supporting macro-economic balance, ensuring stable exchange rate of ruble and reduction of inflation to the level of 5- 6.5% etc.

Structural diversification and innovation-led development would see completion of formation of national innovation system; modernisation of fundamental and applied science and professional education; facilitating modernisation of high-tech sectors of the economy; facilitating growth of competitiveness of processing industry including raw-material processing, metallurgy, chemical, production of construction material, automobile production, food industry and helping development of small-scale and medium-scale businesses .

Global competitive advantage in traditional sectors would help overcoming deficit in energy capacity, completing reform in electro-energy sector, expanding investment projects in the sector, completion of large projects in extraction, processing and transporting oil for meeting domestic demand as well as diversification of its export and realisation of massive projects in transport development.

Strengthening external economic position of Russia envisages formation of custom union with countries of Eurasian Economic Community; expansion of mutual investments; development of sustainable production cooperation links with countries that are technological leaders including creation of joint ventures for accessing global market; completion of process for access to WTO and building of infrastructure for Russia's full participation in the organisation.

Balanced territorial development stipulates creation of new centres of development in Southern Russia, East Siberia and Far East, linked to complex processing of raw-material, development of recreation infrastructure; formation of certain innovative high-tech clusters in European and Asian parts of Russia

Macro-Economic Indicators of the First Stage

(2012 compared to 2007)

Increase in life expectancy (years)	2.5
Rise in GDP(%)	137-138
Growth in labour productivity(%)	140-141
Reduction in energy-intensity of the GDP (%)	81-83
Growth in real income of the population (%)	153-154
Rise in investment in fixed capital (%)	180-185
Expenditure for R&D at the end of the period (% to GDP)	1.4-1.6
Expenditure on education at the end of the period (% to GDP)	5.5-5.7
Expenditure for health care at the end of the period (% to GDP)	5.2-5.4

Source: Kontseptsia dolgosrochnogo sotsialno-ekonomicheskogo razvitiya Rossiskou Federatsii, p.30

As a result of the completion of first stage of the long-term development strategy, average life expectancy of Russians would increase by 2.5 years by 2012 as compared to 2007. Russian GDP would grow up to 137-138% by the year 2012 as compared to 2008 while labour productivity would increase by 140-141%. The end of first phase of the strategy would see a reduction of energy-intensity of the GDP by 17-19%. The strategy aims at increasing the expenditure on education and health care to 5.6% and 5.3% of the GDP respectively by 2012 in comparison to 2007.

Second Stage (2013-2020)

During this stage, the economy would make a jump in raising the global competitiveness on the basis of transition to new technological bases (nano, bio-tech, IT), improving the quality of human potential and social environment, doing the structural diversification of the economy .

The major priorities of social and economic policy during the second stage would include:

A.

In the sphere of development of human potential:

Attaining healthy standards of life; transition to continuous individualised education accessible to every citizen; application of innovative technology in healthcare system and education; providing modern house to everybody; fixing salary according to labour productivity; creation of effective pension system on the basis of insurance and accumulation.

B.

In sphere of creation of high-tech institutional environment:

Adaptation of economic institutes to requirements of global mobility factors of production and transborder production cooperation; ensuring global competitiveness of the banking sector, financial markets.

C.

In the sphere of structural diversification and innovation-led development:

Integration of national innovation system with global innovation system, integration of science, education and business; expansion of the position of Russian companies in global high-tech market, making high-tech production and sectors of knowledge economy significant factors for economic growth; ensuring intensive technological modernisation of mass production on the basis of new energy and resource-saving , ecologically safe technology; formation of centres of global competition in processing industry, sphere of intellectual service and other sectors of the economy; finding solution to the problem of ensuring highly professional cadres to the economy .

D.

In the sphere of global competitive advantage in traditional sectors:

Massive application of new resource-saving technology in electro-energy; expansion of resource base of the economy, active exploitation of oil fields of the arctic shelf and East Siberia; completing the formation of basic transport system integrated into world transport system, rise in export of transport service; creating transport facilities that would facilitate complex exploitation and development of Siberia and Far East and exploring new fields of natural resources; application of new transport and transport-logistic technology, ensuring the raise in quality and availability of transport service; transition of agriculture to sustainable regime of development that would strengthen Russian position in the world agricultural market; rapid development of energy infrastructure, overcoming the deficit in energy capacity, launching of massive projects in the sector .

E.

In the sphere of external economic position of Russia:

Ensuring full functioning of customs union and formation of unified economic space in the framework of Eurasian Economic Community; formation of Free Trade Zone with interested countries; expansion of flexible multifaceted relations with world economic centres, expansion of participation in regional organisations of Asia-Pacific region; transforming Russia into one of the world financial centres; transforming ruble into a leading regional reserve currency .

F.

In the sphere of balanced territorial development:

Complex development of Siberia and Far East; reduction of territorial socio-economic disparity to a level dictated by objective regional differences; bringing a balance between revenue base and expenditure obligation; development of innovation basis of centres of economic growth in Ural, Volga basin, north-west regions.

The Planned Macacro-Economic Indicators of the Second Stage (2020 compared to 2012)

Rise in e xpected life expectancy (years)	2
GDP growth (%)	164-166
Rise in labour productivity (%)	171-178
Reduction in energy intensity (%)	70-75
Rise in real income of the population (%)	164-172
Rise in investment in fixed assets (%)	215-223
Expenditure for R&D at the end of the period, (% to GDP)	3
Expenditure on education at the end of the period (%to GDP)	6.5-7
Expenditure on health care at the end of the period (%to GDP)	6.7 to 7

Source: Kontseptsia dolgosrochnogo socialno-economicheskogo razvitiya Rossiskou Federatsii, p.35

As seen in the above table, the average life expectancy of Russian citizens would rise by 2 years by the end of this period compared to 2012. While GDP growth will be 164-166 %, labour productivity would rise by 171-178% during this period. Energy-intensity during these years would decline by 70-75% while real income of the population would increase by 164-172%. Share of expenditure for research and development will constitute 3% of the GDP at the end of the period whereas it is planned to form merely 1.4-1.6% of the GDP in 2012, the last year of the first phase. The expenditure for education and health care would form 6.5-7 % and 6.7-7% of the GDP respectively by 2020. This is much higher than that of 2012 level, both in terms of percent and volume, and equivalent to the level of developed countries. All this would help Russia in finding its place in the higher league of developed countries by most parameters by the year 2020.

However, State Duma, the lower house of Russian parliament has suggested that the long-term development strategy would be implemented in three stages. The first stage (2008-2012) would build the foundation for an innovation-based economy while the second stage (2013-2017) would include creation of the innovation-based economy and the third stage (2018-2020) would consolidate the results of the innovation-based economy.[13]

Notes

1. Putin's speech in the expanded state council meeting;kremlin.ru/eng/speeches/2008/02/08/1137
2. Grigoriev Leonid, *KonfliktiIinteresov IKkoalitsii, Pro-et Contra* , no. 4-5(38), 2007), p.115-116.
3. Ibid., p.107.
4. Kontseptia dolgosrochnogo sotsioalno-ekonomicheskogo razvitia Rossisskoi Federatsii; "The Concept of Long–term Socioeconomic Development of the Russian Federation to 2020", p.8-9.
5. Sergei Glaziyev, *The Strategy and Concept of Socioeconomic Development of the Russian Federation upto 2020*, p-5.
6. *Kontseptia dolgosrochnogo sotsioalno-ekonomicheskogo razvitia Rossisskoi Federatsii*, p. 22-23,
7. Ibid., pp.14-26.
8. Glaziyev S, Strategiya I, *Kontseptia sotstcalno-ekonomocheskogo razvitiya Rossii do 2020 goda: ekonomicheski analiz*, p-5.
9. Ibid., p.6.

10. *Kontseptsia dolgosrochnogo socialno-economicheskogo razvitiya Rossiskou Federatsii*
11. Ibid., p. 8.
12. Ibid., p. 8.
13. http://engforum.pravda.ru/showthread.php?p=2502118

References

Kontseptia dolgosrochnogo sotsioalno-ekonomicheskogo razvitia Rossisskoi Federatsii; "*The Concept of Long-term Socioeconomic Development of the Russian Federation up to 2020*".

www.economy.gov.ru/wps/wem/myconnect/economylib/mert/welcome/economy/macroeconomy/administmanagementdirect/doc, p-1)

S. Glaziyev, "O Strategii Razvitiya Rossiskoi Ekonomiki", Moscow, 2001.

Obzor, "Sotsialnoi Politiki v Rossii", Moscow, 2007

A. Mohanty, *Genesis of Russia's Market Reforms* (Moscow: Slovo Publishers, 2003).

President Putin's speech in the expanded meeting of the Russian State Council on 8th February, 2008.

Globalising Central Asia in Changing Times: A Critical Note

Kuldip Singh

The winding up of centrally-controlled economies from the former Soviet Union and East European countries was followed by emphatic claims about 'end of history … that is the end point of mankind's ideological evolution and the universalization of Western liberal democracy as the final form of human government'.[1] Those who subscribed to such a view held that the winding up of socialism indicated victorious march of the ideology of liberalism on the one hand and the poverty of the socialist model on the other. Even at that point of time, it was difficult to endorse the view that struggle of ideologies for supremacy had ceased to exist, whereby capitalism had proved victorious over socialism. Such a struggle of competing ideologies should have never disappeared at any point of time in human history nor is it likely to disappear in future. However, under the prevailing circumstances, pessimism about socialist dispensations on the one hand and some kind of liking for Western type market economy was quite natural and on expected lines in the post –Soviet space including Central Asia. This was to happen because, among other things, the dismantling of socialism in Soviet Union resulted from the failure to achieve what was promised in tall claims about socialism, especially in the ones which Mikhail Gorbachev made in the wake of economic reforms initiated by him. He declared with full confidence that socialism was 'capable of coping with the historic task of reaching heights of scientific and technological progress…. The success of Perestroika will be final argument in the historical dispute as to which system is more consistent with the interests of the people….'[2] Sure of the success of his reforms, he declared that 'we are looking within socialism rather than outside it, for the answers to all the questions that arise….'[3] He sought to convince the world that socialism in its pure form was capable of achieving wonders. Therefore, the disappointment with the non-realisation of such ambitious goals set out by Soviet leaders particularly Mikhail Gorbachev, led to endorsement of Western type market economy system and internalisation of the notion that such a system delivered better than the actually existing socialist economies. With actually existing socialist systems gone, not only the defenders of capitalism but also many who for long remained bitter critics of the system of capitalism started arguing that capitalism had no alternative. Capitalism came to be seen as a system capable of curing economic ills of the world, including ones that third world countries were suffering from, which visibly influenced the thinking of newly emerged ruling elites in the post-Soviet Central Asia. These countries could not escape the impact of global march of capital, a strake reality of the post-Soviet era, in which country after country demolished barriers, which hitherto prevented unbridled global reach of world capital. In the globalised world of this epoch there remained 'no capitalism with its exploitation and oppressions, its classes and class struggles, its structural defects and explosive antagonisms', making imperialism too look like a phenomenon of the past.[4]

At such a juncture, the Central Asian countries were expected to be receptive to the sane advices of the IMF that they should develop efficient market economies and integrate them into the global economic system. The validity of these prescriptions was sought to be established on the basis of claims of the Bretton Woods institutions that their views on Central Asian issues were not based merely on their experience with the Central Asian countries, nor even on their involvement with transitional economies in general, rather these prescriptions were based on their vast experience of the world economies at every stage of economic development. The newly emerged ruling elites in these countries were told that the world economy had grown while being closely integrated in terms of trade and capital flows and that globalisation in new situation meant the continuation of similar positive trends.[5] The only specificity of the time was that 'with greater freedom of trade and investment and new breakthroughs in telecommunication and information technology, markets have become much larger, more complex and more closely linked than ever before'.[6] Therefore, the newly emerged countries of Central Asia should avail economic gains, which emanated from increased capital flows that accelerated investment and growth that would create more jobs, reduce poverty and help them to attain human development goals. The IMF fore warned that the countries which failed to expand trade and attract foreign capital ran the risk of being marginalised in the global economic system and falling farther and farther behind the rest of the world in terms of growth and human development. Therefore, it was in the interest of the Central Asian countries to allow market forces to set prices and allocate resources so that the economy could operate efficiently; to discipline fiscal policy that kept government expenditure in line with government revenues, while providing for a satisfactory level of public investment in basic infrastructure and human capital and a well-targeted social safety net and to ensure that the private sector performed its intended role as the main engine of growth.[7] They were impressed upon to introduce transparent regulatory systems so that foreign investors were encouraged to bring in their capital, technology and skills, effective legal system that protected property rights, broad based simplified tax systems and in the process ensuring that reforms were irreversible and were there to stay. Above all, the states in Central Asia were told to disengage from activities which market could perform more effectively.

While being favourably inclined towards these prescriptions of Bretton Woods institutions and as was widely expected in the prevailing situation of capitalist hegemony, the Central Asian countries, prominent among them being Kazakhstan and Kyrgystan, took measures for building market structures and institutions.[8] Uzbekistan's model of economic reforms was qualitatively different from both Kazakhstan and Kyrgystan. Uzbek President Islam G. Krimov, while addressing economic problems of the society as his core concern pursued the policy of what was termed as complete de-ideologisation of the economy. He stood for state retaining its position of chief reformer in the complex transitional period; providing sound legal basis for economic reforms; taking a due care of demographic situation of the country, wherein basic needs of the people were not to be lost sight of and for the creation of market structures in a gradual stage by stage manner.[9] The distinct feature of Uzbek model was that the government retained stakes up to 51% in the share holding companies, which ensured effective state controls over privatised units.[10]

Kazakhstan, the leading protagonist of market reforms, embarked upon the road to radical economic reforms with a view to open the economy and actively integrate it into the world trade system.[11] The country implemented wide ranging privatisation programmes which boosted private sector and on way to market economy system, it modernised financial and banking system for creating investment friendly environment. The government claimed from time to time that because of the implementation of economic reforms, Kazakh economy stood far ahead of others in the region of Central Asia. High growth rate and increased per capita GDP to more than \$ 5100 in the recent time were attributed to the economic reforms introduced in the country, though it was widely recognised that the boom in oil and gas prices was the major factor in the wealth acquired by the country, which even enabled it to establish National Oil Fund to accumulate oil and gas revenues, which the Fund has raised to $ 15 billion. [12]

The market oriented structural and institutional reforms in Central Asia have been uneven and tardy. Kazakhstan and Kyrgystan have moved faster whereas Uzbekistan and Turkmenistan have been slow in establishing market-related institutions. Using widely approved indicators developed by European Bank for Reconstruction and Development, it emerges that the level of reforms in terms of prices, foreign exchange and external trade, privatisation, and enterprise reforms and banking sector has been high in Kazakhstan and Kyrgyz Republic.[13] Tajikistan made significant progress in price reforms, external sector reforms and privatisation, whereas level of reforms in Uzbekistan and Turkmenistan has been low, especially in the external sector and enterprise and banking sector reforms. The transition form state-controlled economy to privatised one was bound to be difficult and uncertain, as not many properly understood the ethos of privatised market-oriented economic system. Being disenchanted with state-controlled economy and under the sway of triumphal mode of capitalism, the Central Asian countries set on the unknown path of market-economy system. It led to many problems, most glaring among them being corrupt practises at various levels of the state administration. However, the leadership remained optimistic about the reforms, little realising that fast mode of doing business in the private sector had no place for lethargic and cumbersome ways of doing business in the state-controlled system.[14] People used to public ownership did not easily inculcate the notion of private ownership and it became difficult for them to accept the credibility of the banks in the private sector. Therefore, the Central Asian leadership's agenda of integrating their economies with the global economy clashed with the ground reality in a big way because what 'was once… a closed, centralised economy based largely on inter-industry barter suddenly looked forward to play global role….'[15]

The over-enthusiastic supporters of reforms lamented that newly emerged post-Soviet Central Asian were not truly globalised. In their assessment, the partially globalised economies were not ideal ones for availing full economic benefits accruing from globalisation. Such claims had been pouring in at a time while some prominent economists held the view that the contention, 'openness enhances growth and economic growth reduces poverty', remained doubtful because it had been found that though economic development in the long run reduced poverty but it was firmly held that certain types of growth, particularly the one that accentuated inequality did not reduce poverty.[16] However the supporters of globalisation being in triumphal mood, a strong tendency was noted on their part to examine drive for globalisation in terms of what countries did in the form of removal of barriers for trade and investment, with less focus on what actually accrued to the common man. Rosy notions, without sound empirical base have been in abundance about countries like China and India depicting economic reforms a success. For instance it is often forgotten that FDI emerged as a major factor in China's economy only in the 1990s, a decade and a half after the liberalisation of the economy and that Chinese economy has very high rate of domestic investment, 40 percent of the GDP of the country as against 20 percent in India.[17] Also India and China may be among the world's fastest growing economies, but these economies cannot be held as the most globalised economies. Tariffs still remain high and none of the two has adopted capital account convertibility. There are several developing economies, which are far more globalised than these two, whereas their growth performance is far below India and China.[18] Therefore, some of the scholars have concluded that the remarkable economic development the Asian people have achieved is in spite of globalisation and not because of it.[19]

At the present juncture, the march of globalisation has entered a new phase when critics see the retreat of globalisation after its intensification more than one and half decades earlier. Now even the World Bank, chief facilitator of drive for globalisation, confesses that a new phase of globalisation has ushered in where in the coming decades, the decisive issue would be how to manage globalisation. At a time when major economies of the world are going through recession and IMF has recently revised its estimates of growth of the world for 2009 from 3% to 2.2%, it would definitely be more difficult for the defenders of capitalism to convince others that cross-border economic integration was good, facilitated flows of trade and investment and led to rapid development of new technologies. The World Bank projections that world economic growth will be higher between 2006 and 2030 than what it was between 1980 and 2005, with 3.1 percent annual rise in the per capita income of the developing countries, leading to the halving of absolute poverty from 1.1 billion to 550 million people with income below dollar one per day, cannot be trusted in the present set of circumstances when indicators point out slowdown in the global economy, in view of meltdown in the US and unexpectedly poor growth in Europe.[20] The diehard supporters of globalisation may still believe that temporary set backs to globalisation, notwithstanding, the drive may continue because even the dramatic events in the past including the demise of Soviet Union did not prevent globalisation. In this context, one may add that the demise of the Soviet Union signaled the crisis of socialism not capitalism. Therefore, it can be argued that contrary to the halting of capital's global march, the collapse of the Soviet Union was destined to accelerate it. However, the contemporary phase of economic recession in the major economies of the world indicates bad times for market-oriented economies, though the precise nature and future fallouts are not fully known yet. Even World Bank confesses that growing inequality in and among nations, rising tensions in the labour markets and increasing environmental pressure are the stress factors in the contemporary global economic system.

In the present uncertain complex scenario, it is interesting to see how these Central Asian countries respond. This is a time when even the staunch defenders of market-economy driven capitalist system are advocating a more active role for the state for bailing out crisis ridden economies, where if the slowdown continues these countries may think of more state centered measures. The indicators available at the moment point out that the Central Asian countries are likely to be more inward-looking than ever before and would be more careful for working out the mode and terms and conditions for integrating their economies with the global economic system. Kazakhstan, the most globalised economy among the Central Asian countries, has responded to the global economic slowdown on the expected lines. The Government of Kazakhstan has held that on its part it was farsighted measure to create the National Fund for accumulating revenues from oil and gas, which would now work as a 'financial cushion' against economic shocks emanating from global economic slowdown .Out of the revenues of the Fund, an amount of 10 billion US dollars has been set aside for extending support for financial and real economy sector, which would ensure safety of bank accounts and deposits.[21] The government has launched the Stress Assets Fund for acquiring mortgaged properties from the banks, thus injecting the new liquidity in to the economy and bailing out the banks from possible bankruptcy. With a view to overcome the ill-effects of the world financial crisis, President Nursultan Nazarbayev declared recently that the government had decided to merge innovating project financing funds and state run national companies for creating mega holding to fortify their national and international competitiveness. The country has taken the initiative to place all state budget and national company purchase orders domestically. The President underlined the necessity of purchasing products from small and middle business enterprises for lending them financial support because many such enterprises do not have enough capital and as such financial support would enable them to save business and in the process make jobs secure. On an optimistic note, the President declared that the country has enough resources to overcome the crisis though he laments that the times have changed today and people have learnt to work and save money. This kind of inward looking tendency on the part of Kazakhstan is noteworthy because the country has been the most enthusiastic supporter of market economy oriented reforms. The countries like Uzbekistan and Turkmenistan as noted earlier have been slow starters in this regard. In the wake of global financial slowdown, this kind of inward looking economic policy has become more pronounced, the trend, which may deepen further if such a crisis persists, as are the indications at the moment. The drive for globalisation may not be halted completely but countries would be more careful and state would surely play a more significant role in the days to come.

It should not be out of place to examine the severity of the crisis, the severity that would determine the mode and intensity of the remedial measures to be adopted by the countries in the different parts of the globe. In this context, it should be reiterated that the great depression of 1930s brought Keynesianism, which was historically recognized as a progress in economic thought, to the centre stage of economic thinking of that epoch. Likewise, the lessons to be drawn from present economic slowdown may also leave a lasting mark on the economic thinking of the countries because the largest economy of the world is headed into a recession that may be as bad as anything the US has faced since the 1930s.This signals bad times for the countries that directly or indirectly depend on the US as the engine of demand. There are no visible signs that it would overcome its economic crisis in the near future. The economists suggest that the US cannot come out of the mess it finds itself in today without more savings, needed for transferring production capacities back to the country which over the years were transferred to other countries, so that it could pay off the debts that recklessly ran up[22]. Moreover, the crisis of 1930s was resolved by labour and popular movements, shifting the burden of crisis on to capital through social wage contract, national unemployment insurance relief and social security, whereas today the crisis is being dealt with by shifting its burden onto the working class[23]. The solution of earlier crisis involved a downward redistribution of income whereas now the strategy is upward redistribution of income through regressive tax policies, financialisation and construction of debt regime. It is here in the shifting of burden of crisis to labour and the middle classes that the economists see chances of it deepening further, rather than being resolved.[24] The massive transfer of US investment capital from federal treasury securities to mortgage based securities played a major role in extending the crisis to the housing sector and in the process turned real estate into unreal.[25] However, in a broader perspective, it is argued that the crisis resulted from the deteriorating of the effective demand, as a direct consequence of the dismantling of Keynesian model and attempting a major upward redistribution of income since the last years of Carter administration. The Keynesian 'social contract' was abandoned in view of rising cost of the empire, the defeat in the Vietnam, the oil crisis, the weakening of the position of US dollar, leading to the termination of Bretton Woods agreements by Nixon administration. From 1970s onwards, the post-war empire based on credit was converted into an empire based on debt, thereby credit substituting wages and national incomes, to boost effective demands and thus temporarily resolving the under consumption crisis arising from the dismantling of Keynesian 'social contract'[26]. To further complicate the already complex situation, there is no long-term Keynesian solution to the problem, as high consumption is no longer ecologically sustainable because in terms of environmental crisis, it would contradict Keynesian solutions more severely and more quickly than wage inflation did in 1970s.[27] Therefore, in the current global crisis, economists see an opportunity to rethink of our economic models for the sake of ensuring sustainable development. With current population of 6.7 billion rising to over 9 billion by 2050, if we let the current trends of credit and leverage, growth and distribution continue, world production and consumption could increase by four to six times, with poverty persisting alongside, this would make development ecologically unsustainable.[28] The world will have to rethink of unfettered growth that has guided economic development for over two centuries because growth without equitable distribution has come to be widely recognised as the root cause of world hunger, poverty, terrorism and increasing instability.[29] The current crisis may finally make us learn the lesson that long term economic security and stability come not from lending money to distant foreigners to buy your stuff, rather from a large, economically secure middle class that has the means to purchase the output and services produced by nations.

In the recent years, Central Asian countries, prominent among them being Kazakhstan and Kyrgystan, have been trying to model their economies on market economy lines, the process which is likely to be halted under the prevailing circumstances. With oil boom coming to an end, revenues from such sales have been drastically reduced. The global recession assuming serious dimensions, it is becoming more and more clear that the countries like US cannot be the buyers and investors; they have been in the recent past. The gravity of the situation is believed to be serious enough that we will have to rethink of our models of growth. How are we to be ecologically sustainable? How markets are to be monitored at the global level when Bretton Woods institutions have been found wanting? How far growth can be continued without being bothered about equitable distribution of gains? These are the searching questions of the contemporary era, which no country, Central Asian being no exception, can afford to ignore. Their frustration with state-controlled economy, in view of the failure of state-controlled economy in the former Soviet Union of which they were a part, was on expected lines. However, now the world is confronted with a situation where economic slowdown in the major economies of the world is being seen as a crisis of global capitalist system. Therefore, the recent phase of globalisation with financialisation as the hallmark may not be continued. The Central Asian countries have been in the transitional phase throughout 1990s and they entered the twenty-first century in the same mode. The impact of present phase would also be felt in the Central Asian countries where already Kazakhstan, which has been the most vocal supporter of economic reforms, has responded to the global crisis by bringing state structures to the rescue of market. The search for self-reliance, the model that the former Soviet Union practiced for a long time, may become more pronounced, to which Central Asian countries are no strangers.

Notes

1. Francis Fukuyama, "The End of History", *National Interest* (summer 1989), p. 4.
2. Mikhail Gorbachev, *Perestroika: New Thinking for Our Country and the World* (London: Fontana 1988), p. 131.
3. Ibid.
4. Randhir Singh, *Crisis of Socialism: Notes in Defence of a Commitment* (Delhi: Ajanta, 2006), pp. 684-85.
5. Michel Camdessus, "Challenges Facing the Transition Economies of Central Asia", Address at the Conference on *Challenges to Economies in Transition*, Bishkek, 27 May 1998, p. 2. http://www.imf.org/external/np/speeches/1998.
6. Ibid., p. 3.
7. Ibid.
8. R. G. Gidadhubli, "Central Asian States: Transition to Market Economy" in P. L. Dash

(ed.) *Emerging Asia in Focus: Issues and Problems* (Delhi: Academic, 2008), p. 393.
9. P. L. Dash, "Can Uzbekistan be a Role Model of Governance in Central Asia", Paper Presented at Seminar on *Regional Cooperation as a Development Tool in Eurasia*, organised by ICAF, New Delhi, 27-29 March 2008, p. 2.
10. Gidadhubli, n. 8
11. Kairat Umarov, "Kazakhstan is an Idea for Regional Cooperation" in P. L. Dash, n. 8, p. 175.
12. Ibid., pp. 175-76
13. Gulshan Sachdeva, "Strengthening Economic Linkages between South and Central Asia", in Kuldip Singh (ed.) *South-Central Asia: Emerging issues* (Amritsar: GNDU, 2005), pp. 125-26
14. P. L. Dash, n. 9, p. 5
15. Ibid., p. 6
16. Pranab Bardhan, "Social Justice in the Global Economy", *Economic and Political Weekly*, Vol. 36, No. 5, 3-10 February 2001, p. 468
17. Pulpare Balakrishnan, "Globalisation, Growth and Justice", *Economic and Political Weekly,* Vol. 38, No, 30, 26 July 2003, p. 3166
18. Ibid.
19. Devendra Kaushik, "Asian Ascent: Bedrock of a New World Order", in P. L. Dash (ed.), n. 8, p. 64
20. World Economy and Development, "Retreat or a New Wave of Globalisation", 4 February 2007. www.wdev.eu
21. Embassy of The Republic of Kazakhstan in India, *Kazakhstan Weekly News*, Vol. 169, 28 October 2008.
22. R. Taggart Murphy, "Asia land the Meltdown of American Finance", *Economic and Political Weekly*, Vol. 43, No. 46, 15-21 November 2008, p. 29.
23. Farshad Araghi, "Political Economy of the Financial Crisis: A World-Historical Perspective", *Economic and Political Weekly,* Vol. 43, No. 45, 8-14 November 2008, p. 30.
24. Ibid.
25. Ibid., p. 31.
26. Ibid.
27. Ibid.
28. Paul Srivastva, "For a New Sustainable Economic Order", *Economic and Political Weekly*, Vol. 43, No. 44, 1-7 November 2008, p.7.
29. Ibid.

Globalisation: Socio-cultural Conflicts and their Implications

Preeti D. Das

We are aware of the fact that globalisation leads to the emergence of a global society. 'It reinforces the realisation of the fact that the earth is a common place for all, irrespective of their ethnic identity'. However, this also globalises the conflicts. Many multilevel conflicts have ethnic, religious, ideological and economic grounds. Attempts are being made to resolve the conflicts or deal with the conflicts in a better way. Concepts like 'cultural pluralism' and 'cross cultural sensitisation' emphasise openness and tolerance in interethnic relations. In this paper, I try to identify some of the major conflicts of socio-cultural nature which have acquired a new and important historical significance due to the influence of globalisation. Identification of conflicts influenced by globalisation poses a basic question like: How globalisation influences cultural diversity and what are the changes taking place in the nature of socio-cultural conflicts? Finally, I try to see the implications of these conflicts.

While talking of a global society, many argue that it has brought the cultures in focus in the global environment, which leads to another question—has it developed a culture which transcends diverse ethnic, economic, racial and religious backgrounds? When we say a global society promotes cultural integration and removes cultural barriers, we also ask this question: Has it developed a space for cultural understanding?

As far as the culture is concerned, my argument moves around the basic definition of culture—culture emerges through a systematic respect for particular customs and habits. Language, religion, social customs reflect the culture of a society. According to Webster's 'The New International Dictionary': culture is the "total pattern of human behaviour and its product embodied in speech, action and artifacts and dependent upon man's capacity for learning and transmitting knowledge to succeeding generations". Culture reflects not only the ideology of a society but it is the very substance of identity for individuals in a society. Thus, wherever human beings form communities, a culture comes into existence. The culture can be formed at various levels: at the village level, at the city level or at the level of a nation. Family, clan, ethnic groups and religion contributes in the formation of culture. Therefore, culture is an awareness of a common language, ethnicity, history and religion. The term culture refers to a variety of totems and boundaries, but religious affiliation has been amongst the most powerful influences.

Individuals and communities which believe in the values of their culture and the importance of its distinctiveness come close to each other and form a society. Thus culture is 'the highest stage of social development, which is an outcome of material production, division of works and exchange'. It is 'overall the stage of socio-cultural development of a society'. Civilisation is nothing but a society itself and includes all the components which are a must for the existence of a society. It is complicated in the sense that it is made up of sub-systems: political, economic, cultural and social.

Though religion plays an important role as far as cultural identity is concerned, slowly, with the change of time, its influence has started weakening in the world ideology.

The process of producing a global culture cannot be without any conflict. It poses a threat to the rights of individuals in a society. Then it becomes important to determine whose rights should be protected—ethnic, religious, racial groups or individuals. Thus the need for proper management of these conflicts becomes very crucial. Kumar Rupsinghe in his article Governance and the Conflict Resolution in Multi-ethnic Societies emphasises the role of governance: 'the notion of governance requires a more expanded notion of conflict transformation'. As per him, 'timely interventions can be made to resolve and prevent the outbreak of violence and war'. He further argues that 'governance of multi-ethnic societies requires the active participation of civil society and the development of a culture of negotiation and tolerance'.

Coming back to culture, it is in itself a very complicated concept as it denotes virtually every aspect of social, political, economical, intellectual, religious and artistic life of people (Tylor, 1924). Though all aspects of culture have a very complicated structure of their own, but the moment culture as a whole comes in contact with other cultures, it develops a fireball around itself and behaves differently and hence becomes more defensive. The founder of cultural studies Raymond Williams stressed (1975:91) "Culture has become the focus for differentiation" in many regions[1]. Of late, the term culture has become, at national and international level, a subject of intense political controversy. Many international organisations have come up with a deeper analysis of conflicts and their resolution. In order to understand implications of conflict, understanding the nature of conflict becomes very important. An overview of the categories of cultural conflicts shows that there could be religious warfare, ethnic conflicts, conflict between cultural cousins or the ideological conflict. At the base of all these conflicts, the concept of self-determination remains a major problem in the international communities. Ever since the collapse of USSR, Russia is facing major problems in handling ethnic minorities. These are not merely identity issues but majority of them prevail to protect their cultural and traditional values.

The nature of ethnic conflicts of Russia like in Chechnya or Volga-Urals region is mainly a fight for independence. These states no longer want to be a part of the Russian Federation. The Buryats are among several 'indigenous' peoples in Russia who are trying to protect their culture, including their language. Their effort to safeguard regional economic resources projects their fear in the field of security of resources.[2].

After the 1994 Chechen conflict, Chechen rebels have once again started their fight for independence. Their main argument was that Russia's military tactics have violated the Geneva Conventions by performing extrajudicial executions, torture (including rape), 'disappearances' and arbitrary detentions.

High level of ethnic conflict is also felt in the Volga-Urals region but the physical violence here is far less than that in Chechnya. One of the major reasons for this could be economic independence and to some extent their nationalising policies

The quest for the formation of 'Great Tatarstan' also poses a threat to the ethnic instability in Russia. The fear is that it would infringe on ethnic claims in Bashkortostan, Ulyanovsk Oblast, Chuvashia, etc. since these regions have quite a large number of Tatars who are currently outside its federal borders.

Another major concern for Russia is the Islamic revival in neighbouring Dagestan which would have huge political implications. Due to the economic importance of this region, even a minor increase in instability would be detrimental for Russia.

Similarly, the Buryatia region experienced a revival of Buddhism as per the 1999 report. Unnamed local officials spoke of Buryatia's 'political stability' as partly relying on a 'tradition of religious tolerance' which enables orthodox Christians, Buddhists and Shamanists to co-exist in Buryatia. Institute for Peace Studies (IPS) notes, however, the involvement of rival Buddhist 'factions' in regional politics. According to Dr. Natalia Zhukovskaya, an expert on Buddhist studies at the Moscow-based Institute of Ethnology and Anthropology, "Buryat authorities are meddling in Buddhist affairs, as an alternative khambo-lama [chief priest] is said to be supported by the authorities". The Buryat Buddhist representative claimed that this support had caused a 'schism' in the Buddhist community. The alternative khambo-lama was reported to have deposed the incumbent. The deputy chairman of the State Duma Committee on Social Movements and Religious Denominations expressed his concern on the use of religion by Russian regional politicians which could trigger violent conflicts[3].

Thus, we see that at the base of practically all of the above mentioned conflicts of Russian society lies the zeal to protect traditional values and religious affinity. Countless views concerning the phenomenon of 'Globalization' exist. More frequently it is viewed as something 'fundamentally new and interpreted as the one threatening cultural uniformity or homogenisation around the world'. It is in one sense taken to represent the new face of 'cultural imperialism'. In effect, it is viewed mainly as 'a threat to the cultural diversity'. In reaction to what is viewed as the erosion of traditional cultures and civilisations, Nader N. Chokr emphasises that we are "...witnessing the re-emergence of a tendency to 're-ethnicise the minds' through renewed and more or less systematic 'cultural revivals' world wide (viz., 'hinduisation', 'ivoirisation', 'sinofication', 'nipponification', 'islamicisation', 'russification', etc.)"[4].

For a deeper understanding of the implications of socio-cultural conflicts of multicultural society in the era of globalisation, I have tried to develop my argument around basic nature of the human being. But before we move on to the implications, it is important to see the structure of a multicultural society. At the base of any structure lie its component units. The component unit may differ based on the field or the level of the structural analysis. The component unit of my structural analysis of multicultural society is the culture of one group. The term 'culture of one group' can be understood as one ethnic group or one community belonging to the same cultural unit. It is not necessary that all the ethnic groups or the communities of one multicultural society should be of the same size. These component units can differ in their size depending on the size of that particular ethnic group or the community. Therefore, we can say that a multicultural society consists of some small and some large units.

In order to form a structure, there has to be some connectivity between these constituent units. Since the size of units is different, the nature of connectivity or bond within these component units also differs. This bond can be termed as 'strong' or 'weak'. Each of these units behaves differently at different point of time. Thus the nature and behaviour of this unit will be characterised by a given timeframe and space.

In order to form a multicultural society, the society has to have a minimum of two or more than two cultures as its component units. When these component units collide with each other, then the tendency is that a part of both the cultures will come close to each other and will merge in order to form a new or a relatively modified unit, whereas some part will be dropped out. Though this part does not get destroyed, it may turn into smaller units and in turn get attached to some other cultural units or lie dormant for sometime as long as it does not come in contact with others. This behaviour of the component units of a multicultural society is very much similar to the behaviour of an atom which is made of electron, proton and neutron. An atom gets attached to another for forming a molecule based on the compatibility between the numbers of electrons they have. Different molecules are required to make a compound. I have tried to apply this basic rule of physics to understand the structure of a multicultural society where if two or more different cultural groups come close to each other, they give birth to an altogether new culture. This new culture does have the atomic characteristics of both the cultures or, in fact, all the cultures which participated in this process.

Though the impact of one culture on the other also depends upon the timeframe, the duration of their contact and the place of their contact, but their contact certainly leave an impact on each other irrespective of their size. Nevertheless, some component units are dominating while others are less dominating. The dominating nature of these component units does not depend on their size but on the strength of even the smaller units.

Based on this principle, I have tried to study the Russian society of three phases: pre-soviet, soviet and present society. In search of their identity, the cultures are looking back as to who they were and are trying to bring back some elements of their culture. However, through the ages, various collisions between different cultures have given a different outfit to those traditions. For example, Russians are no more the same people who they were in the pre-soviet period. Their contact with different communities over the past years in different socio-political conditions, at peaceful times or war times, has changed them drastically without their knowledge of it.

Critics of globalisation argue that 'globalisation will wipe out the cultural identity and put everybody under one uniform'. The fear that the 'distinctive cultures' will disappear was so high that calls were made to 'preserve all the cultures'. Nonetheless, the cultures are bound to change with time and this change is unavoidable. Many scholars look at this change as 'cross-cultural contamination, intermingling and fertilisation' (Appiah, 2006). As has already been observed, culture is a creation of people at different levels. It reflects the beliefs and tradition of a particular group. Everything moves and keeps changing including solids and if they do not change, they are bound to collapse. Similarly, if cultures are not flexible enough to change, they are bound to wither away. Nonetheless, as per the principle of physics, it cannot disappear completely but lies as dormant element. This dormant element gets activated as and when it gets a suitable climate for its growth. However, as an individual's absorption capacity is based on one's inner self, the absorption capacity of each constituent unit is based on its gaseous, liquid and solid components. The component units of multicultural society can also be classified as atom or molecule into three groups: gas, liquid and solid. The units which come under the category 'gas' can easily adopt the changes occurring around them or easily get adopted by others. In such cases, the process of globalisation acts as a medium or a carrier of gaseous units from one place to another. The best example of it can be 'MacDonald culture', 'pizza culture' or 'jazz music', 'disco culture' and many other similar likings of one community get popularity outside their own community. Units which come under the category 'solid' are very rigid and may not change despite being in contact for centuries. Nevertheless, they do change, may be at the surface level but take a longer time than the units belonging to other categories. Religion could become the best example of this unit. It has been observed that in a multicultural state, various festivals like Christmas, Id, New year, etc. are being celebrated everywhere in a modified manner keeping elements of its originality alive. Thus we see that the cultures despite becoming 'global' are unique in their own way and continue to represent a complex of traditional and modern values.

I would like to end with a quotation of Yuri Lotman: "We live because we are different".

Notes

1. Vivienne Orchard , "Culture as Opposed to What", *European Journal of Social Theory,* University of Birmingham
2. *Country Reports 1999* Feb. 2000; UNPO n.d.
3. IPS
4. Nader N. Chokr ,"Consequences of Cultural Complexity",, *China Media Research*, Shandong University, 3(2), 2007

References

Erasov B. C., "Civilizations and Cultures", *Russia and East: Geopolitical & Civilizational Relations*, 3rd edition, Moscow, 1996.

Baylis J.,"The Globalization of World Politics", *Oxford University Press*, 2008.

Longworth Philip, "Russia's Empires–Their Rise and Fall; from Prehistory to Putin", 2005

Elena Rudykina,"Functioning of Regional Component in the Russian Language Teaching Process", *Vogograd State University*, Vogograd.

Preeti Das, "Motif and Structure of Fairy Tales; A comparative study of Russian and Asian Tales", Thesis submitted to JNU, 2000.

Rolan Barthes, "The Semiotic Challenge", translated by Richard Howard, *Oxford*, U. K. 1988.

Debates on "Social Problems of Russian Society: Volunteer Initiatives of Youth" held on 24th October 08 in Media-centre of Izvestia.

State and Democracy in Central Asia

Phool Badan

Introduction

The Soviet Union disintegrated in December 1991. In the aftermath of the dissolution of the erstwhile Soviet Union, the five former Soviet Central Asian republics emerged as independent sovereign states on the map of the world. The collapse of the Soviet system provided an opportunity to the Central Asian republics—Kazakhstan, Kyrgyzstan, Tajikistan, Turkmenistan and Uzbekistan—to stand upon their own feet. As a result, each of the Central Asian countries started to reshape their political system which would be fundamentally different from the past. Since the demise of the erstwhile USSR, the leaders of Central Asian states have introduced liberal measures in their economic sectors and democratic values in political system.

Historical Background

Prior to the Russian conquest, the culture and political life of the Central Asian peoples did not differ greatly from the settled and nomadic population in other parts of the Muslim world.[1] In order to study the nature of political developments in the region, it will be necessary to recount milestones, which have deeply influenced the political culture of the Central Asian region. These are:

- The Arab conquest of the Central Asian region and spread of Islam beginning from the eight century.
- The Mongol-Tatar invasion and conquest of Central Asia in the twelfth century and their subsequent assimilation and Islamisation.
- The rise and fall of the Timurid Empire.
- The Russian conquest of the region during the nineteenth century.
- The October Revolution of 1917 and subsequent Sovietisation and secularisation of Central Asian region.[2]

After the end of its medieval glory, Central Asia was divided into three major native Khanates: Khanate of Khiva, Khanate of Kokand and Emirate of

Bukhara. The Khanates were feudal autocracies which were ruled by *Khans* and *Emirs*, and Islam was the main source of political legitimisation. The system of administration of land tenure and taxation was based on the Perso-Arab administration of Transoxiamia. 'The system of justice was based on the Islamic laws (*sharia*) and the customary laws (*adat*)'[3] and was headed by the member of the religious elite known as Kazi. Initially, the court of Kazis was allowed to operate. But with the introduction of Russian judicial system, the Kazi courts were reduced to subordinate status. 'Kazis were appointed for life and had no fixed administrative district'.[4] But later, the Kaziship acquired hereditary character. The Kazi enjoyed a high social status and economic privileges. Another religious elite was the *Mufti* who was the legal and spiritual head of the Khanates.

In practice the dynastic rulers of the Khanates and their subordinate officials did not generally follow the accepted principles and the legal norms. The rule of the native *Khans* and *Emirs* was cruel and exploitative as was the case with many other societies in Asia and elsewhere. The *bieys,* the wealthy landlords and subordinate feudal officials used to exploit the poor people of the region. Poverty was rampant, disease and illiteracy widely prevailed. To put things in perspective, there were features of many other societies around the world.

Political power structure in Central Asia was of feudal nature, similar to the one prevalent in medieval Europe. Hereditary rulers had nominal control, but the provincial *beks* (governments) were politically independent and carried on constant wars against their neighbours: their sovereigns. The government was autocratic where the ruler's words were law and there was no space for opposition. The clergy enjoyed a high status and respect in a society where illiteracy and superstitions were widespread.[5] The *Khans* and *Emirs* got full support from the institutions like *Kazi*. The people of the region had no right to participate in political process; they were not even aware of the various activities of the government.

The Khans received taxes from the general public as a right. However, the *beks* were exempted from paying these taxes. The *beks* were not even obliged to give an account of their earnings to the Khans. However, they did offer lavish presents to the Khans once or twice a year.[6]

Men were picked up from all parts of the country to keep the roads in repair, to build houses for the *Khans*, to cultivate his grounds and to clean out the canals, and were forced to work without any payment; they were not provided even food. When half of the village population was forced to work like this, the other half was compelled to pay a tax of two *tengas* a day to each of the working man. Anyone who refused to pay the tax was punished with whipping. Sometimes people were whipped to death while others were buried alive at the place of work.[7]

In the aftermath of the annexation of the Central Asia by the Tsarist Government in the second half of the nineteenth century, the Russian Government established colonial administration in the region and functioned under the Ministry of War. Military played a major role in the administration of Turkistan. The offices of the Governor-General of Turkistan region and the governors of its oblasts were staffed with military officers.[8] **The** colonial administration of Turkistan was accountable to the Russian Government. In other words we can say that the Tsarist Government established autocratic type of administration in the region. The people of the region had no political rights and even they were not allowed to know about the policies of the government.

The Bolshevik Revolution took place in October 1917. Soon after the great Socialist Revolution, the Soviet Union became a federation of fifteen national 'Union Republics' and eight autonomous regions. Legally all Union Republics had equal status, but geopolitical factors made the Russian Republic superior to the other. There was a single party system in the whole of the Soviet Union. Opposition political parties were not allowed to operate in the country. Before the October Revolution of 1917, the Bolsheviks promised democratisation of the political institution but, after the revolution, this promise was ignored. All issues were decided by the Soviet Communist Party in the name of 'democratic centralism'.

In the Soviet political system, there was no scope for individual initiative and local autonomy; civil and political liberties were nonexistent and individual participation was also not there. But in spite of these, the Soviet political system was based on rapid economic transformation which was considered as a way of bringing both rapid economic growth and social justice through popular participation. In other words it can be interpreted as an effort for altering material relationship of the society.

The Soviet system was characterised by centralised control, harsh rationing, coercive mobilisation of labour, coercive requisitioning of agricultural produce, elimination of market and absolutist methods. In short, it can be said that the Soviet system was based on the centralised directive system of planned economy in its purest historical form which was implemented by the Soviet authority in the former USSR.[9]

The Soviet system derived its 'political relevance from the explanation of society in terms of class conflict and exploitation'.[10] In this system, the embracing political system is the state and the subgroups derive their corporate personalities from it. Individuals existed only as the 'elementary particles' of the state, which is a highly centralised authority and any dispersal of it is seen as dangerous to the whole system.[11]

So far as Central Asia is concerned, it was part of the former Soviet Union where all major decisions were imposed by the central government and Communist Party of the Soviet Union. Republican bureaucracy received the direction from Moscow, and leaders of the region acted as agents of the Russian Communists. Likewise, the Soviet economic system was based on centrally planned system. There was no place for religious and cultural autonomy. As far as the formulation of basic policy is concerned, central government had the final and decisive say.

Democracy in Central Asia in the Post- Soviet Period

The Soviet Union ceased to exist in December 1991. As a result of its disintegration, the five former Soviet Central Asian republics emerged as independent sovereign states in the region. In the aftermath of the collapse of the Soviet system, each of the Central Asian countries have faced enormous problems. One of the major problems was to establish democratic political system in the region. In this regard, the countries of the region have responded in different ways. Since the demise of the erstwhile USSR, the leaders of the Central Asian states have introduced liberal measures in their economic sectors and democratic values in political systems. During the Soviet period there was single party system and opposition political parties were not allowed to operate in the country. But after getting independence, the Central Asian republics have introduced multi-party system and periodic elections etc. Only in case of Tajikistan the ruling elites rejected the change which ultimately led to the Civil War. But in the post Civil War period, Tajik Government allowed the UTO (United Tajik Opposition) to participate in the government. Tajikistan is a good example which has given political space to the opposition political party like Islamic Renaissance Party. Turkmenistan and Uzbekistan opted for gradual reforms in their political system. Some of the leaders of the Central Asian countries have showed their apprehension and fear that the drastic political liberalisation would promote political instability in the region. So far as Kazakhstan and Kyrgyzstan are concerned, they have opted for more pluralistic forms of political system.

All the Central Asian republics have adopted their own constitutions. The power structure of these states is formally based on the principle of 'separation of power', but in practice the presidents are the centre of all the powers in all the Central Asian Constitutions. There is no place for vice-presidents.

The Constitutions of all the Central Asian republics profess sovereignty, democracy and secularism as their underlying principles. The Constitutions of the Central Asian Republics declare Central Asian countries as secular states. The people of Central Asia have been guaranteed the right to profess and propagate any religion that was not allowed to the native people during the Soviet days. The Constitutions of the republics guarantee the right and freedom to their citizens regardless of nationality, ethnic origin, property holding, religious belief and political convictions. Everyone has the right to life, and men and women have equal rights. The Constitutions also allow the citizens to assemble and hold meeting, rallies, demonstrations and marches peacefully. Citizens of the countries also have the right to form political parties and social associations within the framework of the Constitutional order.

The Central Asian states have established multi-party political systems in the region. There are a number of political parties which are working in the region. The republic wise political parties are noted below.

There are twelve political parties in Kazakhstan. These are: (a) Nationwide Social Democratic party, (b) Democratic Choice of Kazakhstan, (c) Communist Party of Kazakhstan, (d) Village Social Democratic Party, (e) People's Communist party of Kazakhstan, (f) Democratic party of Kazakhstan Bright Path, (g) Fatherland's Ray of Light (Nur-Otan) Party. This is a ruling party in the republic, (h) Alash, (i) Coalition for a Just Kazakhstan, (j) Democratic party, (k) Party of Patriots, and (l) Rukhaniat Party.[12] The Constitution of the Republic of Kazakhstan forbids the establishment of any social organisation which seeks to forcibly change the Constitutional order and undermine the state, security, violate territorial integrity, or promote 'social, racial, national, religious, class or tribal discord'.[13] The Constitution of the Republic, supplemented by a legislation put an absolute ban on any propaganda or campaign directed towards the above aims. The creation of political parties based on religion is not allowed in the Kazakhstan Republic.[14]

In the Republic of Uzbekistan also, there are five major political parties: (a) People's Democratic Party of Uzbekistan. It is a ruling party of the republic. It emphasises upon the principle of law and order in order to keep the country out of extreme nationalism—in other words, Islamic fundamentalism, (b) Liberal Democratic Party of Uzbekistan. This is a ruling party in the country. (c)

Self-sacrifice National democratic Party, (d) Justice Social Democratic Party, and (e) National Revival Democratic Party of Uzbekistan. National Revival Democratic Party of Uzbekistan talks about political, economic, educational and cultural prosperity and national consciousness of the Republic. It pays special attention to rearing a lofty sense of internationalism and nationalism through values common to all human kind.[15]

The political parties in the Republic of Kyrgyzstan have power in politics and freedom to campaign. There are 25 political parties in the country: (a) Agrarian Labour Party of Kyrgyzstan, (b) Agrarian Party of Kyrgyzstan, (c) Ak zhol, (d) Alga Kyrgyzstan Party, (e) Ar-Namys Party, (f) Ata-Jurt, (g) Ata-Meken Socialist Party, it supports the democratic reforms of political system and market based economy, (h) Banner National Revival Party, (i) Beren, (j) Communist Party of Kyrgyzstan, (k) Democratic Movement of Kyrgyzstan. The party believes in ideals of democracy and its main aim is to 'campaign for civil liberties'.[16] It also propagates land reform and its privatisation. The party supports economic and political reforms in the country.[17] (l) Democratic Women's Party of Kyrgyzstan, (m) Erkin Kyrgyzstan Progressive and Democratic Party, (n) Justice Party, (o) Movement for the People's Salvation, (p) Mutual Help Movement, (q) My country Party of Action, (r) National Unity Democratic Party, (s) Communist Party of Kyrgyzstan, (t) Party of the Veterans of the War in Afghanistan, (u) Peasant Party, (v) People's Party, (w) Republican party of Kyrgyzstan. It believes in democracy, (x) Social Democratic Party of Kyrgyzstan. The party believes in the ideal of democratic reforms and market-oriented economy, (y) Union of Democratic Forces.

There are three major political parties in Tajikistan. These are: (a) Communist Party of Tajikistan, (b) Islamic Renaissance Party of Tajikistan, and (c) People's Democratic Party of Tajikistan. People's Democratic Party is a ruling party in the country. Besides, there also are four minor political parties in the republic. The names of the minor political parties' of the republic are: Democratic Party, Justice Party, Social Democrtic Party, and Socialist party.[18]

So far as Turkmenistan is concerned, the country is presently governed by a single party as there are not many parties which exist. However, there are innumerable unregistered opposition political parties such as Communist Party of Turkmenistan, Republican Party of Turkmenistan, Turkmen Union of Democratic Forces, etc. Democratic Party of Turkmenistan is a ruling party in the country.[19]

The Central Asian countries have established election commission and have also introduced periodic elections in their political systems. The elections are conducted by Central Election Commission. The Constitutions of the region advocate free and fair elections.

Kazakhstan held a presidential election on 4 December 2005. There were five contestants in election including incumbent president Nursultan Nazarbayev. He won the election. Opposition candidates were allowed some access to the mass-media. The Organization for Security and Cooperation in Europe (OSCE) criticised the elections, calling them unfair, but noted improvements.[20]

A parliamentary election was held in Kazakhstan on 18 August 2007 for 107 seats. Seven parties were contesting the election. Except Nur-Otan party, none of the party reached the 7% threshold to win the seats. The election was described on state television as 'a real step towards democracy'. The OSCE observers said that the election had showed some progress with same problems.[21]

In the Republic of Kyrgyzstan, presidential election took place on 10 July 2005. There were six candidates in the fray. Kurmanbek Bakiyev won the election with 88.9% votes. In the parliamentary election, the Ak-Zhol party became victorious. The other two parties, Social Democratic Party of Kyrgyzstan and Communist Party of Kyrgyzstan, won 11 and 8 seats respectively.[22]

The presidential election was also held in Tajikistan on 6 November 2006. Six candidates were contesting the election. Emomali Rakhmonov won the election with 79.3% of valid votes. So far as parliamentary election is concerned, it was held on 27 February and 13 March 2005. Seven parties participated in the election. But only four parties were able to make their presence in the parliament. People's Democratic Party of Tajikistan became the victorious party by winning 49 seats in parliament.[23]

In Uzbekistan, presidential election took place on 23 December 2007. There were four candidates in the election. Incumbent President, Islam Karimov, won the election and became the president of the republic third time. He received 90.77% of the valid votes. Observers from the commonwealth of independent states and SCO gave the election a positive assessment.[24] Parliamentary election was held in Uzbekistan on 26 December 2004 and 9 January 2005. Liberal Democratic Party won 41 seats in the 120 seats parliament and emerged as the single largest party. People's Democratic Party Uzbekistan got 28 seats, Self-sacrifice National Democratic Party won 18 seats, National Revival Democratic party of Uzbekistan got 11, Justice Social Democratic Party obtained 10 and Non Partisans got14 seats.[25]

After Niyazov's death, Gurbanguly Berdimukhammedov became the acting president of Turkmenistan. The election for the office of the president of the Republic was held on 11 February 2007. There were six candidates in the election. Gurbanguly Berdimukh ammedov was declared the winner of the election, receiving 89.23% of the polled votes.[26]

Parliamentary elections to the Majlis were held in Turkmenistan on 14 December 2008. It was the first election since Turkmenistan's independence in which theoretically, there were parties other than the Democratic Party of Turkmenistan. About 90% of the members were of the Democratic Party of Turkmenistan and 10% were from the affiliated organisations 'initiative groups'. Thus, no opposition political parties have been set up, but initiative has been taken in this regard. Human Rights observers are of the opinion that 'the conditions are not in place to hold a free and fair election that would be meaningful reflection of the will of the people' but also mentioned that there has been 'some progress'. A small nine-member team from the OSCE observed the elections, as well as small teams from the United Nations and CIS, the first international observers, were allowed to view the election. After the elections, the head of the CIS observations team said—"the parliamentary elections were held in compliance with election legislation in norms of democratic elections and were marked by high voter turnout"[27].

The Constitutions of the region have made provisions for an independent judiciary. Judicial powers are to be exercised by the Constitutional court, the Supreme Court, Supreme Economic Court and the lower courts. The Constitutional Court has the power to interpret the Constitution and resolve the disputes between state authorities, and its jurisdiction is final. Judges of all courts are appointed by the president.[28]

Thus, all the independent countries of the region are marked by a weak judicial system. This system is a heritage of the former USSR when the public prosecutor held wide powers. The system of public defence, public litigation and writ petitions has not been institutionalised. The judiciary as the custodian of the constitution and democratic rights still has to evolve.

Since independence of the Central Asian republics, fundamental reforms have been carried out by the governments of the region in the field of judiciary. Even after 17 years of independence, the reforms are still in process. The judicial reform in Uzbekistan was initiated by Presidential Decree No. 2682 on *the Improvement of the Judicial System of the Republic of Uzbekistan* on 14 August 2000.[29] Kazakhstan has also taken steps to reform the judiciary in the country. In reforming major institutions, the Constitutional law on *Judicial*

System and status of Judges (December 2000) and state programme on *Legal reform* (September 2002) have become the cornerstone documents of the Judicial reform aimed at increasing judicial independence in Kazakhstan. Now we can say that promoting and strengthening of judicial independence is on the top of the agenda in the course of legal reforms aimed to achieve the rule of law and democracy in Uzbekistan and Kazakhstan.[30]

As far as the freedom of media is concerned, during the Soviet period, media was controlled by the Communist Party of the Soviet Union and the government of the erstwhile USSR with the help of the Censor Board, Glavlit. But Gorbachev relaxed control over the media through his policy of openness (glasnost). In the aftermath of the disintegration of the former USSR, the Central Asian countries have provided relative freedom to the means of communication, though this freedom of media is still far from real in practice. However, a welcome initiative has been taken in this direction.

Thus, Constitutions of the region envisage democratic political system but they grant extraordinary power to the president. Besides, the Constitutions of the Central Asian states provide social, cultural, political rights and civil liberties to the people of their respective countries which were denied during the erstwhile Communist regime of the Soviet Union. But these rights and liberties are far less than the rights and liberties available to the people of the developed and democratic countries of the world. But a beginning has been made in this regard. The Constitutions of the Central Asian states allow full political freedom and creations of multi-party democracy. The leaders of the region are trying to reform their political systems. Some of the democratic measures have been taken by the governments of Turkmenistan and Uzbekistan in this regard. But the institutions necessary for the growth of democratic cultures are weak. The institutions which are essential for the development of democratic political system such as separation of powers; multi-party system; free, fair and periodic elections; independent and powerful judiciary; independent mass media; professional bureaucracy and rule of law; etc. have not been nurtured. The size of middle class which is the backbone of democracy is also small in number.

Conclusion

At the end I would like to say that the Central Asian states have been taking the steps for the creation of the modern democratic political system and to widen the democratic space. The democratic movements are weak in the region since these countries are newly independent states. They got independence 17 years back, which is a very short period for establishing democratic system in a country. So, they need some more time for nurturing the democratic political system in the region. It is also important to understand that the Central Asian republics are passing through a transition period. One can look forward to the deepening of democratic reforms in these countries.

References

G. Wheeler, *The Peoples of the Soviet Central Asia* (London; The Bodley Head, 1969), p.93.

Shamsuddin, "Geopolitics of Central Asia", *India and Russia in a Changing World* (New; ICSSR, 1999), p.100.

Shamsuddin, *Secularisation in the USSR* (Delhi; Vikas Publishing House, 1982), p.82.

Elizabeth E. Bacon, *Central Asians under Russians Rule* (New York, Ithaka; Cornell University Press, 1966), p.67.

Richard D. Pierce, *Russian Central Asia, 1867-1917* (Berkeley and Los Angeles, 1960), p.12.

E. Schuyler, Phil Dr., *Turkistan*, (London, Sampson Low, Marston; 1876), p.57.

Ibid.

R. Vaidyanath, *The Formation of the Soviet Central Asian Republics: A Study in Soviet Nationalities Policy, 1917-1936* (New Delhi; People's Publishing House, 1967), p. 33.

Kristian Gerner and Stefen Hedlund, *Ideology and Rationality in the Soviet Model: A Legacy for Gorbachev* (London; Chicago University Press, 1989), p.35.

David E Apter, *The Politics of Modernization* (Chicago, London; Chicago University Press, 1965), p.6.

Ibid, p.35.

"List of Political Parties in Kazakhstan", available at: http://en.wikpedia.org/wiki/List_of_political_parties_in_Kazakhstan

Article 55, "Kazakhstan: Republic Constitution", *FBIS: Central Eurasia*, nos. 48-54, 19 April 1993, pp.68-78.

Article 58 (Paragraph 2), Ibid.

"New Political Party to be set up in Uzbekistan", *Pravda- vostoka*, 25 May 1995, p.1. *Summery of World Broadcast*, part-I, 27 May 1995, p. SU/231G/1.

"Kyrgyzstan", *The Europa Year Book*, vol. II (London, 1997), p. 1968.

"Kyrgyzstan", *Political Handbook of the World 1998* (New York, 1998), p.579.

"Elections in Tajikistan", available at: http://en.wikipedia.org/wiki/Elections_in_Tajikistan

"TurkmenistaniPresidentianiElection",availableat:2007,availableat:http://en.wikpedia.

org/wiki/Category: political_parties_in_Turkmenistan

"Kazakhstani Presidential Election, 2005", available at: http://en.wikipedia.org/wiki/Kazakhstani_presidential_election,-2005

"Kazakhstani Legislative Election, 2007", available at: http://en.wikipedia.org/wiki/kazakstani_legislative_election_2007

"Election in Kyrgyzstan", available at:http://en.wikipedia.org/wiki/Election_in_kyrgyzstan

"Elections in Tajikistan", available at: http://en.wikipedia.org/wiki/Elections_in_Tajikistan

"Uzbekistan Presidential Election, 2007", available at: http://en.wikipedia.org/wiki/uzbekistani_presidential_election_2007

"Uzbekistani Parliamentary Election, 2004-2005", available at: http://en.wikipedia.org/wiki/uzbekistani_parliamentary_election,_2004%e2%80% 93200

"Turkmenistani Presidential Election, 2007", available at:http://en.wikipedia.org/wiki/Turkmanistan_presidential_election,_2007

"Turkmenistani Parliamentary Election, 2008-2007", available at: http://en.ministari.org/wiki/Turkmenistan_parliamentary_election_2008% E2% 80% 93 2009

Constitution of Turkmenistan, Ashgabat, 18May, 1992, no. 691-XII, pp.1-19, "Kazakhstan: Republic Constitution", *FBIS: Central Eurasia*, nos. 48-54, 19 April 1993, pp.68-78, "Kyrgyzstan: Republic Constitution", *FBIS: Central Eurasia*, nos. 99-105, 9 August 1993, pp. 8-101, "Tajikistan: Draft Republic Constitution Presented", *FBIS: Central Eurasia*, nos. 52-56, 18 May 1994, pp.92-103, *Constitution of the Republic of Uzbekistan,* Tashkent, 8 December 1992, pp. 9-36.

Marina Shin, Madina Zhamuzakova, Stanislav Kim, and Lada Mirzalieva, "Implementation of Judicial Independence in Uzbekistan and Kazakhstan in the Rule of Law Context", *Managerial Law*, vol. 46, no.6, 2004, p.88.

Ibid, p.90.

New Challenges to Nation-States in Central Asia with the Advent of Globalisation

Nandini Bhattacharya

The successor states in Central Asia are still in their toddling stage of independent nationhood. From the very inception of their unprepared and unexpected independence in 1991, which resulted from the sudden collapse of the USSR, they had a very difficult and complex journey towards reshaping their state and reorienting their identity. Their immensely important geo-political location has drawn them into international power politics even before they had reconciled with their change in status as full sovereign states. Especially after 9/11, these states had undergone a phase of suspicion from the Western world since they carry Islamic connections. The supra-national yoke of the Soviet entity having been removed, they started rebuilding their states on the ethno-national super-structure inherited from the previous Soviet regime. For a substantial period of time, there was a popular apprehension among scholars and strategic analysts about the growth of another supra-national force in the form of political Islam in this potentially susceptible zone. Though overt Islamisation has not occurred, the importance of Islam and its complicated role in certain areas of the vast region cannot be denied. In order to cope up with the changes and challenges posed by the reality, these states needed to take an intense drive towards confidence building along with difficult measures of economic and political policy. The drive for redefining their identities and reviving their cultural and historical heritage from the lost past became an imperative at this stage.

However, the Central Asian republics met with yet another challenge almost immediately after their independence, which was also barely related to the collapse of the USSR, in the form of globalisation. These immature states, with their myriad of internal problems and complications, had hardly any time for prospective inward speculation. Each of the states, namely Kazakhstan, Kyrgyzstan, Tajikistan, Turkmenistan and Uzbekistan have shown ingenuity in their approach towards the external world from the moment they became independent. The command economy gave way to market economy the moment the Soviet system collapsed. It was this trend of opening up the closed economy that coincided with the general trend of globalisation at the very outset. Linking up with world economy was a basic necessity for these countries at this moment of uncertain beginning. This necessity resulted from the lopsided economic structure that they had inherited from the Soviet system, where this vast territory performed the task of providing raw materials while the industrial finished products used to be supplied by White Russia or European portion. But, even before independence, at the time of Perestroika, while Gorbachev started demanding autonomy and self-sufficiency for these Republics, Glasnost expressed a great deal of local level protests against such push for which they were not prepared so far. However, after freedom, they faced the acute economic crisis which they had apprehended from the time of Perestroika. Economic self-sufficiency was a far cry, dependence on Russia had to be reoriented but at the same time they got the freedom to choose their patrons in order to save their economy from outright collapse. Thus, the entry of Western patrons either as investors or loan providers was obvious at this juncture. Initially, some of the Central Asian state authorities had a lot of expectation out of the foreign involvement for the upliftment of their broken economy. Thus, in the indecisive and insecure economy of a zone where a sudden power vacuum has occurred along with ideological transformation, globalisation had a rather smooth entry. So, for Central Asian states, unlike other third world countries, there was hardly any scope for even the faintest protest before the introduction of globalisation. On the contrary, because of the lack of money and infrastructure, the prospect of foreign investment apparently came as a boon. But, given the complex intricacies of economic dynamism of this region, the impact of globalisation and international network of trade and finance did not bring an easy solution to its difficult problems. In the observation of Stanislav Zhukov, "In the first years after the dismantling of the USSR , it was widely believed by the post-Soviet elites that the globalisation and internationalisation would prove to be an unqualified boon for the national economy in each of these newly independent states. However, this is not always the case; not all states have a chance for development in the global economy. Indeed, the fate of many will be that of economic marginalisation".[1]

Apparently, globalisation of these countries was an ideological shift as well, for it not only changed the economic parameters but also brought them into contact with powers branded as the opponents by the earlier regime in power. Interactions with the 'capitalist' West, which was abhorred so far, now opened up a new arena for these states to experiment with. But this was no easy shift from one system to the other or transferring their dependence from Russia to America. Globalisation in this region had a far more complex and mixed character compared to the other parts of the third world. For here the control of Russia, politically, strategically and even economically, remained quite effective even after the demise of the Soviet structure. Rather, globalisation added more powers to share the exploits of this relatively weak yet extremely viable economic zone. But their interest in these territories was not confined to economic exploits alone; there were strategic issues involved and geo-cultural prospects being quite significant as far as the presence of Islam was concerned. Thus Russia, America and China, the three major powers of the world, got involved in this area, with some common and some special intentions. There are of course many other European and Asian countries of different stature that were interested and involved in the economy of these states.

The peculiar geo-cultural contours of this vast, land-locked zone have much to do with their problems and prospects. It is physically joined with Europe and Asia and can become a natural contiguity to Russia's Eurasian theme and project. The eastern link of the zone with China was a source of uneasiness throughout the Soviet phase which now developed a new dimension with Chinese expansionism and involvement. There too, the revival of historic Mongol tradition gathered momentum in academic platforms. The role of USA was rather remote compared to Russian and Chinese involvement in these territories. But, of course, US interest is significant and its role is effective as far as dynamics of globalisation is concerned. Interestingly, the Central Asian states took membership of the IMF as early as possible while keeping formal links with Russia through their membership of Commonwealth of Independent States (CIS). The range of co-operation and collaboration expected by the newly independent states was thus remarkable.

In the consequent years, the new nation-states became members of a number of strategic, political and economic forums/fora in order to participate in the global dynamism. One characteristic feature of these states in their post-independence phase was to widen their scope of experiments in international relations, which was quite impossible in their previous ideological setting. To begin with, they were all members of the Commonwealth of Independent States under the auspices of Russian leadership. But this union for both economic cooperation and strategic security of the nascent nations was not enough for them and within five years, one of the Central Asian members, Uzbekistan, showed the courage to discontinue its membership banking on other stronger alternatives available. The alternative bloc which developed meanwhile was GUUAM consisting of Georgia, Ukraine, Uzbekistan, Azerbaijan and Moldova. While CIS continued with the membership of Russia, Belarus, Armenia, Kazakhstan, Kyrgyzstan and Tajikistan, GUUAM took a pro-US stance and openly expressed a desire to have partnership with NATO. Although the cold war phase was over, yet the tacit tension between Moscow and Washington got revealed in such polarisations. In fact, there were many such nuances that revealed strong undercurrents within and amongst the Central Asian states regarding strategy, security and economy. In spite of being one broad geo-cultural zone with a very long shared past heritage and a common political bond in the recent past, Central Asia failed more in her intra-regional negotiation and cooperation than in the case of foreign relations. They showed irresolvable disputes on ethnic lines, intolerance and jealousy in the sharing of economic resources and infrastructure and, therefore, responded to an external phenomenon like globalisation from their individual stand point. The similarities and dissimilarities of the material viability and practical situation in each state conditioned their exercise of options available to them.

Central Asia's Adjustment in Global Economic Demands: Its Variations

To discuss the role of globalisation in post-Independent Central Asia, one must therefore reckon with the fact that each of the successor states in this broad geo-cultural zone displayed distinct and diverse trajectories in both internal and external spheres. Economic viability of these states to participate in global economic network remained uneven and lopsided. Although these states in general did not possess much industrial infrastructure or capital resources for their quick development and appeared quite unimpressive by the global capitalist standards, yet the presence of a substantial variety of natural resources made them prominent participants in global economy. Almost all the republics contain natural oil, gas, gold and other metals, grow cash crops and possess hydro-electrical resources in varying amounts. According to an American expert, "The Central Asian states are mercifully blessed with a number of resources that enable them to enter upon the world stage with viable economic prospects. While much of the region's industrial potential is of dubious quality, its resources and raw materials are of much promise".[2]

The above written account describes the basic parameters for Central Asia to take part in the global economic dynamism. Specially, the oil and gas reserves had made this zone appear as an alternative energy base for future. An editorial in the *Washington Post* stated openly, "The broad Western strategy must be to take the immense energy resources of the Caspian Sea area. In this way, the west can diminish dependence on the oil and gas of the uncertain states of the Persian Gulf".[3] But though these resources may provide some sense of security for these countries in the long run, they did not solve the telling economic crisis straddling across the republics. For natural gas, transport became a critical factor and lack of infrastructure imposed a deep impediment. One can begin with the example of Turkmenistan, an otherwise obscure state, which had an enormous reserve of natural gas but lack of direct access to the world market never allowed her to become rich. Turkmenistan was unique in her posture by not taking part in any of the international blocs that had developed in the post-Soviet era (neither CIS, nor GUUAM). This decision of moving alone can be explained by her peculiar situation with huge gas reserves but inadequate transport arrangements. For natural gas export pipeline links are absolutely essential and the countries through which they pass naturally exert considerable control over the entire process of export. Thus, Boris Rumer observed, "The dream of the early 1990s that this country would become a second Kuwait never came to pass. The principal problem of the economy is the lack of access to a market with solvent clients: that is, with end-users of natural gas who are capable of paying for deliveries".[4] Here the Russian linkage continued almost without a break in spite of the break up of the USSR, for the pipeline linking the natural gas deposits of Turkmenistan with its new customers was bound to pass through Russia. This Soviet infrastructural legacy is not easy to overcome or replace. But Russia refused to purchase and re-export the natural gas in big amount from Turkmenistan. Neither was Russia willing to allow Turkmenistan to construct an alternative pipeline for accessing the world market. Thus, the Russian position became obvious—it neither had any intention to help Turkmenistan nor did it allow the new state to fend for itself. But, Turkmen President Niyazov took a bold decision to open up his resources for direct foreign purchase. Immediate interest was shown by the USA, China, Japan, Iran, Turkey and the Gulf countries in this issue, while important international petroleum companies like Shell, Unocal and Exxon agreed to explore the given sites.[5] But further complications developed between foreign powers regarding the creation of new pipelines involving the USA and Russia, USA and Iran, Iran and Turkey and so on.

But notwithstanding all these complexities, an alternative pipeline was made through Iran in December 1997 and Tehran promised to buy a substantial amount of gas for the next twenty five years. But potential investors were still vacillating with the fear of inflated estimates given by Iran. However, Turkmen pipelines through Iran were not approved by the USA for the fear of Islamic influence .Thus, what this complex and yet indecisive picture shows is the range of choice and options open to the small and obscure Central Asian states and how often an independent decision went either against her old patron or the present leader of the world. Though the scope of reaping on her gas exports remained unutilised for his state, Niyazov should be credited for breaking the deadlock and creating an alternative passage to reach the world market by taking enormous risks.

The more prominent states in Central Asia namely Kazakhstan and Uzbekistan took two completely different approaches towards their global economic policy: while Kazakhstan decided on integration into the world economy as fast as possible, Uzbeksitan sought to protect its national economy against the advent of global competition[6]. Kazakhstan decided to link up with world economy at a very fast pace and therefore welcomed a number of foreign investments, infrastructural assistance and expertise for necessary development of the industrial sector. Under this rapid change embarked upon quite consciously by Nabiev, the ruler of the biggest and richest of all Central Asian states, the old inherited economic structure which was gigantic and non-market oriented seemed to collapse. Structures of foreign control were established in all export products, for example, copper, zinc, manganese, lead, aluminium, uranium, electric power stations, coal mines, all petroleum refinery plants, etc. The entire economy of this state got overtly tilted towards the export sector. The focus was concentrated on internationalisation and therefore, the internal economy, which was unrelated to export and foreign capital, suffered major set backs.

Poverty increased markedly and economy in general became totally dependent on the price fluctuation of the world market.

But it is also true that Foreign Direct Investment helped stabilise the Kazakh economy in the initial years. Huge credits were poured into this country by the IMF as well as the World Bank. Undoubtedly, it was the lure of Caspian Sea oil reserves that attracted so much foreign attention and investment in this land. But detractors were dismissive of the gains. Thus, Zhukov conjectured, "having sold off its export producers to foreign companies, the government deprived itself of a source of financial resources that otherwise could have been used to supplement the budget". [7] In fact, the Kazakh government did not only allow foreign investment, but had already surrendered a share of the Caspian Sea reserves to Japanese National Oil Company and the American corporation Phillips Petroleum. Zhukov is not very optimistic about Kazakhstan's future as an oil exporter due to a number of practical difficulties. He argues, "One can cite a host of problems: the influx of investments is more modest than expected, the development of local reserves poses serious difficulties, the quality of the raw materials is inferior, and the problems of transportation remain unresolved.... Whatever the scenario, the development of Kazakhstan is almost exclusively dependent on the strategy of the transnational corporations dealing in oil and gas, as well as the economic conditions prevailing in world oil markets".[8] Analysts like Zhukov feel that Kazakhstan needed to diversify the economic structure along with the petroleum route for quick wealth.

The foreign countries involved in Kazakh economy were many and diverse. There were a substantial number of US and European investors on one hand, and on the other, initiatives to develop trade links by China, Japan and other Asia Pacific powers was also quite evident. Kazakhstan exported coal, petroleum, aluminium, ferrous alloys, copper, mineral fertiliser, nickel and ferrous metals. China seemed optimistic on the prospect of trade with Central Asia as a whole, for she opened up a number of cities on the border, namely Jeminay, Tacheng, Turugart Huocheng for facilitating free trade with Kazakh and Kyrgyz states, although it remained marginal in proportion to Chinese trade volume (only 1% of its total trade turnover). The geographic contiguity of China with Kazakhstan proved to a big advantage point. In the keen observation of Oksana Reznikova, "In the competition for Central Asian oil and gas, China relies upon a number of advantages, the most important of which include the territorial proximity to the region and the rapidly growing demand for energy resources...The export of oil to the east is the most advantageous route for Kazakhstan itself. In this case, the pipeline will cross virtually the entire territory of this country, and hence the tariffs on pumping the oil will go to the treasury of Kazakhstan and not neighbouring states".[9]

The other most important economic power in the Asia Pacific, Japan, took a quicker initiative to take part in the oil economy of Kazakhstan in spite of not having any geographical contiguity. Japanese National Oil Company took initiative to explore oil resources in the Aral Sea region of Kazakhstan and signed agreement to share its future output. But since Japan has no direct access to this land, it was desperate to have an outlet through any possible route such as via China, Turkey, Iran and so on. And among these options, Iranian route was supposed to be the shortest to reach the world market. But Japan could not attain this due to American sanction[10]. There are other countries of the of Asia Pacific like Indonesia, South Korea and so on who have already moved their investment and commercial networks towards this land. However, partnership with the Asia Pacific failed to grow into a formidable alternative for this land, though it holds good promise for future.

In the backdrop of these newly developed connections and economic links of Kazakhstan, her relationship with her old master Russia had to be reviewed. Boris Rumer in one of his books openly admitted that the relation between Russia and Kazakhstan is problematic, to say the least[11]. A customs dispute occurred between them in January 1999 over disagreement on the VAT. Kazakhstan had put ban on 21 categories of food items from Russia. Moreover, Kazakhstan's Siberian link for exports, disregarding Moscow, also created tension between the two. Moscow retaliated by reinforcing their common border and restricting all movements across it, especially of goods. However, such tensions are common between neighbours who after a long period of sharing got divorced form each other. Importantly, these sporadic outbursts on both sides did not imply any permanent breach of contract. These two neighbours tended to band together for geo-strategic cause, much more important than economic sharing. To make this happen, Russia, the previous patron, needed to accept the new commercial partners of Kazakh economy, however jealous she might have felt. Kazakhstan, on the other hand, needed to acknowledge the importance of Russian presence even if Moscow's highhandedness seemed too overbearing at times.

Kyrgystan is another Central Asian republic that accepted the same model. In fact, Kyrgystan was the first of all five Central Asian states to introduce convertibility of her national currency and accepted the IMF Article III thereby leading to unification of the exchange rate. But her economic condition was even more vulnerable as compared to her neighbours. The only solid resource which brought her to export network is the gold mines of Kumtor. Zhukov observed, "The development of gold-bearing deposits here is the only relatively large-scale project in Kyrgyzstan that has attracted foreign investment. In other words, during the span of nearly a decade, foreign investors have been unable to find any other object worthy of interest".[12] Since independence, the entire growth of the Kyrgyz economy had been based solely on the expansion of gold mining. In 1998, the price of gold fell and affected her economy adversely.

But all was not lost for Kyrgystan. In contrast to this apparently depressing scenario, one can cite some relevant portions of the speech by the Managing Director of IMF Michel Camdessus in a conference in Kyrgyzstan[13]: "The Kyrgyz Republic is now at a promising stage of its history. After several years of an extremely difficult transition, your country starts experiencing the benefits of its orientation toward a market economy. Not only has the dramatic decline in output been reversed, but for two years in a row growth of output has been around 7 percent, while the introduction of the som has been key in bringing inflation down from the destructive hyperinflation level of 1,259 percent, where it was in 1992, to the single digit level where it stands now, and you know that further progress is at hand". Although beginning almost with a euphoric note, he immediately admitted the limitations of the new process. In his words, "Allow me to elaborate somewhat on that. These achievements are still fragile and, in the framework of the new programme on which we have just agreed, your government, Mr. President, wants to consolidate them, to make sure that the trends toward increased poverty are also reversed, and that the poorest in the country benefit particularly from the economic expansion of the years to come". He made a strong pledge of support for a supposedly 'ambitious but realistic' programme undertaken up by the Kyrgyz President Akayev, and ensured financial support by IMF to develop efficient market economy and help towards integration into global economy. However, in a speech marked by an overtly enthusiastic celebration of globalisation and its possible benefits, he also mentioned the risks involved in the strategy of extreme dependency on foreign capital: "But if globalisation offers many opportunities, it also holds two major risks. Countries that attract large volumes of private capital are more vulnerable to sudden shifts in investor confidence, which can be very destabilising to their own economies and have negative effects on other countries as well".[14]

Michel Camdessus's fears were not entirely misplaced for Central Asia. Given these uncertainties and poor state of local economy, there developed a strong network of transborder narcotic trade. This was also true for Tajikistan, the smallest, poorest and the most disturbed among all Central Asian states. This is not to argue that narcotic trade was an innovation of the post-Soviet era. It was always there in a clandestine manner and in a low scale across the Afghanistan border. But with the collapse of strong boundaries and restrictions on exchange, this negative economy began to flourish in leaps and bounds. Uncertainty in economic and political life for the general populace and the failure of the regimes to restrain poverty led to the cultivation and shipment of narcotic crops as an alternative occupation. Experts have calculated that the range of income generated through this underground trade was often a big supplement to the general economy. Given the limitations of the existing governments to cope up with the transition economy, people went for the easy alternative available for survival and globalisation facilitated the growth of this negative trait as intensely as for other market items.[15] But drug trafficking is not just exclusive among the poorer republics Drug became a common problem for each and every one of the republics, for the presence of poor and jobless people was increasing in each of them and, given the lure of easy money, the frustrated population could not be kept away just by dry futuristic promises. The issue became so alarming that it was no more kept unaccounted. Boris Rumer claimed in one of his works, "The scale of the shadow economy on the territory of the former Soviet Union, including Central Asia, is immense. In the case of Russia itself, this sector is estimated at 25% to 40% of the GDP. There is every reason to believe that these estimates can be applied to Central Asia as well .Moreover, one must also take into account all the economic consequences of the drug business which—as suggested by press reports and much anecdotal testimony—has become very widespread in the region".[16]

Uzbekistan, the most prominent of all Central Asian states, chose a different course in her economy and negotiated with globalisation from yet another perspective. This was the model to globalise with a strong control of the state over economy. She could sustain her control over export of precious metals like gold and uranium which enabled her to get over both financial and physical dependence on Russia. The other advantage Uzbekistan inherited from the Soviet phase was cotton-culture, which acted as a ready cash-crop for export in the world market and provided some more space for her transition economy to grow and adjust. Moreover, the price of cotton in the world market had sky rocketed in the mid 1990s (24% in 1994 and another 26% in 1995), which came as a blessing for nascent Uzbek state to strengthen her position to a large extent. But this too entailed a lot of risk and uncertainty. As Zhukov conjectured, "The extreme fragility of the macroeconomic situation in Uzbekistan is explained by the almost complete dependence of the national economy on the demand for cotton in the world market"[17]

However, cotton monoculture was a product of the lopsidedness of the classical Soviet economy which Uzbekistan had inherited. During Glasnost, there was a tremendous uproar against cotton obsession by the local intellectuals which was logical enough. Nevertheless, it was cotton that provided her with the initial back up in the difficult transition years. Rumer, however, took a revisionist approach in cotton issue. In his analysis, "Much has been written as well about the harmful consequences of the hypertrophic development of cotton growing in Uzbekistan. But time has now come for a more balanced approach...It is, therefore, hardly feasible to argue that the cotton complex is an inordinate burden for the republic; on the contrary, Uzbekistan gained much more than it lost from the targeted development of cotton growing".[18] However, this strong state with her strong government embarked upon overcoming the limitations inherited from the Soviet era. Two major problems faced by Uzbekistan were insufficiency in food and underutilised energy. Since agricultural lands were all preoccupied with cotton, the country needed regular grain import for sustenance. Even on energy, Uzbekistan lacked infrastructure, although like the other Central Asian states there were sufficient resources. Uzbekistan took the bold step of developing energy base and by the mid 1990s, she became self-sufficient in energy and fuel. But for the development of its fuel and energy base, Uzbekistan had to take the help of foreign capital. The oil refineries in Ferghana and Bukhara were made with all modern facets which enabled them to avoid petroleum import. The other giant project for a natural gas processing came underway in Shurtan. These developments were 'unqualified positives' in Zhukov's observation. But this became possible only with foreign capital as loans and how Uzbekistan pays them back depends on her future planning. Here the picture is not as impressive as depicted by Zhukov.

The other large industry growing with foreign investment is automobile, where the South Korean company Daewoo had invested substantially. Daewoo had invested in a number of electronic equipment projects as well. The Uzbek authority had also launched a joint venture with the US Company Case to assemble agricultural machinery. All these were experiments of a transitional economy which entailed a lot of risk and the foreign indebtedness of Uzbekistan kept increasing along with its commitment to diversify her economic base. Uzbekistan banked substantially on the IMF and the World Bank for further credit supply and development models, while her planning remained lopsided with huge effort in the energy sector. Import of industrial goods continued, while agriculture (cotton) remained the major donor for other branches. Zhukov is alarmed in this context, "The investment policy is creating new structural traps without eliminating the old ones".[19]

The involvement of foreign capital and participation of global economic powers were diverse and plentiful in Central Asia. At one end they exhibited a huge scope for development and prosperity; on the other, the immediate impediments towards their realisation seemed insurmountable. The position taken by the global economic powers was never unconditional. The interests of each of the powers in the zone varied according to their perspective which sometimes found common ground while at other times clashed headlong. Again, all their interests were not confined to economic benefits or commercial advantages. They were invariably linked up with strategy, security, ideology and culture. In fact, globalisation has created more scope for interactions between different geopolitical zones, creating new complications and tensions between and amongst them.

Role of Great Powers in the Globalisation Process of Central Asia

Of all the powers involved in this region, the most prominent and imposing one was obviously Russia, the old patron. The Soviet legacy was still very strong in each sphere of Central Asian economy for it was organic to a gigantic project of an integrated command economy. Especially geographic contiguity with Kazakhstan made it almost physically impossible to withdraw the relationship form either side. Yuri V.Gankovsky, an expert observed, "Economic factors exert tremendous influence on the political situation within Russia and on its policy towards the Central Asian region and vice versa. In the Soviet Union, a common economic system was created, and it functioned".[20]

There were also more complex developments that cut across economic factors. The shadow of Soviet rule was still very strong over each of the republics but their response to it was different. For example, Uzbekistan, the power in the making, who wanted to be the new hegemon of Central Asia, began to avoid Russia in many things: she withdrew from the CIS, received no investment from Russia, restricted Russian mass media in their land and so on. But the other Central Asian states half-heartedly accepted the Russian influence in order to prevent Uzbek encroachment as their new master.

The issue of political Islam also got enmeshed with this already complex interaction between Russia and her former republics. Russia sought to keep an intense vigil on the socio-political development of this entire zone for the fear of a growing political Islam. Russia herself faced sporadic outbursts of Islamic terrorism in certain volatile pockets (Chechnya) within her territories. The need was often mutual. For example, Russian intervention in Tajikistan to stall the civil war and prevent its capture by Islamic fundamentalist regime seemed necessary from both sides. Whatever Uzbekistan might have felt about the Russian shadow looming large at her neighbour's door step, she too had to reckon with the fact that to fight Islamic fundamentalism, Russian highhandedness was still useful. But Russia's future project towards Central Asia got revealed in the propaganda on Eurasianism—old wine in a new bottle. Eurasianism—an apparently geo-cultural notion—tries to bring back the broken frame of Russian hegemonyover the vast zone of Europe and Asia. Ever since the period of Russian empire, this broad sense of Eurasian entity was in vogue. Its reappearance, according to Rumer, at a period of crisis, indecision and uncertainty is not for any ideological goal but for the revival of Russia as a 'super power'[21]. But Russia supposedly continued to pay her 'hidden subsidies' for the old dependencies as she sold her goods at lower price to CIS countries than elsewhere. Thus, economic and strategic relations between the old patron-client nexus gets redefined on a new, transformed context where the outline of the lost world reappeared, reinforcing the inevitable forces of continuity

The other power, which had been closely linked with this geo-cultural zone from the very inception of history, was China. Throughout the Soviet regime there was overt and covert tension between the two socialist regimes over their extension of power in this zone. The Chinese Central Asia shares a lot of commonality with their Soviet counterparts in socio-ethnic terms. The two most contiguous neighbours of China are the Kazakh and Kyrgyz states. Other than extending commercial network in these territories, China began to build up many diplomatic equations with the states in Central Asia.

Significantly enough, China too faced a threat of Islamic resurgence within her borders in the Xinjiang province inhabited by the Uigur people. Uigurs are Turkic speaking Muslims who inhabit both sides of Central Asia. This strong Muslim population in Xinjiang had been fomenting unrest and demanding separation, posing a constant threat to China's integrity. This brought China to the common cause of combating political Islam and its diffusion from her Western flank, Central Asia, Afghanistan and Pakistan. Inorder to combat this negative force and strengthen the common security, a common platform named the Shanghai Five (China, Russia, Kazakhstan, Kyrgyzstan, Tajikistan) was created in 1996 with the goal of preventing Islamic extremism and drug trade. In 2001, Uzbekistan joined in, and all the six states signed a declaration of Shanghai Organisation of Cooperation (SOC) 'for the struggle against terrorism, separatism and extremism'[22]. However, this cooperation between China and Russia in this region born out of a common threat of political Islam was not absolute. There were hidden tensions between the two. China's effort to bring herself to an equal footing with Russia was often perceived as a threat by Moscow who enjoyed unchallenged pre-eminence of this region in the past.

America, the pioneer of globalisation on the other hand maintained a rather superficial commitment in the region at the beginning. Graham E. Fuller, an American scholar openly admitted that, "American national interests in Central Asia are quite limited and are primarily 'negative' in character; that is they seek to prevent or avoid undesirable development in the region".[23] The concept of 'undesirable developments' included the fear of re-emergence of Russian ideological expansionism, fear of nuclear proliferation, danger of further civil war and fragmentation that may destabilise the global political trajectory, and last but not the least, the risk of a radical anti-western brand of political Islam in the zone concerned. The positive interests of US in Central Asia according to Fuller are to promote democratic atmosphere, encourage more civil rights and help in the growth of a free market economy and the willingness to play a role in this economic development. Rumer echoed a similar observation about US aloofness in Central Asia, "In essence, the United states chose not to become directly involved in Central Asia and instead opted for an attentive, wait-and-see policy. In short, the United States declined to exert control over the region, a policy that would simply have required too great an effort and devoured too many resources".[24]

But the US could not maintain this safe distance for long. The event of 11 September 2001 changed the whole American trajectory of involvement since the Central Asian states with their Islamic entity could not be ignored any longer. The state which agreed to host Washington representation was none other than Uzbekistan. The hosting of the US army by this strong state was certainly related to her growing distance and tension with the other two big powers active in this soil. And this was strategically easier for her than her neighbours since Uzbekistan does not share any common boundary with Russia or China. Uzbekistan began to withdraw and disregard the older existing security and cooperation arrangements. Karimov was initially reluctant to join the Shanghai organisation and after five years, he joined the SOC in 2001. But he failed to attend the SOC emergency meeting held in October, the same year, in Bishkek, the Kyrgyz capital. The scope of a security and strategic partnership with US had become far more attractive by then. This visibly overt tilt on part of Uzbekistan created further insecurity and dependence on part of other states like Kazakhstan, Kyrgyztan and Tajikistan on Russian support and Chinese alliance. The hegemonic tendency of Uzbekistan within the zone has multiplied manifold with the Uzbek-American partnership. Hence, the importance of the already existing big powers increased as a defensive mechanism for the rest. Thus, the US could not replace the positions held by the two great powers geographically contiguous and historically linked with Central Asia for ages, though it became a leading actor in this zone. Thus, multiplexity became the order of the day. Here, Fuller's observations regarding the character of US policy are instructive. As for US commitment for the development of democratic atmosphere, there was hardly any attempt to change the dictatorial regime of Islam Karimov in Uzbekistan. This was a political compromise for a lesser evil as against the threat of Islamic fundamentalist onslaught, a trend that fits in perfectly with the basic tenors of American foreign policy. In fact, the example of Saudi Arabia shows that even Islamic fundamentalism is not a problem for the US to adjust to so far as the power remains subservient to American interests. Fuller further stated, "America cannot be policeman of the world, and our presence and advice could well be resented and shunned on occasion".[25] But America's image as the global policeman is constant as far as threats or profits are involved. It has been proved most vividly in case of Central Asia.

The Uneasiness on Global Islam and Relations with Other Islamic States

The threat of political Islam which created such tension and involvement of big powers in this zone needs to be studied carefully for a proper understanding of the cross-currents in the strategic and ideological domains. Central Asia's Muslim links appeared as a possible ideological alternative in the post-cold war vacuum about which there was a lot of apprehension in the entire world. Even Islamic attachment could have taken various directions, for example, the Turkic strand, the Iranian brand or the Turkic-Iranian combine against Arab, or a bigger bloc of Islamic states opposed to the West (including Russia). But, the Central Asian states took very cautious and careful steps to negotiate with these Islamic states for they too are apprehensive of the danger of fundamentalist infiltration. In fact, it was since the fag end of Soviet rule that some strands of Islamic protest movements had been gathering momentum against the existing system. These political groups became more forceful after independence and tried to capture power. The most intense manifestation of this took place in the Tajik Civil War. However, in none of the states could these Islamic forces capture the state-power as such. These states, though totalitarian successors of the Soviet system, continued to carry secular principles. Therefore, it was the mutual need of both the powers within and without to keep political Islam at a safe distance. As a result, even commercial policy decisions suffered between Central Asia and West Asia. The most glaring example of this had been the relation with Iran. Although there were enormous possibilities of growing collaboration between Iran and some other Central Asian states, like Turkmenistan in natural gas projects, and initiatives were taken on both sides for its promotion, the idea was not welcomed by most of the big players in the game. Similarly, Iran's linguistic and cultural proximity with Tajikistan had a good chance of disseminating the spirit of Islamic revolution. However, the US was fundamentally opposed to the prospect of any perceptibly growing Iranian influence in this zone, be it commercial or ethno-cultural in nature. Even for the authorities within these states, Iran was treated as a risky factor. Rumer observed, "The ruling elite and the intelligentsia of

Central Asia are deeply apprehensive of Iranian influence, for they believe that Iran's clerical elite supports and arms the Tajik Islamists in an effort to expand their presence in the region".[26]

The voice of a Central Asian scholar reflect the same observation, "Unlike western anxieties, the Iranian Islamic influence remained marginal. The Central Asia Islam was by a large majority Sunni, and the Shiite movements were not taken into consideration. Only Tadzhikistan let itself to be penetrated relatively, more by linguistic ties than an inclination for the Islamic Republic's religious philosophy".[27] But the only exception remained Turkmenistan with her natural gas project. The reason here was more commercial than ideological since the route through Iran could be the shortest and the cheapest one for Central Asian products to move out. Presently, the only other available route for this landlocked zone to reach the outside world is through Russia. The other possible route could be through China which would, however, be a much longer one to take. However, commercial viability got downplayed by prevailing geo-political considerations. American sanction against this newly created gas transport route though depressing hardly surprises anyone.

The other Islamic country showing interest in this region is Turkey. In the initial years of independence, there developed a possibility of growing Pan-Turkic movement, including the majority of Central Asia taking Turkey as a role model for westernised, democratic Muslim state. But the Central Asian totalitarian states refused to take to democratic ways and shunned the Turkish model. Meanwhile, the limited resources of Turkey to invest in Central Asia also got exposed. Turkish investment in this zone was confined initially to textile and tourism industries and therefore remained limited mainly to Uzbek and Kyrgyz territories. It needs to be mentioned, however, that the apprehension of Turkey being an agent of the US to remove Russian influence, popular in some quarters, appears farfetched in hindsight. Bayram Balci, the Director of the Institute of Central Asian Studies, believes that the Turkish influence was welcomed in Central Asia for a mission of 'spreading a moderated Islam and an Islam highly mixed with Turkish nationalism, ensuring support of the Turkish embassies in this way'. The great strength of these Turkish movements lays in the fact that they also enjoyed, everywhere else except in Uzbekistan, favourable consideration of the local official authorities which saw in it a bastion against Iranian or Saudi Arabian Islam, perceived as overtly anti-establishment and dangerous."[28]

The other major Islamic country involved in the region was Saudi Arabia, which had invested a chunk of their petro-dollars to help building mosques, Islamic centres and universities. Their hidden aim was also to combat the nascent Iranian influence. The two major South Asian powers India and Pakistan also looked up to Central Asia as a new zone for developing interactions. Here again the sub-continental rivalry reflected upon commercial proposals. Thus the Indian demand for an energy route through Iran was countered by Pakistan's preference for an alternative through Afghanistan and Pakistan. The only non-Islamic power in West Asia, Israel, too had a keen interest in Central Asian market and had already invested in certain sectors, much to the indignation of Iran and the Gulf states. But, the most powerful and confident of all Central Asian states Uzbekistan heartily welcomed the prospect of getting Israeli products, investments, technology and agricultural know-how for her betterment. Even on relations with Teheran, Karimov, the strong dictator of Uzbekistan, openly stated his willingness to carry on economic, commercial and cultural relations with Iran without allowing the import of radical Islamic forces.

Thus different Central Asian states took their own individual stand that suited their material position towards global or political Islam of different variants. But, as yet, none of them has agreed to accept any of the Islamic states as their role model or have become their lesser partner. Here again, Bayram Balci observation is worth mentioning:

> "The post-Soviet Central Asia and Caucasus belong to the Turkish-Iranian cultural space but they stand out more strikingly by the Russian and Soviet cultures they are imbued with in quick succession. We now bring a new light to the reconstitution of religious space, confrontation between local Islam and globalised Islam, policies implemented to manage one and check the other, to ascertain the Islamic future towards which this region is heading, situated as it were at the crossroads of several periods of turbulence".[29]

However, a critical essay on the genesis and future of political Islam in Central Asia and its global role highlighted how the interaction between local and global Islam took place and why the authoritarian regimes, with their genuine concern for preventing global terrorism, actually failed to prevent its presence and growth within their society.[30] The authoritarian leaders of these states have a common claim that terrorists coming from outside are threatening their peace and security. In the World Economic Forum in Davos in Switzerland, January 2000, Kyrgyz President Akayev mentioned the danger of terrorist training camps in Afghanistan and its infiltration in Central Asia. At the same platform, the Kazakh President Tokaev apprehended the collapse of all peace plans if Islamic radicalism kept spreading. The Tajik President Rakhmanov lamented elsewhere that it took the world to experience September 11 in order to realise the massive terrorist threat lurking in Afghanistan while Tajikistan had to endure it for long as a neighbour. The Uzbek President Karimov also warned of a 'huge evil-international terrorism, extremism and fanaticism, which has been posing a threat to our peaceful and calm life over the past few years'. In McGlinchey's view, "Of course, the intent of these government pronouncements is to link the growth in political Islam with outside intervention. After all, if foreign meddling cannot be blamed, then Central Asian leaders would be forced to confront an alternative causal explanation—the domestic roots of Islamist opposition".[31] The scope of radical Islam, McGlinchey believes, was created and encouraged by the lack of democratic atmosphere in these countries which none of the current regime seemed ready to deliver. The western world, on the other hand, preferred these anti-democratic authoritarian regimes in their battle against global menace of Islamic terrorism. Thus, a vicious cycle that refuses to address the real root of political Islam from within goes unabated

Central Asia in Quest for Her Own Path in the Realm of Globalisation

The situation in Central Asia is, therefore, a very mixed and complex one. The interplay of global and local factors in economic sphere has created many possibilities, some leading towards possible breakthrough while others reaching inevitable deadlock. Each of the nation-states had been experimenting within their given constraints and opportunities against the backdrop of globalisation. Their negotiation with the global economy has remained at a rudimentary level although ample scope for expansion exists.

Above all, globalisation has been not merely an economic process for these states. Since their independence they were undergoing a very difficult path of redefining their identity, their nationhood and their participation in globalisation often got intermingled with their quest for identities. They still have Russian attachments and may become a part of Eurasian entity. But of course they are Asians with an old historical lineage which they wish to revive. Even within Asian entity they contain many overlapping trans-national attachments—Islamic, Turkic, Mongol and so on—each of which

has something or the other to contribute to their national entity. However, interplay of these diverse factors in various degrees has lead to an ever growing confusion for these new states thriving for a well-defined place in the global hierarchy of wealth. Following the general conception of Wallerstein on globalisation, one can realise that this uncertainty is not in isolation, but is a part of a transition epoch for the whole planet. In Immanuel Waller stein's own expression, "Rather we are located in age of transition, transition not merely of a few backward countries which need to catch up with the spirit of globalisation, but a transition in which the entire capitalist world system will be transformed into something else. The future, far from being inevitable and one to which there is no alternative, is being determined in this transition that has an extremely uncertain outcome".[32]

The new Central Asian states, however, took serious decisions on international arena, both on security and economic issues, and their decisions did not always show uniformity, being part of a common regional entity. How to tackle the presence of so many great powers with both common and conflicting interests has been a real challenge for these states. But on two issues where the states had more or less agreed and received global support are in combating the challenges of global Islam and the acceptance of foreign capital, either in the form of investment or loan, for economic development. But, on both the issues, the external solutions cannot work without addressing the internal situations. It is the complex pattern of interaction of both internal problems and external influences that has created the parameters for the new nation-states to evolve their distinctive responses to globalisation in the light of prevailing internal problems. It is rather important to note the different changes occurring, both due to internal and global factors, and how these forces have intersected and evolved in the changing socio-economic scenario triggered by globalisation. To end, the remarks of Byaram Balci seem most relevant,

> "In conclusion, let us emphasise that all the Republics are confronted with the same dilemma: how to enter globalisation and occupy a place in the international scene and guarantee internal stability at the same time. Above

all, promoting order in a world context where Islamism is perceived as the main source of unrest, most of the Central Asian States are tensed and agitated about their policy on how to manage people belonging to a religious order. Fearing that any concession to Islamist speeches might be misconstrued as an admission of weakness, all these regimes favour intransigence; thus indefinitely putting off any hope of dialogue and national reconciliation"

Notes

1. Stanislav Zhukov, "Adapting to Globalization in Boris Rumer", *Central Asia And The New Global Economy* (New Delhi: Aakar Books, 2003), pp.149-150
2. Graham E. Fuller, "Central Asia and American Interests", in Hafeez Malik, ed., *Central Asia: Its Strategic Importance and Future Prospects* (London: Macmillan, 1994), p. 140
3. (Washington Post, 14th October, 1997, sited in Boris Rumer & Stanislav Zhukov eds , Central Asia: The Challenges of Independence, Aakar Books,2003, Delhi , p-3
4. Boris Rumer, "Economic Crisis and Growing Intraregional Tensions" , in Boris Rumer, ed., Central *Asia And The New Global Economy* (Delhi: Aakar Books, 2003), p. 20
5. Ibid, p. 21
6. Stanislav Zhukov, "Adapting to Globalization", in Boris Rumer ed., *Central Asia And The New Global Economy* (Delhi: Aakar Books, 2003), pp. 154&161
7. Ibid., p. 158
8. Ibid., p. 160
9. Oksana Reznikova, "Central Asia and the Asian –Pacific Region",in Boris Rumer ed.,*Central Asia And the New Global Economy* (Delhi:,Aakar Books, 2003), p. 227
10 ibid, p235
11 Boris Rumer ed., Central Asia: a Gathering Storm?, Aakar Books, Delhi, 2003,p-41
12 ibid.,p-151
13 Address by Michel Camdessus, Managing Director of the International Monetary Fund, at a conference on "Challenges to Economies in Transition" Bishkek, Kyrgyz Republic, May 27, 1998
14. Ibid.
15. S. Zhukov, op.cit.,p-153
16. Rumer& Zhukov eds., Central Asia, Challenges of Independence, Aakar Books, Delhi, 2003, p14
17. Zhukov, op.cit. p-162
18. Rumer& Zhukov eds., op. cit ., p-6
19. Ibid, 168

20. Yuri V.Gankovsky, "Russia's Relations with the Central Asian States Since the Dissolution of the Soviet Union", in Hafeez Malik , ed., *Central Asia: Its Strategic Importance and Future Prospects* (London: Macmillan, 1994), p-121
21. Rumer, Central Asia: A Gathering Storm,op.cit.,p-47-53)
22. Rumer , Central Asia : A Gathering Storm,op.cit., p-55
23. Graham E. Fuller , "Central Asia and American Intersts", in Hafeez Malik ed. Central Asia:Its Strategic Importance and Future Prospects, Macmillan, London,1994.,p-130
24. Boris Rumer, Overview,in Boris Rumer ed.,Central Asia: A Gathering Storm? Op.cit., pp-56-57.
25. Fuller,op.cit., p-132.
26. Boris Rumer, CA, Gathering Storm? Op.cit., P-35
27. Bayram Balci, Islam and Globalization in post-Soviet Central Asia and Caucasus, Director of the Institute for Central Asian Studies(IFEAC) in Tashkent. dated,01.04.2007
28. Ibid
29. Ibid
30. Eric McGlinchey, *The Making of Militants: The State and Islam in Central Asia* Comparative Studies of South Asia,Africa and the Middle East, Duke University Press, Vol-25, No. 3,2005
31. Ibid., pp558-559
32. Immanuel Wallerstein, "Globalization or the Age of Transition? A Long-term View of the Trajectory of the World System", *International Sociology*, 2000; 15;249.DOI, Source: http://iss.sagepub.com/cgi/content/abstract/15/2/249, p-250
33. Byaram Balci,op.cit.

International Trade Development of Kyrgyzstan Within the Central Asian region

Tursunay Usubalieva-Oktai

Positive developments in external trade with neighbouring countries are vital for a small, landlocked country in transition like the Kyrgyz Republic. Kyrgyzstan continually recognises the need and importance of international and regional integration, and is making steps to improve access to foreign markets. Kyrgyz Republic has been striving to develop good relations in all fields with all its neighbouring Central Asian countries and to actively promote regional cooperation by continuing to balance its international relationships in economic ties. In the process of global economic integration, Kyrgyzstan with its market economy and peaceful foreign policy has been trying to achieve considerable success in expanding its trade relations with many countries.

According to the latest Economic Freedom of the World: 2008 by Fraser Institute, Kyrgyzstan is ranked 60th of 141 countries with a rate of 6.96 in terms of the degree of economic freedom present in five major areas: (1) Expenditures, Taxes and Enterprises; (2) Legal Structure and Security of Property Rights, (3) Access to Sound Money; (4) Freedom to Trade Internationally; and (5) Regulation of Credit, Labour and Business.

Moreover, export promotion support and encouragement is defined with ambitious forecast and plans in Country Development Strategy 2006–2010 (approved in May 2007 by the Government of the Kyrgyz Republic), priorities with a focus on foreign economic policy to support openness of the economy and building up, diversification and increase of stability of export. Currently, the country's external trade with the countries of Central Asia remains limited and insufficiently diversified as Kyrgyz exports are concentrated in a few low value added commodities.

In 2007, Kyrgyzstan's foreign trade turnover equalled 3,920.7 million US dollars and increased by 43.8 percent as compared to 2006. Export volume increased by 42.6 percent, amounting to 1,135 million US dollars. Import volume equalled to 2785.7 million US dollars in 2007 and increased by 44.2 percent against 2006. Thus, Kyrgyzstan had a negative trade balance of 1,650.7 million USD with a rise of 15 percent compared to the previous year. In 2001, the positive trade balance was marked, amounted to +8.9 million US dollars; it happened for the second time during 11 years (first positive trade balance was in 1994: +23.1 million US dollars). Worsening of the balance resulted from the demand of manufacturing enterprises in imported raw materials, materials and components for production, including export products. As Figure 1 shows, the growth of foreign trade turnover is observed, there has been a stable growth since 1997.

Figure 1. Dynamics of International Trade of the Kyrgyz Republic, 1997-2007

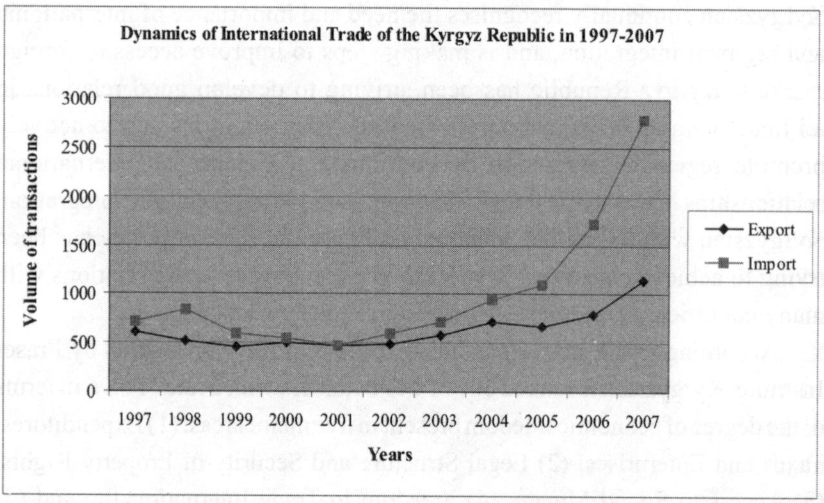

In 2007, Kyrgyzstan exported to over 77 countries. The main volume of export went to Russia (20.7%), Switzerland (19.9%), Kazakhstan (18%), Afghanistan (10.4%), China (6.5%), Turkey (3.7%), Uzbekistan (7.3%), Tajikistan (2.4%), Latvia (1.4%), United Arab Emirates (1.3%), Belgium (1.0%), Iran (1.0%). These countries constitute more than 92.9% of the overall export.

Principal import partners of the Kyrgyz Republic are Russia (35.4 % share in total trade turnover of the KR), the United States of America

(15.6%), Kazakhstan (11.1%), Uzbekistan (3.8%), Ukraine (2.9%), Turkey (1.9%), Germany (1.9%), Korea (1.4%), the Netherlands (1.3%), European Union countries (1.2%). These countries made up 88.4 % of total import volume.

A special emphasis is placed to promote greater regional cooperation in the Central Asian region in the last few years. Differences between the countries of Central Asia in their economic achievements and their political scope might create significant challenges for the smooth circulation of goods, services and people and producẽ tensions which hinder joint approaches to solve shared problems. Improved regional economic cooperation among and between the Republics of Central Asia remains important for their security, stability and sustainable socio-economic development. Several challenges faced in Central Asia, such as developing regional trading corridors, creating energy networks and systems, managing rivers and river basins, and fighting against terrorism and organised crime, are inherently cross-border in character and can only be tackled effectively through a cooperative effort at regional level.

In an effort to expand trade and closely integrate into the international trading system, the Central Asian Republics (CARs) have been pursuing both membership in Regional Trade Agreements (RTAs) (regionalism) and accession to the World Trade Organisation (WTO) (multilateralism). Trade policy issues, and in particular WTO accession, form a central plank of the economic strategy of Central Asian governments, but progress towards this objective remains unequal. Compared to other Central Asian countries, the Kyrgyz Republic has already joined (20 December 1998), but despite its 10 years open economy intentions, it has so far failed to gain significant benefits due to the weak implementation of its own commitments. The main partners Kazakhstan and Uzbekistan are still at different stages of accession negotiations to join the WTO, but the accession of Tajikistan or Turkmenistan remains a more distant prospect. Kyrgyzstan, in its turn, is willing to support accession of Central Asian regional partners into the World Trade Organisation.

The Central Asian countries are regularly invited to adhere to the various agreements and ratify them. In fact, the Central Asian States have joined selected international conventions and agreements but separately and without any uniform regional consensus.

Figure 2. Kyrgyzstan's Foreign Trade Development with Central Asian States 2002-2007

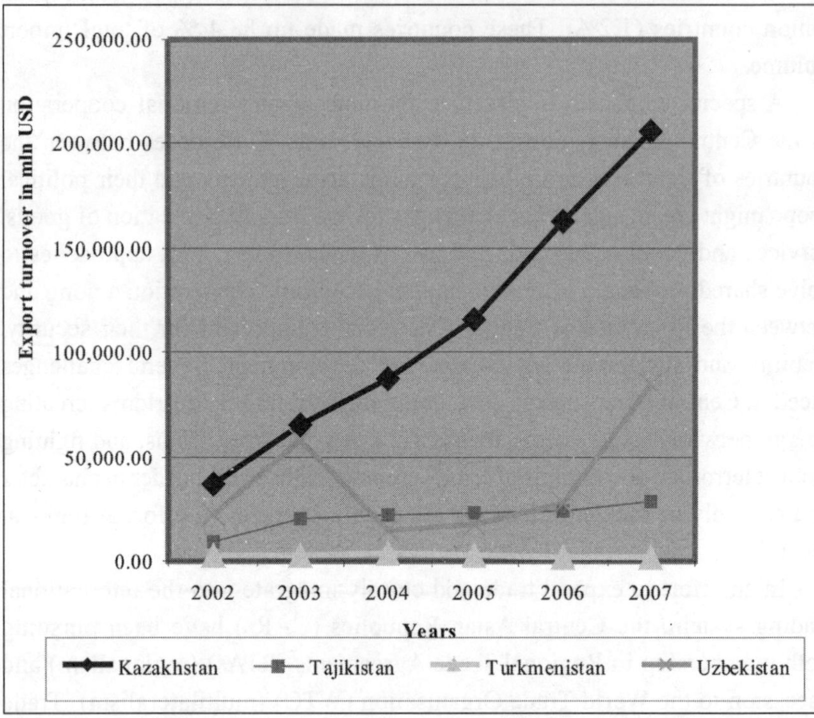

Thus, in 2007 the general volume of trade between the Kyrgyz Republic and other Central Asian countries exhibits a sustainable trend towards growth. Most active commercial and economic cooperation is observed between the Kyrgyz Republic and Kazakhstan (an increase of over 20%), Uzbekistan (an increase of over 13%) and Tajikistan (an increase of over 50%, see Figure 2).

From 2002 to 2007, in its trade relations with Central Asian states, Kyrgyzstan experienced trade deficits with Kazakhstan and Uzbekistan, while its balance of trade with Tajikistan remained constantly positive over the same period.

According to the Kyrgyz Customs Control Office, in 2007, Kyrgyzstan's export volume to Kazakhstan amounted to $206 million (163 million in 2006) as compared to $84 million to Uzbekistan ($28 million in 2006), $28 million to Tajikistan ($22.5 million in 2006) and $1.9 million to Turkmenistan ($2.1 million in 2006).

Kyrgyz import from Kazakhstan rose from $195 million in 2006 to $305 million in 2007, thus Kazakhstan remains the biggest import trade partner, compared to other four Central Asian Republics. Import from Uzbekistan amounted to $103 million in 2007 against 84 million in 2006. The volume of imports from Tajikistan reached $2.1 million in 2007 compared to $2.7 million. Imports from Turkmenistan amounted to $1.2 million in 2007 against $1.7 million in the previous year.

Kazakhstan remains a key foreign direct investor for Kyrgyzstan, particularly in the banking sector. Kyrgyzstan has very attractive tourist spots, which are popular among Kazakhstan on the hot and dusty steppes. Kyrgyzstan has ample cheap hydropower and water, and Kazakhstan needs both. Several enterprises in Kyrgyzstan are designed for deliveries to Kazakhstan, for instance, a large cement factory in Kant just on the border to Kazakhstan. Kyrgyzstan is well-suited to become a service provider for Central Asia in general.

The main cause of Kazakhstan's protectionism against Kyrgyzstan is that the latter is too cheap. While the average wage in Kyrgyzstan is about $100 a month in 2007, it is almost five times higher in Kazakhstan at $434 a month. While standard trade theory suggests that a country would be able to export more if it devaluates, the opposite is true of Kyrgyzstan because it arouses protectionism from Kazakhstan. Hence, the Kyrgyz exports are completely inelastic. Much percent of Kyrgyzstan's trade problems can be solved through Kazakhstan's accession to the WTO.

Uzbekistan is also considered one of Kyrgyzstan major trade partners. Uzbekistan's trade is greatly encumbered, because it remains one of the few state-trading countries in the world. Kyrgyzstan can do little to boost trade with Uzbekistan until it has unified its exchange rate, which will require a major political transformation of the country. The persistence of multiple exchange rates and state-controlled prices in Uzbekistan means that decentralised trade is not possible with anybody. Illicit Uzbeks exports to Kyrgyzstan of state-subsidised petrol, for instance, means that the Uzbek state subsidises Kyrgyz consumers, while the Kyrgyz state loses tax revenues and Kyrgyz petrol suppliers rightly complain about unfair competition.

Relations with Uzbekistan remain difficult, although recently, there has been expanded cooperation, particularly with regard to security issues in the Fergana valley. In the Soviet and post-Soviet periods, Kyrgyz Republic benefited from subsidised energy imports in exchange for timing and limiting the release of water from its large hydropower units. However, following a breakdown in the trilateral agreements on water and energy, Uzbekistan has now invested in additional storage and flow capacity to reduce the impact of excess water releases. Concerns remain in Kazakhstan about the impact of Kyrgyz Republic's seasonal releases. Due to its water resources, the Kyrgyz Republic has potential to play a more important role in regional power trade and in due course may be able to sell power to South Asia. Addressing the shortage of energy to meet domestic heating requirements in winter, however, remains a challenge and requires new investments in thermal heat and power generation as well as further structural reforms.

The disparity between natural resource endowment and living standards in the Central Asian region is striking. The region is rich in natural resources, especially oil, gas, precious metals and hydroelectric power. Nevertheless, trade and economic integration remain a central aspect of ongoing integration scheme.

In reviewing regional issues, it needs to group them into two categories. First are critical issues involving regional public goods that require cooperative solutions—removing trade and transit barriers, developing more effective ways of sharing water and generating energy, managing shared ecosystems, creating more efficient and coordinated transportation networks and preventing communicable diseases. Second are cross-border thematic issues such as human development issues, community linked development and microfinance and private sector development which represent similar concerns as well as opportunities for countries to develop common strategies.

Tajikistan and Kyrgyzstan have liberal trade regime while Kazakhstan too has a reasonably liberal one. Turkmenistan's foreign trade regime is not particularly restrictive on paper but export-import operations are seriously hampered by foreign exchange restrictions and state dominance of the economy. On the other hand, Uzbekistan, a key country to the development of trade given its central location in the region, has a restrictive foreign trade regime with high tariff import protection and numerous non-tariff barriers such as border closures.

The international trade development of Kyrgyzstan with the Central Asian states continues to be hampered by a number of various barriers:

- lack of regional approach to issues: integration customs and economic policies, tariff harmonisation, non-tariff and tariff integrated system;
- complex trade policies that are badly coordinated and lack transparency;
- high costs from poor transport and transit conditions;
- delays at border crossings; waste of time at border crossing points for running the customs formalities;
- numerous administrative and clearance requirements;

- absence of initiatives promoting single window shop and single stop principles;
- lack of dissemination of the routine legal frameworks to the traders;
- lack of common methodology on transit procedures, customs techniques, inspection methodology;
- currency restrictions;
- border crossing limitations such as visa requirements.

Regional cooperation in transport and customs transit aimed at reducing trade costs is particularly important for landlocked countries. This is because landlocked countries heavily rely on transportation by land through the territories of neighbouring countries for international trade. Poor transport infrastructure and restrictive transport and customs transit regulations in neighbouring countries can increase transport costs considerably and make transit times long and unpredictable for landlocked countries. Goods can lose a substantial proportion of their value during transportation if transit times are long. This is especially true of perishable goods (such as fresh fruits and vegetables) or those subject to frequent changes in consumer preferences (such as high fashion apparel).

International trade experience shows that transit brings very substantial profits. The problem is that there are considerable differences in transit fees, customs regulations and tax levels have not been agreed, there are problems with cross-border trade and frontiers are often closed, generally for no good reason. Most importantly, there is no common policy for levying fees on the transit of goods and services. All these factors, of course, have a damaging effect on trade and economic cooperation in Central Asia.

Unlike regional cooperation in trade policy, regional cooperation in transport and customs transit is unambiguously beneficial for the Central Asian states. Moreover, it is essential if these countries are to overcome disadvantages and harness advantages of their location, fully integrate into the international trading system and achieve sustainable development. On the one hand, the countries are all landlocked and situated far from seaports and developed countries. This constrains their trade with developed and other distant countries. On the other hand, the countries are located at the crossroads between East and South Asia and Europe and close to some of the world's largest and fastest growing emerging markets, such as the People's Republic of China, India and Russian Federation. Moreover, Tajikistan, Kyrgyz Republic and Uzbekistan each have exclaves in the territory of the other two.

Movement of people, transport equipment and goods from the exclaves to the other parts of the country they belong to inevitably involve transit through another country. In varying degrees, the Central Asian countries also serve each other as transit countries in international trade.

The Central Asian countries are known for their small economies. Therefore, they need to promote trade and closely integrate into the international trading system to achieve sustainable economic development. Regional cooperation in trade policy can help them do this. In particular, reciprocal trade liberalisation under regional trade agreements (RTAs) can help these countries liberalise trade policy at relatively low costs, reduce the risks of protectionist measures by trading partners, create new trade and improve social welfare. However, it can also divert existing trade and worsen social welfare in the Central Asian region and hinder their full integration into the international trading system, depending on the design of the RTAs and the context in which they are implemented.

In the case of Central Asia, an additional specific objective has been established to promote greater regional cooperation. Mistrust between regional leaders and a tendency to strive for purely national interests puts them at a disadvantage. Central Asian leaders feared losing the sovereignty their countries won with the collapse of the Soviet Union.

In today's globalising world there seem to be a growing tension between the quest for global free trade and the fact that trade liberalisation is more often regionally than multilaterally organised. Indeed, the number of regional integration initiatives is steadily growing up among the Central Asian countries. This trend raises the question of what the impact of regional integration is on the countries involved.

References

Asian Development Bank, *Central Asia Increasing Gains from Trade through Regional Cooperation in Trade Policy, Transport, and Customs Transit,* 2006

Bilalova, S.A. *International Marketing Course Lectures, Teaching Guide for Graduate Studies,* 2nd edition with additions, Bishkek: 2007

Bobusheva, D.S. *Methodical Manual on Academic Course of International Business,* Olimp Bishkek: Printing House, 2006, pp. 23-24

Country Development Strategy 2006-2010 of the Kyrgyz Republic. Downloaded from http://www.gov.kg/index.php?name=EZCMS&page_id=286 as of January 2008

Daniels, John D, Radebaugh Lee H, Sullivan Daniel P. *International Business,* 10th Edition, Pearson Prentice Hall: pp.163-168, 2004

Gwartney, James, Robert Lawson and Serth Norton, *Economic Freedom of the World 2008 Annual Report* http://www.freetheworld.com/2008/EconomicFreedomoftheWorld2008.pdf as of 23 October 2008

National Statistical Committee of the Kyrgyz Republic, *External trade of the Kyrgyz Republic 2002-2006, Bishkek*

National Bank of the Kyrgyz Republic, *Balance of Payments of the Kyrgyz Republic,* 2002-2007, Bishkek

UNDP Regional Bureau for Europe and the Commonwealth of Independent States. *Central Asia Human Development Report Bringing down barriers*: Regional Cooperation for Human Development and Human Security, 2005

UNCTAD, *Trade and Development Report*, Chapter 2, Globalization, Regionalization and Development challenges, 2007

Section II

Sustainable Development, Social Welfare and Human Resources

Trafficking of Women: The Case of Uzbekistan

Marfua Tokhtakhodjaeva

Introduction

Traditional 'soviet' migration changed after the collapse of Soviet Union in post-Soviet area. The scale, content and direction of streams of migration increased. Globalisation trends and radical transformation of local economies has forced people to abandon traditional occupations trying to meet the ever changing demands of new and growing labour market. It is the increased illegal labour migration from poor countries to the more wealthy ones. There appeared streams of crime migrations trafficking men, women, children, and also narcotics and arms. Uzbekistan faced economic hardships that naturally lead to emergence of unemployment, lower wages and increased vulnerability of unemployed. So Uzbekistan is becoming the country of origin, transit and destination for illegal labour migration including trafficking of human beings.

Uzbekistan became a source country for men, women and children trafficking after 1991 when the 'iron curtain' was opened; institutional and legislation base could not give adequate responses to this new situation of migration. The transition period has had negative ramifications for the economies of post-Soviet countries. Poverty, high level of unemployment, lack of social welfare net became widespread; as a result, the illegal transnational business of human trafficking became reality in these countries.

Uzbekistan is most the populous country in the Central Asian region; it is said to be the main country of origin in region. There is human trafficking inside and outside the country and commercial sexual exploitation is very common in the region. The trade of human beings easily goes beyond the border of region and establishes such strong networks that focus on making profits out of people, especially youth. These crime networks continue their activities. Few cases of punishments of dealers cannot stop trafficking of persons. The reasons behind the spread of human trafficking are an absence of adequate legislation, corruption in governmental bodies, a weakness of new political and social institutions, low level of legal awareness of population and understanding the reality in by them. Most of the former soviet people are socialyl naive and have no real information about the life in destination countries and do not know the damages of illegal status for them in alien countries. All these reasons have increased their vulnerability to trafficking.

There are many forms of trafficking of persons in Central Asia: trafficking of men for hard labour required for construction in far off rural areas and for military exploitation, trafficking of women for commercial sexual exploitation or for child bearing are a few examples. Children are also increasingly becoming the victims of trafficking and are engaged in prostitution or hard field labour in rural areas. The problem of child labour is common for post-Soviet countries. The topic of the paper is trafficking of women, its routes, factors that contribute to the trafficking, dealers and victims. Victims are trafficked into different activities. However, the commercial sex industry remains the sector that creates the highest demand and generates the highest profit.

As a result, the situation of human rights is humiliated in a great scale in Uzbekistan as in the countries of destination—violence, forced labour, kidnapping, prostitution have become common here, so the trafficking of persons is a problem not only for the governmental bodies and officials, but also for the society where the security of citizens is under a threat.

Trafficking Routes and Schemas

The trafficking routes from Uzbekistan reaches such countries as Kazakhstan, Kyrgyzstan, Russia, Gulf countries such as United Arab Emirates, Kuwait, Bahrain, Saudi, Egypt , the South and South-East countries as India, Pakistan Thailand, Malaysia, South Korea, Japan. Main streams in trafficking of women and statistics data of deportation cases of victims of trafficking are maximum from these countries. Also there is information about victims being trafficked to Georgia, Iran, Turkey, Syria and Israel as well as to various European countries and US. Within the region, Tajik women are known to be trafficked to Uzbekistan. Uzbek women, in turn, are brought into Turkmenistan, Kazakhstan and Kyrgyzstan. Kazakhstan is country of destination for trafficking labourers from Kyrgyzstan, Tajikistan and Uzbekistan. Although estimates are difficult to come by, some observers say that up to 10 000 people are trafficked from Central Asia region annually; most of these are young women forced into prostitution. In 2005, International Organisation for Migration (IOM) estimated that more than 5000 Uzbeks are trafficked for sexual exploitation and forced labour annually.

Most places for recruiting women are cross-border illegal labour markets. There are 12 on the borders of Uzbekistan within Kazakhstan, Kyrgyzstan and Turkmenistan. Recruiters collect groups of 10–15 women here for transportation to an abroad location usually. Dealers promise them work in milk farms, cotton fields, hotel cleaning, domestic services, etc.

Case. *Nigora Khodjaeva from Namangan collected group of 20 rural women between ages 20–25 in November 2007. She recruited them in local illegal labour markets. She promised them job opportunities in farms, restaurants services and shop's services and arrived with them to a countryside house in Antalya. She took their passports and forced them in to prostitution. (www.centrasia.ru/newsAphp4?=1199656620).* There are many employment, model and marriage agencies in towns and capital; they give advertisements about non-professional job opportunities, recruiting young girls from fashion schools for 'arranging their marriage abroad'. Dealers advertise about recruiting dancers, models, and service's workers in hotels and restaurants for work in abroad locations. They organize (buys) visas (sometime even passports), tickets and transportation to destination countries and women are indebted for these 'services', also for food and housing. Trafficked women should pay these debts over a long run; in fact they become slaves of recruiters. There are common cases when traffickers beat them, give them narcotics and women become dependent on narcotics, their dept increases and the sex workers become real slaves. There are cases when women and girls work as subjects for producing pornographic materials.

In cases involving land travel to Russia or neighbouring Central Asian countries, the issue of travel arrangement comes down to paying transportation expenses, routine bribes securing the good will of law enforcement officials. Illegal migrants prefer travelling in groups. In some cases, there is travel by air though airports entail stricter control and thus the necessity for to carefully manage all travel arrangements.. Usually travel companies arrange this process as business or shopping trips. The traffickers usually are in contact with travel agencies in countries of destination.

There are a few illegal transit camps on the border of Israel and Egypt, South Korea and Vietnam for trafficking sex workers from Central Asia. Mediators between dealers and border officers called 'stalkers' organise the illegal crossing of these borders. Women live in camps for a few days in hard conditions. There has been information about transportation of 60 women from Central Asia to the camp in South Korea. Illegal transportation of persons across the borders is under the control of crime groups who organise trafficking of persons. There are many 'orders' for young Uzbek virgin girls from Saudi and this business is profitable for dealers. They organise the trips for non-adult virgins with false passports and false 'mothers'. The cost of one non-adult virgin is 10 thousand USD. According to official information, during one year, five thousand prostitutes, among them Uzbeks, left Almaty airport and only a few returned in 2005.

Factors Contributing to the Trafficking of Humans

The main reasons behind the increase in trafficking of women are:

- The will of women to change their lives for better and reach a higher level in a short time; the root of trafficking is the will to migrate in hope of finding better income generating opportunities and better life. Jobs in abroad are generally perceived as an easy way to escape from poverty and labour market exclusion. Women who are trafficked seek a higher earning;
- The will of traffickers to receive high profits in a short time;
- The region's problems with law enforcement and corruption are additional incentives for traffickers; some officials in police, justice system or custom service are involved in trafficking process.

The target of traffickers in Uzbekistan is mostly the young generation. A serious economic decline has been observed after 1992; poverty has drastically increased and now affects almost 40–70 percent of the population. Women are more vulnerable economically than men and have become victims of poverty. Women are in a worse position in labour market and have poorer chances of reach good paying jobs and good positions.

Women are more vulnerable than men socially because they are the subject of control of community and their mistakes are not promised. Traditional Uzbek women are expected to rely on their male relative or husband for economic support and particularly vulnerable when the social and economic support of men fails The practice of arranged and sometime forced marriages is an especially important social institution in Uzbek society which seems to have particular bearing on the problem of trafficking. The practice of arranged marriages becomes important leverage for social promotion of women. This situation can partly explain why traffickers have found it easy to deceive young women by promising them marriage to wealthy foreigners.

Interview: Khakima, 29 years old; "I am from Surgan-Daria province. My husband left home for Novosibirsk and few times sent our family money but we have no information about him for the last 3 years.. We had no money for surviving so I left my two children with my mother-in-law and came to Tashkent to earn money for my children. For the past nine months, I have been living in Keles (30kms from Tashkentoin the border with Kazakhstan) and everyday I go to illegal labour market and become chart worker and take work in field or domestic services in Kazakhstan. There are many women from all regions of Uzbekistan. I pick up cotton, clean the houses, animal farms, pick up vegetables in plots an etc. I was on my way to earn money for my children. Last year me and 8 women were taken by a woman named Rahima to a farm to pick up cotton. She said that we should work for 10 days and we can earn as much money as we pick up cotton. We did not know that she was selling us to this household as slaves. After 10 days, we asked for our money but the owner of the farm said that he had paid to Rahima and we should work as long as there is cotton in the field. We understood that we were in a trap but few of us knew the way to the border and we ran away at night and with difficulty returned to Keles, very hungry and tired and without money. It was our luck that the owner had no dogs and the distance was no so far (December 2004. Materials of NGO 'Tashkent Women's Resource Centre').

Uzbek society still remains traditional despite 70 years of Soviet era. Despite the legal equality of sexes, independence restored national identity as adherence to traditions including the secondary status of women in social conscience. According to the traditional mentality, good education is not a duty for woman because her first and foremost goal is marriage and children. Access of women to higher education became limited. Nowadays, money is needed for higher education and the family prefers to pay money for the education of boys than girls. There exists cultural violence against women that has limited the future sustainability of women. It is important for the young generation to have an opportunity to work, to have a choice of work and the required skills for work.

Aysha Kasimova considers: "When I came to Turkey I saw that women in Turkey were more free than the Uzbek women. There are many demonstrations for their rights; there are real womens' activism and not beauracratic activism as in my country. I worked in middle class family. Women in this family are more self-assured than in my country. I was a servant but felt myself more free here. So I will come to Turkey, I will work hard because here I have an opportunity to earn more money than I can earn in Uzbekistan, I see another life, I get to learn new things that I cannot learn in Tashkent, there this is not easy but here there is more freedom. I have learned to build my life myself. (Interview of Marfua Tokhtakhodjaeva. June 2008)

Activist N.Karimova considers: " I think for a long time Uzbek people and the government hid the problem. We are a secretive society that does not like to share their problems with the world. A good Uzbek women had to be first the daughter, then wife and finally a good mother. The girls who went abroad were not considered to be good girls. People thought any girl would do this are just doing it be a prostitute. They did not realise the true deception of traffickers. Most of these girls need the money and that is why they agree to go".

Polygamy has been restored in Central Asia as an Islamic tradition but not legally. So only one marriage can be formally registered and only one wife has the right to claim property and custody for her children, others have no legal protection. Absence of jobs leads to migration from the country and the desire to work overseas.

Human trafficking is built on divesting situation of people and their inability to sustain their lives. Young people who are trying to find work after graduating from schools, colleges, universities, divorced women who have no skills for a good job become the target group for traffickers. Being unable to find a job, they are easily attracted by traffickers. Having poor understanding about law and life abroad, they give their passports to dealers who buy them a ticket and in turn they are indebted of big sum. Victims arrive in country destination and here they cannot escape without documents and they are objects in hands of traffickers.

Tatiana, 27 year old: My family—my mom and two sisters, ran away Dushanbe at 1994 at the time of civil war in Tajikistan to Tashkent. We came to my mom's sister at first, later we rented a room in a little old house but we had no propiska. So my mom could not find the job and she worked as chart worker, because of the lack of money. I stayed in my school and went to illegal labour market too. I was recruited for service in wedding and there I was raped. This man gave me more money and said that he liked mem and he rented a little apartment for me. After some time he passed me to his friend and etc. So I became a sex-worker. In 1998 I was recruited to work in Thailand, and I have been working here: six months in Thailand, one in Tashkent where I rested a little and had medical services. Usually, my recruiter took my passport and returned it only before my departure to Tashkent. I did not know how many clients pay but before departure the boss of brothel gave my earning money. This money I used for paying for propisk. Later I bought a little apartment for my sisters (my mom died in 2001) and gave them opportunity to study. I work for them. In 2004 I was arrested by police and deported from Thailand without money. But my recruiter bought me new passport and I am continuing my business but now I have big debt to recruiter(Materials of NGO 'Tashkent Women's Resource Center',2005)

One of the factors that contribute to trafficking is everyday domestic violence. Women, who are victims of everyday humiliation, beaten and lack economical resources for development of their children, try to find new sources for surviving. Domestic violence is often the reason for divorces. Divorced young women who have no skills and property can be easy of victims of traffickers. These women would like to find opportunity to earn money in season rural work in neighbourhood countries. They come to cross-border illegal labour markets, sometimes with elder children, and they are recruited by traffickers for sexual exploitation in neighbourhood countries in the little brothels at far off small towns in Kazakhstan or they do hard rural work and become the victims of sexual violence by their bosses or male workers who work with them in fields. They cannot run away without passports and money from far farms. Rural women and children from Uzbekistan become the victims of trafficking of forced labour at the farms and fields. Rural women remain the main vulnerable group of labour migrants due their lower labour skills, existing gender stereotypes and sexual coercion.

One of the main reasons of trafficking of persons is corruption in police, custom and prosecutors services and the alliances of corrupted officials with crime networks. Traffickers go unpunished even when they do not provide documents for travel of victims, including non-adults, thanks to the support of their partners in police. The cases of corruption of policemen and officials in trafficking of persons are seldom opened, but sometimes alike cases are opened. For example, the investigation of crime of policeman B.Umurov, the son of member of Uzbek parliament Ms M.Burhanova, showed the criminal past of his mother. She was a trafficker and she collected groups of girls for sexual exploitation in Thailand, UAE and Turkey. Her partner who helped her to prepare documents for victims was another son of hers who worked in Prosecutor office as an investigator. The author of this information in media considers that some other members of parliament have a criminal past too. (4)

Main characteristics of trafficked women are:

- Single or divorced women aged 20–30 living in capital or the provincial centres;
- Head of household usually with at least one child;
- Mostly from ethnic minorities and rural origins;
- Usually no higher education.

They were promised high wages abroad as shop-keepers, maids, cleaners, or the bride of a rich man.

The first step that makes the trafficked persons most vulnerable abroad is the separation from their travel documents. It is common practice of recruiting firms in many Gulf countries to ask for travel documents to be deposited in the hands of relevant authorities or firm agents at the time of departure.

In these cases, usually slips of papers are provided to employer or inviting agency that is present at the time of departure. There is problem related to the lack of registration and visa expiration that renders the victim even more vulnerable with the local authorities.

Forms of Trafficking of Women

Human trafficking in region is an easy, highly remunerative and low risk business. Inhabitations and obstacles remain minimal. Trafficking in persons from Uzbekistan takes many forms. Trafficking young women and girls for commercial sexual exploitation is most common.

Children are also increasingly becoming the victims of trafficking and are engaged in prostitution. The problem of child labour is common too.

Zukhra, 40 years old: "Many women work abroad because there are no good-payment works in my native town Djizak. They work mostly in Russia and Kazakhstan. My friend from Tashkent called me and said: "Would you earn money in Kazakhstan? She promised 1000 USD in each month. I agreed to leave for East Kazakhstan to work as cook in the local hotel. I have three non-adult children and I wanted to earn money for their education. I invited my friend Zemfira and we moved to the town Ridder. The man named Ahmet met us at railway station and we arrived at the hotel. He was polite and attentive. He took our passports for visa and presented us to hotel restaurant's boss and we began to cook there. After one week, the boss forced

us to have sexual relations with clients, when we refused we were beaten and the during the next one month, the situation was the same. Thanks to the police raid we were saved from violence. Police asked for our passports but passports were in the hands of Ahmet. Police had arrangement with Djizak police. After more than two months, we returned to the native town without money and in depression. But this case is more happy than what it could have been" (Interview of Marfua Tokhtakhodjaeva , December 26.2007)
Trafficking for childbearing and for marriages exists too but information is very limited.

Women have been mail-order brides, marriage agencies have been very active especially at the turn of 21st century, there are many advertisements about opportunities of marriage with 'wealthy foreigners' from South and South-East Asia, Middle East and Europe. Now the activity of marriage agencies have moved to Internet and the real scale of their activities is not known.

Another major form of trafficking is trafficking for illicit intercountry adoption. There are a few cases involving Uzbek citizens exporting newborn babies to Israel. An Uzbek woman was arrested in Tel-Aviv airport carrying a 1-month-old baby girl. The woman later testified that she was asked for a healthy child from white parents.

Governmental Responses

Criminal Code of Uzbekistan prohibits recruiting persons for the purposes of sexual or other exploitation through fraud. It also prohibits keeping brothels and pimping. The code also criminalises forcing women to perform sexual acts, forced unlawful deprivation of liberty is punishable, making and distributing pornographic material is punishable too. For most part Criminal Code in Uzbekistan does not consider taking women abroad for the purpose of sexual exploitation to be a separate crime, although most legislations condemn the persuasion of female into prostitution, the abduction of people and the illegal detention of persons. Unfortunately, the legal practice gives only a few cases of punishment to traffickers in cases involving officials and cases of corruption of officials impact the cases of trafficking of women. There is no definition on trafficking of persons as a crime, the persons and crime groups who are part of this crime.

The government involvement in combating human trafficking has been weak in Uzbekistan. There have not been monitoring efforts to combat trafficking by civil society because most civil society institutions like NGOs and human rights groups were crushed by government in 2005. There do not exist mechanisms for struggle against trafficking of persons and cooperation in regional and international level between neighbourhood states officials is poor. So, nobody knows the real scale of this crime. These are evidence of weaknesses of legal struggle against the trafficking of persons.

The governments of Central Asian countries could not effectively respond to these challenges due the lack of cooperation among local and national authorities, absence of reliable statistics of victims and analysis in this field, poor legislative framework, low awareness of population and authorities on this topic, shortage of experience and expertise of relevant government and non-government actors in dealing with trafficking issues as well as shortage of resources for job creation.

The usual perception of officials towards these women is brutal. They are regarded as prostitutes and receive almost no help. The same attitude exists towards victims of trafficking, shared at the national level. Many authorities from Ministry of Interior and Foreign Ministry' consular departments do not identify trafficking as a problem in Uzbekistan. They explain, "When commercial sex workers go abroad, they are fully aware of what they are letting themselves into. These women, going to the destination countries to world, in illegal commercial sex activities shouldn't blame anyone when they run into trouble".

Little attention is given by local authorities to the issues of trafficking. Uzbek women travel to neighbouring countries to become sex workers. Ministries of Internal Affairs recognise that corruption exists and some officials are involved in trafficking of persons, but information about these cases is not available. Some customs, border, security, transport and airport officials are involved and collect a share of the profits. Data is limited. Some publications in media seem to indicate that trafficking of persons has increased during transition, but absence of free media after 2005 and opportunities to do independent studies is forbidden, which does not give the true picture to show the situation.

Nadejda, 20- year- old talks about a case of corruption in Tashkent airport: "I was invited by my friend from Afghanistan to UAE. I was stopped by passport control, because last year I was deported from Turkey. The officer kept me till I gave him 100 USD. I was in the room with a group of 15 girls, they too paid the same sum. It was only after that we received permission to go to plane."

In order to help present and future victims of trafficking, the government of Uzbekistan signed cooperative agreement with Russia, Germany, China, India and has been working with governments of Kazakhstan and Kyrgyzstan and Ukraine to investigate criminal cases of trafficking of persons. The government with the help of IOM has set regional telephone hotlines in seven Uzbek provinces to provide legal advice to persons considering going abroad for work and legal assistance to those who have already fallen victim to traffickers.

Also it has undertaken measures against some tourist firms involved in trafficking of persons and revoked their licenses. Measures have been undertaken to review the activities of employment agencies. There is information that Uzbekistan government has prepared a draft on trafficking legislation and has submitted it to legislature.

Interview N., officer Uzbekistan National Security service officer: "Criminal charges in that case were brought. 30 persons, including the organiser of the group MS Chuprikova; her daughter who was married to citizen destination country and was entrusted with meeting the victims on their arrival; passport department officials from region in central Uzbekistan, who were involved in forging the victims' passports; two border control officers from Tashkent airport; and several other women, who were assisting the operations of the company"

In 2002–2003, 512 persons were convicted of pandering in Uzbekistan. And law enforcement officials were investigating 23 cases of recruitment and illegal trafficking of 30 victims abroad for sexual exploitation. Another case involved an organised group that set up a tourist company which trafficked young women between the ages 18–25 to Gulf countries. It prosecuted 101 persons comprising 80 convictions at February 2004. The penalties ranged from five to eight years of imprisonment. Cases such as trafficking and recruitment for sexual exploitation were identified.

Committee of Women of Uzbekistan has established the Centre for Rehabilitation and Adaptation of Sexual Traffic Victims However, the centre has not been operational because of a lack of financial resources.

Uzbekistan had signed the Commonwealth of Independent States' Agreement on Cooperation in Fighting Illegal Migration in September 2003. This document is the first to specifically address the issue of trafficking of persons in CIS countries. It is aimed at exchanging legal, operational and investigative information related to human trafficking between the police authorities of CIS.

Conclusions and Recommendations

- It highlights the incidence of trafficking in human beings from Uzbekistan which has become a social trend.
- Trafficking of women is a problem as there is human rights humiliation and hundreds of women lose their health and security. A small number of transnational sex dealers and corrupted officials have stable and increasing profits and create victims of trafficking. To avoid women trafficking, it is important to change the attitude towards traditional gender stereotypes that promote superiority of men over women and measures need to be taken for eliminating domestic violence.
- Trafficking of persons is the result of economic decline, bad governance and increasing unemployment.
- Due the cultural and structural violence, women are denied the right of an equal being and it is this reason of lack of knowledge, professional skills and dignity that make women easy victims.
- Traditional nature of Uzbek society and the weakness of economy influence the trafficking of women from Uzbekistan. The communal nature of Uzbek society where anonymity is difficult encourages recruiters to rely on information they can spread among neighbours and relatives.
- Underlying social and economic roots of trafficking of humans reveal the realities of fertile environment for increase in trafficking.
- Rising awareness, public debates on role of women in society, public information campaigns and increased employment opportunities for women should help decrease risks and realities of trafficking.
- Education should incorporate civic education and include human rights issues, nature of gender violence and sexual harassment, discuss some traditional practices like dowry, arranged marriages and the suitable age for marriage. It is actually required to organise awareness workshops among journalists, doctors and law enforcement officials and decision-makers.
- Absence of free media and independent studies on social and economic situation is a barrier to increasing awareness of people about the damages to women rights as human rights.
- Media, schools, community leaders, government officials should conduct activities for increasing awareness about human trafficking issues.
- Government and legislation system should adopt adequate legislation on trafficking of persons and establish monitoring on cases of trafficking of persons.

Bibliography

"Central Asia: Special Report on Human Trafficking", UN Intergrated Regional Information Network, 21 October 2003

US State Department Trafficking in Persons Report. June, 2007

www.centrasia.ru/newsA.php4?st=1192912440

www.uzmetronom.com/2008/01/17/mama_ roza_ v_olijj_mazhlise.html

IOM and OSCE. Trafficking in Women and Children from the Kyrgyz Republic. Geneva. IOM.2001

BBC Monitoring International Reports, 20 July 2003

Trafficking in persons report, Office of Monitor and Combat Trafficking in Persons.2004

How Globalisation Impacts Tajikistan's Youth: Exploring the Human Development

Najam Abbas

Ensuing from the fact that it has been 17 years since Tajikistan declared independence, how well is the country geared up towards exchange, interactivity, connectivity and cooperation, both regionally and globally? A question worth exploring is how effective are the attempts to benefit from globalisation as a helpful means for improving living conditions, particularly of the largest and expanding youth population?

This paper centres on the experiences of young people in the context of mountain settings in Central Asia, and examines to what extent an interface with globalisation allows the youth to make constructive contribution to the society, generate social capital vital for a civil society through creativity in the education phase and connectivity in their practical life. Is it globalisation that causes uncertainty, amidst many other factors shaping the pathways to future in terms of their educational and occupational attainment? To what extent the attitudes of society and its provider systems mediated through policies and practices act as barriers, gatekeepers or enablers?

The investigation of the broader impact of globalisation experience is essential for a proper understanding of the Central Asian youth in their peculiar socio-spatial context such as in the Pamir Mountains. Such a research will contribute to a clearer understanding about the nature, direction and outcome of youth transitions concerning their academic and work prospects under the present and future global processes.

A principal aim of this paper is to understand how the process of globalisation influences youth in achieving their aspirations by focusing at youth living in Tajikistan's mountainous settings. This requires (1) an understanding of the way the young people make sense of their lives and their future amidst global changes, and (2) a closer familiarisation with factors shaping or shadowing the youth's pathways to a meaningful adulthood through education and work.

While globalisation is expected to bring more education opportunities through increased opportunities, this paper explores if there is any impact on youth's education and career when globalisation visits their isolated mountain region. It will help us cast a close look at the challenges faced by Tajikistan's youth coping with ensuing changes. There remains a need for studies that can help develop our understanding between different facets of disadvantage and continuing social exclusion.

An analysis will also help us learn about the relevance of present direction of education to longer term affects of globalisation. It will also facilitate an understanding of the local setting in shaping the peculiarities of pupil orientation and performance capability. In other words, the youth will play a significant role and it will be the nature of its human capital that will determine Tajikistan's future development. Based on this fact, the extent to which the country's young human capital is determined, evolved and utilised will play a crucial role in how Tajikistan keeps pace with the ongoing globalisation.

Globalisation—Societies in Transition and Youth Transition

According to the Oxford Companion to Politics, globalisation can be conceived as a process (or set of processes) which embodies a transformation in the *spatial* organisation of social relations and transactions, expressed in transcontinental or interregional flows and networks of activity, interaction and power (see Held and McGrew, et al, 1999). It is characterised by four types of change: (1) a *stretching* of social, political and economic activities across frontiers, regions and continents; (2) the *intensification*, or the growing magnitude, of interconnectedness and flows of trade, investment, finance, migration, culture, etc; (3) a *speeding up* of global interactions and processes, as developed transport and communication increases the *velocity* of the diffusion of ideas, goods, information, capital and people; and, (4), the growing *extensity, intensity* and *velocity* of global interactions.

The term globalisation captures elements of a widespread perception that there is a broadening, deepening and speeding up of world-wide interconnectedness in all aspects of life. Looking from a regional perspective in the five Central Asian states that emerged as independent countries in 1991, the challenges for young people making the transition to adulthood are greater today than ever before. The post-1991 economic transformation has placed young people in an unprecedented context which has impacted forcefully and directly on their life immediate life chances. The options available to today's young people will facilitate or constrain their success as adults.

Factors such as globalisation and shift from centrally planned economy to new market economy have made the context unprecedented. This is further compounded by the bids for modernisation that bring with it new ideas and lifestyles that can conflict with traditional norms and values. It is yet to be seen what the potential economic benefits are, and how the gains are distributed, or do they generate a new set of problems associated with rising inequality and social polarisation. This is what makes the young people's transition in the post-socialist societies rather unusual.

Since the start of Tajikistan's interface with globalisation (beginning with its independence in 1991) to what extent the earlier order is giving way to 'a new context marked by fluid networks and boundaries, new mobility and new uncertainties'[1]. Are older form of social integration such as full employment, mass trade unionism and participation in political parties giving way to concerns about fragmentation and disconnection? More specifically, does the country's youth get more or fewer opportunities to become a part of the national, regional and global workforce? A related question is that whether the youth's academic and professional upbringing is actually contributing towards development of the human capital. The efforts to develop a market economy require studying a range of issues related to effective human development strategy. For a country transiting to market economy, it is essential that academic and professional research efforts pay attention to the youth's potential contribution in the country's over all human resources.

What Does Globalisation Bring for Tajikistan's Youth?

It is important to think about both the subjective and objective sides of globalisation. These are not two separate issues, but merely two perspectives on the same phenomenon, asserts Leslie Sklair, adding: "The subjective side looks at globalisation from the point of view of the individual whose life is affected by globalisation and whose own decisions (for example, media use, job situation, voting behaviour, consumption choices) in their turn play a part in affecting the structures of globalisation; the objective side starts from the forces of globalisation themselves (mass media corporations, global economic forces, institutions that structure politics, global marketing) and how they create and condition opportunities for individual choices for different groups of people. It will be silly to assume that we have to choose one or the other. We obviously have to consider both."[2]

It appears that when approaching globalisation, most Tajik opinion makers are mindful of its pros and cons. Many are noted taking a cost-benefit analysis approach voicing concerns over its desirable and undesirable affects. These elements tend to call for measures protecting the country against 'unfavourable' consequences and appear less active to pursue any positive dividends that globalisation can bring to the people. Professor Kosimsho Iskanderov reminds that as Tajikistan is located at the periphery of global processes, it follows the global tendencies cautiously to minimise the negative consequences of this process, allowing minimal effect on the national interests of the country while reaping its positive aspects. This is reflective of the prevalent thinking among Tajikistan's scholars. Some are weary of adapting to conditions that globalisation may and face their unpredictable implications. Others appear interested in the carrots of globalisation and staying clear of any sticks in sight. 'Tajikistan is undoubtedly interested in utilising those possibilities of the globalisation process which allow economic development in the country. Above all it needs to attract foreign investment although it is hard to imagine that the international financial institutions will not pose their conditions. One way or the other, the country can become dependent and will be compelled to accept such conditions. Therefore, it becomes pertinent to adapt mechanisms to protect national interests.'[3]

In the words of Tajikistan's President Imomali Rahmon, "On one hand, globalisation is considered as a stimulus for developing closer relations between people and countries allowing technical means including information technology for new accomplishments. On the other hand, by way of indirect consequences, globalisation has deepened the divide between the developed, developing and non-developed countries and has posed pressure on national and cultural traditions of the people. More obvious has become the stance of some developed countries claiming a superiority that boosts a clash of civilisations approach. President Rahmon is quoted to have said that "the most alarming, even dangerous consequence of globalisation and what it is related to is the decline in values, morals, traditions and other elements of social life, without which real some existence of a human being is simply impossible."[4] This, in effect, reflects a protective perspective with which Tajikistan wishes to approach globalisation with its kids' gloves on.

Professor Iskanderov notes that less developed economies find it hard without attracting foreign investments. No doubt an easy transfer of capital, information, peoples, and goods globally—if effectively utilised—could bring benefits to less developed countries. However, the negative consequences of globalisation require to be studied hard. Tajikistan is interested in globalisation for the sake of stability and progress while at the same time in protecting its citizens, nation, and national culture from any negative or harmful consequences. This implies that in Tajikistan, opinion makers prefer an interface with globalisation that is regulated by conditions.

In an article in the East Times published from Russia, the preferred approach to globalisation is thus described: "Tajikistan proposes all efforts in order to utilise the possibilities brought by the globalisation process for the spheres of education, science and healthcare. Globalisation has allowed the country to receive financial aid for addressing a host of serious social issues such as unemployment, poverty alleviation and environmental problems etc."[5] However rather than displaying any initiative, many resort to a cautious approach which reflects their inhibitions and misgivings about globalisation.

The above passages make it clear that when approaching globalisation, most policy makers in Tajikistan resort to a cost-benefit assessment. Many wish to ward off any undesirable affects.

These elements tend to make a trade off between progress in the society and protecting it from external influences, between increased development and heightened security, between keeping pace with the changes or keep them at a distance, asking for accelerated pursuit towards globalisation or an apprehensive one.

Yet a new generation of scholars believe that globalisation draws a new map of the world, new mechanisms of interaction and new ways in which people live in the world. The possible options of transformation require observing and understanding the logic of its evolution in local and regional context, stresses Tajikistan's scholar Rustam Hydarov. In his view, the "most crucial aspect of globalisation has to do with the fact as to what extent it can transform the human development". An analysis of the following components helps measure up how appropriately a Central Asian society like Tajikistan can keep pace with globalisation? The fact that how appropriately the process of globalisation has been perceived and practiced as a fact of life at large can allow a nation ride on the wave of globalisation to further the reforms for changing the society to serve its people better and efficiently.

The future progress of reforms, opening up reaching out and collaborating with the outside world depends largely on how appropriately the process of globalisation has been perceived and practiced as a reality, writes commentator Rustam Hydarov. In his words, "That is why the impact of globalisation on transformation occurring in Tajikistan requires a comprehensive analysis. It is insufficient to look at globalisation only through the prism of economic and geopolitical interest of one country or bloc. It also has to do with how you wish to be identified and with whom you wish to side with in the international arena. The changes taking place around us have a tendency of ongoing transformation for coping with. There is a need for new methodological paradigm that allows to fully comprehend the global processes".

The Tajik scholar articulately puts the young generation's expectations as follows: The possible options of transformation require observing and understanding the logic of its evolution in local and regional context. The fundamental requirements of globalisation envisage three components to be in place: a developed market economy; a pluralistic political system; and most importantly, a functional system that promotes development of human capital.

The most crucial aspect of globalisation has to do with the fact as to what extent it can transform the human development, emphasises the Tajik scholar. But in general, is the country keeping pace by keeping a distance with what globalization could bring, asks Hydarov while raising an even more pertinent question: As a transition society, how successfully Tajikistan is creating a politically pluralistic setup to allow the promotion of its' human capital?

A question worth exploring is how effective are the attempts to benefit from globalisation as a helpful means for improving living conditions. Perhaps such question ensue from the fact that it has been 17 years since Tajikistan declared independence, how well is the country geared up towards exchange, interactivity, connectivity, and cooperation both regionally and globally?

The following passages explore possible answers to this question:

Concerns about how global forces are altering the passage into adulthood are all the more urgent because of the changing demographic profile of countries such as Tajikistan. Between 1992 and 2002, Tajikistan's population increased from 5.5million to 6.25million, by almost 14 percent. The rural population increased from 3,807,000 to 4,597,000. Meanwhile, during 1992–2002, GDP decreased by 64 percent, about 1.8billion dollars to about 692million dollars. Per capita GDP decreased almost three times, approximately from 325 to 112 dollars. [6]

A peculiar feature of Tajikistan population's composition is the proportion of its youth. Those aged between 15 and 29 years comprise 26–27% of the total and such tendency is expected to continue over the next 15–20 years. Related with this expanding group is a rising tendency in birth rate, number of marriages, employment activity and the need to acquire new skills. In other words, the youth will play a significant role and it will be the nature of its human capital that will determine Tajikistan's future development. Based on this fact, the extent to which the country's young human capital is determined, evolved and utilised will play a crucial role in country undergoing economic transition[7].

From a historical perspective, Bryan S. Turner reminds us that "the flow of people has become more rather than less restrictive….while there may be an increasing global flow of goods and people, there is a parallel 'immobility regime' exercising surveillance and control over citizens and aliens".[8]

While more youth from Tajikistan are migrating than ever before, they are also more likely to get low-productivity, low-paid and vulnerable jobs, with no social protection, basic rights or voice at work, according to experts at the International Labour Office (ILO). While Tajikistanis continue to enter the regional workforce in great numbers, this fact must not obscure the glaring inequities that still exist in workplaces throughout the world, experts at the ILO say, adding: "The workplace and the world of work are at the centre of global solutions to address equality and the advancement of youth in society. By promoting work opportunities for youth, we are empowering societies and advancing the cause of economic and social development for all".

The world is facing a growing youth employment crisis. Latest data from International Labour Office indicate that of the world's estimated 191 million unemployed people in 2004, about half or nearly 86 million are aged between 15 and 24.

The **Global Employment Trends for Youth 2006** report emphasises that today's youth face serious vulnerabilities in the world of work and warns that a lack of decent work, if experienced at an early age, may permanently compromise their future employment prospects. The report adds urgency to the UN call for development of strategies aimed at giving young people a chance to maximise their productive potential through decent employment.

The impressions gathered through field interviews reflect that the experiences of today's young people, as well as the implications of transition for them, vary enormously. For some young people, particularly those in rural areas, the outward patterns and rhythms of life may appear to be largely unaffected despite some opportunities the changes may have brought to towns.

Because of rapid population growth, young people who are poor are about as numerous today as they were in the past despite declining poverty rates; current estimates imply that roughly 70% young people in Tajikistan are growing up on less than $1 a day. Additionally, the continuing growth in the absolute numbers of young people as well as the lengthening period of years spent unemployed ensue a rapid and continuing growth in young peoples' need for education, as well as for recreation and other health services. Further challenges include relatively poor learning outcomes in school among enrolled students and persistent disadvantages for young women, young people from low-income families, and young people living in the least developed countries.[9]

Making Sense of Youth Transitions in a Mountainous, Transitory Context

It is important to understand more fully the web of patterned interactions that can undermine young people from achieving their aspirations. This requires (1) a closer familiarisation with factors shaping or shadowing the youth's pathways to a meaningful adulthood through educational and occupational attainments; and (2) an understanding of the way the young people make sense of their lives and think about their future.

To determine the role that the present education plays in shaping exclusionary and inclusionary transition, it is necessary to establish if the present education setup is helping youth towards appropriate career pursuits. While for many, opportunities accompanying the new economic era remain few, the risk of exclusion remains greater. A significant number of people lose their hold on the labour market, then on the social and political participation in their community where you often see people who live their separate lives often characterised by a combination of destitution and apathy.[10] In post-socialist transitions, absence of recruitment opportunities and maintaining the job for those who get one becomes an issue of vital significance. One may recall evidence of this happening in Poland where many among the unemployed were young people coming from secondary technical schools and failed to get jobs in the contracting industries for which they had been trained.[11]

To a large degree, the nature and quality of young people's future lives depend on how the transition to adulthood—a critical stage of human development—is made and how well they are prepared to take on new roles and responsibilities. What factors enable the youth negotiate through this critical period is a stage of life that has yet to receive sufficient focused attention?

Field interviews conducted with youth in Tajikistan in 2007 reflect that the experiences of today's young people, as well as the implications of transition for them, vary enormously. For some young people, particularly those in rural areas, the outward patterns and rhythms of life may appear to be largely unaffected despite some opportunities the changes may have brought to towns.

For a number of reasons, Badakhshan deserves attention where poverty rates are rising and population immigration rates are proceeding at unprecedented levels. Moreover the risks of disengagement and even exclusion for young people are very high and increasing. Furthermore, recent data on school participation suggest that in some settings since the 1990s, school enrolment figures may not reflect attendance rates.

Growing pressures on school systems may further compromise school quality, which is already poor. Fewer Pamirian young people marry or bear children during adolescence as compared to previous generations; many lack opportunities to use this lengthening adolescent phase of their lives to acquire needed education and training.

For youth growing under economic transition, poverty and isolation, limited growth prospects considerably constraint (if not cripple) their successful transition.

How to measure the degree of globalisation in a given local context? Can it be qualified? Perhaps globalisation can be measured by: 1) the sum total of contacts and connections of a locality with distant localities; 2) the speed at which these contacts occur; and, 3) the local awareness of these contacts and connections.[12] [Steinberg, 2006, p. 31]

As Fredrik Barth wrote that modernisation "ties essentially all local communities together in a kind of complex global plural society, and every basis for isolating and classifying a part of this network seems to have been lost". [p.36]

For exploring what happens to youth's education and career when socio-economic transition visits their isolated mountain region, it is useful to look at the challenges faced by Pamiri youth coping with the transition. The key problems and challenges that come forth have to do with the utility of education and purposefulness of a youth's adult life. Those who complete their education and enter the labour market face far more difficulties than their parents had faced. This reflects the present generation's vulnerability to the education system inabilities and the labour market's limited capacity to absorb. There remains a need, however, for studies that can help develop our understanding between different facets of disadvantage and continuing social exclusion—a concept which requires defining what aspects we are going to raise. This study take notes of these insights to understand what factors influence young adults growing in places encountering many factors like isolation, education, unemployment, deteriorating living and academic standards, lack of opportunity to travel or study abroad; these are inter-linked and inter-related.

Thus, to what extent the Pamiri society enables its youth to make constructive contribution to the society, generate social capital vital for a civil society, through creativity in the education phase and connectivity in their practical life. During the stage of life course, as young people make the transition from student to adult worker, there is always a degree of uncertainty, as many other factors are shaping the pathways to future in terms of their educational and occupational attainment. They may be divided in three important categories namely:

- structural—the nexus of economic, physical and social factors that lead to identifying the difficult localities, isolated by distance and concealed by their mountainous terrain;
- personal constraints, some internal and psychological; and then,
- the attitudes of society and its provider systems mediated through policies and managers' practices also act as barriers, gatekeepers or enablers.

Growing up in geographically isolated, economically deprived mountainous rural settings, how do young Pamiri people get by in hard times and hard places? Are they at a risk to encounter further challenges in the post-transition era? The respondents' accounts go beyond the environs of learning process and relate to a wider realm of young peoples' lives and their futures. An analysis of these accounts can help us learn about the relevance of present type of education to longer term transitions. It will also facilitate an understanding of the local setting in shaping the peculiarities of pupil orientation and performance capability. The analysis will explore if there is a lag between qualifications acquired and jobs pursued? If yes, to what extent it is an outcome of an individual's choices and actions or whether conditions that await the school leavers assume a structural character?

Among other matters, the narrative sheds light on issues such as the role that the present education plays in the shaping of exclusionary and inclusive transitions? Such a query requires one to establish if and to what extent the present education setup is helping youth towards appropriate career pursuits. If there are social problems, where do they emanate from? So it all boils down to limited options in academic and career choices. So if you take the incidents of social breakdown occurring in the society like suicides, drug addiction, street fights, turf wars and other pathologies taking place in Badakhshan, you will find that the narrative casts some light on the probable causes behind such a phenomenon.

From whichever perspective one approaches the Pamiri people, (s)he realises that despite their education and hardworking nature, the society is yet to function efficiently to allow optimal intellectual, professional and economic attainment. The study puts a finger on root causes for some possible/inherent weaknesses. The paper will draw upon qualitative research to determine what processes and symptoms of social exclusion are being experienced. The rich narrative gathered through field interviews of 120 respondents to represent 20 different categories of the Tajik society will serve as an input towards a more holistic analysis of the prevailing situation. The diverse dimensions alluded to by the respondents suggest that the investigation of a broader range of transitional experience is essential for a proper understanding of the youth in their peculiar socio-spatial context. The data contributes a clearer understanding about the nature, direction and outcome of youth transitions concerning their academic pursuits and work prospects as well as career trajectories they end up with.

An analysis can become more appropriate if it takes note of the social, demographic and economic peculiarities of the youth population in a particular geographical and historic setting. This also necessitates determining the education pursuits among the youth and to what extent they contribute towards the human capital. The enthusiasm and level of activity among youth is also important to note. This on its part helps to determine to what extent does the youth act as a specific socio-economic group on its own. The assessment can serve as an input towards future measures for developing a long-term approach for improving the youth's future role and participation.

Young men and women growing up into their adulthood encounter a period of social, psychological, economic and biological transitions. While difficult in themselves, these changes become far too challenging for many young people growing under transforming societies as they involves tougher choices and fewer options.

In the context of the Pamirs in post-Soviet Tajikistan, there are several pertinent questions worth examining by all those vying to contribute to lifting the community spirit, strengthen social bonds, promote civic virtue, develop community networks and contribute towards a civil society:

In terms of education the emphasis tends to be on quantity not quality;

In terms of travel, the borders are more regulated;

In terms of outreach, collaboration with foreign and local NGOs is yet to warm up;

In economic terms, entrepreneurship remains hampered with regulations.

To what extent the globalisation of information influences Tajikistan's development approach?

In theory, internet connections are available in Tajikistan's major cities. However, both affordability and access remain an issue. While the information technology and communicational revolution can serve as tools to improve the quality of living widely, 'yet access to the new technology is severely limited not only through economic penury, but also through educational inadequacy'.[13]

On one hand it is observed that the commercial aspect of communication regarding the use of mobile phone is allowed but forms of expression are kept under strict rules and regulations.

Scholars such as Iskandershoev say that "although the information revolution and the universal internet access have made the world transparent, it is not always accurate when it comes to national culture identification, political traditions and value perceptions. In connection with the expanding internet use, it is immensely important to reinforce the ideals of high morality and the promotion of centuries old spiritual values in the society. On this account, globalisation does not bring any rainbow prospects for the poor countries. However, a carefully selected vision of national interests and a mechanism to protect them, besides a correctly thought out policy by the government and the civil society that takes account of the dynamically transforming international situation allows Tajikistan to utilise the positive aspects of the globalisation process in the interests of its people with minimum costs for the country".

The above quote offers some valuable insights into the mindset of those who form the general opinion on what globalisation is and how to approach its various facets.

Another relevant question is how globalisation impacts national demography through waves of in-migration or out-migration and what are its consequences on the composition and shape of a Tajikistan's labour market?

In terms of migration, the young labour is under employed;

The teachers' brain drain leaves education worse off;
Youth's outflow leaves the potential underutilised.

A considerable number of development agencies, academic institutions, as well as individual researchers have interest in looking at the means and way the Pamiri people can benefit from globalisation to enrich their social capital and improve their human development potential. As a timely report, this study will identify the dimensions and direction of unemployment. The discussion concerning these parameters suggests some policy interventions to deal with social exclusion and the low level of social capital which above all requires efforts to break the cycle of dependency and unemployment. It may also be needed to pay attention to social exclusion and to check if those who have been long-term unemployed are becoming resigned to their circumstances. The sense of fatalism cultivated by a prolonged unemployment can itself become an impediment to any measures to change this state of affairs.

Many global institutions are examining the possibilities to improve conditions in Badakhshan through mountain tourism, mountain rural entrepreneurship etc. But is there an adequate emphasis on a key component in such pursuits, the youth? A casual search through literature on development issues regarding Tajikistan may not establish much emphasis on youth emerging from those publications.[14] This study stresses that no matter what effort is being made and will be made, the youth's role and issues related to enabling youth or withdrawal factors that disable youth would remain of key concern. In other words, the youth will play a significant role and it with be the nature of its human capital that will determine Tajikistan's future development. Based on this fact, the extent to which the country's young human capital is determined, evolved and utilised will play a crucial role in a country undergoing economic transition[15].

Youth is the focus and the bridge between different aspects that we are trying to interconnect between the worlds of education and work. According to Ken Roberts, the sociological approach has been uniquely able to use the evidence from young people as a window through which to identify the impact of the ongoing macro-changes in former communist countries among different socio-demographic groups in the wider populations (Roberts 2003: 484). Moreover, "it was important to study young people because this age group was in the front line of change in the transforming societies —the most at risk of unemployment, and also the best placed to respond to new opportunities in the private sector economies. [Scholars] also argued that young people would supply insights into the kinds of adult generations that post-communism was producing".[16]

More so, as a report on Global Employment Trends for Youth warns that massive youth unemployment poses a social menace, breeding vulnerability and feelings of exclusion and worthlessness which may lead to 'personally and socially destructive' activities. The efforts for improving economies will remain partial unless the potential of young people can be used in a productive way without which neither they nor economies as a whole will face a bright future. It is observed that many young people live with deprivation, impermanence and fragile relationships with intermittent and infrequent employment becoming a norm.[17]

"While passing from childhood to adulthood, young people undergo a thorough set of status changes. There are changes in their political and legal rights and liabilities, their welfare entitlements, and in their positions as consumers. However, education-to-work and family/housing transitions now command special attention", emphasises Ken Roberts adding, "nothing else is likely to be comprehensible until these transitions have been properly analysed and understood."[18]

Education is not proving helpful to youth to find a decent earning and to be able to contribute to the society. Thus the learning part of the youth's life is not efficient enough. It may be noted that the working part of the youth's life too is full of uncertainties. The information provided by this study's informants will draw attention to and explain why all this is happening.

Social capital in the context of a mountain society in transition

Despite high level of literacy, there are little opportunities to place the educated people in any productive activity, resulting in a serious underutilisation of youth's learning that cannot translate into decent employment at adequate wage levels. Even skilled, university educated workers have problems finding decent jobs. This results in a painful human (intellectual, emotional and financial) waste that goes into an unending quest for more education is leading to a 'gulf between human investment and low-skill, low-pay labour market'. Stressing on gaining more from what conventional education has to offer may not be sufficient as it is a growing economy which facilitates a growth in jobs.[19] Another aspect of the transition to note is that the ensuing changes rather than facilitating opening of further borders and increase in travel facilities have witnessed further restrictions on mobility of goods, persons and ideas. Instead of bringing additional growth opportunities, the changes in the economy have brought insecurity and inequality.

While referring to different dimensions of the education-work gap, the point to be emphasised is that simply stating that there is some unemployment/underemployment that exists or just pointing out towards a gap between education and work, will remain insufficient if we do not fully appreciate its various dimensions and the implications that it brings, economic, social, and perspective concerning the psyche/mindset as it evolves for the individual, for his family, and for his community. The education-job gap, or unemployment, is the key issue—a global problem, with 1 billion people unemployed or underemployed in the world. At least six dimensions of the underemployment of the knowledge and skills of the workforce may be distinguished in contemporary societies.[20] These are: the talent use gap; structural unemployment; involuntary reduced employment; the credential gap; the performance gap; and subjective underemployment. In his book touching on the sociology of education, work and socioeconomic policy, Livingstone notes: "The growing gap between the unprecedented extent of collective knowledge of the people and the diminishing number of meaningful, sustaining jobs has become the major social problem of our times" (p. 1). Taking a broader picture of the global scene, Livingstone notes that there is no shortage of skilled people and in many places they are overeducated.[21] This situation is acutely felt in the context of Badakhshan owing to the changing patterns of employment/labour market (with particular attention to the closure of traditional industry and the growth of unemployment).

The above lines attempt to determine if the prevailing state of unemployment has to do with the educational qualifications presently provided at the educational institutions? If there is a link between the available options and future needs, what changes are necessary? Is the education system determining what specialisations will be demanded in future? What factors will allow enabling the young men and women join opportunities to contribute to the society rather then end up as jobless and dependent on others.

Youth, Transition and Social Change

When someone reads the literature on education in Tajikistan, it mostly refers to rebuilding and rehabilitation efforts taking place since the end of the Civil War in 1997. Examining the issues on an institutional plain, one may note that there is further need for clarity of vision, coherence of thought, action and practices. Emphasising on education alone may not bring the necessary improvement unless the other aspects in the context of transition are considered when education initiatives are being taken.

What happens to the youth after their education, this needs to be the priority concern, whether appropriate programmes need to be developed for providing adequate preparation and qualification. Otherwise, merely providing access to education may not provide a solution by itself.

Yet another perspective worth stressing is that tracing the path from the school to the work place is not sufficient. What is needed is to take into account a wider realm of young peoples' lives and future. There are issues that have to do with the purpose and utility of education imparted. When we point to marginality and disadvantage, it is common to both rural and semi-urban youth, but something particularly affecting the rural population in addition to the above is that they are socially excluded. Every problem aggravates multi-fold when it comes to the rural areas.

Why is there a need to look at globalisation through the lens of human potential development?

Many approaches to reduce poverty usually focus on reviving idle plants in urban locations. This may imply that 70% of Tajikistan's population in the rural areas is not incorporated in employment growth opportunities. They are marginalised and excluded primarily due to the fact that for the last 15 years, no new jobs have been created in the rural areas. The social exclusion approach can go deeper to suggest that among the rural population, there is a particular set of people in the mountainous locations who are further disadvantaged. So, using concepts like social exclusion would open the doors to further analysis of their disadvantages, and the way it is introduced in the transitory context.

Owing to the collapse of the system that existed there and due to the fact that nothing has replaced it effectively, there is a process of de-facto denial, of quality education, of supplies for the education system; a lack of quality health service as well as of the supplies for medical care. Thus contribution made towards the uplifting and upbringing of the younger generation is not adequate enough. It becomes necessary to look at social exclusion from the aspect of denial caused by the fact that merely being born during the transition has made growing up become similar to trekking along a path which is full of barriers and obstacles. So it is a new approach and analytical tool to many concepts that are inter-connected, inter-related, inter-linked or used synonymously. Vulnerability for example, emphasises that while poverty establishes or determines the percentage of people with some specific sources or a lack thereof, here we need to look what further discomforts and deprivations people encounter and how these make them weak in their potential contribution that they could make.

All attempts to modernise and reorder a society during a transitory phase risks a breakdown if any essential safeguards and precautionary measures are not put in place. This is to provide safety valves and outlets if the changes do not work as envisaged or there are spheres where a transitory society doesn't function efficiently enough or there are breakdowns. If you have a growing youth population but the education system produces youth who are not fit for work or the work environment is not adapted to conditions to take in and absorb the youth, it will lead to a negative impact on the economy, the networks will be disrupted, cultural and social degeneration will occur, and it will have an adversary impact on political system and civil society too. This in itself becomes pathology of sorts (study of the nature of a malady and its causes, processes, development and consequences) because it is not addressing its immediate needs or taking care of it as expected.

Factors such as access to and availability of choice to the youth determine which career path the young generation would take. Interventions such as by AKDN aimed to empower the communities for effective functioning development and growth, need to look deeper if the transition has brought some barriers that impede the pursuit to academic attainment and professional accomplishment. However looking only through the broader lens of poverty may not capture all dimensions closely. Therefore, this study uses social exclusion as a way to posit social capital. Once the significance and value of social capital would crystallise further that there is something which is not there which is absent, lacking or inadequate. Then it would only add to the significance what social capital has to do. Leading development academic Amartya Sen believes that a social exclusion framework reinforces the understanding of poverty as capability deprivation. Thus scholars such as Kaushik Basu plead for widening economists' understanding of exclusion beyond the analysis of income and productivity.[22]

For evaluating the impact on global development, it is advisable to look into components which serve towards improving the standards and functioning of the society. As a study of post-socialist transformation asserts, poverty appears among all social categories as they lose from the transformation. Above all, it concerns the unemployed, some of the unskilled workers, the majority of the rural population (particularly former peasant workers), and owners of small farms, and even part of lower-level intelligentsia.[23]

Social capital being multi-faceted requires paying sufficient attention to the aspects that would hold individuals together. 'Social capital is defined by its function. It is not a single entity, but entities having two characteristics in common: they all consist of some aspect of social structure, and they facilitate certain actions of individuals who are within the structure'(Coleman

1990, p. 302). It is said that social capital increases the efficiency of action. While physical and human capital facilitates productive and economic activity, knowledge too has been recognised as a valuable source. Marshall, for example, suggests that "capital consists in a great part of knowledge and organisation." But the present circumstances put forth the question whether contemporary knowledge imparted at Tajikistan's educational institutions serves an efficient and productive purpose?

The concept of human capital embraces the acquired knowledge, skills and capabilities that enable the person to act in new ways. One wonders to what extent 'intellectual capital offers a resource and a capability for action based in knowledge and knowing'? [24]

The significance of social capital (the social glue that holds people together in families and communities) becomes even greater in an increasingly uncertain yet fast changing society. It has to do with the essential contribution of networks and trust in promoting well-being of the individuals. This is especially so in settings where 'persons' actions are shaped, redirected, constrained by the social context; norms, interpersonal trust, social networks and social organisation are important in the functioning of not only the society but also of the economy.[25] Primarily it is 'the web of social relationships that influences individual behaviour and thereby affects economic growth'.[26]

Clearly the interest of a global development initiative such as AKDN is to improve the standards of living, bring spiritual enlightenment and intellectual development to the Ismaili community which was cut off from the rest of the world for 70 years. For that there is a need to identify what factors would facilitate and enable the society to become well-knitted, effective, well-governed, with rule of law, having transparency with representation, participation, engagement and involvement and empowerment. The UCA is one of the facets of that attempt to help people improve their being. For years, experts in mountain development assembled to look at some parts of addressing the problem of poverty.

Most publications with reference to transition in Tajikistan usually refer to how many people fall below the poverty line, how many above and what progress has been made in last ten years or so. These discussions are useful but not sufficient enough as there is a need to dig further and deeper. Attention needs to be drawn to two specific dimensions: (1) what is lacking? (2) where to begin addressing those limitations and shortcomings?

Conclusion: Why Tajikistan's Youth Are Yet to Reap Globalisation's Rewards?

A number of passages quoting authoritative sources from Tajikistan make it clear that when approaching globalisation, most policy makers in Tajikistan resort to a cost-benefit assessment, many desiring to ward off any undesirable affects.

These elements tend to make a trade off between progress in the society and protecting it from external influences, between increased development and heightened security, between keeping pace with the changes or keep them at a distance, asking for accelerated pursuit towards globalisation or an apprehensive one.

The opinions quoted in the paper are reflective of a cautious and conditions driven mindset and an approach which remains anxious of change rather than being eager for it. Such attitude helps to explain why there is more inaction and less inclination to benefit optimally from globalisation.

Yet a new generation of scholars believe that globalisation draws a new map of the world, new mechanisms of interaction and new ways in which people live in the world. The possible options of transformation require observing and understanding the logic of its evolution in local and regional context stresses Tajikistan's scholar Rustam Hydarov. In his view, the "most crucial aspect of globalization has to do with the fact as to what extent it can transform the human development. An analysis of the following components helps measure up how appropriately a Central Asian society like Tajikistan can keep pace with globalisation. The fact that how appropriately the process of globalisation has been perceived and practiced as a fact of life at large can allow a nation ride on the wave of globalisation to further the reforms for changing the society to serve its people better and efficiently".

Thinking about both the subjective and objective sides of globalisation merely enable to consider two perspectives on the same phenomenon. An open minded approach can help Tajikistan's youth determine what aspects of globalisation can help them bring better opportunities through processes of greater activity, interaction and exchange, both regionally and globally.

Notes

1. Kevin McDonald, "Globalization, Civil Imagination and Islamic Movements", in Dr Amyn B Sajoo, *Muslim Modernities: Expressions of the Civil Imagination*, London I.B. Tauris, 2008, p. 183
2. Leslie Sklair, *Globalization: Capitalism and its Alternatives*. Oxford University Press, Oxford, 2002, p2.

3. Kosimsho Iskanderov, Tadzhikistan e processi globalizatsiyi, Vremya Vostok, OT 7.08.2008.
4. Ibid.
5. http://www.easttime.ru/analitic/1/10/462.html
6. Tajik Television first channel, Dushanbe, in Tajik, 20 Feb 2002
7. Munir Pulotov, Formation and Evolution of Youth Human Capital under transition to Market Economy: A case study of Tajikistan, Economic Faculty, Khujand State University, Tajikistan, 2001 (in Russian).
8. Bryan S. Turner, "Revivalism and the Enclave Society", in Dr Amyn B Sajoo, *Muslim Modernities: Expressions of the Civil Imagination*, London I.B. Tauris, 2008, p. 138
9. See Youth unemployment at all time high, http://www.ilo.org/public/english/bureau/inf/magazine/52/youth.htm
10. Dahrendorf 1995: 15 cited in Ibid., p. 69
11. G. Weclawowicz, *Contemporary Poland*, London, UCL Press, quoted in David Byrne, Social Exclusion, Open University Press, Buckingham, 1999, p. 85.
12. Jonah Steinberg, The anatomy of the Transnation: The Globalization of the Isma`ili Muslim Community, Ph.D. dissertation, University of Pennsylvania, 2006. pp. 31 & 36.
13. Amartya Sen, Why Human Security, paper read at the "International Symposium on Human Security", Tokyo, July 2000, p.4.
14. See for example AKF Annual Report 2005 (published July 2006), http://www.akdn.org/akf/AKF%20Annual%20Report%202005.pdf
15. Munir Pulotov, Formation and Evolution of Youth Human Capital under transition to Market Economy: A case study of Tajikistan, Economic Faculty, Khujand State University, Tajikistan, 2001 (in Russian).
16. *Ken Roberts,* "Change and Continuity in Youth Transitions in Eastern Europe: Lessons for Western Sociology", *The Sociological Review*, Volume 51 Page 484 - November 2003
17. Global Employment Trends for Youth, Global Employment Trends Model, internal database, ILO, Geneva. Godfrey, M. 2003. http:// www.ilo.org/public/english/employment/strat/download/getyen.pdf
18. Ibid. p. 487
19. William DiFazio, *The American Journal of Sociology*, Vol. 105, No. 3. (Nov., 1999), pp. 904-906. Also R. James Sacouman, The Canadian Journal of Sociology, September 1999, www.ualberta.ca/~cjscopy/reviews/educjobs.html
20. See details in D.W. Livingstone. The Education-Jobs Gap: Underemployment or Economic Democracy. Toronto: Garamond Press, 1999, 360pp.,
21. D. W. Livingstone, Beyond Human Capital Theory: The Underemployment Problem

available at http://www.oise.utoronto.ca/depts/sese/csew/livngstone.htm accessed on 11 October 2006.

22. For more on above discussion see Arjan de Haan, Social Exclusion: Towards an holistic understanding of deprivation, April 1999, Social Development Department, Department for International Development, UK, p.4, http:// www.dfid.gov.uk/pubs/files/sdd9socex.pdf accessed on 12 October 2006.
23. G. Weclawowicz, *Contemporary Poland*, London, UCL Press, quoted in David Byrne, Social Exclusion, Open University Press, Buckingham, 1999, p. 84.
24. Nahapiet, J & Ghoshal, S, "'Social Capital, Intellectual Capital and the Organizational Advantage", *Academy of Management Review*, 23(2), (1998).
25. James S. Coleman , "Social Capital in the Creation of Human Capital", *American Journal of Sociology*, volume 94 , p.96
26. Pennar, K. 1997. "The Tie that Leads to Prosperity: The Economic Value of Social Bonds is only Beginning to be Measured", *Business Weekly*, pp. 153-155.

Youth of Uzbekistan in Conditions of Globalisation

Dilafruz Buranova

Uzbekistan attained its independence only a few years ago in 1991. During the later years, much has been done for the development of statehood and expansion of democratic norms, which includes building up a vibrant civil society. Uzbekistan is taking steps for building a civilised democratic state. This is necessary for facilitating transition from a planned socialist economy to a market economy. It was really a period of search for everything—from politics to societal values. At the time of independence, Uzbekistan faced many social, economic and political problems such as economic stagnation, food shortage, breaking up of economic relations with former Soviet republics, anxiety of a society as a result of various adventurous political forces, discontent in a society due to the activities of power structures, etc. As a whole, chaos and instability followed in the post 1991 phase

Just after attaining independence, Uzbekistan followed the footsteps of neighbouring former Soviet republics in stabilising the socio-political and economic system of the country. The first half of the 1990s of the last century was spent on stabilising the transitional socio-political system. After mid 1990s, efforts were made to initiate new programmes and policies for helping the country in chalking out new strategies and meeting new challenges. All these measures were aimed at ensuring socio-political stability of the country. What distinguishes the Uzbek model of developmental strategies with that of the other Commonwealth of Independent States (CIS) members was that in Uzbekistan, a new course of action was charted out without a 'shock therapy' model, where emphasis was laid on bringing socially vulnerable sections of the society to the mainstream.

Coupled with the dismantling of the Soviet structure, Uzbekistan as a nascent state faced another challenge from globalisation. This was especially true in the first half of 1990s, when the notion of globalisation was at its peak. This process also influenced the Uzbek state/nation-building process. Stabilising socio-political system, while engaging with the forces of globalisation, was a challenging task before the Uzbek leadership in the initial years. The Uzbek political elite under the leadership of President Karimov initiated this process of reforming all spheres, viz. economy, social relations, political system, the state, agriculture, sphere of national interests, ideology and others.

One of the central and key questions of reforming a society is dealing with the problems of young generation. In Uzbekistan, a large chunk of the population is of young age. According to an estimate, the number of young people at the age of 18 years and below is 10, 360,000, or about 40 percent of all population, and those of 30 years and below come to 17, 80,000, or 64 percent. In fact they constitute one-third of the total labour force. Apart from this, they also constitute one-third of the voters of the country.

Realising the importance of youth in the state/nation-building process, the Uzbek political leadership charted out special measures aimed at revitalising the role of youth in the social structure. These include providing assistance to youth in their educational development, providing employment opportunity etc. In the post-Soviet phase, these measures were carried out on a priority basis. Looking at the development of youth movement in the country, one can say definitely that there was an improvement in the facilities for youth in order to fully realise their potential. It is due to governmental measures to a great extent that these youth movements are making contact with their counterparts abroad.

The dawn of independence was an important milestone in the history of the youth movement in Uzbekistan. The attainment of independence provided a new opportunity to Uzbek youth to chalk out a new action plan necessary for spiritual and moral development of the country. However, this transition was not a smooth one. One important aspect of this transition involved developing an attitude among the young population of the country to respect ancient traditions, customs and cultures of the country. In our country there is a tradition to respect one's elders. These values should be imbibed in the minds of youth today. The Uzbek government realised that apart from existing moral and social customary rules, these age-old customs and heritage can be protected through legal measures also.

It is not only the spiritual and the moral development of the young population which is given attention, the Uzbek leadership is also giving priority towards the improvement of educational and employment potential of the young people. This is being realised by providing proper educational facilities as well as other incentives necessary to develop their full potential.

Since independence, efforts have been made to realise the full potential of youth in Uzbekistan. Some of these measures are:

Firstly, there has been a sincere effort to free the youth movement from the ideological framework of Marxism and Communism and also from the influence of radical and chauvinistic forces. Secondly, steps have been taken to create popular youth movements across the country.

Since the early years of independence, the State has been the main reformer of the youth policy. The following measures were taken to improve the socio-political and economic life of the people:

- recognition of the social status of youth;
- creating conditions for catering to the interests of the youth;
- the creation of the Right to Education and Employment;
- working out the system of privileges and encouragements;
- implementation of the government programme of personnel training;
- support for rights and freedom;
- development of various public associations and the organisations.

The core of state policy is based on a principle of recognition of the constructive role of youth in the reform processes.

The state youth policy is supported by the following statutory acts and state laws: Decrees of the President of the country, Laws of *Oliy Majlis* (Parliament), Decrees of the Cabinet of Ministries and Government Programmes.

Some main laws on the development of the youth in Uzbekistan are 'About Bases of the State Youth Policy in Republic Uzbekistan'(20 November 1991, with amendments in 2004), 'About National Personnel Training Programme' (29 August 1997), 'About Education' (29 August 1997). Other laws include those related to Family Code, Labour Code, Citizens Code, as well as government programmes like 'About Additional Measures to Strengthen the Health of Women and Rising Generation', 'For Healthy Generation', 'Government Programme on Development of the Sports among Population', 'The Government Programme on Youth Support' (1991, 1994, 2008) and others.

Sincerity of the Uzbek government in improving the conditions of Uzbek youth can be inferred from the fact that more than 80 legislations have been passed since independence regarding youth policies. The first such policy was enunciated in November 1991. The law has defined the main principles of a youth policy as:

- care of well-being and future of the youth;
- legal and social protection of the youth;
- preserving the continuity of generations, national and cultural interrelations and traditions, spiritual communication of generations;
- support for youth initiatives, guarantee of freedom to the youth in choosing ways to pursue their interests;
- encouraging participation of youth in government programmes and policy on development of a new society;
- civil liabilities for the youth.

According to the 'Law on Education' (29 August 1997), all citizens are provided with free secondary education. Uzbekistan is among the few nations with practically full literacy level, which is still increasing. The education level in 2003 reached 99.34 percent.

Education is one of the priority areas of the government with an allocation of 7.4 percent of GDP to this sector. The government guarantees provision of education and provides equal opportunities to receive education at all levels, including pre-school, school (primary, secondary, secondary specialised), pos- graduate education and research activities.

Each person who reaches the school age is required to attend school and complete nine years of education. After finishing school, young people are offered a wide range of professional education at secondary specialised and vocational schools and universities. Like the European system, in Uzbekistan also a number of mechanisms are aimed at strengthening the educational system. Strict measures are taken by the government to maintain the quality of education in the country. Today 65 high schools of the country train 300,000 students in 850 specialities. As many as 200 secondary specialised schools are functioning in the Republic. The whole education system of Uzbekistan covers over 6.5 million students

The 'Law on Education' guarantees everyone an equal right to receive education irrespective of sex, language, age, racial and national identity, belief, religion, social origin, residence, duration of residing in the Uzbekistan territory. Teaching in average educational institutions is conducted in seven languages: Uzbek, Russian, Karakalpak, Kazakh, Kirghiz, Tajik and Turkmen. In 88 percent of schools teaching is conducted in the Uzbek language, 5.5 percent teach in Russian, 2.5 percent schools use Karakalpak, 2 percent have Tajik, 0.4 percent schools teach in Kirghiz and 0.2 percent teach in the Turkmen language.

To face global challenges, efforts are going on to provide internet supported education and the government is also encouraging computer-aided education in the country. The government has also instituted scholarships in the name of historical figures like Biruni, Ibn-Sina, Navoi and Ulugbek. To encourage girls' education, government has sponsored a scholarship named as *Zulfiya* (a well-known female Uzbek poet). In July 2003, a new scholarship was instituted named as *Istedod*, basically funded by the Presidential administration. This fellowship helps students in getting education in foreign universities across the globe. The government is also improving the sports facilities in the country by providing various financial incentives to the youth. The major objectives of government's youth policies are to protect the interests of the youth and provide congenial environment where they can prosper.

A number of NGOs have been working for the youth since independence. The Social Movement of Youth 'Kamolot' is a powerful youth organisation uniting more than 4 million (more than 20 percent of young people of the country) youth between 14 and 30 years of age. It carries out its activities in more than 20 directions on various projects in the Republic. 'Kamolot' supports youth in their creative possibilities, assisting their participation in meeting the actual problems of a modern life. Various branches of 'Kamolot' exist all over the country. A children's organisation 'Kamalak'(Rainbow) was created as a part of this movement.

Youth newspapers like 'Turkiston', 'Youth of Uzbekistan' and a magazine named 'Yoshlik' are published. There is also a TV channel 'Yoshlar'(The Young People). Besides, ten youth NGOs have been created. They take an active interest in issues such as protection of ecology, propaganda for a healthy way of life, working out of youth initiatives, protection of a young family and the child, rendering humanitarian help and many others.

With the active encouragement from business groups and other high officials of state, the Foundation 'The Forum of Culture and Art of Uzbekistan' was created in May 2004. It organises scores of youth projects and receives applause from the Uzbek youth. A number of activities for the betterment of youth are carried out. It also provides vocational education and other support aimed at harnessing the potential of youth in the country. Together with non-state charitable organisation 'Mehr Nuri' (the Mercy Ray), it has developed a special project called 'Programme of Educational Grants', which is meant for comprehensive support to students of higher educational institutions of the country to perfect and increase their creative and educational potential.

In May 2007, a Presidential Decree 'On additional measures on financial and moral support to young families' was issued. The Decree outlines a number of measures aimed at protecting the interests of the youth.

In January 2008, Uzbekistan adopted a law 'On guarantees of the rights of the child'. On April 8 the same year, *Oliy Majlis* (Parliament) of Republic Uzbekistan ratified the Convention of the International Labour Organisation № 182 "On prohibition and immediate measures for eradication of the worst forms of child labour" with effect from 1999. It is especially remarkable that the year 2008 was declared by the Uzbek President as the Year of Youth. In this connection, a state programme 'The Year of Youth' was adopted in the country. It is aimed at the all round development of the youth in the country including their political status and activities.

In conclusion, one can say that Uzbekistan in the post-Soviet phase is taking utmost measures to improve the life and liberties of the population, especially that of the youth. The programmes and policies outlined by the Karimov government are helping the cause of youth and are providing opportunities for their participation in the national mainstream. The role of civil society also in this regard cannot be minimised.

Surviving Economic State Reforms: 'Illegal Practices' As a Way to Make up for Ineffective Transition Towards a Welfare Economy in Ukraine

Abel Polese

This paper suggests that 'corruption' (or better what is labelled as corruption), in Ukraine, is not the cause but the response to state inefficacy and incapacity to carry out reforms that evenly distribute welfare.

By performing what are labelled as 'illegal acts', citizens make up for the incapacity of the state to act as welfare dispatcher and thus allow the system not to collapse. In addition, those practices allow a more even distribution of resources and economic development that, even if not credited by macroeconomic indicators, allows people to overcome problems like inflation or shortages resulting from mismanagement of economic policies.

On the one hand the state did not give up its right, and obligation, to act as welfare dispatcher for public workers, students, doctors and patients and all those in the need for social support. On the other one, the incapacity to carry out the necessary reforms (rising up wages and working out decent retreat schemes) has resulted in an increasing tension in the relationship between the state and the citizen that is at the grounds of Ukraine's inefficacy

Ukrainian public institutions have been accused of being permeated by endemic corruption and public workers to take advantage of their position. This paper reverses this point of view: once the state is unable to compensate citizens, the only way they have to survive is to engage in some informal economic transactions that Western law codes classify simplistically as 'corruption'.

Informed by primary participant observation and informal interviews gathered in hospitals, schools, universities and public offices, this paper offers an alternative vision on under-the-table practices that, initiated in the USSR, have been 'institutionalised' and are a major component of Ukraine's economy since 1991.

Historical Context

Ukraine achieved independence in 1991. Well-positioned, with a wide access to the Black Sea, rich in coal and steel and cultivable land, it seemed destined to a prosperous future. This was, at least, the opinion of the national committee that students and workers took when striking blaming Moscow, in 1990, for all the economic problems Ukraine had. It was generally believed that Kiev, once released from the financial and political burden of the Soviet Union, would start a rapid transition to economic stability and growth to become a welfare state on the model of its western neighbours.

Reality revealed different. The first elected president, Leonid Kravchuk, was soon to be blamed for being unable to carry out economic reforms and letting corruption spread around as a cancer in the country. Early elections were held in 1994 and eventually won by Leonid Kuchma, who promised to carry out the economic reforms Kravchuk had failed to implement. However, like his predecessor, Kuchma did little to secure an economic development of the country and corruption kept being one of the main problems of Ukrainian economy. A turning point might have been the 1998 financial crisis that threatened to extend from Russia to Ukraine. Oligarchs and other main economic actors accepted to appoint, though for a limited period of time, a team of competent economists, including current president Viktor Yushchenko, to secure the country from the economic crackdown that had ruined a number of Russian businessmen. For the first time national economy saw a real economic growth and hopes of a transformation appeared.

The reformist government was short-lived (1999–2001). Once the economic elites felt saved from the financial crisis, the current Cabinet of Ministers revealed too burdening for them and Viktor Yushchenko got sacked. In 2004 the Kuchma era ended and Yushchenko was elected at the presidency of Ukraine, promising solid economic and social reforms to bring back Ukraine on the right economic path. The main problem is not the lack of welfare in the country but rather an uneven distribution of financial and material resources, which are concentrated in the hands of a few oligarchs and a growing, but still low, number of middle class people.

Once foreign investments began to increase, the private sector blossomed and wages accordingly rose, if compared to the average income, in this. The problem is for those who do not have access to this part of the job market, especially those working in the public sector.

As a rule, public workers should be supported by the state in order to carry out their duties and should have enough financial tranquillity to work properly. Reality turns out to be different.

In Ukraine, in most of the public sectors, the state has so far failed to play its role as a welfare dispenser. Liberalisation of several sectors has not been accompanied by the creation of *super partes* controlling organs and dynamicity of the economic life—and prices—is not followed by a dynamicity of wages, at least for the public sectors where workers see their purchasing power decrease day by day. In January 2003, average wage in the educational sector was 349.43 hr. (Ukraine currency Hryvnia) and in the health sector 293.41 (1 Euro was 5.60 hr. in January 2003) while in financial activities it was 1117.54 hr. In January 2006, those values were 684,96 and 560,96 (1 Euro was 6.40 hr. in January 2006), indicating growth. However, one has to remark that those values are before tax, and are still extremely low—an average wage in finance was 1727.64 hr.—and unable to compete with the rising costs of goods and services. For example, the price of services increased 27.4% between September 2005 and September 2006.[2] As a result, several categories of workers—teachers, doctors, police officers and pensioners—are unable to live on the revenue the state is providing and need to make up for the shortfall somehow.

In a standard welfare state, it is expected that the state collects taxes and uses the money received for the advantage of its citizens but Ukraine seems unable to act this way.

This contribution focuses on two case studies of sectors that are public and should be managed by the state but their organisation is so peculiar that it is difficult to see them as public. In particular, this paper will focus on the educational and health sectors and their management (and mismanagement). From my fieldwork it looks clear that bad management by the state has generated a parallel socioeconomic system to make up for inconsistency of state policies making those public sectors de facto private in Ukraine.

This public/private ambiguity is of utmost importance in the consolidation of a transitional state as Ukraine because it has several consequences. Once a sector that is in theory of property of the state is de fact not, the relation of the state with the citizen comes to be affected. In particular, the state looses credibility once it fails to act as welfare dispenser as expected. The very meaning of the state is to take care of tasks on behalf of the community since it would be too burdening for the citizens to carry them out individually. But, once the state fails to do that, citizens may feel they have no formal obligation towards the state.

My main thesis is that this anomaly in property relations in Ukraine distorts the relationship citizens have with the state. In other words, once the state fails to act as a state, there is no reason why the citizen should respect it as a state. A state that has no respect is not a state. Power is endorsed to the state by the citizens; once they do not support the state and refuse to give out their power, the state looses its sense and is comparable to a primitive society, where social networks and clan affiliation are more important than affection. Once a state fails to act as welfare dispatcher, it might loose its very reason of existence.

This is a vicious circle, people respect state law if they see an advantage in this behaviour, and Ukraine gives little advantage, a number of people ignore economic and juridical principles on which the Ukrainian society should be based, lowering the level of income of public budget and this limited availability of money impacts the capacity of the state to take care of its citizens.

This situation proposes Ukraine as a failed state (or quasi-failed since it is still able to secure some basic needs) and it is of crucial importance to the construction of a Ukrainian statehood and nation building in the country. In the end, a parallel system based on money and acquaintances is developing; the state has little voice in it and one could suggest that privatisation has gone much beyond what it is believed and include part of the public sector, a fact that contributes to the loss of credibility of the Ukrainian state. A further critical point is that Ukrainian nationhood is not yet consolidated and measures of nation building, trying to gather people under the same state, are being adopted. But with little will to subscribe to the socioeconomic project of the Ukrainian state, even national consolidation may be affected, for economic nationalism has a role in it.[3]

To illustrate my argument I have organised the paper in four parts. The next section provides some theoretical concepts whereas the following three are case studies based on the material I have collected in Ukraine in 2002/2006 when I was teaching and researching in Odessa and Kiev. The final part shall glue together all the evidence gathered and propose an explanation of the phenomenon.

When a State is a State?

A state is a set of institutions and practices with enough authority to administer a determined territory limited by some borders. This includes the authority to set up rules to govern the population living within the state territory. To refer to Weber's[4] definition of a state, it is the organisation that claims a monopoly over the legitimate use of physical force in the enforcement of its order. A further development of the state may be considered as the welfare state, in which the state takes care of all its citizens, though this vision has been criticised for not granting enough liberty to the citizen. We do not need to go as far as the welfare state, it is sufficient to remind that a state often hosts two main sectors: public and private (one should not forget the so called 'third sector' but this is not fully instrumental to our discourse).

The public sector is managed directly by the state. It is the state that is responsible for creating the jobs and the conditions that will help it to function. Once this is set, there will arise the need to form and then hire a number of people who will work for the state and for the benefit of other citizens. The private sector, where existent, is not under the direct control of the state. However the state might want to create the institutions that prevent abuses on other citizens.[5] For example, labour unions are allowed to negotiate with the employer on the working conditions in private companies and avoid exploitation of workers.

In a state, the individual will have to hand off some of its liberty for the benefit of the whole community, and thus its indirect benefits also. This will come in the form of taxes: I pay the state to set up a set of hospitals so that I can get medical assistance when I need it, or free education for my children; this can come in the form of physical work or serving the army to secure a defence against potential invaders. The important thing is that the individual is linked to the state through what Rousseau has called 'the social contract': the state guarantees some benefits and the individual pays in time, resources or labour. When there is no central coordination of such efforts for the benefit of the community, we might be in presence of what can be called an archaic society, where decisions are made on the basis of pre-defined hierarchies, helped by social networking and the relationship amongst citizens is different: if I need medical assistance, I go to my neighbour to ask for help instead of asking the state to find me a doctor whom I might not know at all.

However, the border between an archaic society and a modern state in crisis is often blurred. This is also due to the fact that the category of 'politics' shall face several farther divisions (juxtaposing democratic tendencies to local dynamics) and modern politics have gone through a process of complication.[6] A failed state, like Ukraine, which is unable to act as a regulator of welfare even in big cities has similar characteristics to this description of archaic societies.

Traditional approaches to explain this lack in Ukraine have often reckoned with ethnic ties, geographical and linguistic factors. Catherine Wanner instead has proposed a model of national identity in Ukraine based on economic opportunities.[7] I intend to move further in this direction and analyse the role of the state in the building of a civic community in Ukraine.

Why in Ukraine is there a low political participation, economic contribution to the national economy and problems of statehood and identity? I am suggesting that one of the reasons is the incapacity of the state to run the state and thus it fails to gain the respect and cooperation of the citizens.

A starting point may be the theory of power by Gene Sharp[8] who reflected on why political leaders have the authority they have. Political leaders are the guide of a state because people endorse them; this may be conscious—through elections—or unconscious—by avoiding to act against them like in the case of a dictator. By the same token, a state has some authority because there is an implicit agreement: the state provides with basic needs of the citizen and the latter grants it some authority in a number of aspects of daily life.

The state in normal conditions acts for the good of the community: it protects its people from foreign invasion (army and political diplomacy), it defends the individual from abuses from another individual (courts and police), it takes care of people's health (hospitals), it educates its people (schools and universities) and provides them with economic means to survive (work).

This can be done in two ways: either the state takes care of all those issues—centralised state—or it leaves the individuals free to organise themselves—liberal state—but creates the necessary institutions to avoid abuses and secure correct functioning of the market (Fukuyama 2005). For instance, the state can either manage the health sector itself or open the market and let people fund private hospitals but then set up institutions to avoid price abuses, monopolies and guarantee access to health care to all its citizens.

Sharp stated that authority is granted by the people. Therefore, a functioning state is a state enjoying respect and submission of its people. But this respect is not automatic and, once gained, has to be preserved. What would lead an individual to refuse acknowledging the role and authority of the state? Bovi[9] answers that people contribute to community expenses when they feel there will be a return, that is they pay taxes when they reckon that this money will be invested by the state for the welfare. Conversely, if people feel no advantage will derive from paying taxes, there will be a higher tendency to fiscal evasion. For instance, a high level of corruption deceiving people would cause them not to expect any return from their investment in the state (taxes) and therefore they would try further to avoid paying taxes.

In terms of everyday life, we can reckon with two categories of persons: those who, when ride public transport, pay the ticket and those who do not pay it. Or better those who think it is correct to pay the ticket and those who think it is legitimate not to pay. Paying the ticket means to contribute to the development of the public transport, the individual gives money to the state which, in turn, will invest it and keep the transport functioning and possibly improve quality standards. In other words, the money the citizen invests is coming back in the form of services. This is true when the individual is used to a direct relationship with the state, *do ut das*, but when the individual lives in a state where the administrative elites give priority to their own personal advantages at the cost of the community, it does not expect anything from the state and will tend to invest as less as possible. People from welfare state tend to pay the ticket much more spontaneously than people from failed welfare states and it is only apparently, or partially, correlated with income. It is a deeper question depending upon the way the individual sees and feels the state.

When the state does not function properly, citizens will have to get access to services, deemed normal in welfare states, through friends or acquaintances (*po znakomstvu*),[10] through exchanges of favours (*po blatu*)[11] or through offer of commodities[12] or money (vzyatka) whose classification as 'corruption' is, to say the least, simplistic.[13] In Ukraine, there is a property ambiguity related with the public sector. The public sector is public only on paper, de facto it is private and this modifies standard relations of the citizen with the state.

The next sections will deal with three case studies to show how people have made up for the incapacity of the state to act as welfare dispenser and how this affects participation of citizens in political, economic and social life of the country.

Pay Private, Get Public Education

The Ukrainian 1996 Constitution mentions that primary education is free of charge in Ukraine and states that the state shall strive to guarantee higher education free of charge, when possible.

As a general rule, we can distinguish two types of schools: private and public, depending on the way to finance vital activities. When a public school deems that the state budget is not enough, or when it wants to widen the range of activities and offer better facilities, it may address to the private sector and look for extra funding. In Ukraine it is extremely difficult to find a school that survives merely on the state allocated money. Normally a hybrid system is set and the school asks the families to contribute to the school budget through donations, commodities and/or work in case of poorer schools. The principle is 'you get what you paid for' so that wealthier families will address to those schools that are reputed the best, and where they will have to pay accordingly[14] and poorer families will send their children to less demanding schools where the kids (or even the parents) might be asked to help in painting walls or in general to the maintenance of the school.

Officially, schools are not allowed to pay their teachers more than the state-set salary and should use the extra income for extracurricular activities. So how can better schools secure better teachers? First of all more expensive schools can secure better facilities that can enhance the school reputation and attract better teachers.

Teachers, in turn, will be attracted by the reputation of the school but also by the social connections they might get in a given school. In a school hosting wealthier children, they have more chances to get presents, they might be asked to give private lessons at higher prices and I do not exclude a sort of incentive: prizes given by the school as a way to overcome financial regulations, overall these schools are financially more rewarding for teachers as compared to others.

The situation in the universities is similar. Public universities shall return to the state any extra income they have at the end of the year. The distinction between good and bad universities, apart from historical reputation, is done on the entrepreneurial capacity of the university or, better, of the faculty that seems to have life as self-standing institutions. To enter a faculty of international relations, foreign languages, medicine or other degrees leading to a top job is extremely difficult but entering an average faculty of history or ethnography is relatively easy.

Teachers will have more or less the same income all over the country but a rating of universities exists, both for students (when they decide where to go) and for teachers (when they decide where to teach). Better universities are not only a matter of preparation of students but also a matter of contacts and opportunities. If all your colleagues come from the economic elite of the country and you study with them, you are likely to get a number of friends and connections at the end of your studies that will ease your life in the job market, in addition to the good reputation of the university that will enhance your CV.

Teachers, in turn, shall use the good university as a base for future contacts. Like in the school case, they are more likely to get in touch with wealthy students and might get some advantages out of it, in addition to teaching in a prestigious university that will ease your search for a 'part-time' job in a private university, which has no limit in wages like public ones, and boosts your prestige in social networking.

It is natural that there is a rush for the best universities and the extreme gap in demand and offer has two main effects according to the elementary principle of economics. The number of students longing to enter a university is high and accordingly higher are those wishing to enter one of the best universities of the country. Extra students mean extra income for the university, so the university will accept a number of students higher than it can manage. Second, entering a university like the Shevchenko in Kiev is extremely competitive and there might be people willing to sell a place at the university to round up their income as long as there are people ready to pay for this.[15]

When knowing only half of the story, that is that teachers get extra money from sources other than their salary, supporters of the welfare state would blame corruption in the country[16] but I have already maintained[17] that we are witnessing a privatisation of the educational sector, the state being unable to take a decision: either to acknowledge that salaries do not correspond with the cost of life in Ukraine and allocate a higher share of the budget,[18] or liberalise schools and universities in Ukraine and overcome those financial machinations that burden the schools with extra money and prevent the state to collect taxes on extra incomes that do not necessarily pass through the school accounting office.

I do not intend to justify herewith the act of selling an admission test for some thousand dollars, in which case I agree that both parts are to blame, but I would like to introduce an extra variable in the evaluation of the results of the educational sector and stress the share of responsibility the Ukrainian state has.

The question is now on perception. What is the perception of the state by people who are not helped by the state to get access to an education, which is their right? The state exists but its merit is not to dispatch education and make it accessible, conversely it has a feudal role: it owns the universities and gets a profit from it without caring for the welfare of its citizens. The state does not control the educational sectors, it merely owns it. People who work in the sector control it and get advantage of their position; this is much more similar to privatisation than to the public management of education. Where is the relationship between the citizen and the state when the citizen cannot appeal to the state but has to go to the state representatives who act on their own to gain access to a university? The state here is absent and the citizen gets no advantage from the social contract it is engaged with.

Where are All the Doctors Going?

The hospital case is also illuminating. According to the Ukrainian constitution, medical care should be free of charge. What happens in reality?

Conditions of Ukrainian hospitals are quite bad, as they are overcrowded and equipment are in general obsolete, which lowers the standards, despite the good will of a good number of doctors and nurses. Private hospitals have been increasing in number in recent years and, in the choice between a private and a public hospital, the number of Ukrainians preferring the public one is extremely low. In both you pay, perhaps in the private one a bit more but this saves you from long queues and also, the private ones are generally much better equipped than public hospitals. It is generally accepted that in public hospitals you pay a bribe and the standards are low whereas in private ones you pay a fee and everything goes smoothly.

This might be true but to a certain degree. In a public hospital you might have to pay or you might not, depending upon a number of social and interpersonal rules that I shall try to explain but the starting point is the wage which the university staff gets. Standard wages of doctors were around 200/300 US dollars—while administrative staff and nurses get much less—at the time of the fieldwork (2005/2006), an amount of money largely insufficient to survive if one reckons that in a big city, a one room apartment in an average area costs around 300 dollars.

A potential patient enters a hospital and asks for a consultation. Medical care is free of charge so this will be given in the end. The incognita is what kind of service it will get and when.

It is not uncommon to see that a high number of people are waiting before you; you might also want to be checked by a given doctor and get some extra attention.

Those are the services you have to pay for, not necessarily in money or in commodities. You might be lucky and have to wait only a few minutes and find a doctor in a good mood, or might not. The less uncertainty you want, the more you have to pay. If you want to be checked straight away, you might want to go to a nurse and make her understand that your case is 'urgent'. You will then be expected to pay for the 'express check-out' so that you can either slip a banknote into her pocket or leave it on the table of the doctor who will collect it only after you leave the room. Possibly it should be one single banknote so that if you want to offer 20 hryvnia (3 Euro ca. the standard fee in Kiev during my fieldwork), you do not have to use smaller notes, not to talk of asking for change! You have to put the exact sum onto the table.

Another case is that you know the nurse or the doctor, in that case, you will not have to pay but the service will be proportionate to your prestige before that person. If you are a close friend, you will be sent to the doctor almost immediately whereas if you just know him, you might have to wait some time.

You could opt for another strategy *po znakomstvu*—a friend is interceding for you with the doctor. In that case, waiting time and service will fall in between the first two cases; you will be treated better than an unknown but worse than a close friend.

Finally you could just gain the sympathy of the hospital staff if you have a brilliant personality or simply if you can get empathy from the doctor or a nurse, in that case you will 'pay' the service with emotions rather than money.

On the doctor's (or nurse's) side the discourse is similar. Normally in Ukraine, a doctor working in a public hospital tends to help people, but the modality and the way he does it are extremely variable. As a doctor you will have your routine work, checking people who have health problems and will have to face lack of equipment and huge crowds of people longing to see you. You might try to do your best given the available machines but still will be concerned that your salary does not allow you to live in a normal way.

When somebody is ready to acknowledge your role by rewarding you with a present, you might not want to loose the opportunity to get an extra income. I am reticent to use words such as bribe as these words have a moral judgment that I would like to avoid in this context. Even Ukrainians, when talking of donations to the doctor, are more likely to call them a sign of thankfulness than in other cases (when they pay police officers or teacher). I have already argued that once a public worker is not rewarded by the state, its role of public worker is ambiguous and the money it gets from other sources might not necessarily fall into the category of 'bribe'.[19] What is important to the discourse here is the give-take dynamics and the role of the state. Some doctors will demand money, some others will expect it but not lay a claim on it. The core of the discourse is that there is a whole parallel system functioning and that the distinction between public and private is extremely fluid in this case.

What would happen if doctors would be allowed to receive extra money from patients? Immediately what is now labelled corrupted system would become a hybrid private-public one. In Ukraine there are already such cases. The most interesting I have found was a sanatorium in Mirgorod where patients are now free to buy a service and there is an accounting office so that 'bribes' have to be paid to the sanatorium, not to the doctor.

This difference in form is extremely important for its effects. Bribing is harmful, and punishable, for it takes away from the taxable income. Once a payment is made under the table, this eludes state control and people do not pay taxes on it. In turn, this slims down the state budget and the state has to lower the level of welfare granted to its citizens. A payment under the table in a hospital downplays the state and therefore the hospital cannot invest on new equipment, a loss of welfare for the citizen. At the source of all this, however, there is state incapacity or lack of will to provide doctors with a normal wage. Doctors will have to make up for this lack and engage in a number of informal exchanges that will damage the state.

According to most western reports, the situation is clear: corruption is galloping across the country[20] and is most visible in hospitals. According to the author, a parallel system is making up for state ineffectiveness.[21] What is the message that the citizens get? Like in the case of schools and universities, the state owns the capital but is unable to manage it. A doctor will not act as a representative of the state when checking a patient but as a representative of its family as it is only limitedly a public worker. Public worker means to be committed to work for the state in exchange for the means to survive by the state but the state fails to carry out its obligations as wages are too low to survive.

The citizen will therefore perceive the state as absent or, in the best case, negligent. Why should a citizen respect the state and pay money when it will not get back through services from the state? Why should it at all feel as a citizen of that state? It will rather think that, in common with the doctor, it has an enemy, the state which is underpaying the doctor—prompting it to look for extra income, at the expenses of the patient—and which is offering a mediocre health care to citizens.

The State, the Welfare and the Welfare State are Not Synonyms

A state that is not a state is unlikely to prompt citizens to act as such and Ukraine is an evident case. Soviet legacy and incompetent state management have de facto enormously reduced the role of the state to some basic functions and returned to a pre-modern society, where citizens are glued together by belonging to the same state but do not rely on it for most of the everyday questions. Social networking and individual connections are much more important than a direct relationship with the state that fails to act as welfare dispatcher and thus the citizens have to turn elsewhere in their quest for welfare. Once the state fails to secure basic needs, state morality might not apply anymore[22] and acting 'against' the state is a duly consequence: smuggling is illegal because it takes away revenues from the state but, once the state, through its economic system, is damaging the citizen, why should the latter grant money to the state?[23]

There are other spheres of daily life that would lead to the same conclusion, such as social health with almost inexistent pensions and a low level unemployment aid, a half functioning executive ready to sell its services and a chaotic labour market.[24] What is relevant to this analysis is the relationship between a malfunctioning state and civic participation to the development and stability of the state itself.

Ukraine is a country marked by a relatively low political and civic participation and tendency to tax evasion. This can certainly be rooted in historical factors like the legacy of the Soviet Union; however a constructivist approach may also help. There is a lot to be understood by analysing the relationship state-citizen in nowadays Ukraine. In modern societies, contribution to a state may not be anymore than the result of constraints by a higher authority but a choice of the citizen. A welfare state is not based on coercion but on free participation of its citizens and a spontaneous contribution of the citizen to the state can only be prompted by a correct behaviour of this latter. The social contract upon which a welfare state is based is a *do ut das* agreement where the citizen shall feel worth to invest time and money in its state which, in turn, must secure a return and protect the citizen.

The state should be present in a number of aspects of the citizen's life, at crucial moments but also in everyday life, and in this respect it is extremely important what the citizen may expect from the state.

Ukraine provides its citizens with an amazingly ineffective combination of state management tools. The state is public, the private sector is private but the public sector is private—or worse it has the disadvantages of the public and private at once. It has the service and equipment of an indebted public sector, prices of a private sector and a quasi-monopoly typical of unhealthy economic environments, with the state owning this monopoly and the impossibility to appeal against it. It is quite unlikely that somebody will attempt a process against the state for damages received by a bad management of a hospital.

The message citizens receive is that the state is not taking care of their welfare or that the state is unable to do it. In both cases perception is negative; it is a careless or weak state that is unable to gather enough respect to prompt citizens to have loyal relationship with the state.

As a citizen I shall try to get maximum benefits but I will not expect anything from the Ukrainian state. A wealthy family will have the money and the connections to get access to good medical service and send children to a good university, in some cases a private one. But wealthy citizens are a minority in Ukraine and although they have a major voice in political, economic and civic life of the country, the masses are also extremely important. As an average Ukrainian, I shall address to friends, friends of friends or acquaintances to get a decent medical treatment and engage in a relationship of mutual dependence with other people I might barely know. Likewise if I want my child to be well-educated, I shall try to secure access to instruction through informal channels but this is not the essence of the state, which should act for the wealth of the whole society and which should be a mediator between citizens. I need a doctor, I address to the state and find one through the state, this is the welfare state path. In Ukraine, if I need a doctor I might want to skip the passage through the state, I will find one thanks to peers' help. But this is a path typical of primitive or pre-modern societies where the state is absent or weak. If I have conditions of a primitive society and its disadvantages, why shall I support a state? Why should I enjoy social drawbacks of a stateless society and economic burden of a state-based one?

'I shall not' is the answer and this is why people might want to refuse the role of the state in Ukraine. As a result, reticence in serving and honouring the state is extremely high. Distrusting the state will also mean not to be willing to participate in its activities such as choice of political leaders, civic actions or engaging with a national identity as people feel such a gap between them and the state (or do not feel the state at all) that they will see no reason to participate in something that does not belong to them.

Conclusion: A New Conception of the State?

Although institution and state building in Ukraine are considered advanced, Ukraine is still far from being able to offer a social contract with advantages for its citizens. Giving up some egoistic sentiments for the good of the community is not yet actual in Ukraine because citizens cannot see what kind of advantages they are going to get by renouncing their selfish instinct.

In a well functioning state, the citizen invests some time and money into the state which, in turn, will secure some advantages to the citizen itself, such as protection in daily life, education and social benefits. In Ukraine the state fails to pay back its citizens and leaves them alone in the daily fight for survival; hospitals and educational institutions are only two cases of the larger list of institutions that fail to grant the citizens what they should.

Such weakness or negligence of the state results in lack of trust in institutions and the state which in turn affects the attitude and behaviour of the citizens. They will have more difficulties in identifying with the state and will not understand why the state must be rewarded with time or money by them if they cannot get anything back from it.

To better the situation, the Ukrainian state has a range of options in between two extremes: either privatise a part of the public sector and create a set of institutions ready to defend the citizen if the private entrepreneurs take advantage of their condition in order to avoid monopoly or other harming options; or, on the other extreme, totally reform the public sector, increase wages and invest a quantity of money that can then be claimed back from the citizens once decent services are secured. It is up to the politicians to decide the strategy to follow, the only thing I can remark here is that the system is going to implode if it keeps on following this existing path.

Notes

1. Participation in the conference and research for the article was possible thanks to a Marie Curie Fellowship, grant no. PIOF-GA-2008-219691
2. All those data are from the Ukrainian Statistical Committee, http://www.ukrstat.gov.ua/ (last accessed 8 November 2006)
3. Takeshi Nakano, "Theorizing Economic Nationalism", *Nations and Nationalism,* Vol. 10, No.3 (2004): pp. 211-229
4. Max Weber, "The Theory of Social and Economic Organization", *New York: Free Press* , 1964
5. Francis Fukuyama, "Foreword" in *Report on the Transparency International Global Corruption Barometer 2005* (2006), available at http://www.transparency.org/policy_

research/surveys_indices/gcb accessed 15 August 2006

6. Daniel Bell, "Ethnicity and Social Change", *Ethnicity: Theory and Experience,* edited by N. Glazer and D. P. Moynihan, Cambridge: Harvard University Press, 1975
7. Catherine Wanner, "Money, Morality and New Forms of Exchange in Postsocialist Ukraine", *Ethnos* 70, no.4 (2005): pp. 515-537. See also Catherine Wanner, *Burden of Dreams*, Pennsylvania University Press, 1998
8. Gene, Sharp, *The Politics of Non Violent Action,* Boston: Porter Sargent, 1973
9. Maurizio Bovi "The Nature of the Underground Economy-Some Evidence from OECD Countries", JIIDT, Vol. 7 (2003): pp. 60-70
10. Markku Lonkila "Informal Exchange Relations in Post-Soviet Russia: A Comparative Perspective", *Sociological Research Online* 2 no.3, (1997) www.socresonline.org.uk/socresonline/2/2/9.html
11. Alena Ledeneva, *Russia's Economy of Favours: "Blat", Networking and Informal Exchange*, Cambridge: Cambridge University Press, 1998
12. Jennifer Patico, "Chocolate and Cognac: Gifts and the Recognition of Social Worlds in Post-Soviet Russia", *Ethnos* 67, no.3 (2002): pp. 345-368
13. Caroline Humphrey, *The Unmaking of Soviet Life: Everyday Economies after Socialism,* Ithaca, NY: Cornell University Press, 2002; Abel Polese, "'If I Receive it, it is a Gift; if I Demand it, then it is a Bribe' on the Local Meaning of Economic Transactions in Post-soviet Ukraine" *Anthropology in Action 5, no. 3 (2008)* forthcoming
14. Zerkalo nedely, see http://www.zerkalo-nedeli.com/nn/show/427/37370/ (accessed 4 June 2006).
15. Abel Polese, "De jure oder de facto? Die Gesundheits- und Bildungssektoren in der Ukraine" *Ukraine Analysen* no. 16, (2006): pp. 2-4
16. See Zerkalo nedely, but also Transparency International or Freedom House reports
17. Abel Polese Paying for a Free Education; *Transitions On Line*, Prague (8 August 2006): pp. 1-3
18. Y. Gorodnichenko, and K. Sabrianova Peter, "Public Sector and Corruption: Measuring Bribery from Micro Data" *IZA Discussion Paper* No. 1987 (2006), available online at http://www-personal.umich.edu/~ygorodni/private-public-Gorodnichenko-Peter-2006-01-25.pdf, last accessed 13 March 2007; W. Miller, B. Ase Grodeland and T. Y. Koshechkina, "Victims or Accomplices? Extortion and bribery in Eastern Europe", in *Economic Crime in Russia* edited by A. Ledeneva and M. Kurkchiyan, London: Kluwer Law International, (2000): pp. 113-128
19. Abel Polese, "Ukraine: the State is Public, the Private Sector is Private, the Public Sector is…?" Paper presented at the "Workshop on Property" New European College, Bucharest (14-15 June 2007)
20. Transparency International *Report on the Transparency International Global*

Corruption Barometer 2005 (2006), available at http://www.transparency.org/policy_research/surveys_indices/gcb (last accessed 15 August 2006)

21. Abel Polese, "Border Crossing as a Daily Strategy of Post Soviet Survival: the Odessa-Chisinau *Elektrichka"*, *The Anthropology of Eastern Europe Review*; Vol. 24 (1), (2006): pp. 28-37
22. Wanner, op. cit. 2005
23. Polese op. cit. 2006 and 2007
24. Polese op. cit. 2006

Profiling the Impact of Globalisation in Central Asian Republics: A Perspective

Mushtaq A. Kaw

Globalisation defines a trend of transformation from local and regional to the global phenomenon and characterises the coexistence of a relationship based on surplus, trade, market and capital. Such a globalising trend in international trade antedating medieval times was stalled by unlimited state control, excessive taxes and traditional means of transportation and communication[1] besides two great wars and their corresponding anti-imperial 'nationalist' interlude in the twentieth century. These factors, either individually or in aggregate, contributed to slashing down the level of foreign trade and capital investment in the developed and the developing countries. However, the given trend picked up as a sequence of unprecedented technological advancement and the pro-activism of several leading transnational financial corporations (Hereafter TNFCs). Unluckily, in 1970s, the TNFCs encountered economic crisis due to low returns on their capital investment, rigid national policies, exorbitant prices of goods and high levels of taxation. To tide over the crisis, the TNFCs mandated , say in the case of the Third World countries, that they should necessarily (i) reduce business tax, wages and inflation, (ii) promote mobility and capital investment in industry and financial services, (iii) privatise state enterprise, (iv) liberalise imports to render the exports efficient for foreign earnings, (v) ensure equitable sharing of resources , (vi) render borders soft to allow hassle free trade, (viii) and permit infrastructural development, roads, highways, railways, pipelines, telecommunication and electronic networks. In a way, they emphasised on a unified and flexible economic order that sought to integrate national, regional (pan European, pan-Asian, pan-Arabic and pan-American) and world economies towards policy of *laissez faire* and neo-liberalism, which invariably recognised both developed and the developing countries as co-partners in the cross-border trade and foreign capital investment.[2] Consequently, by the end of twentieth century, the Gross Domestic Produce (GDP), per-capita income and other socio-economic indicators of development registered a tremendous progress in the Third World Countries notwithstanding the belief of the 'Cultural Imperialists' that 'globalization is the reincarnation of the Western imperialism/ colonialism'; hence, oriented to co-descend and stigmatise the Third World countries for securing optimum benefits to the transcontinental corporations themselves than the people of the world at large.[3]

While that is there, there can, however, be no denial to the hosts of benefits accruing from the rapid technological advancements in information technology and volatile capital flows. As elsewhere, these new engines of growth redefined human interface in diverse paradigms especially in Korea, Japan, China, India and Central Asian Republics (Hereafter CARs): courtesy huge foreign capital investment in the CARs by the world famous companies on banking, trade, construction, hydropower generation and hydrocarbon exploration and transportation. These included *Chevron Corporation*(US), *Agip* (Italy), *Gazprom* (Russia), *Unocal* (US), *Mobil* (France), *British Petroleum and British Enterprise Oil*, *Anglo-Dutch Royal Dutch/Shell*, *Statoil* (Norway), *Repsol* (Spain), *National Company of China* (NCC), *Mitsui* (Japan), *Petrons* (Malaysian), *Merhav* (Israel) and *INDC* (Iran) etc. While Swiss and Turkish corporations invested in oil and gas exploration in Kazakhstan, Uzbekistan and Turkmenistan, *Daimler-Benz* of Germany, *Daewoo* of South Korea in car industry, the *BAT* of United Kingdom made investment in cigarettes making and tool manufacturing. Turkey launched Eurasia Television Network from Ankara to Central Asia to popularise her cultural influence in spoken Turkish language.[4] So did other Eurasian firms invest in mining, energy and telecommunication industries.[5] Korean and Uzbek firms, the *UzDaewoo Auto Joint-Stock Company* and the *General Motors-Daewoo Auto and Technology*, cooperated to manufacture auto spare parts through *UzDaewoo Auto Company* in Asaka in the Eastern Andijan region. Chinese consortiums sponsored projects on road building, oil and gas transportation, hydropower generation and power lines from and across Kazakhstan, Kyrgyzstan, Turkmenistan[6] and Tajikistan. [7] The Russian companies, *RusAI* and *Oleg Deripaska*, financed projects on hydropower generation and aluminium processing at Rogun and Turzunzade respectively in Tajikistan. Indian firms, *ONGC Mittal Energy Ltd* and *Nuclear Power Corporation of India*, invested on energy explorations in Kazakhstan and hydropower generation in Tajikistan. In addition, the transcontinental funding agencies , the *Asian Development Bank* (ADB),

World Trade Organisation(WTO), *European Union*(EU) [8] etc. floated loans and funds for infrastructural development and energy generation and transportation from CARs to international markets.

As a natural concomitant of above investments, the CARs particularly Kazakhstan, Uzbekistan and Turkmenistan followed by Kyrgyzstan and Tajikistan experienced the emergence of mammoth business houses, banks, industrial set ups, construction plants, hydropower and hydrocarbon projects and telecommunication systems. These are changing the entire façade of CARs and capacitating them to huge foreign exchanges, strengthen national currencies, generate jobs, raise life standard and open up vistas of social sustainability and economic restructuring. Such benefits are steadily percolating down to villages which are gradually changing their face and transforming them into leading urban hubs pointing thereby to a horizontal and vertical growth in the CARs including Tajikistan and Kyrgyzstan, the two poor economies, with lesser resources and distant location from the established world markets, marine and transportation hubs. By all means, however, Kazakhstan offers the best model of socio-economic development following large scale multinational companies and massive foreign investments. The UNDP reports,[9] field experiences of the present investigator and the search findings of the eminent Kazakh economists like Bolat Tatibekov, are altogether supportive of marked improvement in the life standard of the Kazakhs over the last several years. While the country is not devoid of the poverty, its level is substantially diminishing compared to her counterparts. The below poverty level which had increased till 1998, dipped from 34.6% to 9.8% during 1999–2005. Likewise, the purchasing power in terms of foodstuffs, goods and services improved almost at the same level. The number of people whose income was below food basket cost declined from 16.2% to 1.6% during 1998–2005, a ten times recovery.[10] In a way, average monthly income of Kazakh men increased from 14034 *tengis* in 1999 to 34648 *tengis* in 2004: that of the women also improved from 9485 to 21445 *tengis* during the same period.[11] The literacy rate recovered at all levels[12] and so did the rate of child mortality from 35 to 20.1 between 1991 and 2003 per thousand births[13]: indeed all because of Kazkhstan's abundant hydrocarbon resources, volatile trade, immense exposure to and cooperation with foreign countries, multinational companies, firms and consortiums for mutual benefits. Such type of growth is traceable in Uzbekistan, Turkmenistan and other Central Asian states of course with varying degrees.

Politically, globalisation smoothened inter and intra-state conflicts among the CARs probably in tone with John Stuart Mill's belief that 'integration would prove an instrument of conflict management in domestic situations'. For economic and other benefits, the contending parties would prefer peace, dialogue and settlement to conflict and war. The political realist, Winston Churchill, also upholds Mills' views on the multiple advantages that follow from the merger of the nation-states[14] and resolution of a wide variety of those conflicts that characterised the 'writings of Herodotus, the father of history, Karl Marx, the proponent have-nots, Samuel Huntington, the advocate of Western civilisation'.[15] Quite precisely, globalisation sought to neutralise, if not out rightly eliminate, an assortment of ethno-national, religio-cultural and economic conflicts among the CARs. Even their border disputes with Russia and China, were relatively settled for mutual benefits emanating from the global trade.[16] This sort of conflict management spontaneously forged a sense of mutual co-existence among the CARs, though this juxtapose exposed them to popular indignation for the restoration of fundamental and democratic rights. The intermittent popular outbursts in Kyrgyzstan, Uzbekistan and trans-Caucasian states against the authoritarian regimes explain the extraneous influences that globalisation brought forth during economic amalgamation. Indeed, it exposed the hitherto landlocked and stereotyped peoples of Central Asian to the progressing world communities, which eventually, sought to widen their political horizon and socio-economic and cultural make up. Such an awakening was the offshoot of the educational integration of CARs with the reputed institutions in US, Turkey, Korea, India, Japan, Russia and China which the Central Asian youth visit for the pursuit of the degrees in engineering, medical, M.Phil, Ph.D etc. True educational reforms in CARs had the nation-building agenda to which indigenisation of native languages was a specific feature. But these were simultaneously aimed at (i) marginalising Soviet educational system, (ii) building up foundation for a quality-based education, (iii) and creating comparable educational institutions with Europe.[17] Under the circumstances, learning English language and education across the Seas ceased to be a taboo as both are the potential mediums of earning job and education with in the global framework. Little wonder to observe Central Asian youth taking Western education in Europe and Asia and the level of illiteracy instantly declining in CARs. Kazakhstan, for one, substantially reduced illiteracy and the gender disparity as is vindicated by almost the same percentage of the Kazakh boys and girls at the primary and secondary levels. The women's participation in the legislative bodies of the country also swelled due to educational priorities of the Kazakhs: 7.7% by 2004 in the Senate comprising 39 members and 10.4% in the country's Parliament or

Majlis of 77 members. To recall, the said rate had immediately contracted after the Soviet demise.

Culturally, globalisation facilitated the rural-urban movement, a phenomenon unheard of Central Asia till recent past as the region was known for '... the low rate of movement of the population from their local rural environment to urban centres...each inhabitant's loyalty remained at the local level', the village and its local customs, traditions and kinship ties.[18] Globalisation brought them out of the Arcadian life and boosted their large scale migration from the socially isolated and economically backward to quite advanced and richer zones housed by peoples of divergent ethno-national and ethno-regional backgrounds. There they jointly work in multinational companies and business houses and share their thought and harmonious tradition of "cultural pluralism" which finds support from Laura Adams's writings: 'globalisation is a process that contributes to international integration and homogenisation' and stimulates 'diversity by providing venues for the propagation of new ideas about local identities'.[19] The points in reference are the nascent metropolitans of Central Asian states, which symbolise quite integrative educational, economic and cultural centres. The same is true of the population in Eastern Turkistan or Xinjiang where, for instance, the restaurants represent a real blend of distinct tastes and ethnic identities, the Chinese owner, Uighur receptionist, Kyrgyz cook, Kazakh server and Tajik customer. Even the higher educational institutions in CARs characterise the blend of Indian, Chinese, Russian, Pakistan and Japanese students through mutual influences in food, dress and culture, which eventually leads to the formation of the 'cultural entropy'. Such a phenomenon is especially publicised by those young Uzbek, Kazakh, Turkmen, Kyrgyz and Tajik girls and boys who visit developed European and Asian countries, USA, Japan, Turkey, China, India, etc., for education, job and trade . They return home with new experiences about alien culture, individual behaviour and collective attitudes, which they later transmit to their native conditions. Many of them take up jobs in multinational companies, shopping malls, business houses, cafes, bars, restaurants and quietly conducted night clubs in the important metropolitans of the CARs. During an informal chat, a Kazakh national from Almaty, maintained that "globalisation does not distance but unifies cultures which is a blessing to pool together human energy, diverse ethno-national and geographical identities notwithstanding varying materialistic ends and interests". This kind of universal brotherhood is, therefore, based on the principle of 'each for all and all for each' as it effectively swamps rigid ethno-cultural structures. Having diversified sources of income, globalisation empowered the Central Asians to formalise a wide variety of customs and rituals related to the human belief, birth, death and marriages, the hallmark of Central Asian history and culture from early times. With flow of money, they organise such ceremonies with great deal of extravaganza and entertain visitors, mourners and guests alike with quite a wide variety of food, juices, tea, drinks, etc.

However, it would be simply naïve to consider globalisation as an absolute programme of human development. Together with advantages, it brought the Central Asians face to face with complexities of life; which is why perhaps the ongoing global recession is making its impact on CARs also. Some experts opine that had there been no globalisation, the spill over of recession would have been localised. More so, they believe that globalisation, exceptions apart, failed to produce a genuine middle class in Central Asia. The neo-rich class mostly comprises the political and the educational elite which are, by and large, disinclined to ameliorate social inequality and rural-urban void. The official data is fudged by the CARs to present a rosy picture of the growth and development, they further believe. Hence, poverty, unemployment and low life standard reign supreme especially in Kyrgyzstan and Tajikistan, which together perpetuate crimes, endemic corruption and a stressful society[20] to avoid which, the Tajiks often take recourse to arms smuggling and drug trafficking as short-cut means of social survival and elevation. Of the six routes originating from Afghanistan, three routes traverse Khorog, Panj and Moskovsky in Tajikistan. [21] The Khorog-Oash-Aandijan route, the 'Opium Highway', is treaded by the Tajik youth to smuggle opium from Afghanistan to European markets across Tajikistan, Kyrgyzstan, and Russia. In fact, opium smuggling absorbs a lot of poverty-stricken and unemployed youth in the whole Gorno-Badakhshan Autonomous Oblast (Hereafter GBAO) on two counts: one, it remains the dominant source of their survival in the rugged terrain and second, it is fairly lucrative as can be easily gauged from the report of Andrey Nikolayev, the former Director of the Russian Federal Border Service: "A certain amount of heroin costs $100 in Badakhshan province in Afghanistan. Once it is smuggled across the River Panj into the GBAO in Tajikistan its value increases to $1000. As it is taken through Oash in Kyrgyzstan it increases to $10,000, when it reaches Europe it costs $100,000".[22] Interestingly, the Tajik women contribute a great deal to its trade in the Pamir region despite heavy penalties. They also engage in the 'suitcase' or small international trade. Thus from Alamty Kazakhstan, the heroin consignments are afforded by different gender ethnic groups including the children to Russia and thence to Europe due to soft borders and free global trade .

Likewise, trafficking of women is facilitated by the phenomenon of world transforming into a 'global home'. Eminent sociologists, like Marfua Tokhtakhodjaeva from Uzbeksiatn[23] and Sofia Kasymova from Tajikistan[24], have expatiated upon the underlying factors of prostitution and flesh trade in the countryside of CARs.[25] Field studies also reveal that a large number of innocent girls, lured by job and business, are transported across in groups to perform illicit and immoral acts. Similarly, for making a living, a large number of Central Asian workforce annually migrates to Russia and other foreign countries. During their out-stay, they make new marriages which contributes to alarming social tensions in their home land. In sequence thereof, they either divorce their actual spouses or leave them half way to live by themselves: attend the family and small farms or else migrate to urban areas for job, which at times, pushes them into the web of the prostitution and flesh trade. This type of transitory or perennial out migration, the offshoot of population explosion, scarce resources, uneven growth rate, varying wage scales, unemployment, etc. also find support from the immense opportunities thrown open by globalisation, the soft borders, flexible visa regimes, boom of the multinationals and foreign capital. Quite exactly, scores of Central Asians annually migrate to Russia, China, Korea, Japan, India, Turkey, USA, etc. for education and career building. In fact, the said trend had set in immediately with the Soviet demise in 1991. The new-born Soviet Central Asian states, under transition, failed to address the immediate challenges. For the fear of ethnic cleansing or for earning employment, a large proportion of non-Turkic and non-Iranian ethnic groups migrated from the CARs[26]though it was correspondingly reciprocated by the inflow of equal and even more number of Kyrgyz, Uzbek, Tajik, Kazakh, Turk, Uigur and Dungans into CARs at their embryonic stage. The net result was that the titular population swelled from 62.3% to 79.9% in Kazakhstan during 1989–2000; 71.4% to 77.6% in Uzbekistan during 1989–2002 ; 40.1% to 53.4% in Kazakhstan during 1989–1999 ; 52.4 % to 65.7 % in Kyrgyzstan during 1989–2001 and from 72% to 91% in Turkmenistan during 1989–2001.[27] The further expansion of the Turkic groups in CARs would precipitate marginalising the ethnic minorities and lead to what Karl Deutsch terms as the 'obliteration of unity of nation states in all such situations whose populations are already separated into social groups with different languages or cultures of necessary way of living'.[28] It would be equally fraught with serious consequences for the migrant Central

Asians in all such situations 'where there is migration and where groups of people who lived earlier in isolation, become ethnocentric to accommodate in heterogeneous conditions'.[29]

Nevertheless, it should not be presumed that out migration of Central Asians stopped after 2000. It continues unabatedly as tens and thousands of unemployment and poverty-affected Tajiks, Kyrgyz and Uzbeks of Russia and Kazakhstan are driven to out migration for employment and better wages. Fairly speaking, it has become the only source of living to many Tajik and Kyrgyz families leave apart the accruing remittances to the respective nation states of Central Asia. The remittances amount to $260 millions in Tajikistan and $160 millions in Kyrgyzstan (only via Western Union). Reportedly, the money transferred by Kyrgyz migrants makes the half of the national budget. This is excluding the contribution of unregistered remittances and hand-to-hand transfers. Another obvious benefit of out migration is that it absorbs surplus work force by 10–15% in Kyrgyzstan, Uzbekistan and Tajikistan. However, one should not loose sight of the fact that the phenomenon of out migration contributed to the youth drain in CARs. Migration of highly qualified specialists is a very big loss to the CARs as hoards of workers, qualified and educated youth from Tajikistan, Uzbekistan, Kyrgyzstan, Kazakhstan and Turkmenistan immigrate to Canada, UK, USA, Japan, Turkey, etc. for high-paying jobs.[30] In the process, the respective countries loose the services of a potential human resource otherwise necessary for the growth and development of the respective countries especially when they are going through transition from central to market economy, to which effect, as was desired by the transcontinental funding agencies, they enforced measures to promote privatisation of all means and forces of production and encourage real competition and genuine labour and trade market. It is a different thing that the full form of private proprietorship on the analogy of Transcaucasian states is yet to grow in agricultural and industrial sector of the CARs. The Soviet state units of agricultural production, the *kolkhoze*, still exist with a different name of *shirkat* . The peasant's right to land ownership, free production and marketing is yet regulated.[31]

Educationally, globalisation is blamed to affect radical change in the priorities of the CARs, from education to business, which experts attribute to 30% slash in the literacy rate, for instance, in Kazakhstan during nineties and to a equal proportion in other Central Asian states. The number of first year university students reduced to only 3340 in Turkmenistan in 2000.[32] The option of the subjects for studies also changed because of the emphasis of globalisation in international relations and business administration. The premier subjects of math, physics, biology, known in Soviet times, took a back seat which is exemplified by the 50% contraction in the percentage of physicists, mathematicians, biologists in Kazakhstan around 1990–96. Geology and sciences declined by 40% while number of littérateurs increased by 7%, vetenarians by 14% and lawyers by 50% during the same period.[33] However, history and languages continued to have a space in the educational set up under the nation-building agenda. During the process of educational restructuring, the native languages were recognized as the official languages and Russian was simply accorded the status of a *de facto* language **for administrative, academic and political performance**[34] **which genuinely** frustrated the regional intelligentsia of different language and cultural backgrounds for the fear of loosing promotions and privileges.[35] Thus the Russian language and its text in school libraries were gradually substituted by the native literature. [36] In Kazakhstan, by 2000, the number of Russian training schools reduced by 60% and in Turkmenistan by 71%.[37] In Tajikistan, the textbooks at Russian-speaking schools were not updated for more than 10 years for the same reason. [38] That **the officialisation of the native languages was a big 'language shock' to multi-ethnic Russian speaking social groups is there, it deprived them of a common medium of communication and employment in** industries, management, science, etc.[39] The rich content and unifying spirit of the Russian language [40] was, therefore, cut across partly by the language policy of titular nations and partly by the gradual inroads of the English rather the globalised language in the Soviet space.

That most productive belts are converted into industrial zones by the multinational companies thereby causing health, ecological and environmental hazards, is indeed there. The globalisation is juxtaposed to leave dreadful impact on the cultural ethos of the CARs. True it combined divergent ethnic groups in the above explained cases, but in others, it is proving to be a predator. A Kyrgyz scholar rightly opines that "with economic unification, the nomadic life style is experiencing a potent threat of extinction", a fact which is exactly in tone with the opinion of the 'cultural imperialists' that 'global cultural and technological influences eat up indigenous identities by displacing local values and practices antedating pre-historic times'. On its account, a substantial percentage of rural population is in the process of shift from rural to urban areas at the cost of the age old cultural ethos. A point in reference is the break down of the joint family tradition and the weakening of community and fellow feeling so characteristic of Central Asia villages since early times. During an informal chat, a Chinese scholar from the Chinese part of Central Asia (Xinjinag) forthright termed globalisation as a 'double-edge sword: on the one hand, it enriches traditional Chinese culture and instills new vigour in it, one the other, it expunges some of its valued elements". Historically speaking, the given trend of the destruction of traditional values and customs set in with the Soviet occupation of Central Asia and their corresponding development programmes on the Socialist pattern though Glenn radically differs with it: "...The creation of state and collective farms (*Sovkhozy* and *Kolkhozy*) has tended to be based on local villages and have therefore resulted in a syncretic fusion of the tribal/clanic structure and the agricultural production unit". [41] He is supported by Barnett who argues that "the groups were relocated to new areas...they generally moved *en masse* so that the kinship structure was retained...the state and collective farms were ethnically mixed" and so were the ethnic groups and the kinship units kept in tact.[42] Contrarily, however, the rural-urban mobility in the wake of Sovietisation damaged village communities and their allied values for the simple reason that, on movement from the basic village to the *Sovkhozy*, the peasantry was subjected to an altogether different conditions: from individual and self-sufficient units to state regulated farms, from choice of free peasant production to a centrally controlled cropping pattern, from a relatively independent to a choked atmosphere of communes where everything was governed by the Soviet state. Therefore, by dislodging peasantry from their native villages,[43] the Soviets undid the very basis of villages and their age long customs based on kinship, family, primordial and ethno-tribal ties. [44] The simple reason was that the Soviets wanted to make socialism as the 'the only source of guidance'. The further setback to the Central Asian cultural ethos is underway due to industrialisation, urbanisation, rural-urban mobility, new market forces enshrined in the entire edifice of globalisation. During educational and material pursuits within the integrated economic framework, the migrant rural folk, the young boys and girls, are caught up in a peculiar type of conflict between legacy and modernity and in the process, they are distanced from their family, village, land, customs, traditions, taboos, practices and in fact from the whole treasure of generations bequeathed heritage. They experience a change in every walk of life and from a simple life pattern to a globalised culture of jeans, cafes, restaurants, bars and liquor shops, etc. They are overwhelmingly absorbed by the Western movies, literature and music at the cost of the most enthralling and scintillating classical *Sufiyana* music. The traditional musical instruments, the *tabla, santoor, rabab*, *sittar,* etc. are nearing extinction in the train of the pop. Music videos, a practically unknown medium in pre-independent Central Asia, are frequently used to explain glorious past and national identities of the CARs. The popular Uzbek singers, like Sevara Nazarkhan and the trio 'Setora', produce such songs and videos which are broadcast on the youth television channel, *Yoshlar* (Young People) on weekly basis indicating a great deal of global cultural influence .

The social customs and practices related to marriages, the hallmark of Central Asian culture, have also undergone new experiences due to the inflow of extra money in the region. Because of which the people have got into wasteful resource cult as they organise the marriage ceremonies with great deal of extravaganza and immense expenditure on entertaining the guests with an intricate variety of meals. They doll out huge quantum of dowry to the groom in cash and in the form of cars, TVs, refrigerators, washing machines, and other electronic goods. On the day of marriage contract, the newly married couple is held out in Benz, Mercedes and other spacious cars of the foreign make. Similarly, the rituals regarding death and burial are extravagantly performed, symbolic of a social obligation than a sacred and holy act of attaining peace unto the deceased. Consequently, such ceremonies have become ritualistic both in form and content as these are organised to replenish the coffers of the priestly communities and entertain the visitors/ mourners with the belief that it would augur well for the life of the deceased in the world here and hereafter. Therefore, the rehearsal of such ceremonies, lasting for days, months and years together, are facilitated by the additional sources of revenue stemming from the globalization in Central Asian villages, towns and cities. While the affluent sections of the society manage them conveniently, the poor just afford them by begging and borrowing. In a way, the globalisation has hastened the cultural void among three broad social segments: (i) those who dwell in villages, follow customs, traditions, beliefs, taboos, rituals, practices etc. in letter and spirit, (ii) those who combine the Western culture with their traditional cultural survivals, and (iii) those who terminate the traditional customs and practices as obsolete in the face of the Western culture. In these circumstances, globalisation, leave apart its monetary dividends, is contributing to social tensions which, at times, are compounded by the generation gap and the conflicting perceptions of the older and younger generations about life and its nuances.

To wrap up, globalisation represents a coin with two faces, one bright and another dark: one symbol of economic prosperity and another social conflicts and contradictions in Central Asian context. No doubt it is exposing the peoples of the region to the new trends of scientific and technological temperament and improving their quality of life and social sustainability. But such benefits are, more or less, specific to particular strata of the society whereas the larger segments, especially in villages, are devoid of them. This is why the villages do not indicate a worthwhile improvement and they relatively wear a medieval look despite the enforcement of numerous schemes of economic restructuring as warranted under the norms of globalisation. In addition, globalisation is contributing to environmental and ecological disasters as huge firms, factories, business houses, occupy the spaces that were actually meant for agriculture operation. These release carbon monoxide and other industrial pollutants which are detrimental to the health and ecology as a whole. On top of it is the threat to the rich cultural ethos. Since globalisation offers ample scope of human growth and development, rural-urban shift is, as such, becoming inevitable leading thereby to the disintegration of the otherwise joint families based on compact kinship ties and primordial values. Their spontaneous extinction is giving way to a new space rooted in money and material than peace and solace. In view of this, there is a great need of preserving the Central Asian culture from the onslaught of globalisation. Let us not be averse to change for onward march to civilisation but let it not be at the cost of the rich heritage of the nation states of Central Asia. Last but not the least, Central Asia is since known as a home to a cluster of multi-ethnic and multi-national groups, who have been always at war with one another for regional leadership, power, resource and territorial sharing. One does foresee the role of globalisation in neutralising such inbuilt inter and intra-state conflicts but one can't really guarantee their final settlement unless the Soviet fallacies are set to right through the intervention of some apex global and regional organisations.

Notes

1. Mushtaq A.Kaw, "Trade & Commerce in Chinese Central Asia", *Central Asia: Introspection*, eds., Mushtaq A. Kaw & Aijaz Bandey, CCAS, University of Kashmir, 2006. pp. 47-61.
2. Jeremy Breacher and Tim Costello, eds., *Global Village or Global Pillage: Economic Reconstruction from the Bottom Up*, by, South End Press, 1994, pp. 1-9.
3. Prof. T.K.Oomen, Keynote address, National Seminar on "Globalisation & Social Sustainability", Department of Sociology, University of Kashmir, Srinagar, October 12-13, 2008.
4. "Turkey Pushing Eastward-By Satellite", *Washington Post*, March 22, 1992.
5. Shirin Akiner, " Politics of Energy in the Caspian Sea Region", *Regional Survey of*

the World: East Europe, Russia and Central Asia, Third edition, UK, 2003, n. 27, pp.11, 215-17; Murat Kenisarin, "The Energy Sector of Uzbekistan: Present State & Problems", Central Asia and the Caucasus , no's.2(26) and 34, 2004, pp.126, 128; Turkmenistan Natural Resources, Library of Congress: Cf. http://www.countrystudies.us/Turkmenistan/20.htm

6. Robert G.Sutter, *China's Rise in Asia: Promises & Pearls*, Lanham, 2005, pp.26-30, 108-09; James C. Moltz, "China's political and economic relations with Kazakhstan and Kygyzstan", *Central Asian Survey,* Vol. 17, No.2, 1998, pp. 231-35.
7. *International Monetary Fund*: Republic of Tajikistan, March 8, 2007.
8. Fouskas K. Vassilis , *Zones of Conflict: US Foreign Policy in Central Asia: Structural Reform and Political Change*, London, 2003, p. 22; Bruno Coppieters, "Central Asia Region in a New International Environment", *NATO Review*,Vol.44, No. 5, September 1996, pp. 26-31.
9. First Report on *UN Millennium Development Goals in Kazakhstan*, UNDP, Kazakhstan, 2002.
10. "Population Living Standards in Kazakhstan", *Statistic Yearbook.* Agency on Statistics of the Republic of Kazakhstan, Almaty ,2004.
11. "Females and Males of Kazakhstan", *Short Statistic Bulletin*, Agency on Statistics of the Republic of Kazakhstan, Almaty, 2004.
12. *First Report on UN Millennium Development Goals in Kazakhstan*, UNDP in Kazakhstan, 2002; *Short Statistical Yearbook of Kazakhstan,* Agency on Statistics of the Republic of Kazakhstan, Almaty, 2006.
13. "Population Living Standards in Kazakhstan", *Statistic Yearbook.* Agency on Statistics of the Republic of Kazakhstan, Almaty ,2004.
14. Winston S. Churchill, "Foreword", *An Idea Conquers the World*, ed., R.N.Koudenhove-Kalergi, London, Macmillan, 1953, p. X.
15. *The Economic Times*, New Delhi, July 25, 2008.
16. Witt Raczka, "Xinjiang and its Central Asian Borderlands", *Central Asian Survey*, Vol. 17, No.3,Oxford, 1998, p. 384; Guangcheng Xing, "Security Issues in China's relations with Central Asian States",(eds.) Y.Zhang & R.Azizian, *Ethnic Challenges Beyond Borders,* London, 1998, n. 1,pp.65,209; *China's Policy Priorities,* Lanham, 2000, p. 65; K.Warikoo, "Central Asia and China : The geopolitical Imperatives", (ed.), Shams-ud Din, *Geopolitics and Energy Resources in Central Asia and Caspian Sea Region*, New Delhi, 2000, p. 260; Yasmin Melet, "China's Political and Economic Relations with Kazakhstan and Kyrgyzstan", *Central Asian Survey*, No. 31, p. 245
17. Henri Fruchet, "The Use of History: the Soviet Historiography of Khan Kenesary Kasimov" and Robert Lowe, "Nation Building and Identity in the Kyrgyz Republic", *Central Asia: Aspects of transition*, (ed.) Tom Everett-Heath, London/New York,

2003, pp. 106-32.

18. John Glenn, *The Soviet Legacy in Central Asia*, London & New York:Macmillan & St.Martin Press, , 1999, pp. 91-96.
19. Laura Adams, "Globalization in Central Asia: Notes on Centrality and Marginalization", *Journal of Central Asian Studies*, vol. VI, no. 2, pp. 6.
20. Emomali Rakhmanov, *Tajikistan in the Mirror of History*, Vol. 1-2, London: River Editions Ltd., 2006, p. 1.
21. *International Crisis Group*, "Recent Violence: Causes and Consequences", *Central Asia Briefing*, October 18, 2000.
22. Roger N McDermott, "Border Security in Tajikistan: Countering the Narcotics Trade?", *Conflict Studies Research Centre*, ISBN 1-904423010-8, October 2002, K 36.
23. "Trafficking of Women: The Case of Uzbekistan", Paper presented in the International Seminar on *Globalisation and Eurasia*, Centre for Russian & Central Asian Studies, School of International Studies , Jawaharlal Nehru University, New Delhi, November 9-12, 2008.
24. "Labour Market Globalisation & Status of Women in Post-Soviet Tajikistan", Paper presented in the International Seminar on *Globalisation and Eurasia*, Centre for Russian & Central Asian Studies, School of International Studies, Jawaharlal Nehru University, New Delhi, November 9-12, 2008.
25. "Labour Market Globalisation & Status of Women in Post-Soviet Tajikistan", Paper presented in the International Seminar on *Globalisation and Eurasia*, Centre for Russian & Central Asian Studies, School of International Studies, Jawaharlal Nehru University, New Delhi, November 9-12, 2008.
26. 16,199,154 to 14,953,131 Ukrainians, Germans, Tatars, Byelorussians, Azerbaijanis, Poles, Chechens, Bashkirs, Moldovans, Mordovans, Armenians and Greeks migrated from Kazakhstan and 50,000 to 90,000 Germans, Crimean Tatars, Jews, Turks-Meskhetians and others migrated from Uzbekistan during 80s and 90s: the similar was the proportion of out migration in Kyrgyzstan , Tajikistan and Turkmenistan.
27. Valeriy S. Khan, " The State Ideologies in Post-Soviet Central Asia: The Ethnic Dimension", International Seminar on Central Asia in Retrospect and Prospect, Centre of Central Asian Studies, University of Kashmir, Srinagar, J&K, India, August, 2006.
28. "Social Mobilisation and Political Development", *American Political Science Review*, No.55, 1961, pp. 493-514.
29. "What is an Ethnic Group", *The Ethnicity Reader: Nationalism, Multiculturalism and Migration,* eds., Montserrat Guibernau & John Rex, Oxford & Malden, 1997, p.21.
30. Stephen Dalziel, "London's Russian's", *BBC World Service on Assignments* (July 10,

2000); Saskia Sassan, *Globalisation and its Discontents*, p. 8.

31. Mushtaq A.Kaw, "Changing Land Tenures, Agrarian Reforms and Peasantry in Central Asian Republics (CARs)", *International Journal of Central Asian Studies*, Vol. XI, Institute of Asian Culture & Development, Seoul, Korea, 2006.
32. Eric W.Sievers, *The Post-Soviet Decline of Central Asia: Sustainable Development and Comprehensive Capital*, London/ New York, 2003,p. 54.
33. *The Post-Soviet Decline of Central Asia: Sustainable Development and Comprehensive Capital*, p. 66.
34. G.Tett, "Soviet Mullahs Who Threaten Gorbachev", *Financial Times*, 17 August, 1991.
35. Gelner Ernest, *Nations and Nationalism*, Ithaca : Cornell University Press, 1983, pp. 162-66.
36. Катагощина И. Т. *Кризис идентичности как фактор миграционных процессов на постсоветском* Восток, 2001, № 6, с. 79.
37. Независимая газета. 2000. 30.09.
38. *Тенденции бедности и благосостояния в Таджикистане в 90-х годах.* Аналитический доклад. Душанбе, 2002, UNICEF, с. 27.
39. Саралаев У. К. *Роль языка в международном общении.* - Диалог цивилизаций на Великом шелковом пути. Материалы международной конференции. – Бишкек, 2002. – С. 449.
40. Байтенова Н. *Межэтническая интеграция.* – Алматы, 1998. – С. 129.
41. *The Soviet Legacy in Central Asia*, pp. 91-96.
42. Rubin Barnett, "The Fragmentation of Tajikistan", *Survival*, 35/4, Winter 1993–94, p. 76.
43. R.A.Pierce, *Central Asia, 1867-1917*, Berkeley, 1960, p. 70.
44. Geoffery Wheeler, *The Peoples of Soviet Central Asia*, London, 1966, p. 71.

Labour Market Globalisation and Status of Women in Post-Soviet Tajikistan

Sofia R. Kasymova

Process of globalisation or cooperation, interaction and interrelation of Tajikistan (as well as other post-Soviet countries of Central Asia) with the world community started developing[1] from the beginning of 1990s in the last century, from the time of getting independence and forming of the national state, accompanied by transformation of economic, social and political structure of the society. There is no doubt that the process has its appreciable impact on gender order, and changes that have been going on during the last years in traditional life of Tajik women can easily prove it. In public discourse the assessment of the changes is ambiguous and inconsistent. We see on one hand the deterioration of the economic and social situation for the majority of Tajik women during the post-Soviet period. The argument may be the increase in discrimination against women; encroachment on their right to work, property and other rights; restraint of personal liberty and the right of choice. The causes are the following: the consequences of disintegration of the Soviet economic and social structure, unstable transition to the market economic relationship, abatement of patrimonial policy of the state and intensification of traditional patriarchal norms and practices[2]. On the other hand, there is also the appearance of having a positive character, new forms of women's social and labour activity, such as women NGOs. there are more opportunities, widening limits of social and special mobility of Tajik women, such as domestic and foreign labour migration.

Thus, in this article the author considers the process of globalisation, especially labour market globalisation, as a phenomenon having a dual character. Also in the article the author analyses different aspects of the consequences of globalisation that have an impact on the life situation of different social groups of Tajik women, especially qualified working women and country women, who work in the agrarian sector of economy. The empirical base of the article consists of sociological research materials (interviews, focus-group discussions, observations). The research was conducted in the years 2005–2008 in different regions of Tajikistan and focused on the problem of women employment, the question of gender equality and labour migration[3].

From Global Changes to The Problem of A Family Survival

During the last 15 years, the employment structure in the economy of the Tajik Republic has considerably changed. One of its notable characteristics is the increase in women employment from 40% in 1991 to 46.1% in 2006, accordingly labour activity among men dropped from 60% to 54%[4].

The breaking up of the former economic system after the collapse of the Soviet Union brought a decline in living standards of both rural and urban population. Reconstruction of the national enterprises in cities and farm enterprises (collective farms, state farms) in rural regions, aimed at adoption of market economy in Tajikistan, in most cases brought an end to underemployment[5]. As a result of privatisation, most of the powerful officers, who used their administrative and network resources, managed to get the public and so called collective socialistic property to their private ownership. Majority of the population, especially women, who were taking up minor positions (under the command) in the employment structure of Soviet Tajikistan not only stayed out of the process of industrial and agricultural enterprise, but also lost their guaranteed salary, assuring minimum subsistence. Wage levels dropped[6]. In fact, such a phenomenon can be considered to be hidden unemployment. There were jobs and there was work, but they could not provide salaries sufficient for meeting the essential needs of a worker and his family. If earlier a man as a family head could materially support a big family with the income from his work (as well as with the social welfare provided by the state in the form of social security, free education and health care), the new conditions dramatically curtailed his ability to do so. Reduction of labour demand is accompanied by growing of its supply from both sides: of men and women. It refers to dramatic decline of living standards of most families and impossibility to survive having a salary of only one member of a family. Women are trying to find all ways to earn money not only because of the death or absence of their men, but usually because of the meagre salary of the head of a family. In most cases women play an unusual role of a bread-winner. It means that women make a great contribution to their families, especially to large ones. During the Soviet time, housewives were reckoned as dependants who were in the charge of men (bread-winners). If we compare the present and the Soviet periods, we will see that working age of women has changed: today some girls between the ages 10–12 can do nothing but to start working in order to earn some money necessary for their families. At the same time in Tajikistan, old women also continue working, because average superannuation allowance in the country is equivalent to subsistence minimum.

Thus, the population of Tajikistan (both men and women) has been experiencing social shock that has considerably changed their lives. Globalisation influenced everyone equally, but the results are not the same, especially for women of different social groups. A Russian researcher M. Malisheva[7] writes that globalisation widens the gap between different social groups of women; its influence is unbalanced and depends on the level of the country development, on education and professional qualification of women, on their employment, on national traditions. We can consider it using the example of two social groups of Tajik women: qualified working women and country women—the former, Soviet collective farmers and the latter, housewives and mothers of many children.

Qualified Women: Freedom of Choice Plus Limited Opportunities

Qualified women is the smallest but the most active and productive group among other social and professional groups of Tajik women. These women live (as a rule) in cities. They are the product of the soviet gender policy of emancipation of Muslim women, who were a part of social and political elite of the Soviet state. At the post-Soviet time, they along with workers and farmers suffered because of difficulties of the transitional period, used different ways to find a job, tried to work in different spheres mastering new forms of activity. The process has made not only quantitative but also qualitative changes in the working structure of Tajikistan. Data of official statistics (from 1995 to 2003) show that the number of women working in the industrial fields and in the sphere of health service decreased[8]. Two main factors influenced the situation: 1) mass migration of Russian-speaking population, representatives of which formed the basic segment of qualified workers (it also refers to women), and 2) forced transfer of the great number of specialists to other sectors of economy. The cause was a cut in budgetary expenditure in the sphere of health services, education, culture, science and the displacement of women from the sectors that in the condition of market relations became profitable.

All these circumstances make women adapt to the changed situation and train for a new profession. So, they practice shuttle trader business[9]. Today among the representatives of the business, there are many women who are qualified economists, accountants, teachers, doctors, lawyers and so on. From the interview (A., 42-year-old, business owner, Dushanbe): *"Since the year 1994 I have been practising* shuttle business, *it has been a very difficult period for all of us. Both, my husband and I worked, but the money we earned was enough only for food. We could do nothing but to leave our work and start our own business. I started going to Bishkek, Alma-Ata, to buy goods and have to travel places for selling at the market. Today I do not remember that I am a qualified engineer, that I used to work at the textile factory— this is a pity that I can not realise myself as a professional worker, but it is our life. Anyways, today I have enough money for living"*. It is shuttle business that paved the way for women to market economy. In the most cases women are involved in the sphere of individual working activity that is realised on the patent or license basis. Women form the bigger part of all the sellers: in the year 2001 among 24,7 thousand sellers, 50,5% were women[10]. The last statistic data show that 32% of women (of the total number of working women) are engaged in private sector of economy of Tajikistan[11].

Some qualified women are re-trained for the work of housemaids, employees of commercial firms, agencies, international organisations, where they make some special work, but they get handsome salary for it. The author believes that this group of women-specialists irreversibly lost their professional qualification, thus reducing the limited numbering of Tajik women-specialists. On the other hand, professional education and previous working experience have let these women adjust to a new sector of economy.

Today qualified women workers have also started working in the public sector. Appearance of women NGOs is a new phenomenon in the public sector of the economy. Their initiators are western international humanitarian organisations. They help to organise such NGOs and finance them. The majority of the leaders and workers of both national and international NGOs are teachers of schools and universities, scientists, doctors and economists. As researchers say, in the beginning of 1990s, NGO attracted the attention of many people where they could earn more money than in the state sector. Another positive side is the possibility to work more independently. From the interview (Z., 45-year-old, leader of a NGO, Dushanbe): "*Some time ago I worked as a specialist in one in one of the ministries. At the soviet time I had much work. In the 1990s we came to our ministry and spent all the days doing nothing. Since there was nothing to do, I left my job. I spent a lot of time trying to find a job that I liked. Soon I started working as a volunteer for an international organisation. Gradually, I learned to work in another way (at the ministry we were just executors), to do a lot of things independently. I can say that I have got another speciality. I learned English, developed my computer skills. Today I have many more opportunities. I have always dreamt of becoming an advanced student, defend a graduation paper, but I knew that it was very difficult for me. Now I am a candidate of science. From my own experience I know that today it is much more interesting to work. If I am experienced and broadminded, I can earn an honest livelihood".*

Also more and more women have started working in the spheres traditionally monopolised by men. More women, especially Tajik, work today for law enforcement agencies, custom-house and armed forces, where usually men work. Many women work in judicial bodies; today 20% of judges are women[12].

Both quantitative and qualitative characteristics have changed at labour market. Here many aspects are important: gender component, labour relations and individual's attitude to work. As it has been already noticed, in the post-Soviet period, the main factor behind the growth of women employment is the economic reason (most women work in order to maintain themselves and their families). At the same time some women, especially well-qualified women, are not satisfied working just for money. From the interview (I., 33- year-old, the manager of international organisation, Dushanbe): *"I have a good job and I am satisfied with the salary, but it is not enough for me. I understand that I can not develop since I do only technical work".* Many women are interested in developing in building a professional career. One-third of the interviewed women (191 women) would like to be managers or directors, half of the interviewed women want to have a more prestigious position than that they have now[13].

The influence of globalisation on labour market has led to the demolition of traditional norms and stereotypes concerning the work of women. Today we may observe a different attitude of men towards their working women (wives, daughters, sisters). In the Soviet period, one of the main obstacles for involving Tajik women in the sphere of public-paid labour was the prohibition to study and work from the side of husbands, parents and/or other relatives of a woman[14]. Today the problem is not as topical as it was before. According to some data of a public questioning poll, most of women, 74% (of 191 women) noted that their husbands are glad that their women earn more money than the other members of the family, they also approve of their non-domestic work[15]. It can be explained in the following way. Initially, women started working in order to maintain their families with men being unable to earn enough money. Thus men could do nothing but to accept it; later, in many families because of their long absence (labour migration, penitentiary imprisonment), men could not control their women and women had an opportunity to decide independently whether they wanted to work or not.

Mass involvement of women in paid work revealed the gender discrimination existing in the public sphere. Under the new conditions, women basically engage in those spheres of employment in which there is little or no competition with men—public sector, agricultural sector, small business, non-manufacturing budget spheres such as health services, education, culture and social security system. The structure of labour force demand in modern economy is unfavourable for women, both on the official level and in shadow economy. In the private sector new employment as a rule is strictly structured by gender. On the other hand, if formerly the women's right to work was defended by labour law, today the same law has no mechanism of realisation under conditions of transition to the market economy. The evidence to it can be the fact of active supplanting of women experts from banking system, insurance, tax and customs organisations, since these spheres under the conditions of market economy have become more prestigious. The number of women in those sectors of the economy which have become most profitable, as a result of the new market conditions, have steadily declined. Thus, the number of women experts in finance, credit, tax and customs organisations, where average wage levels increased from 2.13 to 174.89 Somoni per month from 1995 to 2003, reduced from 3,600 to 2,100 in the same period[16].

Very often women have nothing to do but to realise their labour potential under extremely adverse conditions, accepting different forms of inequality and exploitation. From the interview (D., 40 years old, Vahsh region): *"My neighbor told me about a private cotton mini-plan, situated in our district. I got a job there. I have already worked there for 5 months; working conditions are very difficult, only a few people can stand them, many people can not continue working after one month. The floor is concrete; it is very cold in the industrial premises, people are working, standing all day long, and we have only one day off. If we fall ill, we can not take a sick leave; so if we do not come to work, our absence is considered as truancy. We (20 women and 20 men) work in two shifts (eleven hours in each shift). We have one hour lunch. It is our director who provides us with lunch. Our salary is 50 Somoni per month. I earlier used to work as a teacher. Then for some time I was unemployed. That is why I decided to start working at the plant, though I know that I will not be able to work there for a long time. Many people get serious illness after this work".*

The situation aggravated, as a Ukrainian researcher T. Zhurzhenko writes: "*...by the state's abandonment of its social contract",* (having in mind the post-soviet area) "*the government simply refuses to carry out measures of social protection previously guaranteed, like direct economic support of families with low incomes, and the provision of a broad range of benefits and services that formerly facilitated the women's burden of double employment"*[17]. Fundamentals of the Soviet policy of social security still remain in Tajikistan. Also the law makes provision for some kinds of benefits, allowances and social payments for working women, but in general the rate of payments is too low to have an influence on the improvement of the economic situation of women and their families.

Country Women: From the Soviet Collective Farms to Informal Employment

Most of Tajik women are country women: out of 3447.8 thousand women 2538.2 thousand (more than half) are country women[18]. In the last few years, the life of country women has been changing; many authors explain the changes in terms of worsening of their life conditions as compared with the Soviet period[19]. Two groups of problems, the course of which is the general socio-economic and socio-political processes of the modern Tajik society, influence the situation of country women.

The first group of the problems refers to the processes of transition to the new market society or divestment of government property of agricultural enterprises and reconstruction of collective farms, which led to the loss of the guaranteed work in collective farms and state farms, where the majority of country population worked. In the Soviet period, agricultural sector was the only main sector where country people could work since they had little small opportunity to get a job in any other sector. Because of this, there was hidden unemployment in countries called the 'redundancy of manpower resources'. In the post-Soviet period, the situation has been worsening because of the minimising government social support to mothers of many children, most of whom live in villages and because of commercialisation of the educational and public health systems.

Like in the Soviet period, women remain the main labour force in the agricultural sector; this tendency is increasing, the number of collective farm women has doubled in the seven years from 1995 to 2002[20]. In 1995 there were 100 working men as opposed 46 working women, in 2003 there were already 139 working women. It shows that the number of working women has been increasing. At the same time, average wages in agriculture are amongst the lowest of any sector of the economy[21]. Women cannot help but work for scanty earnings and firewood.

Land reform and the transition to new forms of management have had a negative impact on the economic and social status of rural women[22]. From the interview (M., 38- year-old, a former state farm worker, now unemployed, Muminabad district): "*Our state farm was disorganised, the property was bought by rich people, we have no job here*". According to a research, 90% of people working in the fields, where they sow cotton, and 70% of people working in other regions, are women and girls. Snapping is carried out by hand by women and girls. According to different data, about 9% of farms are headed by women. Specialists think that the percentage is overrated, since sometimes women are the heads of farms only on paper; in reality the farms are governed by other people, more often it is husbands, brothers or other relatives of the women[23]. Such practice limits women's access to the land, credits and other resources. Following the land reforms, many former farmers, especially women, were left without a job and land, being at the same time nominally members and quite often heads of peasant farms or workers of agricultural enterprises. This exact fact makes the paradoxical situation clear where on the one hand, the number of women engaged in agriculture keeps increasing, and on the other, the same workers de facto are unemployed; this in turn forces them to agree to doing any work and make no resistance to discriminatory practice. Here is a quote from an interview of a 38-year-old odd-job woman V., "*There is no work in the entire district, except in the field, and one has to accept all terms suggested*". According to official statistics, in 2003, 2102 women versus 1061 men worked under trying conditions, the number of women working under harmful conditions expands and to the majority is associated with agriculture.

The second group of problems was initialised by external labour migration growth. Labour migration is one of the most significant outcomes of the labour market globalisation, both in scales of expansion and in strength of the effect on other social processes. The opportunity to offer their work force and professional skills to labour markets of foreign countries becomes one of the available and legal strategic ways of survival for many Tajikistan citizens. At the given period, labour migration ensures considerable cash facilities inflow to the country economy, twice as big as the state budget, representing one of the restraining factors of social tension escalation in the Republic. According to different estimates, the labour migration engages between five hundred thousand to one million Tajik citizens, who are mainly male. Thus, according to the research conducted among those who went out of the republic in search of a job in 2002, 85% were males and 15% were females. During the last few years, we can observe a tendency towards increase in number of female labour migrants among Tajik women that in aggregate indicates expansion of their special and social mobility. Even during the late Soviet period (end of 1980s of the twentieth century), despite official Soviet state policy of gender equality attainment, general body of Tajik women was under tight control of their family and community and rarely went out of their house independently.

Mass and long-lasting departure of men from their families, out of their villages, region and country in search of a job resulted in the increase of female activity in labour socially paid for. Since physical (temporary and/ or permanent) absence of a man in house makes a woman take over the responsibility for family survival, this responsibility pushes a woman out into the labour market, replenishing the number of unemployed and/or people used in informal sector of economy. This can be presumed from the changes that have taken place in the labour market: reduction of employment rate in governmental sector and enlargement in private sector, unemployment growth, diminishing of social guarantees to workers. Most of the new female labourers are ex-rural housewives, plenty of which do not have practical experience and qualified work skills. Almost the whole of this female labour army is occupied with hard, unqualified, poorly-paid labour in consumer services, petty street trade, public catering, and living in permanent dependence upon the employer and intense competition. There is no doubt that all these characteristics are peculiar to informal economy sector. Mass implication of women into the informal economy is an identifying feature for the former Soviet Union regions. As the universal practice implies, initiation and expansion of informal employment is connected firstly with economic crisis, reduction of workplace number in the official sector, with an impossibility to financially maintain family at the expense of paid work for hire execution. According to some estimates, about 400 000 to 500 000 women in Tajikistan are engaged in the informal sector. They outnumber those in the official sector of the economy by a huge marfin. The limited opportunities in attempt to earn a living in their village or district force the countrymen to look for a job in cities.

Dynamics of the republic migration process all over the Republic shows that people coming to Dushanbe outnumber those who left the city: for example, in the year 2003 there were 5979 people who came and 3946 people who left the city. At the same time in Khatlon region the tendency is just the opposite: the number of people who left the region has doubled[24]. The immigration process 'country-city' which started during and after the Civil War (1992–1997) has not finished yet. If at the very beginning of the period it was the forced choice for many countrymen (pursued and persecuted refugees), then later many people started moving to cities in search of better life. Among these categories, moving to cities alone or with the family, there is a greater number of women. As it has been already noted, these women are employed in informal sector of economy: more than half of the women working in the markets of Dushanbe are former country women who are living in Dushanbe permanently or temporarily. In some markets, their number has reached 80% of the total number of all female traders. Many women of this group are in difficult living situation. It is connected with complete or partial break up of former family relations: some of them are widows of the civil war, the husbands of the others have gone to Russia as labour migrants, and the third have divorced. Their life situation may influence their choice of place for living; it is known that it is easier to find a job in a city than in a village, in a city it is easier to earn money to maintain the family.

The process of adaptation of country people and especially of women to social psychological conditions of the city is going on very painfully, very often it incites them to non-normative behaviour. Therefore, the number of country women who have moved to the city become prostitutes, some of them perpetrate a crime, something which earlier happened very seldom. From the interview (A., 26-year-old, divorced, has 2 children, a prostitute, Dushanbe): "*Do you think I work with pleasure? Of course not. I have no way out: I have no registration here; I do not have a flat or a house, I don't have a job, there is nobody to help me. So, I have nothing to do but to live one month with one man, the next month with another man; I am doing it for my children*".

Currently the life strategy of country women in the sphere of employment has a dual character. On the one hand, socially paid work is considered to be temporal forced mean of survival. The question *If you had such an opportunity would you like to leave your job (not to work at all)*? was answered positively by a third of the interviewed (48 women of 191), most of these women (36) who are country women do not want to work, they want to stay at home, of course at the condition that their husband will earn enough money to maintain the family. The author thinks that the attitude of country women to any job is based upon traditional rules: '*it is better for women to stay at home; it is men who must work*'. On the other hand, the attitude of country women to any job is based upon many years experience of hard physical labour, almost every country woman has such an experience. From the interview (K., 53-year-old, Bohtar region): *"I have worked in the cotton field from the time when I was a 6-year student of a secondary school. Everyday I got up at 5 o'clock in the morning. By 6 o'clock I was already in the field. At that time* (she means the Soviet period– S.K), *we almost had no off days though we worked from the early morning to the late evening. We could take rest only in winter. Anyway, our work was well paid; we had enough money for living. Today we work in summer and winter, when it is cold and hot outside, sometimes we work being hungry, and our salary is enough for only a week. I am getting older, my health is weak and I am tired of the hard physical work. But I need to work even for 20–30 Somomi*".

Another indicator is also typical: more than half of the women who said that their income is 100% of their family budget are country women. Thus, if on the one hand labour is considered as a factor of social well-being of both men and women, at the same time some country women hold the position of dependency that is the Soviet gender policy, which supported mother-worker by various forms of social guarantees. Maybe, because of it they are still expecting the government and now international humanitarian organisations to help them and take care of them.

Labour-Market: Traditionalism in front of Globalisation

In the aggregate, all these moments bring us to the changed traditional division of labour in the public sphere, this factor increases gender segregation in the spheres of professional occupation. The way how it happens can be considered by the example of women assimilation in new professional spheres which traditionally were supposed to be the spheres of men. The East market area has always been the place of men, and accordingly, it was men who went into trade business. Also it has always been men's duty to do shopping. Even in the Soviet period, many men did not allow their wives to push in the crowd in the market, considering it socially unacceptable for a self-respecting man.

In Tajikistan 'charter' or 'shuttle business' is a phenomenon of the post-Soviet economies that was started by women. This type of labour demanded non-traditional and non-normative conduct from the women involved and meant that they could, at least for some time, leave the house unaccompanied by their husbands. These women could start and conduct negotiations with ('other') men, could independently dispose of their own money, and could make their own decisions about some family matters. All these changes have gradually altered the traditional image of a Tajik woman, which can not be unnoticed by men. "*...Changes for women stipulate changes for men and men's reactions on the changes should be interpreted by these terms...*", these are the words of an American sociologist M. Ferry taken from his research on the problems of changing gender roles in the relationship between husbands and wives.□ Following the idea, we may conjecture that in this definite period of time, men can not fully realise the changes going on in their or/and not their women, because all these phenomena refer the level of psychological stress. For most families charter business was the only survival option in a situation of economic chaos and social instability. At the same time, when a woman becomes a 'co-breadwinner' or the only breadwinner in the family, it generates conflicts. As one woman put it, "*the neighbours are laughing at my husband— look, you are sitting at home, and your wife earns the money for the bread—so he beats me up*" □. This may happen because the joint performance of a breadwinner's role can be perceived as a threat to men who construct their ideals of masculinity on this economic basis. [25] A woman's income strengthens her power in the family as it decreases her dependance upon the husband, especially as money has traditionally been considered to be an essential source of family power relations.

It may happen that husbands and other male relatives pursuing their own ends will demonstrate their tolerance towards untraditional occupation of their women, but the society, also studying its own interests will not accept the situation, demonstrating a very negative attitude to the women. Female 'shuttle' traders experience the pressure of psychological rejection from the side of the society, this rejection is expressed as doubts regarding their 'normative behaviour'. According to M. Tohtahojayeva, such a situation is typical for the Uzbek Republic. In the newspaper Vatan, one journalist wrote: "... *A woman, who became a* breadwinner*, is not considered 'a real eastern woman' anymore, she is not a woman who stays at home and lets her husband solve all the problems*"[26]. Maybe, all these ideas follow from the traditional discourse of the primordial guilt and peccability that is the integral feature of each woman, it may be the total distrust of the society to a woman, who has no right to live and is under the command of her husband-master. We must add that it also refers to women who in search of living migrate to Russia.

Their attempts to live and work independently in a foreign country make them potentially vulnerable. It explains why many of them start living with their fellow countrymen formally or informally as husbands and wives, the fact of 'belonging' to a concrete man means that other men will not woo them.[27] Many women, selling their goods in the market or working in the consumer services, feel psychological discomfort because of 'sympathy' and disrespect from the side of other people, they realise their weakness because they are not able to change their traditional situation. Some of them say with regret: "*...if my husband were alive or (another variant) if my husband were a real man, I would never start working in this sphere...*".[28] It should be noted that such a situation (even in another variant) is also typical for other post-Soviet countries. V. Sukovataya wrote that in Ukraine most people are sure that 'business is a bad thing, which a 'normal' woman will never strive for it because it is incompatible with the role of wife and mother'.[29]

Conclusion

Labour market globalisation is a phenomenon that has a dual character. Undoubtedly, its influence is enormous, but the results depend on many factors such as: availability or lack of material, financial, professional, educational, informational resources of certain social-demographic groups of people. Thus, in post-Soviet Tajikistan, emancipated women, who had working experience, were well-educated and lived in cities found themselves in the most favourable situation, managed to react immediately to the changed situation and planned their successful strategies. Country women who were poorly educated and not qualified had to suffer in the bad living conditions.

Labour market globalisation has its influence on traditional institutes of marriage and family, on personal interrelation between men and women. Thus, the growing labour activity of women has made them economically independent; these women can fully or partially maintain their families. As a result, in such families, traditional gender roles of the husband—breadwinner—and the wife—housewife—have changed, resulting in gender conflicts. Social mobility of Tajik women has really increased and so has its positive and negative aspects.

Notes

1. It is characterized by international capital flows to the economy of the country, active work of international (foreign) humanitarian organizations, technological advance (mobile communication, internet), integration of the country financial market in the world market. The borders of space and social mobility of Tajik population widened because of increase of the number of labour migrants and progress in intercultural relationship.
2. Cf.: *Tajikistan. Report on Human Development* 1999. Dushanbe, 2000. *Tajikistan: in the way to gender equality.* Dushanbe, 2003. *Tajik NGOs' Alternative Report on Realization of the Convention on Liquidation of all forms of Discrimination Against Women*. Dushanbe, 2006.
3. Cf.: S. Kasymova, *Women Position in Labour Market and in the sphere of Employment: the ways of poverty elimination in Tajikistan. Gender Analysis on the basis of the results of Sociological Research. Report on the research).* Dushanbe, 2005. S. Kasymova, *Gender equality*. Informational and analytical bulletin «Mirror» № 7 (37). (2005): 55-73.
4. Cf.: *Tajikistan: 15 years of independent statehood. Statistical collection.* Dushanbe, 2006. P.103.
5. In the year 1999 the level of gross domestic product made up 40% of the level of gross domestic product of the year 1990. If before getting independence Tajikistan took on human development index 88th place among 174 countries, in the year 1999 the country took only 108th place. See: *Tajikistan. Report on human development 1999*. Dushanbe, 2000. P.22.
6. Average monthly salary in the last quarter of 2005 was 83,58 somoni (26,8$). Cf.: *Tajikistan: 15 years of Independent Statehood. A statistical collection*. Dushanbe 2006. P. 128. For the last years the rates were changed several times, but they still do not correspond to minimum of subsistence.
7. Cf.: Malisheva M. *Contemporary patriarchate. Social economical essay*. Moscow: RAS, 2001. P.18.
8. Cf.: *Labour and Employment in RT. Statistical collection*. Dushanbe, 2004.
9. A shuttle trader is a small trader who resells goods which he/she buys abroad or in another region of the country personally. Imprescriptibly features of the business are: limited supply of goods, which a shuttle trader can bring, direct participation in the process of purchase of goods, in the processes of transportation and realization of goods.

   Cf.: S. Olymova, I. Bosk *Labour Migration from Tajikistan*. Dushanbe, 2003. P.47.
10. Cf.: Elena Kislicina, *About Small Enterprise Development in the Republic of Tajikistan in 2001*, in: Health and Population. Annual Scientists' Public Magazine, 111 (2002):

P.36.

11. Cf.: *Women and Men of the Tajik Republic*. A statistical collection. Dushanbe, 2007. P.120.
12. Cf.: *Tajik NGOs' Alternative Report on Realization of the Convention on Liquidation of all forms of Discrimination Against Women*. Dushanbe, 2006. P.28.
13. Cf.: S. Kasymova, *Women Position in Labour Market and in the sphere of Employment: the ways of Poverty Elimination in Tajikistan. Gender Analysis on the basis of the results of SociologicalRresearch. Report on the research*. Dushanbe, 2005. P.51.
14. Cf.: M. Gafarova. *Women of the Soviet East*. Dushanbe: Irfon, 1987. P.34.
15. Cf.: S. Kasymova, *Women Position in Labour Market and in the sphere of Employment: the ways of Poverty Elimination in Tajikistan. GenderAanalysis on the basis of the results of Sociological Research. Report on the research*. Dushanbe, 2005. P.29.
16. Cf.: *Labour and employment in RT. Statistics collection*. Dushanbe, 2004. P.24.
17. T. Zhurzhenko *Women Employment under Conditions of Transitional Economy: Adaptation to the Market or Marginalization?* / A Ukrainian woman in the transitional period: from the social motions to the polity. Kharkov, KSI, 1999. P.231.
18. Cf.: *Women and men of the Tajik Republic. A statistical collection*. Dushanbe, 2007.
19. Cf.: K. Partoyev, M. Mahmadaliyeva, *Reform in the agrarian sector of the Tajik Republic*. Dushanbe, 2006.
20. From 117,0 to 235,1 thousands people See: *Labour and employment in RT. Statistics collection*. Dushanbe, 2004. P.24.
21. *Tajikistan in Figures 2004*. A Short Statistical Collection. Dushanbe, 2004. P.49.
22. Cf.: The law of RT "*On the land reform*" from 03. 15. 1992 №594, The law of RT "On farms" from 05. 10. 2002. №48.
23. Cf.: K. Partoyev, M. Mahmadaliyeva, *Reform in the agrarian sector of the Tajik Republic*. Dushanbe, 2006. P. 48
24. *Regions of the Tajik Republic*. Statistics collection. Dushanbe. 2004. P.27.
25. M. Ferry, *Feminism and Family Research*. Gender Issue 2. S-Peterburg, 1999. P.86.
26. cf. M. Sharipova, *Violence with Regard to Women in Tajikistan*. The Context of the Investigated Phenomenon, Dushanbe 2002 (abstracts collection of the Scientific Information-Patent Centre of RT, №1. №13(1447).
27. M. Ferry, *Feminism and Family Research*. Gender Issue 2. S-Peterburg, 1999. P.86.
28. M. Tohtahojayeva, *Tired of the Past. Reislamization of the Society and Women Situation in Uzbekistan*. Tashkent, 2001. P.304.
29. Observations and selected interviews with women, working at the Moscow markets, conducted in 2000-2002.
30. cf. M. Sharipova, *Violence with Regard to Women in Tajikistan*. The Context of the

Investigated Phenomenon, Dushanbe 2002 (abstracts collection of the Scientific Information-Patent Centre of RT, №1. №13(1447).

31. V. Sukovataya, *Women Enterprise in the Soviet and post-Soviet History*. Another view. Minsk. 2002. P.2.

Aspects of Providing Security in International Law-Making of Kazakhstan

Beibit Shangirbayeva

International law-making activity of the contemporary Kazakhstan aims at ensuring long-term national interests such as self-preservation (security) and development of the country, including building domestic economic capacity, which in whole promote integration into the world economy and world community based on principles of partnership. Well-balanced and multi-vector foreign policy of the Republic of Kazakhstan is reflected in its international law-making.

Kazakhstan as a state situated at the juncture of different civilisations plays a significant role in guaranteeing the regional and global security. The issue of ensuring and strengthening the security is particularly of current importance as of the moment in view of the forthcoming chairmanship of Kazakhstan in the Organisation for Security and Cooperation in Europe in 2010.

The Republic of Kazakhstan creates and develops legal norms on ensuring regional and global security, participates in lawmaking activity of international organisations of different levels. Kazakhstan's practice in this issue includes different initiatives provided for through bilateral and multilateral diplomacy.

After its proclamation as an independent state Kazakhstan built a legal basis for self-preservation of the country, including security. According to the Constitutional Statute 'On State Independence of the Republic of Kazakhstan' dated December 16, 1991, the Republic of Kazakhstan is a subject of international law, is eligible to enter into international organisations, systems of collective security and participate in their activities (article 13). This Act was the first legal basis for Kazakhstan's participation in the collective security system. According to the Kazakhstan's Constitution dated

August 30, 1995, Kazakhstan has proved its willingness to 'take an adequate place in the world community', to respect the principles and norms of the international law (Article 8) by including the norms of the international agreements and other obligations of the Republic into existing law (Clause 1 Article 4).

Lately the political science has had a broad understanding of the term 'international security', from the point of view of not only increasing a military potential ('hard' factors), but also the ability to face economic, social, demographic, ecological, cultural, informational and other challenges ('soft' civil factors).

Analysis of the international law-making of the Republic of Kazakhstan in the area of security ensuring shows that the practice of international relations covers the issues of ensuring not only the national interests but the global interests of the world community as well.

The key foreign policy initiatives of Kazakhstan for guaranteeing security are as follows:

The initiative of the Head of the State on building collective security in Asia and convening a Conference for Interaction and Confidence-building Measures in Asia (CICA)—the first foreign policy initiative of independent Kazakhstan (1992, UN Session 47);

The objective of CICA is to strengthen the regional security as a sub-system of the global stability, although the interaction and confidence measures shall include politico-military, economic, ecological and humanitarian aspects.

CICA's documents are Almaty Act and Declaration on Eliminating Terrorism and Promoting Dialogue Among Civilisations (2002); CICA Catalogue of Confidence-Building Measures (2004); Declaration on the Second Summit Results; Agreement on CICA Secretariat, in compliance with which the Secretariat shall be based on the territory of Kazakhstan (June, 2006). Analysis of the content shows that the Declaration is of political nature where the governments express their willingness to cooperate for strengthening the peace and development and where the Republic of Kazakhstan is assigned to be the Chair of the Conference in promoting dialogue and developing the CICA process.

Currently this Forum includes 17 countries, 9 countries have the status of observers and each participating state defines the directions of developing cooperation in Asia based on their topical issues.

The forum is peculiar in its effort to unite five nuclear powers and involve different Asian countries, including conflicting ones. Implementation of this initiative promoted non-availability of the negative past, negative history of Kazakhstan's relationships with any of the countries.

CICA calling initiative, current and future work of Kazakhstan in implementing this idea are the contribution of our country to the peace, safety and stability, cooperation of the countries, strengthening multi-lateral dialogue in Asia. Kazakhstan facilitated the establishment of the forum between the countries 'for political dialogue through developing uniform approaches to the security and cooperation based on consensus', which is, certainly, the participation of our country in developing generally recognised principles and norms of the international law.

Activity in UN system: participation in the Resolutions of the UN General Assembly that ratify and develop basic principles of the international law related to security issues (Participation in building international legal practice).

The Republic of Kazakhstan as a participating country co-authored the drafts of the adopted Resolutions of the UN General Assembly. For example, our country at the UN 48th Session co-authored 25 resolutions, which include decision on strengthening cooperation and providing observer's status in the General Assembly to the Conference on Security and Cooperation in Europe (CSCE) and Organisation for Economic Cooperation (OEC), Resolution 48/58 on the Middle East Peace Process. These facts prove the 'active participation of the delegation of the new state in discussing topical issues of the international agenda and search for the mutual resolution of the urgent issues that face the world community'.

It must be specially noted that Kazakhstan has been actively and successively supporting the principle of non-use of force and threat of force in solving international problems to strengthen the international peace and security. In line with this principle, one of the obligations of the countries is to 'conduct fair negotiations to facilitate a universal agreement on global and total disarmament under efficient international control'.

The Minister of Foreign Affairs of the Republic of Kazakhstan at the UN 49th Session officially declared support for the permanent and unconditional prolongation of the Nuclear Non-Proliferation Treaty of 1968. The main idea of the Treaty is that 'each nuclear-weapon state party to the Treaty undertakes not to transfer to any non-nuclear weapon states nuclear weapons and each non-nuclear-weapon state party to the Treaty undertakes not to receive the transfer of nuclear weapons and manufacture it'. Further, at the 60th Session of the UN General Assembly, the Minister of Foreign Affairs of Kazakhstan

K.K. Tokayev confirmed that Kazakhstan 'is firm and successive in its support of non-proliferation regime' of the nuclear weapons and is planning to enter into International Nuclear Terrorism Convention.

The UN Summit held on September 13–15, 2005 dedicated to the 60th anniversary of UN and its formation issues testifies the urgency of the proposed by Kazakhstan initiative on calling UN Special Session on the role of this international organisation. Even on March 21, 2006, the UN Secretary General Kofi Annan advocated the draft reform in line with which the decision-taking process on international peace and security shall be fulfilled on the basis of fair geographical representation of the countries with the view of their contribution to the development of the world economy and strengthening international security. The existing world geopolitical realities require for the necessity to conduct rule-making efforts of the countries in the form of changing and amending the UN Charter.

Kazakhstan also participated in the Drafting Committee for drafting UN GA Resolution 51/195 'Emergency International Assistance for Peace, Normalcy and Reconstruction of war-stricken Afghanistan and the situation in Afghanistan and its implications for international peace and security'. The Resolution was underlain by the provisions of Almaty Summit of the member-states (Kazakhstan, Russia, Kyrgyzstan, Tajikistan and Uzbekistan) of October 4, 1996. Thus it serves as a practical example of the norms of the regional agreements to form the basis of the international decisions. Moreover, Kazakhstan's contribution is evident to the regional security as a sub-system of the global security.

The above examples of Kazakhstan's participation in drafting UN GA's Resolutions, voting for them, prove the official position of Kazakhstan with regard to the international legal issues.

Treaty Law-making

In the area of treaty law-making, Kazakhstan is the participant to multilateral universal conventions, multilateral regional agreements, bilateral negotiations on various issues.

In the area of treaty law-making as of today Kazakhstan has signed such treaties as CHB–1, NNT (Nuclear Non-Proliferation Treaty), TCTDNW (Treaty for the Complete Prohibition and Total Destruction of Nuclear Weapons), Hague Code of Conduct against ballistic missile Proliferation, Krakow Initiative aimed at detection and prevention of illegal circulation of weapons of mass destruction and their supply sources, etc.

During nine years with the UN cooperation, a Treaty to create the zone free from nuclear weapons in Central Asia was being drafted. At the CICA Second Summit the member-states also supported the promotion of the initiative to sign this treaty. According to this Treaty it is prohibited to produce, purchase and station nuclear weapons on their territories, except for the use of nuclear energy for peaceful purposes. Thus, the Treaty to create the zone free from nuclear weapons in Central Asia was signed on September 8, 2006 in Semipalatinsk between Kazakhstan, Kyrgyzstan, Uzbekistan, Tajikistan and Turkmenistan.

Closing of Semipalatinsk polygon was the first in the world historical precedent of voluntary closing of the nuclear polygon. Following that the Closing of Semipaltinskiy Polygon was a decision of exceptional importance for the 'whole world community', as after the testing grounds of Nevada, *Lob-Nore* on New Land 'fell silent'. Small power nuclear tests held by France on atoll Mururoa in September 1995 gave a rise to a wide negative response of international community and even adoption of UN special resolution. Protests in the whole world made Paris to earlier cease nuclear tests.

Today Kazakhstan cooperates with the International Atomic Energy Agency and fulfills its nuclear activity under the control of this organisation, being the member of the multilateral organisation Disarmament Conference.

Another contribution of Kazakhstan to the system of regional security is its participation in the setup and work of the Shanghai Cooperation Organisation (hereinafter referred to as SCO), drawing increasing attention each year of the world community, in particular USA, Japan, Turkey, South Korea, EU, international organisations such as ASEAN, NATO, OSCE, UN. The SCO member-states are Kazakhstan, China, Russia, Uzbekistan, Kyrgyzstan and Tajikistan; Mongolia, India, Iran and Pakistan have the status of observers.

The organisation was set up based on the Agreement on Confidence Building in the Military Field in the Border Area (April, 1996) and currently includes the goals of fighting terrorism, separatism and extremism, transnational crime, illegal migration, development of trade and economy, investment policy, cultural cooperation, etc.

Within SCO, there are effective acts such as Shanghai Convention on Combating Terrorism, Separatism and Extremism, Agreement on Mutual Help to Liquidate the Consequences of Natural Disasters, Agreement on Regional Anti-terrorism Structure (hereinafter referred to as the RATS) and Programme of Multilateral Cooperation till 2020 which envisages establishment of common economic space and other documents. RATS participates in preparation of international legal documents in the area of combating terrorism, separatism and extremism. The concept of cooperation in the area of combating terrorism, separatism and extremism was approved; probably some of the aspects of this concept will be derived by Kazakhstan when adopting a new concept of national security. This year activity resulted in setup of new structures such as Business Council and Inter-bank Association, for the first time the post of Secretary General of the Organisation was established for which a representative of Kazakhstan was elected.

Taking into consideration the increasing role of regional organisations, a special body on regional organisations issues was established within UN system upon the proposal of Kazakhstan. For example, Collective Security Treaty Organisation, of which Kazakhstan is a participant, is a member of this UN Committee. In the view of Kazakhstan, regional organisations may promote and assist UN in resolving specific issues in the regions.

So, based on the example of Kazakhstan's participation in the international law-making process within the system of regional international organisations, it can be noted that Kazakhstan has made a significant contribution to the generally recognised principle of international law as a principle of countries' cooperation set forth in the underlying international documents.

Thus, Kazakhstan's state practice in the area of international law-making on ensuring security is currently carried out:

- through participation in the work of global and regional international organizations on ensuring global, sub-regional and regional security respectively;
- through foreign political initiatives aimed at global disarmament, strengthening confidence measures, participation in establishment of the zone free from nuclear weapons in Central Asia;
- through ratifying important international legal treaties in the area of security and initiation and development of new international treaties; etc.

In whole, Kazakhstan's practice aims at support of the principle of non-use of force and threat of force in resolving international problems to strengthen international peace and security.

Notes

1. This article is dedicated to the author of the Eurasian conception of human rights Professor Zh. Busurmanov

Section III
Civil Society, Informal Networks and Local Governance

Forming a Civil Society: The Uzbek Experience

M. Usmanov

Globalisation is the key element which is shaping both internal and external foreign policy making of Uzbekistan. The same force is also responsible for strengthening the democratisation process of the country as well as facilitating rapid modernisation of the country. In essence, globalisation implies rapid expansion and complication of interrelations and interdependence of people and states, expressed in processes of forming a global information field, the world market of capital, goods and labour force, internalization of environmental problems and others.

Globalisation covers all spheres of social life: economic, political, social, state-legal, military-strategic, etc. The positive aspect of globalisation lies in facilitating the level of economic well-being of people. It helps to promote all-round intellectual and cultural development, to ensure universal peace and safety; to liquidate distribution of the nuclear, biological and chemical weapon, rational use of natural resources, saving of environment, etc. as necessary conditions of people's survival.

Apart from these above mentioned positive aspects, globalisation is also connected with integration into world economy and simultaneous preservation and development of a state's own economic potential; integration into world information space and maintenance of information safety; development of world culture and preservation of one's own national identity, etc. It can be argued that globalisation is a panacea which can cure all ills and no nation-state can escape from this process.

The notion of democracy is also closely related to the term 'globalization'. In this context it is pertinent to mention here that there cannot be a single model of democracy for all the countries of the world. Modern tendencies of development of democracy are characterised by numerous models of democratic organisation of the power, traditions of the people, historical conditions, where different institutes of civil society, various poles between branches of the authorities exist due to different social institutions and collectivist values. Different religious, moral and mental values influence the existing democratic models.

The Uzbek civil society which owes its origin to local customs has shown its viability on the basis of continuous caring of the people, material maintenance and legal protection of the masses, the constitutional declaration of their main rights and legal interests, and principle of the relations with the individual as a basic value. These democratic measures establishing fair and human mutual relations of the person and the state, proclaiming economic, political and ideological freedom of the individual, constitute the core of civil society. Civil society should strive for 'All for the sake of the person and for the sake of his future'.

Uzbekistan after attaining independence is following a liberal model where traditional civil society is adjusting itself with changing realities. The basic task before Uzbek policy makers is to create a system where lawful state and civil society can co-exist. This will ensure ushering of democracy. The civil society is a social space where the law not only has a command, but also promotes self-development of the person, ensures realisation of the interests of the citizen and maximises his rights and freedom. Freedom and law operate simultaneously, complementing each other. In other words, while state laws should not restrain rights of humans and citizens, laws should be observed by everybody, implicitly and explicitly. In our understanding, democracy first of all means democratic thinking and consciousness of the people and their democratic skills. This was facilitated by political and social reforms within the country. Thus the main task of the civil society is to raise the consciousness of people.

A closer look at the development of civil society in Uzbekistan shows that Tashkent is adopting a pragmatic policy in implementing the policy through a stage by stage approach where civil society can co-exist with the larger democratic political structure.

The analysis of achievements and prospects of social, economic and political reforms testifies that the selected strategy of formation of a fair, strong civil society was and remains the only right way in real historical conditions under which Uzbekistan has been developing since its independence. A stage by stage realisation of this strategy has helped in the following manner during these past seventeen uneasy years:

Firstly, in the process of developing its own model, according to Uzbekistan's national interests and progress while discarding the old totalitarian Soviet system, the state functions as the main reformer of the public relations. Assuming an evolutionary way of development providing careful preservation of national tradition of the Uzbek state has provided a lot of assistance to the newly developed institutes of civil society.

Secondly, 'From strong state to strong civil society' is the basic policy objective of the present Uzbek government. Strengthening local self-government, ensuring mass participation in the public spheres which can strengthen the rural local government, delegating functions to local layers of administration, are some of the positive steps the present government is undertaking.

Thirdly, it is necessary to strengthen the political culture of the people by enabling them to participate actively in the socio-political process of the country. Liberalisation of public life by strengthening the role and value of NGOs and public institutions, gradually introducing rights and duties of citizens into public organisations and raising the political, cultural and social activity of people in this way are some of the basic tasks before the Uzbek government.

Fourthly, to develop 'an open society' and to carry out further democratisation and liberalisation in all aspects of public life, state and public organisations, the following steps need to be taken: enhancing the role of political parties, further democratisation of government, modernisation of the country, strengthening independent judicial system, protection of rights and freedom of the person, encouraging greater political activity of the people and establishment of parliamentary control over financial base of NGOs.

Fifthly, since these civil society institutes are in a transitional process, the main task before the government is to strengthen them by providing assistance like autonomy in governance, financial assistance, legal assistance, etc. These measures will increase the efficacy of the civil society organisations as well as provide them an opportunity to work efficiently and effectively in transitional conditions.

Chapter 13 of the Constitution of Uzbekistan deals entirely with 'Public associations'. In article 34 of the Constitution, the right of citizens to unite into public associations is enshrined, the state maintenance of observance of the rights and legitimate interests of public associations is provided, non-interference of the state and public organisations into each other's activity is separately mentioned. The constitution has also provided laws on public associations, self-government institutions of citizens, NGOs, trade unions, public foundations and on rights and guarantees of their activities. Charity and variety of other such activities have been legally approved.

The success of these laws can be inferred from the fact that at present, there are around five thousand NGOs that are operating in the country due to the protection offered by the Uzbek constitution. The number of NGOs in the country demonstrates the fact that theUzbek political elite is committed to provide a space to civil society organisations so that democracy can flourish in the country. Another interesting aspect of Uzbek civil society is that all aspects of human life are covered by local public associations. The partnership is essential in the sense that there are certain functions that both state and society together can address properly. Apart from the state and society partnership, another noteworthy trend in the Uzbek civil society is the flourishing number of NGOs working to promote women's welfare, reproductive health and awareness on environmental issues, etc. To coordinate the activities of NGOs, the National Association of NGOs of Uzbekistan (NANGOU), which unites 300 NGOs, and another forum, the National Civil Forum, which brings together a number of NGOs, were formed in 2005. To augment the financial conditions of NGOS, the Uzbek government has allocated more than 500 million Uzbek sum. This fund was allocated to 92 NGOs.

To regulate state and NGO partnership, a new regulation was brought in 2007 titled as 'Guarantees of activity of NGOs'. This law is aimed at providing protection to NGOs. The basic objectives are as follows:

- giving guarantees for NGO activities (freedom to function, access to information, property rights);
- protection of their rights and legitimate interests (protection of business and intellectual activity from wrongful decisions of state organs, activity (inactivity) of their officials, etc.);
- support to NGOs (state grants and placing of state orders to financially help NGOs).

Only free, independent and self-sufficient NGOs and other civil society institutions can effectively carry out tasks which are assigned to them.

In June 2008, the Chambers of Uzbekistan Parliament passed a Joint Decree 'About measures on strengthening support to NGOs and other institutions of civil society'. This is another step on the way to maintaining independence of NGOs.

The Joint Decree envisages the system of financial sources of NGOs and other institutions of civil society, which are independent and based on domestic principles. The questions connected with the volume of financial support from the state budget for supporting NGOs' activities, distribution of these sources, monitoring of their use have been transferred from the executive to the Parliament of the country.

Public fund on support to NGOs and other civil society institutions has been formed by *Oliy Majlis* (Parliament) of the Republic of Uzbekistan. Specially created Parliamentary Commission, consisting of deputies of Legislative chamber, members of the Senate of *Oliy Majlis* and also representatives of NGOs and mass media, regulate finances of the Fund.

Mahalla plays an important role in the system of civil society, being a unique system of self-management by the citizens. In Uzbekistan, the most ancient traditional institution of self-government—*Mahalla*—functions.

Mahalla acts as a bedrock on which the socio-cultural well-being of human society was traditionally based in Uzbekistan. It acts as a nodal agency for the formation of civil society in Uzbekistan. During the independence years, it became possible to strengthen and develop legal basis of their activity and to develop this institute as an integral part of a political, economic and spiritual life of the society and to create material and financial conditions for its development. At present it is possible to assert that democratic processes occurring in the country have allowed to cardinally change the status and importance of *Mahalla* institute. Today they are carrying out more than 30 functions which earlier used to be the prerogative of local authorities. *Mahalla* has turned into an effective, enjoying all-round support of the people self-government body which is capable of solving vital problems of people.

Mahalla plays an important role in creation of small enterprises for young population. Organisation of housework, rational and effective use of farms, delivery grants to needy and socially vulnerable sections of population, solution of problems of public control are taken up at the *Mahalla*. The reconciliatory commissions at self-government institutions of citizens have been formed. The advisers on religious education and spiritually moral education are exclusively women with a lot of life experience, and with skills of rendering social-psychological help.

In November and December 2008, the Uzbek government held elections at local level to elect 9,067 chairmen (*aksakals*) and more than 85,000 of their advisers including 7,476 chairmen of *Mahalla* Committees, 1,331 chairmen of villages and 160 chairmen of rural settlements. For the organisation of elections, corresponding Commission of *Kengash* of the Parliament Senate is formed which consists of representatives of the two chambers of Parliament, 'Mahalla' Foundation, Social Youth Movement 'Kamolot', the National Broadcasting Company of Uzbekistan, Institute for the Study of Civil Society and others. The main aim of the commission is to realise the complex organisational and legal actions for preparation and carrying out elections in full conformity with the current legislation and democratic principles of openness and publicity.

Globalisation and the Role of State in the Formation of Civil Society in Uzbekistan

M. Abdullayev

Globalisation is one of the most prominent features of the twenty-first century. Its essence contains a sharp expansion and complication of interrelations and interdependence of people across the globe. The interaction cuts across the globe, encompassing multitude of socio-cultural groups throughout the global map.

Thus, the globalisation phenomenon covers almost all spheres of public work, including policy, ideology, culture, way of life and also the condition of mankind's existence. This is why the most acceptable definition of globalisation includes the objective process of rapprochement, internationalisation and interdependence in all spheres, both among the countries as well as masses. On the economic front, it implies level of development of a country as well as interdependence among countries. However, the unequal level of development accentuates the conflict situation. At a more local level, it denotes changing attitudes and values of the masses within a social structure. Uzbekistan, which is under a process of transition, is also not immune to the above-mentioned changes. The social system of Uzbekistan is facing the challenge of the globalisation process. Most of the political scientists and economists are trying to asses the impact of globalisation on state institutions and state structures. They are examining how these institutional structures are facing the onslaught of globalisation. In the era of globalisation, the society feels the increasing overloads caused by the easing or rupturing of traditional economic and social communications, social stratification, inter-ethnic and inter-confessional conflicts. It has to be mentioned that under the condition of globalisation, the most important task before a nation is to strengthen institutional structures of governance—state. In fact, this institution can provide the necessary synergy to perform multi-dimensional role of the state, from providing necessary economic assistance to the masses to mitigating conflict.

The state structure has to be consolidated side by side with the civil society institutions as well as local governments. Political stability is possible only when these institutional structures can interact with the social institutions, viz. civil society groups, pressure groups and the lower layer of administration. This process of integration, called the state socialisation, helps in meeting the challenge of globalisation, the precondition to successful integration of a national society into the world community. One can also assume the fact that there is some sort of 'paradox' in the phenomenon of globalisation. Globalisation has also influenced the processes of political, economic and social development and the formation of a civil society in Uzbekistan.

The main task before the political elite is how to construct a state that can encompass the whole gamut of social structure and facilitate development of new ideological paradigm based on public consciousness, which facilitates the strengthening of a lawful state and a civil society in the Republic of Uzbekistan. In the era of globalisation, it is imperative for the state to interact with civil society institutions in a way that strengthens the local governance. Apart from local level NGOs, one has to mention international NGOs. In this context, some aspects of the activities of international NGOs in transnational civil societies need to be mentioned. The latter is in fact playing an important role in shaping the nature of international relations. They are playing a crucial role in influencing internal political situation in various countries. As we know, 'colour revolution' in some countries arose as a result of such activities. Well organised transnational organisations are spread all over the world. It is obvious, if you have received financing from an external source, you will be accountable to the requirement of these sources. This is why the present Uzbek government is regulating the activities of such international NGOs, for maintaining the internal political stability.

Another important threat that the global society is facing today is related to environmental problems. It is caused by the degradation of environment which is vital for health of the person. The situation is so dangerous that the governments, international organisations and financial structures are involved in charting out strategy for overcoming the ecological crisis. Realising the gravity of the situation, the United Nations even chalked out a special measure to save the Aral Sea from drying up. A special fund also came up with the financial assistance from the UN to save the Aral Sea. To protect the ecological heritage of Uzbekistan, the 'Ecological movement of Uzbekistan' has been created.

Looking from a theoretical perspective, political socialisation is an important component of state-building process. Through this process, society undergoes a radical change and is able to identify itself with the changing realities of social structure. The higher the level of changes, the greater is the impact on social structure. This is even more applicable to the Central Asian society where transitional socio-cultural values are predominant, both at individual and societal levels. Incidentally, this is one of the main reasons why the political elite give emphasis upon spiritual nation-building process of the country. This might help in smoothening the nation-building process of the country. The present political stability of the country has partly been attained due to the strong emphasis upon spiritual values of the country. The motto of 'strong state to strong civil society' is the guiding principle of the present day Uzbek leadership which has helped them to maintain and reinforce societal stability.

Conclusion

A strong society is the backbone of a transitional social system. This is due to the fact that unless and until a strong society comes into being, it is very difficult to transfer important functions to civil society groups. This does not mean that the state will diminish its role. On the other hand, it should leave certain functions to these social groups so that some sort of a democratic stability can be achieved. In other words, the state has a capability to maintain national interests whereas public and personal interests will be provided by public structures and organisations, and also other representative political institutions. Since these civil society networks are in a nascent form in Uzbekistan, they look towards the state structures for implementing programmes and policies.

It needs to be mentioned here that kinship organisations like *Mahalla* in Uzbekistan's context can provide a good example of how a strong civil society can play an important role in maintaining a strong social system and also in generating spiritual values . This is necessary for maintaining social harmony in a transitional social system.

Looking from a theoretical perspective, all the countries of the world are in a process of integrating themselves with globalised world. Uzbekistan is not an exception to this phenomenon. The global connectedness provides an opportunity to a state to imbibe positive aspects associated with it. In this way, it will help in maintaining domestic political stability as well as in generating new forms of culture. In the context of Uzbekistan, one has to mention the fact that within a short period of transition, both civil society and state are working together harmoniously for ensuring collective well-being of the masses. The process of globalisation is also influencing the state and civil society institutions to work harmoniously.

Role of Mass Media in the Formation of Information Society in Uzbekistan

Jamoliddin Khakimov

The twenty-first century has gone down in the history of mankind as an information society, whose specific feature is the supremacy of information. As practice shows, he who has information is the leader in society. As we know, globalisation is an objective phenomenon of the present, an expanding process while the work of transnational systems and phenomena develops. Globalism is the result of a breakthrough in the field of information technology as well as scientific-technical, economic, social and political progress. Globalisation is considerably displayed in growing mutual dependence of states, their national economies and in the field of information exchange.

Information society emerges not only on the basis of production and the use of computers and data communication networks, but chiefly on the basis of formation of mass public demands for information and its quick circulation. As is known, globalisation has both positive and negative aspects. Positive aspects of globalisation include the improvement of mechanisms of inter-state interaction, better coordination, concordance and cooperation among the states that are useful not only for the developing countries, but for the developed states as well.

Negative aspects are connected with the use of globalisation by some countries for their selfish ends. For example, conditional character of national borders in information sphere makes it possible to: interfere in internal affairs of other states; with the help of biased information, stir up inter-ethnic, inter-confessional discord; dispose citizens to unlawful unconstitutional actions, etc.; corrupt young people by circulating visual and other obscene materials and encroach on public morality. Today technical abilities of mass media have developed so much that by penetrating into global and local nets, one can cause material or moral damage to an individual and national security interests.

It should be said that a special role in Uzbekistan is given to the development of information and communication technologies. A presidential decree of 30 May 2002 *On Improving Computerisation and Introduction of Information and Communication Technologies*, another presidential decree No. 117 of 8 July 2005 *On Additional Measures To Develop Communication Technologies* and a number of laws and documents adopted by the country's Supreme Assembly create a legal basis for further development in the sphere. The state policy in the field of information is directed to guarantee consistent and full realisation of principles of freedom of speech and citizens' right of getting information set by the Constitution of the Republic of Uzbekistan.

Mass media in Uzbekistan has been looked at as an efficient instrument for forming a new way of thinking and understanding among the population and for this purpose, they should become free and objective spokesmen of the people's views and will and active protectors of their interests. The first step towards strengthening mass media as 'the fourth power' was the constitutional ban on censorship. Chapter XV of the Uzbek Constitution says that 'mass media are free to function in accordance with the law'. Uzbek media legislation includes a number of laws including the laws On Mass Media, On The Protection of Journalists Professional Activities, On Principles and Guarantee of Freedom of Information, On Publishing Activities, On Telecommunications, etc.

Today there are necessary organisational, legal and technical conditions for the formation and development of public, non-governmental structures and institutions in information sphere. There are Creative Journalists' Union, International In-service Journalists' Training Centre, National Association of Electronic Media, Public Fund for supporting and developing independent print media and news agencies of Uzbekistan and other public organisations functioning in the country.

Work of local media and the development of the national media space make it possible to say that the process of media liberalisation in the country has entered another stage of its development. Analysis of the dynamics of the country's media market development shows that there are a growing number of new participants entering in this domain. So, starting from 2004 annual growth rate of non-governmental print media has been over 30 percent against only seven percent in the state sector. There are at present over a thousand media units operating in the country. During the last decade, the number of print media doubled and now there are about 900 newspapers and magazines which are published, along with four news agencies, 100 TV and radio channels, a number of Internet agencies and news services functioning in the country.

All necessary conditions are being created in the country to gradually switch to digital format of broadcasting. The realisation of the selected strategy of liberalisation of all aspects of public and state life enables media to take an active part in civil society formation.

It is generally known that during the epoch of globalisation, the system of circulating information also obtains a global nature. To properly determine the ways of improving the skills of journalists in information society, it is needed first of all to clarify the major parameters of information society and secondly to underline specific features of journalist activities in new conditions.

The first and the second aspects include the following:

- globalisation of information processes;
- annual avalanche-like increase in volume of information, including professional one;
- a sharp increase in the number and quality of information and communication technologies;
- a considerable change in the form and methods of journalist activities in new information situation;
- a considerable fall of the state potential to protect its population against information from foreign sources;
- higher self-consciousness and independence of mass audience.

Before answering the question on what and how journalists should study to meet these demands, one should remember a truth—only those journalists who master industrial and creative technologies of working in information society can deservedly protect their population against negative information. Otherwise they will lag behind and no ideology can save them. Therefore it has become imperative to react efficiently to professional news in the field of journalism and supply the audience with the latest news.

With the recognition of Uzbekistan as an independent state, its international status has improved and its media has started integrating with the world information community. This has also influenced international relations of the country in the sphere of media. 'Jahon' news agency of the Foreign Ministry has been formed along with such international newspapers and magazines like 'Uzbekistan Today', 'Biznes Vestnik Vostoka', 'Delovoy Partner Uzbekistana', 'Uzbekistan Airways' and others. Also an independent news agency 'Turkiston-pres', a news service 'Region Inform', the Internet site 'Uzreport.com' and other online resources that are full of interesting and authentic information were set up.

Trends of development of the world journalism are such that the appearance of modern computer technologies and wide circulation of information promote further democratisation of all societies. By regularly, efficiently and convincingly influencing people, journalism has grown into a comprehensive socio-political system through which everyone can express his/her own opinion on the issues of discussion and take a direct part in political life of his/her own and even other societies.

Uzbek journalists have special tasks. Along with acquiring the leading world experience, they have to preserve their centuries-old culture and protect it against erosion. As the world practice shows, market journalism is prone to it. Why does market journalism inevitably turn yellow? Because the bulk of readers, listeners and viewers who pay for newspapers and magazines, radio and TV programmes or for the goods advertised by them, more willingly learn about various incidents or scandals and less attentively read educative, scientific, spiritual or moral reports. But during polls people do not acknowledge that they prefer entertaining reading to serious reading. The editors who studied public opinion and corrected the newspaper policy towards positive or moral material had to face an immediate sharp fall in the newspaper circulation and alienation of advertisers.

The share of entertaining material is growing as mass media is becoming freer. On the one hand, this is good since pluralism of views is established and the best decisions are taken and so on. But on the other hand, this brings about various negative and quite serious results. Journalism in Uzbekistan has not yet fully entered market relations. This is very important for the country, building not only a strong but also a civilized civil society.

The programme policy of mass media of the world's developed countries half a century ago strictly divided material into such groups as informative, social and political, educational, popular scientific, literary artistic, musical-dramatic, sports, programmes for children and for women, etc. Analysis of contents of the press, radio and TV of Uzbekistan shows that there are still traces of such classification of material in local media. But that division is becoming weaker with every year and it is not excluded that shortly Uzbek journalism would become in this sense similar to the journalism of Russia, Germany, Japan or the US.

In many countries, media units comprise informational newspaper, social and political TV programmes, cultural radio reviews, etc. But these are only superficial differences. In terms of their real content, practically all media are divided into three aspects: news, education and entertainment. The number of entertainment items in media is rapidly growing across the world while the share of educational material is falling. So, in about two decades the world population will have only two types of programmes: news and entertainment. We can only guess how poor will be the man's spiritual world!

This is a spontaneous strategic programming of the world journalism. The second important point is its informational load, clarification of the content of media reports. We can say without any exaggeration that here we see an aggression and violence of information against human nature. This is caused by a great amount of information cast on individuals and preference given to reports on scandals, disasters, elements of terrorism.

German specialists were the first to express their alarm about this, critical of internet and the follow-up Internet mania. Internet domination across the world is obvious today. Internet has justified its name of a world net that is more strongly entangling all peoples, nations, large and small ethnic groups. An exclusive peculiarity of Internet lies not only in being a means of global communication (as experts say, a very important 'instrument of open society'), but also in being a unique medium for mass media functioning. In this connection, web resources of the net are both an aggregate of diversified sources of information products of media companies of international scale and a universal channel of quick circulation of views, ideologies and points of views, considerably influencing media image of states. To occupy a deserved place in that rapidly developing global information market, it is very important to fill in and optimise the domestic segment with high-quality, diversified, fresh and pluralistic information products.

Globalisation of information space and increasing influence of transnational media companies and media industries as a whole has put forward new demands on specialists' training in this sphere. One thing is to prepare journalists for the local media market, and another, holding trainings for Internet journalists, who need to clearly understand that in this case, it is the matter of global information market, although it is first of all the matter of national segment. In educational circles there is a notion of universal journalist, a journalist having professional skills of working with technologies, including ability to acquire, process and create text, audio and video, in other words multimedia information.

Conclusion

To sum up, commercial spirited media of market and democratic western type societies conflicts with the public psychology and communal life of Uzbekistani people. Information then falls in the category of goods while it has to be a spiritual wealth. The improvement of skills of journalists is becoming more important. Education acquired in a higher educational institution soon becomes outdated because of growth of information about science of this education.

In market conditions it is necessary to pay serious attention to professional ethics of journalists. The situation here is aggravated by the fact that in information society, ethics of a journalist as a separate author and ethics of journalism as a social institution can contradict each other. Journalists of Uzbekistan are required to seriously assess the development, depict it reasonably, analyse it competently and to be patient and also wise. The country's journalism is often required to show initiative, dynamics and speed up social progress. In other words, where journalists should be convincing and competent, journalism should act vigorously. This in turn leads to a different understanding of ethics.

Ethics of Uzbek journalists is a harmonic combination of common human and national values and norms of journalist activities. They are based on international principles of professional ethics worked out under UNESCO auspices and are called 'democratic minimum' of journalists. They were adopted ultimately at a consultative meeting of international and regional professional journalist organisations in Paris in November 1983. They are as follows:

- People's right to get truthful information.
- Journalist's adherence to objective reality.
- Social responsibility of journalist.
- Professional honesty of journalist.
- General availability of media and public participation in their activities.
- Respect for private life and human dignity.
- Respect for public interests.
- Respect for common values and diversity of cultures.
- Elimination of wars and other evils opposing mankind.
- Promotion of new international order in the field of information.

In general, ethical approach of Uzbek journalists in the process of civil society building is divided into the following stages: ethics of searching and selecting theme; ethics of communicating with people during the collection of information; ethics of evaluating the facts; ethics of proving the put theses; ethics of mutual relations with the audience and ethics of mutual relations with colleagues.

Policing and the Role of Civil Society

Nirmal Kumar Azad

Key words
Policing, civil society, interaction, engagement, advocacy, human rights, counseling, communal harmony, management, intelligence, investigation, reform, support, evaluation, outreach, privatisation, accountable, transparent

Abstract
The role of civil society in policing in India is promising and still at a nascent stage. Many organisations have been working to reform the system though multiple efforts. The democratisation process of the system is worked through advocacy, training, sensitisation and partnership. It needs improved interaction, commitment and hard work to bring accountability in the system. Efforts are on by both the civil society and the government to improve things and make the system user friendly.

Introduction
Policing in India like any other jurisdiction of the world is an important tool for keeping law and order in place and solving people's problems. With time the nature and scope of Indian police has changed from the likes of solving problems of citizens agitating for drinking water to tackling extremist activities. The evolution of policing in India has seen many phases and the oldest system may be traced back to the era of *Chandra Gupta Maurya* and the bureaucratic structure as envisaged by *Kautilya*.[1] *Mughal* period in India also saw the institution of policing mixed with general administration where a *faujdar*, responsible for a district (*sarkar*), was responsible for maintaining law and order along with other administrative functions. *Ain-e-Akbari* does talk about *kotwal,* the keepers of peace in the city. Police became a part of the criminal justice system during the British period and many reforms have taken

place since then. The function and nature of internal security arrangement as well as the police as an institution has changed over time, based on the agenda of the rulers and the general expectation of the people. There have been many demands for change in the style and functioning of the rulers and one such important watermark was witnessed during the *sepoy* mutiny of 1857. The British sensing the necessity established two important police commissions which paved the way for a robust policing system in the country. After independence, policing in India has been established based on the rule of law and the general mandate of neutrality and impartiality.

There have been almost negligible formidable people's movement impacting policing before imperial onslaught but the frequency increased during the British period and remained more pronounced after Independence. Policing in democracy has to adapt itself on the basic principle of democracy which is it should be for the people, of the people and by the people. Many civil societies have pitched in to improve and reform the function and attitude of police. Nevertheless, the contribution of Indian National Congress and other political and non-political organisations could not be underestimated during British period, but the role of present civil societies has been more critical in shaping the mood of the general people asking for positive change in the system. Such civil societies are of varied types—formal, informal; organised, unorganised; different social, ethnic and religious groups; and others such as student, labour, agricultural workers, environmentalists, etc. In their own way, based on their priorities, these civil societies have been playing an important role in making policing more relevant, democratic and user friendly.

The present paper has tried to scan a wide range of secondary sources which helped in getting a perspective on the present topic. It has also included the analytical framework based on the interviews of the members of law enforcement agencies (the police) and the members of different civil society groups. Many archival reports, reports of the government and other non-governmental organisations were analysed for the paper.

Difference in Perception

The perception of police in the civil society and the vice versa remains open and wide. Such difference in perception is based on historical facts and the nature of jobs that are mandated to them. Police has been regarded as an oppressive organ of the government, acting as a tool to fulfill the economic aspiration of the rulers. Civil society by and large considers police to be partial towards the rich, the influential, the politicians and the henchmen of politicians. They are regarded as discourteous, indifferent and hostile towards others. They are seemed to be rude and even brutal in behaviour. They use filthy language, are abusive and arrogant. In one such instance, the Indian Police Commission 1902–03 concluded that 'what wonder is it that the people are said to dread the police, and to do all they can to avoid any connection with the police investigation'[2]. In another case, the National Police Commission, 1979 has written about a learned judge who observed 'A prisoner suffers for some act or commission but a witness suffers for no fault of his own. All his trouble arises because he is unfortunate enough to be on the spot when the crime is being committed and at the same time foolish enough to remain there till the arrival of the police'[3]. Both these observations signify that people in general are suspicious of police, feel they are untrustworthy and at times look at them with enmity.

It is not only the public which perceives police in a negative light but on the other hand the police also perceives public with the same amount of distrust. The police feels that people seldom cooperate in their effort to maintain law and order and also in investigation of cognizable and non-cognizable cases. They have their own reasons for such feelings. But by and large, reasons for non-cooperation as viewed by police are: disinclination to get involved with police and court; lack of civic sense in public; fear of reprisal; factional and partisan sympathies and general distrust of police.

Dissatisfaction of police stems from their feeling that the respect for law has decreased among the general public. Such emotions have been expressed by citing example of traffic management in Delhi. Many members of the Delhi police feel that they receive little cooperation from public in traffic management. During peak hours, people show little respect for the law; rather they want to jump the red light and reach their destination. In the process, their action creates more problems for the police which is otherwise understaffed. For core area of policing like investigation, crime prevention and collecting intelligence, the cooperation of the general public is not just required but is also an urgent necessity. Similarly, the police in Chhattisgarh feel that the cooperation is far fetched and it gets compounded when some member of the civil society joins hand to champion the cause of left extremist outfits in the state.

The situation has not become so alarming so as to think that both the police and the civil society can not see eye to eye. According to a study as highlighted by the National Police Commission, 1979, the wide difference in each other's perception can best be attributed to the fact that there is little interaction between the police and the civil society. The commission has further highlighted that such difference in perception varies from rural to urban areas. There are many civil societies which are working with the police to improve their credibility and work culture, thereby bringing in a systemic reform within the police. Many such organisations feel that though there are many challenges and difficulties even for making an entry into the system, the road ahead is not dark. It just requires patience, hard work and commitment to bring about the change.

The Cat and Mouse Game

When it comes to define police-public relations, it seems that it is a cyclic and never ending game. The games of Tom and Jerry are replicated where both antagonists are in direct and indirect confrontation. On one hand, the civil societies raise certain kind of demands to be met by the state and on the other, the state responds with positive actions and at times with repression in the form of police action. The following schematic diagram may throw some light on the type of relation that the police and the civil society experience while working in their own domain.

Fig 1

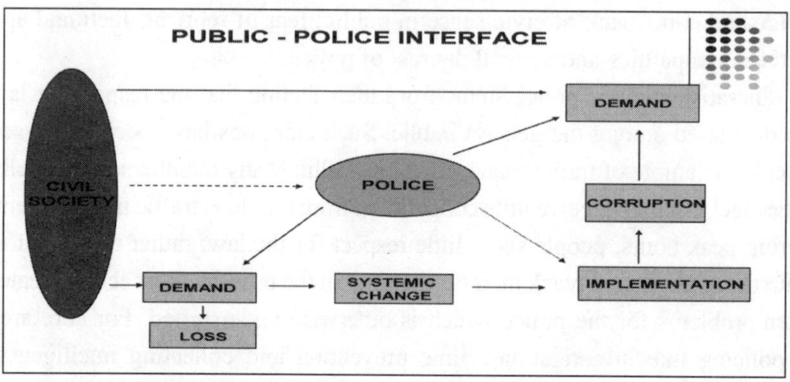

The above diagram suggests that civil society at a particular time in a particular geographical space generate certain kinds of general and specific demands. Civil societies may indulge in a variety of methods in making such demands like picketing, protest, *dharna*, strike and other legal and not so legal processes. Consequently, the state tends to bring in order, either through a dialogue or police action or both. Subsequently, the actions of civil society either intensify or lose its steam. In the event of prolonged genuine mass upsurge, the state might concede their demand thereby augmenting some systemic changes. Such changes can be brought about by bringing in new order/ rules or by modifying the present mode of dispensation. To implement such changes, the role of police also comes in along with other governmental agencies. With time, the implementation, if not monitored, may become tardy and slow. Corruption and other malpractices become the order of the day. Again the civil society becomes active in asking for yet another set of demands. And therefore, same kind of action gets repeated resulting in almost similar kind of result like a cat and mouse story. Many perceive that the interface between civil society and the police is not as simplistic as it has been suggested through the above diagram, rather it is more complex. Civil society and the police in recent years have started interacting on a more regular basis at different levels and these interactions have thus been more meaningful and concrete.

Civil Society' Engagement with Police

Present study shows that there are few non-governmental organisations in India which are working with the police, for the police or against the police. A survey of such organisations suggests that these could be categorised into three major divisions:

Civil Society-Advocacy, Policy and Research

There are organisations in India which are working to bring about reform and change in the existing functioning of the police. Their efforts through networking and advocacy at higher decision making level have given some hope for bringing positive and meaningful reform in the processes of the Indian policing system. Mr. Prakash Singh[4] filed PIL in Honourable Supreme court of India for implementing recommendations of the National Police Commission which can keep the police away from external influence. Organisations such as Commonwealth Human Rights Initiative (CHRI) have actively supported this effort and also pleaded in the case. These organisations have been impacting the decision making processes by holding seminars, workshops and creating an atmosphere where people would be asking for reform in the system. Advocating through their case presentation to the members of Parliamentary Standing Committee and Consultative Committee, briefing legislatures to raise questions in respective Houses and also meeting respective Minister with relevant agenda, CHRI has been trying to initiate processes of democratisation of policing. Other organisations such as Lawyers Collective, Human Rights Law Network and Amnesty International etc. are also working to bring change in the police functioning in India.

Civil society-Grassroots and Public Educators

These are the organisations working at the village level trying to impart education on people's rights and livelihood. The interaction takes place both at formal as well as informal level. Educating people in legal matters and capacity building improve people's perception about their rights and duties. It is not just one individual who is a target but the efforts are made to educate the community at large. Holding *sabhas*, meetings, *baithaks*, *nukkad*, posters and banners help to reach out to people in more meaningful way. Problem solving method, increasing social interaction with individual or the groups, reaching to a common understanding to demand justice are some basic techniques that the civil societies working at village and *taluka* level resort to. Among different organisations in this category, the work of Multiple Action Research Group (MARG), SOCO trust (Tami Nadu), organisations working under National Campaign for *Dalit* Human Right (NCDHR, Delhi), and MAJLIS(Mumbai), etc. is worth mentioning. They have been relentlessly working to improve the social condition of the people and also sensitising the police in different areas.

Civil Society-Legal and Media Activism

Organisations in this category operate through court processes such as PIL, researching and media campaigns. Widely used PILs have been filed in the area of police firing, alleged fake encounters by the police and the alleged police delinquency in investigation. The PIL filed by Andhra Pradesh People's Unity for Civil Liberty (APPUCL) resulted in the framing of NHRC guidelines on encounter deaths. PIL filed by Sheela Barse proved that there is an urgent need for reform in the plight of women in custody. The campaign by media in cases like *Nithari* killing, Jesica Lal murder etc. proved that there are selfless media, individuals and civil societies working to overhaul the system.

Civil Society-Support in Policing

There are many civil societies—the NGOs, traders association, clubs, youth associations, student associations, etc. that have been helping police in their duties. PRAYAS (Delhi), Public Concern for Governance Trust (Mumbai), Action Research Intervention of Tata Institute of Social Sciences on psychosocial counseling centres, etc. are some organisations which have given their credible support to the police in different parts of India. The research suggests that the support extended by civil societies to police can be categorised under the following heads:

Maintaining Communal Harmony

There may not be very structured groups at the village level which are helping police in their effort to keep communal harmony, but they are committed and motivated. Police maintains names of reputed people from different communities who help them during different festivals like *ramnawmi, dussehra, holi, chhath,* etc. These groups are not only helpful during festivals but also during normal days. They help in keeping normalcy during riots and communal divide. Holding meetings, canvassing for *bhai-chara* among the local population are regularly done by them on voluntary basis. They are known by different names in different places like *shanti samiti* in Bihar, peace committee in parts of UP and Delhi etc.

Traffic Management

Very rarely have people been seen assisting police in managing traffic on day-to-day basis. But on important occasions like processions, *sabhas*, marriages and festivals, the volunteers are seen cooperating the police force in regulating traffic. Their association with police is friendly and full of warmth. They require basic training in traffic management.

Intelligence Collection

Civil society has become a storehouse of knowledge and information. Important information of local and national importance is given by these organisations. They give information to police for maintaining law and order and in carrying out their investigations. Because these organisations are well networked, they have the capacity and capability to know details of the case and its ramification.

Crime Investigation and Crime Prevention

Code of criminal procedure provides for the people cooperation in investigation such as making arrest, search and seizures etc. Role of witness becomes another important part of police investigation as well as prosecution. Many local organisations help police in carrying out investigations. Role of Resident Welfare Committees in Delhi have become important in giving inputs to the police officers for investigation and crime prevention. In Jamia Nagar area of Delhi, *Nagrik Surakshan Samiti* and the Jamia Nagar Coordination Committee have been active and supporting police in their day-to-day work.[5] In places like Bihar, Uttar Pradesh and many other states, the role of *Gram Raksha Dal* is an important supplement to crime prevention. The members of these village level groups patrol their area to ward off criminal activities such as robberies, dacoity and others. In Bihar's Champaran district, the role of *shahidi jathas* is worth mentioning. It is said that these organisations came into being in parts of Bagaha, Bettiah to check the growing number of cases of kidnapping for ransom.

Reform-Training

Many organisations like CHRI, MAARG are constantly working to improve police functioning by training police personnel at cutting edge level in the area of human rights and police-people partnership. The experience of democratic policing as initiated by CHRI is worth mentioning where a dialogue process between the police and the public was established in areas like Mana of Chhattisgarh state. Developing training module, teaching and interacting with men and officers in police academies and training colleges, the civil societies have done a yeoman job in creating a humane face of the police.

Prosecution

Many civil societies in India have come forward to help prosecution in terms of assisting in witness production and witness protection. Preparing briefs for the public prosecutors in case of Gujarat riots has helped the government to seek justice for the aggrieved people from the district courts. Preparing witnesses and training them to face the court for deposing help the aggrieved in getting justice.

Infrastructure Support

Many non-governmental organisations like different traders associations, clubs and *vyapari sanghas* have extended their hand in meeting out some of the infrastructural and welfare need of the police force. Constructing police barracks, shelters, providing them with water coolers, fan, facilitating medical facilities, constructing police *chowkis* are some of the infrastructure support given by civil societies in India.

Critical Evaluation

Civil societies have also been criticising police actions which help the force to maintain accountability to the public. Their actions are watched by the NGOs, media, press and others which help them in working within the law. In India, presently there is no scope for social audit for the police force but it is expected that their participation in evaluating police action in future is going to increase.

Police and its Outreach Programmes

It is not just the civil societies which are working to help the police in their duty but also the police who is trying to reach out to public to get their support and assistance in solving problems. Some of the initiatives taken by police are[6]—Friends of Police in Tamil Nadu, Trichy experiment, *Samarth Yojna* of Coimbatore, Tuticorin experiment, *Prahari* of Assam police, *Aaswas* of Assam police, *Maitri* of Andhra Pradesh, *Mohalla* committee in Mumbai, *Parivar Paramarsh Kendra* of Madhya Pradesh police, etc. The basic purpose of these outreach programmes is as follows:

- To establish rapport with the public and to convey that police is a service provider like any other governmental agency;
- To take people's willing support to carry out policing. It may be in the area of traffic control, or in other areas such as patrolling, crime prevention etc;
- Such outreach programmes are carried out with some activities which are in all probability linked to policing. But sometimes, these may not be linked to basic policing and can rather be off-beat activities such as cleaning drain in some area so that people can feel the humane face of police.

These outreach programmes are a pro-active concept that lends a psychological approach to policing. These are police-public partnerships where citizens have been empowered with the help of the police. One basic demerit of these partnerships is that these are neither long-lasting nor institutionalised. Its longevity depends on the intention of police chief in the district. An activity initiated by a police officer may not find its taker once he is transferred out of his present responsibility.

The Way Forward

The role of civil society in policing in India has not taken a deep root because of historical and systemic reasons. Civil society has been playing roles in different moulds—from a critique of police functioning to a facilitator. There is a great scope for civil societies to play a role in future policing, thereby solving people's problem in a more holistic and meaningful way. Recently, Second Administrative Reform Commission[7] suggested some of the present functions of police that are amenable to privatisation. As suggested by Shri S. N. Pradhan, an IPS officer, following are the areas which are amenable to privatisation-

- Crime prevention/ routine policing—traffic management, patrolling streets, collecting intelligence, surveillance, antecedents check/character verification, counseling, etc.
- Crime investigation and control—collecting physical evidence, disposal of dead bodies, maintenance of case exhibits and records, forensic services, medical services, etc.
- Prosecution—execution of summons and processes, escorting and production of prisoners in court.
- Law and order—supply of crowd control weapons, maintenance of equipment and arsenal, security of vital installation, etc.
- In-house support outsourcing—housing, inventory control maintenance and supply, accounts, file management, etc.

The above duties of police which can be outsourced as suggested by Shri Pradhan is a matter of debate and discussion. The concern of security and other sensitivities have to be taken into account before these tasks are assigned to the private parties. Here comes the role of civil society which can very well choose the functions that they can do to assist police. Of late, Police Act Drafting Committee (PADC)[8] has come out with the Model Police Act 2006 with some recommendations that reflect a better coordination between police and public. The Act has suggested establishment of Village Defence Parties and Community Liaison Group[9] in rural policing and Citizens' Policing Committee[10] in urban areas. In both these locations, the participation of public is urgently required.

Conclusion

Analysis shows that the role of civil society in policing in India is limited. There is a need for regular interaction to make the system functional and people friendly. It calls for some changes in the existing functional framework of policing in the country so as to accommodate some of the genuine demands of the civil society. Presently, it is felt that the civil society could help police as being a watchdog for keeping checks and balances in the system. Also, it can support police through research and training module in different areas of policing. Public opinion documented by civil societies should also be fed to the police on regular basis in order to evaluate their performance. And above all, civil society should become a genuine partner in making policing more democratic, equitable and accountable to the people.

Notes

1. *http://rajpolice.nic.in/ab-historyIP.htm*
2. Government of India (1980), *fifth report of the National Police Commission*, p.48
3. Ibid, p.47
4. Is a retired police officer.
5. *Indian Express* , Nov. 20, 2008
6. *www.humanrightsinitiative.org*
7. Government of India, (2005) *5th Report of 2nd Administrative Reform Commission*, p. 103
8. Ministry of Home Affairs, GOI, (2006) *PADC Proposed Bill The Model Police Act, 2006*
9. Ibid, p.50
10. Ibid, p.61

References

Government of India, (2005) *5th Report of 2nd Administrative Reform Commission*

Government of India (1980), *fifth report of the National Police Commission*

Mathur, K. M. (1991), *Police in India*, Gyan Publishing house

Ministry of Home Affairs, GOI, (2006) *PADC Proposed Bill The Model Police Act, 2006.*

Oomen, T. K. (2004), *Nation, Civil Society and SocialMmovement*, Sage Publishers.

Tandon, Rajesh and Mohanty, Ranjita (2003) *Does Civil SocietyMmatter?* Sage Publishers.

Indian Express, Nov. 20, 2008

Resource Website: www.humanrightsinitiative.org

Resource website: http://rajpolice.nic.in/ab-historyIP.htm

Dynamics of Societal Responses to Environmental Change in Jammu and Kashmir

Sally Daultrey

Abstract

Rapid environmental change in the Jammu and Kashmir (J&K) region, within the broader dynamics of climate change across the western Himalayas, is impacting the quality and availability of natural resources with implications for the livelihoods of its people. Population migration in the region places further stress on the already fragile environment and limited natural resources, and displacement of people leads to loss of indigenous knowledge about survival and resource management (especially of its limited water resources and arable lands) in the challenging environment of the Himalayas and Karakoram.

The prospects for environmental stability and security for its population should be considered within the broader dynamics of the relationship between India and Pakistan, as the physical location of the disputed J&K region affords strategic links for both India and Pakistan, to China, Afghanistan and Central Asia. The ongoing border conflict associated with the unresolved status of the Kashmir Valley is resulting in the loss of property, knowledge, status and stability for its people.

Population migration and instability is not directly linked to the impacts of environmental change, however, the effects of climate change are compounding the stresses placed on the region's fragile environment and the observed societal responses. Collective action in response to environmental change may arise from within the region, rather than being imposed on it from outside (directly coupling the self-construction of a society to its physical surroundings), for example in the eastern part of J&K due to its physical geography, partial political autonomy and strong coupling of its peoples' livelihood to available natural resources. Integrated modelling techniques present an opportunity to apply a range of qualitative and quantitative approaches to understanding the dynamics of societal responses to environmental change and resource competition in Jammu and Kashmir. A participatory approach to research in which its subjects influence the representation of the rules which govern the model and critically evaluate its outcomes, would enrich our current understanding of the present conditions and future prospects for the environment and population of India's northwest frontier.

Introduction

How do we analyse the changes underway in J&K? The features of 'natural' systems (water, climate, physical geography) can be coupled with 'human' systems (infrastructure, geopolitical, population dynamics, livelihoods) and 'responses' (competition and conflict) to explore, to a first-level approximation, the dynamics of human interactions and environmental change. The complexities associated with coupling different types of model and the value of using prototype models to investigate relationships between landscape and social change have been widely discussed[1] (Matthews et al (2007); Bithell and Brasington (2009); Lempert (2002)). Despite the challenges, such an approach may be particularly useful where there is deep uncertainty about the characteristics of the system and little or no agreement by stakeholders on how 'correct' decisions should be arrived at (Lempert (2002)). For Jammu and Kashmir, constructing a simple model may enable a first-level investigation of regional vulnerability and responses to climate change, in combination with other global stressors. This paper identifies the key features of the systems which should be included in such a model, proposing an integrated approach to analysing the complex physical, societal and political variables present in J&K.

Systems analysis

Physical Environment and Geography

J&K is situated in India's far north-west, between the Himalaya and the Karakoram mountain ranges. The region borders Afghanistan, Pakistan, China and the Tibetan Plateau (Xijiang), affording strategic links to China for both India and Pakistan.

Altitude ranges from 2700–7650m, with three distinct climatic zones: sub-tropical (Jammu); temperate (Kashmir) and cold, high-desert (Ladakh).

Annual precipitation across the region ranges from approximately 1116 mm/yr in Jammu; 650 mm/yr in Srinagar; ~90mm/yr in Leh. Ground-level temperatures in Ladakh range from -40.0°C (in December to April) to +35.0°C (July and August).

Jammu and the Valley of Kashmir support fertile farmland and montane forest, while Ladakh has very sparse vegetation with productivity peaks only during the short summer season. Grey-brown and hill soils support vegetation in the Valley of Kashmir; mountain and podzolized soils rich in iron oxides dominate Kargil district and east into Ladakh, with the landscape punctuated by sparse fertile oases along the banks of the Indus and its tributaries.

The region supports unique fauna and flora and is home to more than a dozen endemic and/or endangered mammal species including the Blue Sheep (*Pseudois nayaur*), Ladakh Urial (*Ovis orientalis vignii*), Snow Leopard (*Uncia uncia*) and the Wild Yak (*Bos grunniens*). The rich variety of medicinal plants found in Ladakh[2] has an important role in the social and spiritual life of the Ladakhi and in the traditional *Amchi* system of medicine.

As in any ecologically sensitive mountain region, rapid changes in the environment of the J&Kregion—within the broader dynamics of climate change across the western Himalayas—are impacting the quality and availability of natural resources, with implications for the fauna it supports and the livelihoods of its people. Decreasing soil moisture, declining glacier coverage, reduced snow formation and shifting seasonal patterns of precipitation all have important consequences for the environment of the western Himalayas and the flow of water into the Indus basin.

At the regional level, simulations using a Regional Climate Model (under a scenario similar to the IPCC's (Inter-governmental Panel on Climate Change) emissions scenario SRES-A1B) indicate that by 2050 average precipitation will be reduced to less than 1mm per day in the arid regions of northwest India and Pakistan. This, coupled with higher surface temperatures, could lead to a sixty percent decline in soil moisture in the region over the next 40 years.[3]

Precipitation over the Himalayas is thought to be strongly linked to the monsoon cycle further south. Sontakke et al (2008) analysed monthly rainfall data for ten stations in the Western Himalaya[4] (*figure 2*). Earliest monthly rainfall record for Srinagar is available from 1891; for Jammu and Udhampur, from 1901. Averaged annual series for the Western Himalaya for 1891–2006 overall indicates declining rainfall for the period 1960–2006.

Hunt and Dash (2007) found that reduction and variability of the summer monsoon rainfall can partly be explained by the combined effects of climate change and the physical influence of the mountains on the monsoon flow[5]. The presence of aerosols (dust particles in the atmosphere), clouds and air flows around the Indian mountains in a warming atmosphere also have an essential role in determining regional climate. In a warming atmosphere, reduced stability in the troposphere pushes the tropopause higher, shifting warmer boundary-layer air upslope from lower altitudes. Over time, this change in air temperature produces deeper clouds and increased rainfall on the mountain slopes, leading to reduced snow formation, melting of snows upslope and reduced glacier area. Reduced volume of ice means less water flowing from the mountains into the rivers during the spring and summer. Rees and Collins (2006) investigated the effect of declining glacier area on river flow and showed that over the next 150 years, assuming warming of 0.06 degrees per year, the downstream effect of declining glacier area will be greatest in the smaller and more highly glacierised basins of the Western Himalayas, where precipitation is already scarce.

Several recent examples of reported events in Ladakh suggest that changes in the natural environment of this type are already occurring[6]. During the winter months, the Zanskar River (a major tributary of the Indus) has traditionally provided an ice-road connecting isolated villages during long winters, allowing the seasonal migration of people and animals. In the last decade, ice is forming less frequently and for shorter lengths of time—or not at all. Further examples of marked changes in precipitation over the region include a flash-flood devastating the village of Phyang in August 2006, and the arrival of locusts in Khaltse district in the summer of 2006, last recorded (in paintings at a nearby monastery) more than a century before. A farmer living at 4,200m in Ulley, Leh district, reported that for the three successive winters to 2007, snow leopard had been sighted at lower altitudes for longer periods than usual during the early spring (in search of water), presenting a threat to juvenile cattle.

Society and Governance

In the 2001 census, the total population of J&K was registered at about 1.55 million people, of which 75% were living in rural areas. About half have access to drinking water on tap (of which 32% on the premises). 75% of the rural population have electric lighting for at least part of the hours of darkness. Cooking fuels are a further indication of a connection between landscape and livelihood: 56% use firewood and 12% use cow-dung cake. 22% use liquefied petroleum gas (LPG), brought in by road.

Population density (and projected population density, to 2015) ranges between 25 and 200 people per square kilometre, highest in the Valley of Kashmir and in Jammu and likely to remain so for the next decade[7]. In 2003 the estimated total number of migrants throughout the region was approximately 1.8 million, of which two-thirds were between districts (for example seasonal labourforce, road workers, family visits). In the last 20 years, the population of Leh has more than tripled in size. The average annual urban population growth rate in Leh since 1981 is estimated at 5.92%—compared with 2.95% for the whole of India[8]. This growing population will need land, water and food supply to supplement local production, which is limited by environmental conditions and available skilled workforce. Displacement of people (particularly from rural areas) is leading to loss of indigenous knowledge about resource management practices, especially of limited water resources and arable lands, presenting the Ladakhi and Kashmiri people particularly with a dilemma in the face of competition for comparative economic prosperity, education and healthcare to be found in the towns and sustaining of traditional farming practices in the rural areas.

Infrastructure

Physical infrastructure is a key requirement for enabling mobility of a population, in terms of transport of goods, people and animals, access to, exchange and communication of information.

Roads and Telecommunications

Roads in the western half of J&K are connected to India's national highway system through Jammu in the south. By contrast the eastern regions are characterised by a challenging working environment and therefore less developed transport infrastructure. Khardangla, Tanglangla and Changla passes are the highest motorable roads in the world; just two roads connect Leh with other regions to the south (to Manali) and to the west (to Srinagar). In April 2006 the Leh-Srinagar route was declared a National Highway[9]. Developing roads is an important feature of strengthening regional integration and therefore receives funding from central government. The HIMANK project of the Border Roads Organisation[10] was set up in August 1985 exclusively for the development of Ladakh's transport infrastructure, to maintain open lines of communication year-round primarily for military purposes (especially in Siachin). HIMANK enabled road access during the 1999 Kargil war.

The co-benefits of large infrastructure projects such as hydropower schemes and airports are clear, such as improved regional transport infrastructure and telecommunications for the local population. The construction of bridges, replacing rope-bridge crossings, enables year-round surface transport access to remote villages. One example of where improved access has brought change, benefits and challenges is on the marginal ranges of the Changthang plateau in the south-east of the region, where the Changpa nomads produce some of the finest cashmere (*pashmina*) in the world, since the 8th century AD. The survival of their animals and livelihood is entirely dependent on the quality and availability of grazing. Today the Changpa receive grants from the Government of India for cattle-feed during the long winter months. Border road access (largely due to increasing military presence in the area) is opening up the Hanle Valley region to vehicle access, allowing the Changpa to sell directly, avoiding the need to use middlemen to sell their products (although some sources have indicated that Kashmiri traders are paying Changtang herders less than market value). In 2003, pashmina wool earned around 25USD per kg. Annual per capita income from cashmere wool was reported at approximately USD115 for Tibetan refugees and about USD80 for the Changpa[11].

Improved communications enables the two-way flow of information that supports competition within the local economy. A reliable and open communications network is also a precursor for enabling democratic representation within civil society. The demonstrations in Srinagar in July 2008 could be interpreted as democracy at work: the presence of a mobile telephone network allowed supporters of the activism to communicate with each other and organise their actions more rapidly, but also for news of the event to reach the rest of the world more promptly than in similar historic events.

Electricity Network

The Government of India defines rural electrification as remote villages and hamlets where a minimum of 10% of the households are provided with electricity.[12] The western regions of J&K are connected to the Northern Grid. Ladakh is not presently joined to the grid. Peak power demand in J&K was estimated to increase from 1437 MW in 2001–02 to 1923 MW in 2006–07, of which total supply in 2005 was estimated at 500–600 MW.[13]

The most developed source of power in J&K is conventional run-of-river hydropower, providing about 1,800MW capacity. In total the Indus watershed contains ten major dams along its length[14]. According to the Government of India's Central Electricity Authority, to date J&K has developed less than ten percent of its total hydropower capacity[15], partly due to the challenging terrain and unstable political conditions. Dams in the western part of the province are particularly at risk from seismic activity (as seen for example in the October 2005 earthquake in Kashmir)[16]. Further promising sources of power within J&K include solar, geothermal and micro-hydropower. Surveys indicate Puga Valley has around 40MW geothermal potential[17], as yet undeveloped.

Under its Industrial Policy 2004–2015, the Jammu and Kashmir State Industrial Development Corporation has offered subsidies for industrial development in the region, including for small-scale power plant.[18] Incentives include 100% subsidy on the purchase and installation of units of 10–1000 KW capacity and exemption from electricity duty and state excise duty for the first 25 years of operation. Hydroelectric projects are also eligible for support under the international Clean Development Mechanism (CDM) scheme, which rewards developers for power schemes that can demonstrate low net emissions of carbon dioxide during the lifetime of the scheme. CDM projects in J&K include the 45MW run-of-river Nimoo-Bazgo Project in Leh District and the 44MW run-of-river Chutak Project in Kargil District, which will both be connected to the Northern Grid via a new 220kV line connecting Leh with Srinigar. Both projects are scheduled for completion by 2011[19], at which time they will be transferred to the National Hydro-Electric Power Corporation, under a *Build-Own-Operate-Transfer* (BOOT) system. A Memorandum of Understanding between the central and state government grants 12% free power to J&K as a 'royalty' and a 15% share of unallocated supply quota[20]—although whether this recovers the full lifetime cost of the development to the local environment and population is unclear at the time of writing this paper.

Infrastructure and Conflict

Hydropower projects within the Indus watershed have been the focus of dispute, protracted inquiry and internationally-mediated agreements on both sides of the border since Independence in 1947, for example the Kalabagh project in Pakistan (a 3.6GW dam first conceived of in 1953 and as yet unbuilt) and Baglihar in J&K (a 900MW run-of-river scheme, completed in 2004).

In 1952 the World Bank stepped in to mediate the growing dispute over the Indus Basin, which eventually produced the Indus Water Treaty in 1960.

The treaty has survived a war in 1965 and continuing tension between the two countries. Although physical violence in Kashmir is not directly attributable to disputes over the governance of the Indus[21], tension over the status of Kashmir does affect access to water (physical access, development rights, land ownership) throughout the region, as India presently controls the upstream source of the Indus (and its tributaries) which flow into Pakistan. In Kashmir, as in any cross-border region under dispute, large hydropower projects may not *directly* be the cause of conflict but can *become* the focus for existing political tensions and conflict.[22]

Disputes over hydropower projects in the Indus basin usually focus on political issues of access rights and ownership at the time of consultation and construction. Environmental impact assessments for new projects are mandatory but the wider mid-term to long-term effects on the surrounding ecosystems and the populations they support are not always thoroughly understood. The high-desert ecosystems of the mountainous regions of J&K and the green Valley of Kashmir are vulnerable to exploitation and development (for example, higher than global average lead and strontium pollution in Dal Lake in Sringagar[23]). The use of toolsets for ecological assessment, such as that developed by ASSESS-HKH (funded by the European Commission and concluded in 2008)[24] could provide a useful baseline assessment before major infrastructure projects commence.

Political Relations

The conflict over claims to Kashmir by India and Pakistan is the world's oldest unresolved international border dispute and is the subject of five resolutions by the UN Security Council since 1948[25]. The United Nations has monitored the Line of Control (LOC) between India and Pakistan claims to Kashmir, since 1949 (at a cost of approximately $17m in 2008–09[26]). Azad Jammu and Kashmir (AJK), to the west of the LOC, is a self-governing state of eight districts with a total population of approximately 3.3 million[27]. AJK is referred to by India as 'Pakistan-occupied Kashmir', just as Pakistan refers to Jammu and Kashmir as 'Indian occupied Kashmir'. Jammu & Kashmir, to the east of the LOC, is divided into three administrative regions (Jammu, Valley of Kashmir and Ladakh). Ladakh, the largest of the three, enjoys quasi-autonomous status within J&K, under the governance of the Ladakh Autonomous Hill Development Council. J&K has its own multi-party government and was granted special status in the 1948 Constitution of India, giving it autarchy in all matters except for defence, foreign affairs and communications matters. Subsequent modifications to this arrangement include the enforcement of the Armed Forces Special Powers Act in 1990[28], which has been the focus of strong criticism by human rights groups[29] who view it as oppression by the state.

Claims to Kashmir are part of nation-building aspirations for both India and Pakistan. Following the Sino-Indian conflict in 1962, warming relations between China and Pakistan affirmed the importance of Kashmir to India. Harshe (2005) has suggested that by holding on to its claim to Kashmir, India could continue to press its claims over Aksai Chin (in the east of Ladakh) which is presently occupied by China, and contain any threats to the Punjab (to the south) [30].

A key concern for the long-term stability of the region is its association with terrorist groups with strong links into Pakistan and China. The reported incidence of acts of terrorism and violent conflict within the region, on both sides of the LOC, has decreased in the last decade[31] but the region remains far from stable. Kashmir once again became the focus of international attention in July 2008, after a dispute erupted in Srinagar over the allocation of lands to build facilities for pilgrims visiting the Amarnath Shrine[32]. Some 200,000 pilgrims visiting the sacred site in the mountains to the northeast of Srinagar place considerable pressure on an already limited transport infrastructure, public transport service and politically sensitive balance of power. Violent riots in Srinagar during the summer of 2008 illustrated the tension between the resident Muslim population and Hindu interests. As in any complex dispute over rights to land and property, the resident population bore the cost of the conflict. A protest blockade by proponents of the land allocation deal prevented already limited movement across the LOC, with consequences for the local economy (for example, Kashmiri fruit growers claimed losses during the period in excess of $475,000[33]).

On 7 July 2008 Chief Minister Ghulam Nabi Azad resigned and J&K was placed under President's Rule. On 24 September 2008 India and Pakistan agreed to resume peace talks[34], under the 'Composite Dialogue' process launched in 2004[35]. As India prepares for elections, the future of Kashmir and the regional long-term effects of the ongoing conflict remain unclear. Resolving the international status of Kashmir is likely to remain an intractable problem, until such a time as the dynamics and aspirations of the societies which make up the region's resident population are understood, and permitted to determine their representation.

Systems Relationships, Dynamics and Integration

Each of the systems are complex and non-linear, with dynamic boundaries. Some boundaries are fixed (mountains, rivers, policed border-lines), some are abstract (ideas and information exchange, identity)—all are porous. The number and frequency of 'transactions' across boundaries (animals, people, goods, information) is typically controlled by local interactions between elements ('agents') and influenced by external changes (climate, natural environmental variables, arrival of new people or ideas).

How will these systems respond and adapt to the impacts of environmental change? Gilbert et al (2006) suggest that collective action to deal with environmental problems typically arises **within** the system, rather than being imposed from outside, directly coupling the self-construction of a society to its effects on the agents' physical surroundings.[36] This feature is particularly observable in rural regions of J&K, where livelihoods are directly related to the quality and availability of natural resources.

Environmental change is among the many factors that may lead to population migration and increased competition for resources, setting up the conditions for conflict to occur. Scholarly analysis of the potential for conflict as a *direct consequence* of environmental degradation is limited: adopting an integrated approach is the key. As Clark (2007) points out, we should not look for single agent causality in connecting environmental change with physical or political conflict, because this obscures the role that environmental degradation has in larger political and social processes, all of which are important factors in driving competition and migration.[37] Homer-Dixon (1994, 1996 *in* Clark, 2007) suggests that competition arising from environmental stress and acute conflict is most likely in those countries where the institutional capacity within the country for adapting to environmental stresses is weak, identifying three pre-conditions of scarcity that are fundamental in creating the conditions for conflict:

- decreased quality and quantity of renewable resources;
- increased population growth, and increased per capita consumption; and
- unequal access to resources across local populations.

Further, ecological marginalisation (where population growth and unequal access to resources prompts migration to regions that are ecologically fragile) coupled with competition between power elites for renewable resources which are declining in quantity or quality, may lead to conflict situations. This is a particular risk for development sites along the Indus through Jammu & Kashmir and into Azad J&K.

The complexities associated with coupling together the dynamics of human and ecological systems and environmental change (e.g. Bithell and Brasington, 2009)[38] and the value of using a prototype model to investigate the relationship between landscape and social change have been widely discussed[39] (e.g. Matthews et al, 2007). Lempert (200) suggests that such an approach may be particularly useful where there is deep uncertainty about the characteristics of the system and little or no agreement by stakeholders on how 'correct' decisions should be arrived at[40]. Based on the key features of the systems at work in J&K, a simple model may be elaborated to describe the interactions between environment, people and decision-making within the governance systems. The validity of the results might be tested using local-level case studies where adequate environmental and social data can be obtained. For example, O'Brien et al (2004) investigated the exposure of India's agriculture sector to the impacts of climate change, using a combination of vulnerability mapping and local-level case studies to assess impacts and responses and create a 'climate change vulnerability profile' for India, the results of which could serve as a basis for targeting policy interventions[41].

The political and social fractures in J&K are important features influencing decision-making within the state. Earnest (2008) has used a model approach to show that in resolving complex multi-party disputes, a large number of states coordinate a solution to the problem more easily than small groups, because larger groups create denser networks that communicate preferences more efficiently[42]. A participatory approach to research, in which its subjects influence the representation of the rules which govern the 'model' and are invited to critically evaluate its outcomes, would yield the most detailed results for understanding the stressors and reactions within the system and the dynamic connections between each component of the model.

Conclusion

The prospects for environmental stability, peoples' livelihoods and future economic development in Jammu & Kashmir are vulnerable to the effects of environmental change, particularly declining quality and quantity of natural resources. Changes in the natural environment may further complicate the political and social responses to internal and external stressors. Changes to property rights and resource distribution in favour of politically stronger elites (e.g. the State Power Development Authority) may compound the problems of resource scarcity that are due to environmental change, especially for less powerful ethnic minorities. Hydropower development along the Indus and its tributaries may distort and increase land values along the river, leading to competition between regional and state power elites for the control of land and property. This inequity may lead to the displacement and expulsion of minorities, resulting in the loss of indigenous knowledge about resource management practices and good environmental governance.

Population migration, resource competition, conflict and instability are multi-component non-linear systems each with their own complex dynamics, and the processes within these systems are inter-connected. The impacts of environmental change (such as rapid climate change) and the changes brought by globalisation (such as the arrival of telecommunications and transport networks) are compounding the stresses placed on these systems, reducing the capacity of people and ecosystems to adapt and respond. Adopting a systems-level approach to analysing the situation in J&K allows us to identify the critical vulnerability points and suggests that achieving environmental and political stability will require collective action from within the system. A fully-integrated analysis ideally requires a participatory approach to research in which its subjects influence the representation of the rules which govern the model and critically evaluate its outcomes.

The value of this approach is in enriching our understanding of the role of indigenous knowledge in resource management, enabling and informing agile responses to environmental change, and building adaptation capacity for the indigenous population and environment of India's extreme northwest frontier.

Notes

1. Matthews, R.B., Gilbert, N.G., Roach, A., Polhill, J.G., Gotts, N.M. (2007), Agent-based land-use models: a review of applications, Landscape Ecology 22, 1447–1459
2. Manoj Kumar Misra IFS (Retd.), Sunil S. Gokhale (2003), Base Line Information on Medicinal Plants Conservation and Sustainable Utilisation, Ladakh, Foundation for Revitalisation of Local Health Traditions (FRLHT), Bangalore (report sponsored by UNDP/GEF, MoEF, Government of India)
3. Houghton, J. (2004) Global Warming: The Complete Briefing, Cambridge: Cambridge University Press, p161
4. Sontakke, N.A., Singh, H.N. and Singh, N. (2008), Chief Features of Physiographic Rainfall Variations across India during Instrumental Period (1813-2006), Research Report RR-121, Indian Institute of Tropical Meteorology
5. Dash, S.K. and Hunt, J.C.R.H. (2007), Variability of climate change in India, Current Science, 93 (6), 25 September 2007

6. Personal communication, Tsering Norboo, Ulley (2007) and Stanzin Gai, Leh (2008); 'Living with Change' (Stanzin Gai for WWF, forthcoming, 2009).
7. United Nations Environment Programme Global Environmental Outlook Data Portal, available online at http://geodata.grid.unep.ch/ [accessed 20 August 2008]
8. Goodall, S. K. (2004), Rural-to-Urban Migration and Urbanization in Leh, Ladakh: A Case Study of Three Nomadic Pastoral Communities, Mountain Research and Development, 24 (3), 220-227
9. Government of Jammu and Kashmir, Ladakh Autonomous Hill Development Council Kargil, 'National Highway declared', April 2006, http://kargil.gov.in/news/news.htm#Srinagar_Kargil-Leh_Road_Declares_as_National_Highway [accessed 1 August 2008]
10. HIMANK Project of the Border Roads Organisation, http://bro.gov.in/indexmain.asp?projectid=39 [accessed 1 August 2008]
11. Namgail et al (2007), Pastoral Nomads of the Indian Changthang: Production System, Land-use and Socioeconomic Changes, Human Ecology, 35 (4), 497 – 504
12. Government of India Ministry of New and Renewable Energy, Rural Villages Electrification Programme for the year 2008-09. [online] Available from http://mnes.nic.in/adm-approvals/rve-adm.pdf [accessed 5 September 2008]
13. Jammu and Kashmir State Development Report, State Planning Division, Planning Commission, 2004, [online]. Available from http://planningcommission.nic.in/plans/stateplan/sdr_jandk/sdr_jkch3a.pdf [accessed 21 August 2008]
14. Revenga, C., Murray, S., Abramovitz, J. and Hammond, A. (1998), Watersheds of the World: Ecological Value and Vulnerability. Washington, DC: World Resources Institute. [online] Available from http://earthtrends.wri.org/text/water-resources/map-355.html [accessed 5 September 2008]
15. Government of India Central Electricity Authority, Status of hydropower development in India (July 2008). [online] Available from http://www.cea.nic.in/hydro/Status%20of%20Hydroelectric%20Potential%20Development.pdf [accessed 17 August 2008]
16. Bhat, G.M. et al (2005), October 8 Kashmir Earthquake: Impact on Geoenvironment and Structures in the Karnah and Uri Tehsils of Kashmir (India), University of Jammu Centre for Disaster Studies and Research [online]. Available from http://www.eeri.org/lfe/clearinghouse/kashmir/reports/Jammu_India_Report.pdf [accessed 21 August 2008]
17. Harinarayana et al (2004), Magnetotelluric studies in Puga valley geothermal field, NW Himalaya, Jammu and Kashmir, India. Journal of Volcanology and Geothermal Research, 138 (3-4), 405-424
18. Jammu and Kashmir State Industrial Development Cooperation Industrial Policy, [online]. Available from http://jksidco.org/industrial_policy.html and key features

http://jammukashmir.nic.in/govt/SFIP2004.pdf [accessed 21 August 2008]

19. National Clean Development Mechanism Authority, India [online]. Available from http://cdmindia.nic.in/cdmindia [accessed 10 September 2008]
20. Jammu and Kashmir State Development Report, State Planning Division, Planning Commission, 2004, [online]. Available from http://planningcommission.nic.in/plans/stateplan/sdr_jandk/sdr_jkch3a.pdf [accessed 21 August 2008]
21. Kalpakian, J. (2004) Identity, conflict and cooperation in international river systems, UK: Ashgate, p155
22. Iyer, R. (2007) Towards Water Wisdom: Limits, Justice, Harmony, New Delhi: Sage, p. 107
23. Pandit, A.K. (1999) Freshwater ecosystems of the Himalaya, New York: Parthenon, pp. 79-80
24. Moog, O. et al, ASSESS-HKH (Development of an Assessment System to Evaluate the Ecological Status of Rivers in the Hindu Kush-Himalayan Region), supported by the European Commission under the sixth Framework Programme [online]. Available from http://www.assess-hkh.at/ [accessed 17 August 2008]
25. Government of Azad Jammu & Kashmir. Available from http://www.ajk.gov.pk/site/ [accessed 1 September 2008]
26. United Nations Military Observer Group to India and Pakistan has monitored the ceasefire line between India and Pakistan in the State of Jammu and Kashmir since 1949 [online]. Available from http://www.un.org/Depts/dpko/missions/unmogip/ [accessed 10 September 2008]
27. Government of Azad Jammu & Kashmir. Available from http://www.ajk.gov.pk/site/ [accessed 1 September 2008]
28. The Armed Forces Special Powers Act enforced in 1990, permitted military personnel to arrest without warrant, shoot-to-kill and destroy property and provided protection from prosecution for military personnel found responsible for serious crimes. See Government of India Ministry of Law and Justice, 1990 [online]. Available from http://mha.nic.in/pdfs/Armed%20forces%20_J&K_%20Spl.%20powers%20act,%201990.pdf [accessed 1 September 2008]
29. India: Repeal Armed Forces Special Powers Act, Human Rights Watch, August 2008 [online]. Available from http://hrw.org/english/docs/2008/08/18/india19628.htm [accessed 1 September 2008]
30. Harshe, R. (2005), India-Pakistan Conflict over Kashmir: Peace through Development Cooperation, South Asian Survey, 12 (47)
31. Government of India Ministry of Home Affairs, Level of Terrorist Violence and Security Situation in J&K - An assessment (As on 31.10.2007) [online]. Available from http://mha.nic.in/uniquepage.asp?Id_Pk=306 [accessed 1 August 2008]. See

also http://jammukashmir.nic.in/normalcy/

32. Financial Times, 7 July 2008, 'Kashmir chief minister quits over shrine'; 'Police kill three protesters in Kashmir', 25 August 2008 [online]. Available from http://www.ft.com.
33. BBC News Online, 11 August 2008, 'Police fire on Kashmir protesters', [online]. Available from http://news.bbc.co.uk/2/hi/south_asia/7553317.stm
34. BBC News Online, 25 September 2008, 'India and Pakistan pledge talks' [online]. Available from http://news.bbc.co.uk/2/hi/south_asia/7634864.stm [accessed 25 September 2008]
35. Government of Pakistan Ministry of Foreign Affairs [online], http://www.mofa.gov.pk/Pages/Brief.htm [accessed 10 September 2008]
36. Gilbert, N., den Besten, M., Bontovics, A., Craenen, B.G.W., Divina, F., Eiben, A.E., Griffioen, R., Hévízi, G., Lõrincz, A., Paechter, P., Schuster, S., Schut, M.C., Tzolov, C., Vogt, P., and Yang, L. (2006), Emerging Artificial Societies Through Learning, Journal of Artificial Societies and Social Simulation, 9 (2) 9, 2006 [accessed online] Available from: http://jasss.soc.surrey.ac.uk/9/2/9.html
37. Clark, W. (2007), Environmentally Induced Migration and Conflict, Expert report for the German Advisory Council on Global Change (WGBU) [online]. Available from http://www.wbgu.de/wbgu_jg2007_ex04.pdf [accessed 5 September 2008]
38. Bithell, M. and Brasington, J., (2009), Coupling agent-based models of subsistence farming with individual-based forest models and dynamic models of water distribution, Environmental Modelling and Software 24, 173 – 190
39. Matthews, R.B., Gilbert, N.G., Roach, A., Polhill, J.G., Gotts, N.M. (2007), Agent-based land-use models: a review of applications, Landscape Ecology 22, 1447–1459
40. Lempert, R. (2002) Agent-based modeling as organizational and public policy simulators, Proceedings of the National Academy of Sciences, USA, 99, 7195–7196
41. O'Brien, K., Leichenkob, R., Kelkarc, U., Venemad, H., Aandahla, G., Tompkinsa, H., Javedc, A., Bhadwalc, S., Bargd, S., Nygaarda, L., West, J., (2004), Mapping vulnerability to multiple stressors: climate change and globalization in India, Global Environmental Change 14, 303–313
42. Earnest, D.C. (2008), Coordination in Large Numbers: An Agent-Based Model of International Negotiations, International Studies Quarterly (2008) 52, 363–382

Civil Society in India: A Partner in Democracy

Doel Mukerjee

Introduction

A mature democracy has two arms—the state and non state, which often do not synchronise their actions but exist in a space to fulfill the obligations of a democracy. Amongst the non-state actors, civil society has been a vibrant and evolving group within the politicalscape of the country. It is important to understand the role of civil society in the context of the prevailing politics and hence the democratic state in India. Sometimes due to this political sphere, the space which is occupied by the civil society is reduced and subsequently brings it in conflict with the state. Hence civil society becomes uncivil due to political actions and yet, as we all know that in a democracy there is need to have a free voice of the people and this is what civil society has attempted to provide in India. It has contributed by contesting state policies, attempted in bringing the marginalised and poor people into the fold of the democratic process, provided alternate development strategies and has built bridges between the policy and reality.

The present paper examines the progression of civil society from pre Independence to the present period and argues whether civil society has been a partner in democracy building or has it slowed the process with unrealistic arguments which are contrary to fast development. Also the paper questions whether civil society matters in a democracy?

Who is Civil Society?

Most people in academics and even activists find that the definition of civil society is a contentious issue as there are a multitude of agencies which are functioning in the political–social space. Several organisations have close political affiliations and mirror the images of the state while some others are clearly anti-state. Yet in all of this, a common understanding is what the book Invisible Yet Widespread, has defined, "Civil society is not an institution; it is rather, a process whereby the inhabitants of the sphere constantly monitor both the state and the monopoly of the power within itself". Therefore in a sense civil society is the source of democratic activism. Interestingly, in the same book while discussing Pachayati Raj, Tandon has defined civil society as a collection of individual and collective initiatives for the 'common public good', He also makes a much-needed differentiation between government and governance. Governance does not merely denote 'government'; *rather, it is a process of looking after public resources for the common public good.* In that light, India has a perfectly legitimate, democratically elected government, but its governance of the country's economic and social resources leaves much to be desired.

It is in this socio-economic vacuum that different types of civil society have contributed to different aspects of the democratic agenda such as finding space for *voicing* issues related to the priorities and practices of governance which are further used as a *movement* to create collective pressure for government reform. According to Rajni Kothari[1], civil society is not a space to foster greater involvement in state politics, but one in which to engage a new politics outside of the state. In other words, civil society is an alternative domain of people-centered politics. In this domain, a whole range of organisations emerges that aim to address people's real needs and concerns. These people-centered organisations constitute a 'grassroots model of mass politics…in which people are more important than the state'.

Although the civil society and its grassroots may be only bringing out the aspirations of the people, yet some theorists identify the role of civil society in a democracy as having political elements which facilitates better awareness with a more informed citizenry, who make better voting choices, participate in politics, and as a result hold government more accountable. The statutes of these organisations have often been considered micro-constitutions because they accustom participants to the formalities of democratic decision making. In this process civil society actors have now obtained a remarkable amount of political power without anyone directly electing or appointing them. Currently in India some civil society groups such as the Resident's Welfare Associations in Delhi and NGOs such as Lok Satta have transcended to become political parties in an attempt to establish a new political culture which will place the citizen at the centre of governance.

Therefore it can be expediently said that civil society does not represent one modality for democratic practice but may be seen as emerging from different civil relationships with various groups in different contexts.

Genesis of Civil Society in India

It is possible to classify the genesis of civil society into four important phases—the pre-independence, 1950–70s, 1970–90s and 1990s to present period. In each phase, there have been popular movements by various types of groups such as farmers, students, factory workers, civil liberties groups, NGOs and media amongst others. Each movement, confrontation, dissent and interaction with the state has led to the strengthening of the Indian democracy and has helped in protecting the rights of the people, especially those who have little stake in the prevailing power dynamics.

Pre-Independence Phase

The **pre-independence phase** has a long history of civil society movements in the form of labour movements, peasant and tribal uprisings amongst others. The National Movement spear headed by Mahatma Gandhi resulted in the withdrawal of the British colonialists from India. This is perhaps the largest civil society movement in the world in terms of participating numbers. The movement had some enduring features that still influence many NGOs in India, namely through volunteerism, grassroots mobilisation, peace and non-violence with nature and between humans, peaceful civil disobedience and constructive village work in areas like education, health and livelihoods.

1950–1970s

The period after Independence in 1947 was the unfolding of democracy when many voluntary groups which were influenced by the Gandhian perspective for national reconstruction were established. The country had embarked on a massive modernist agenda of industrial development, paying little attention to agriculture, which was the basic livelihood of over 80% people. Most of the land was owned by the upper caste Zamindars and there was little that belonged to the rural lower caste poor. This worsened the lives of the rural poor. In the early 1950s, Acharaya Vinobha Bhave started the Bhoodan Movement (gifting land) and later the Gramdan Movement (village gifting movement) to solve the problem of lack of land with the poor people, especially those from the lower castes. During this time important visionaries such as Jaiprakash Narayan (a socialist and a Marxian) were influenced by the Sarvodaya (upliftment for all) ideas of Vinobha Bhave which later became the Total (non-violence) Revolution. This will be discussed a bit later in the paper.

Inspite of the Bhoodan movement, the wretched situation of the farmers did not improve. In 1967, in Naxalbari in West Bengal there was widespread peasant uprising which followed the Maoist ideology that considered violence as a legitimate tool of resistance which was in direct contradiction to the Gandhian principles. The naxalite movement was held together by various factions of the Communist Party. In this uprising many middle class urban students joined. By 1972, through massive and repressive police actions, the state was able to suppress the movement which resulted in the dwindling of middle-class support. The movement spread to Central India and remained largely under a rural leadership fighting for land, water and forest resources.

Another students' movement was taking shape under Jaiprakash Narayan in 1974 in Bihar which gradually developed into a popular people's movement known as the Bihar Movement. It was during this movement that JP2 gave a call for peaceful Total Revolution together. During this time due to state repression in West Bengal, the People's Union for Civil Liberties (PUCL) in 1976 and the Citizen's for Democracy were established as the first civil liberties group in the country. In 1976 National Emergency was imposed by the government which was a rude shock to a nation that had thrived on an uninterrupted flow of democracy since it had gained independence. There were detentions without trial for a large number of people, news censorship, trespassing without legal sanction of private premises, telephones and letters, and constitutional amendment curtailing basic rights to life and freedom in the name of national security leading to crisis. During these dark days of the Indian democracy, thousands of people joined mass rallies to protest against the anti-democratic acts of the government and mobilised public opinion to safeguard democracy. Elections were held and by 1977 and a new government came to power.

However, by that time the civil society had experienced state repression where in certain parts of the country young students were branded as extremists and liquidated. This brought the need for a strong non-partisan civil rights movement to protect the rights of the people. During the Emergency another important civil society group joined in becoming the watch dogs of democracy which gave advent to investigative journalism and this continues till today. Studies on prison conditions and police actions were conducted by the civil society which gained further momentum with the government's own constitution for Police and Prison Reforms Programmes such as the

Constitution of the National Police Commission and the All India Jail Reforms Committee[3] immediately after Emergency due to the widespread reporting of police excesses.

During this period the rapid industrialisation policy of the government funded the growth of several cottage industries along the lines of cooperatives and NGOs. Some of the cooperatives established were National Dairy Development Board, Farmers Fertiliser Cooperative etc. Also as the country's five years development plans came into existence, several of the development works were rested with NGOs. This period also saw large scale discontentment against policies to construct large dams which subsequently led to displacement as in the case of Hirakud (Orissa) and Bhakra (Punjab). Till today several thousands of people are yet to receive compensation. The issue of displacement was raised first in the case of Hirakud and brought to the Assembly and later nationally. Movies were also made documenting the miseries of the displaced people. But lessons were not learnt and again in the 1980s, the Narmada Dam was constructed which resulted in wide displacement but this time the campaign by civil society groups was more organised as people across the country joined together on a single platform under the Narmada Bacho Andolan. Other people and civil society initiatives were seen in displacements due to mining and quarrying as in Orissa, Bihar (now Jharkhand etc).

Here it will also be important to mention that several trade unions were established in the late 1940 and early 1950s[4]. The trade unions helped the workers to articulate their rights and secure them to gain full facilities for their recognition and effective representation of their interests. Fair working conditions of life and service were also ensured and progressively raise their social, economic and cultural state and conditions. Example, in the 1960s and 1970s, the Mumbai-Thane industrial belt witnessed successive working class strikes and protests, with multiple trade unions competing for the allegiance of workers and political control. In the 1980s, some of these trade unions became considerably militant and joined the political discourse.

1970–1990s

This is another interesting period for civil society as the aspirations of the common people were dejected by the apparent failure of the naxalite and cooperative movements. Also the leftist movement made a dent on the stability of the country especially Central India. The middle class and the civil society in rural India found opportunities as NGOs started highlighting the reasons for government programmes not yielding positive results for poor and marginalised and presented alternate models for development through people's participation. With this new model, NGOs covered the vacuum where the government could not reach in programme areas like education, primary health care, drinking water, sanitation, small irrigation, forest regeneration, tribal development, women's development, child labour, pollution safety, etc. Later some of these models were included in government programme and policies. These NGOs were also apolitical. From this period onwards the government also began to set aside money through a variety of schemes for the funding of NGOs. This included the establishment of a separate institution called the Council for People's Action and Rural Technology (CAPART) to fund NGOs working for rural development. Later it set up an apex national committee with a secretariat in the National Planning Commission. Also during this period, foreign funding agencies came to India providing support in different sectors. At present the NGO sector alone is estimated[5] to have a strength of 1.2 million of which more than two-thirds are based in rural areas.

This period witnessed environmental movements as people had to face situations as the Bhopal Gas Tragedy. The survivors of this tragedy have mobilised survivors and other groups across the country and have agitated for proper rehabilitation and compensation for survivors of the disaster. Other important groups in this category are those who took up the issues of marginalised people and continued to fight for their rights and aspirations in the form of social movements as the dalits, the adivasis, women and minorities.

In the women's movement the first issue to receive attention was violence against women, specifically in the form of rape, and 'dowry deaths'—the killing of young married women for money/goods they brought with them at the time of marriage. This was also the beginning of a process of learning for women as most protests were directed at the State. Because women were able to mobilise support, the State responded by changing the law on rape and dowry, making both more stringent. It seemed at that time that a great victory had been achieved. It was only later that the knowledge began to sink in that mere changes in the law meant little, unless there was a will and a machinery to implement these. And that the root of the problem of discrimination against women lay not only in the law, or with the State, but was much more widespread[6]. Similarly the Dalit Movement although was able to get the SC/ST Prevention of Atrocities Act passed in 1989, yet the implementation of act was difficult due to vast ignorance across the country.

One extremely significant development took place post-1980s and after the Emergency era as a result of an informal nexus of pro-active judges, media persons and social activists. The apex court decided to reach out to the people and it devised an innovative way where a person or a civil society group could approach the Supreme Court/High Court and seek legal remedies in cases where public interest was at stake. Justice P. N. Bhagwati and Justice V. R. Krishna Iyer were among the first judges to admit PILs in the court. Filing a PIL is not as cumbersome as any other legal case and there have been instances when even letters and telegrams addressed to the court have been accepted as PILs and heard by the court. The first reported case of PIL[7] was in 1979 which focused on the inhuman conditions of prisons and undertrial prisoners. The PIL was filed by an advocate on the basis of a news item published in the newspaper, highlighting the plight of thousands of undertrial prisoners languishing in various jails in Bihar. The proceedings led to the release of more than 40,000 undertrial prisoners. Right to Speedy Justice emerged as a basic fundamental right which had been denied to these prisoners. Other cases were also taken up by civil society to contest women's rights, child rights, environmental rights, dalit rights and others.

1990s to Current (Post Liberalisation)

The NGOs were meant to play a largely supplementary role to the government in the 1970s and 1980s, making their scope of work very limited. However, this changed in the 1990s due to the growing disenchantment of ordinary people as it was viewed that the state was favouring industries and multi nationals which resulted in the resurgence of civil society. However, another important occurrence was that the Tenth Plan laid the foundations for a more intensive government-voluntary sector partnership. Government-NGO partnership got a boost in this period where development related work included self-help groups, micro credit, livelihoods and also a new aspect came into the picture where proactive NGO participation was ensured in policy formation and programme implementation.

Acknowledging the folly of relying exclusively on the government to reach various benefits to the underprivileged sections, the Tenth Plan placed a lot of emphasis on involving civil society, especially voluntary and non-profit organisations, in the development effort. The nine-point formula involved the voluntary sector such as NGOs, voluntary organisations, CBOs or community-based organisations in implementing development and welfare programmes in planning, helping them develop core competencies and professionalism, encouraging the growth of the sector in States where there was a vacuum, and involving them in evaluating the targets of the Tenth Plan.

Panchayati Raj Institutions (local governance councils) are one area where although the government has initiated the policy on ground activities, the capacity building and research components are entirely provided by the NGOs. In places where the panchayats have been a success story, such as Kerela, West Bengal, Himachal Pradesh, Karnataka, pockets of Madhya Pradesh and Andhra Pradesh, there is evidence of partnership building of the two arms of democracy. It is important to say here that there has been support in such development activities from the international donor community, although the quantum of funds is not very extensive. In all this engagement and interface in the development process, two major outcomes have taken place: empowerment and self help which are accepted forms of democratic processes. As the state does the tightrope walk between fiscal consolidation and the need to spend on development, policy-makers are constantly seeking the right formula that will help them get more value for money. Some pointers, though not exactly new, can be found in the Tenth Plan, which focuses at length on the issue of effective governance. The Eleventh Five Year Plan also focuses on partnership building with civil society and public-private interventions through inclusive growth.

Other than the state sponsored initiatives, this period has witnessed several traumatised responses to situations by the civil society as in the period between 1970s–90s. The dejection and the phenomenal corruption in different sectors have seen grassroots to policy level campaign on right to information by Masdoor Kisan Shakti Sangathan (MKSS) in north-western Rajasthan. This campaign against corruption, public welfare and accountability was taken up by the most disadvantaged people. Similar interventions were made by Parivartan, a small group working on corruption, in Delhi using the Right to Information Act. Interestingly, a consortium of NGOs under the banner National Campaign for People's Right to Information supported the government to draft the RTI Act based on the field experiences and knowledge from global best practices.

Similarly a group of journalists and academics started the Association for Democratic Reforms to reduce corruption of the legislators and Parliamentarian during elections. This group successfully started a civil society watch dog group in several states in the last elections. Corruption in other areas such as police, prisons and judiciary has taken some of the civil liberties groups to work in these areas. In prison reforms, the work includes capacity building of prison inmates and sensitisation of staff, working on a contemporary Prison Manual and bring out stories of overcrowding of undertrials and poor prison conditions. The story on police reforms has been dynamic during this period where civil society has supported in drafting of a Model Police Act, capacity building of citizens vis-à-vis their rights and sensitisation programmes, campaign against torture etc. The judicial accountability campaign for more openness in judges' recruitment and analysis of judgments are other areas of intervention. Of late there have been several public campaigns of cases where the people and media were pre-empting bias and corruption in the justice systems. However, such acts are in desperation by the ordinary people to bring in some semblance of democracy in their lives.

During riots and violence, it is always the civil society which has stepped in to provide the first support to the aggrieved. There are innumerable examples in support of this from across the country. The recent incidents of protest against setting up of industries on agricultural land in Orissa, West Bengal, Jharkhand underlines the rise of civil society movements in the last decade in the context of land acquisition by industry aided by government, and more recently in the context of the Special Economic Zone Act. In almost all protests, the movements tend to echo and support one another in demanding repeal of both Land Acquisition and SEZ Acts. The villain in most movements appears to be the political leadership, which is seen colluding[8] with the industry.

Due to this genesis, at present there are four generic groups under which the NGOs can be classified:

- The first group are the traditional development NGOs, which work in rural areas on literacy programmes, crèches for children and clinics, encourage farmers to experiment with new crops and livestock, experiment with traditional art forms and endeavour to fill all the gaps left in the development process by the government. There are many examples of voluntary organisations, perhaps the most celebrated example being the Treatment Centre for Leprosy Patients run by Baba Amte in Central India.

  Other aspirations have taken the form of self–help groups (SHG) which came into existence with the failure of the cooperatives. Most of these SHGs were supported by NGOs, the National Bank for Agriculture and Rural Development (NABARD) and other banks. MYRADA (an NGO in Karnataka) made an important intervention in this area. Gradually some of these SHGs have also taken to demand for rights and empowerment.
- The second group of NGOs are those who research a particular subject in depth and then lobby with the government or with industry or file petitions

in the courts for improvement in the lives of the citizens. The Centre for Science and Environment took up a campaign against pesticides in soft drinks can be placed in this group. These groups are often well networked with other grassroot organisations.

- The third group comprises activists as they see activism as their primary means of reaching at their goals, because they do not believe that they can get the authorities to move in any other way. Narmada Bachao Andolan (Save Narmada Campaign) opposed the construction of a series of large dams. The members of NBA believe that large dams worsen water scarcity for the majority of the people in the long run rather than solve the problem, and they opposed the displacement it entailed upstream of the dam. When the NBA found that it could not persuade the planners in India to agree to its point of view, the NBA members held demonstrations, peaceful rallies and opposed the construction of the first of the big dams. As a result most of the NBA members went to jail a number of times. Inspite of all efforts, the Apex court has taken the decision that the construction work should go on.
- The fourth group is those one working in the non-traditional sector such as justice, governance, electoral and administrative reforms, corruption, etc.

Conclusion

But the question that tinkers the mind is: Does civil society matter in a democracy?

NGOs still have a long way to go before they can substantively influence the political process and make a huge impact in governance and democracy. Many have made a good start. In the 2004 elections, the Congress and its allies formed the United Progressive Alliance and supported demands by NGOs in the Common Minimum Programme for tribal rights over forest land, enacted laws on the Right to Information and guarantee at least 100 days of state-sponsored employment for the rural poor[9]. Women's organisations were reasonably successful in advocating on the Domestic Violence Act 2005, Sexual Harassment at Workplace Bill, Immoral Traffic Prevention Act, etc. Amongst the several battles, the Women's Reservation Bill still seems to be an illusion mainly due to opposition from the political parties. There are numerous gaps left by the government, sometimes by intention, lack of funds and lack of awareness. These are the gaps that many NGOs have tried to fulfill. Some of them work in areas that the government does not want to get into like fighting discrimination on the basis of caste. Most Indian politicians do not really want to upset the existing caste hierarchy in their constituency because they are dependent on votes of certain caste groups. In the process, implementation of laws prohibiting discrimination on the basis of caste is often ignored. It is here that the civil society has been able to step in a small way.

Another interesting feature in India has been that politicians tend to listen to NGOs when they deal with causes that can alienate and upset voters. Pollution and the drying up of water sources are two examples. In cities, middle class residents have begun casting their votes for better civil services. They have come together in officially registered organizations called Resident Welfare Associations (RWAs). Delhi's RWAs forced the government to reconsider a World Bank sponsored project for the privatisation of water distribution, citing concerns about rising water access rates. RWAs have also learned to question the business claims of private power companies, file objections with power regulators and are even contesting municipal elections with positive results.

However the collaboration between the state and the civil society has not exactly been smooth. Nor is it likely to be in future. There is suspicion on both sides. For an activist, the civil society space is reducing every day due terrorism, insurgency etc which gives the State adequate reason to interfere in every aspect of life. For NGOs and civil society, it has been particularly difficult as the government wields control over resources with a carrot and stick policy, withholding funds and granting of Foreign Contribution Regulation Act from organisations which have protested against corruption or inefficiency and have rewarded those that do not rock the boat. Several organisations have been blacklisted in recent years. Such actions only worsen relations between the government and the civil society. The latter insist that the blacklisting has been arbitrary in many cases, not backed by proper inquiry and done without giving the group an opportunity to explain themselves. The government however has always denied any witch-hunt on its part.

In addition to the above, at present civil society operates in limited space and is generally confined to particular regions and can only help a limited population. Ongoing internal debate exists within the NGO sector as they struggle to find models that can be successfully implemented across diverse regions. One school of thought is to build a partnership with the state in order to take advantage of the government's reach and resources. Another school believes in functioning without state support. However, inspite of the wariness, the government is aware of civil society's ability to innovate and deliver services efficiently, and has shown interest in partnering with them as widely seen in the Eleventh Five Year Plan documents on inclusive growth. For the first time, the state has framed policies keeping in mind the human resources available from the civil society, especially the NGO sector. The traditional areas of support and partnership in village development, local governance, livelihood, health, education etc continues. Even in areas such as justice sector working on innovative projects in police, prisons, and courts with civil society intervention has been initiated.

The urgent need of the hour is to promote dialogue platforms on cross cutting development issues between the state and civil society to understand and identify the existing gaps in the country. Government and civil society partnership can remain edgy and it should be so, because the idea is not to get co-opted to the existing systems and create cliques, but to deliberate and constantly find alternatives to government policies. The state can only think along a certain line, but someone has to think out of the box for all those who don't fit into the regular scheme, and who can do it better than activists, practitioners, experts, field workers, journalists, trade unionists and all those who can voice a concern for a better India.

Notes

1. Rajni Kothari, Political Scientist
2. Jaiprakash Narayan was popularly known as JP
3. These Commissions and Committees are also popularly called the Dharamvira Committee for Police reforms and Mulla Committee for Jail reforms
4. This is other than the All-India Trade Union Congress (AITUC); others established were Indian National Trade Union Congress, United Trade Union Congress, Bharatiya Mazdoor Sangh, National Front of Indian Trade Unions (NFITU in late 60's), Centre for Indian Trade Union (1970).
5. Estimate provided by PRIA (Participatory Research in Asia)
6. Urvashi Butalia, The women's movement in India: Action and reflection
7. Hussainara Khatoon v. State of Bihar, AIR 1979 SC 1360
8. Singur highlights rise of civil society movements in India, S Menon, Business Standard.
9. National Rural Employment Guarantee Act

References

Rajesh Tandon, Ranjita Mohanty, ed. *Does Civil Society Matter? Governance in Contemporary India*; Sage Publications, 2003.

Madeline Otis, Re-Imagining Civil Society in India, Brown University Thesis, 2005

Invisible, Yet Widespread: The Non-Profit Sector In India, , PRIA, December 2002

S Menon, *Singur Highlights Rise of Civil Society Movements in India*, Business Standard, Sept 2008.

Aloysius P. Fernandez, *History and Spread of Self help Affinity Group Movement in India*, Myrada, 2007

Urvashi Butalia, *The Women'sMmovement in India: Action and Reflection*, Communique (Nos. 42-43, (1997) July-Aug

Banishree Das, Dr Nirod Kumar Palai and Dr Kumar Das, Problems and Prospects of the Cooperative Movement in India under the Globalization Regime, *XIV International Economic History Congress, Helsinki 2006, Session 72.*

Amit Mitra and M.A.J. Jeyaseelan, Civil society, Globalization and Sustainable Development, *Seminar,* No 507

Lessons Learnt from NGOs Working on Bank Operations, World Bank, New Delhi, Sept 3 2007

Patralekha Chatterjee, Civil Society in India: A Necessary Corrective in a Representative Democracy, *Development and Cooperation* (No. 6, November/December 2001, p. 23 - 24)

Jayantha Dhanapala, The United Nations and Civil Society, Disarmament Affairs, Rotary International 2000.

Panchayati Raj System in India and the Role of Civil Society

Vikas Jha

Introduction

The enactment of the 73rd and 74th Constitutional Amendments in 1992 was a defining moment in the history of democratic evolution in India. These amendments provided the constitutional framework for establishing local self-government institutions in rural and urban areas. It turned the nearly fifty years of centralised model of development on its head and paved way for democratic decentralisation where emphasis was on bottom-up and participative planning, access of community to control over natural and human resources and implementation of development programmes.

The democratic decentralisation has led to creation of 240243 elected bodies at the grassroots and election of 2851600 representatives at three tiers: gram panchayat, intermediate panchayat and district panchayat in 2007. Reservation for marginalised section of society in all three tiers has provided political presence to 37 percent women and 30 percent deprived sections of society. The changes in terms of representation at the local level has been tangible but experience of functioning of these self-governing institutions in last fifteen years makes it quite apparent that effective local self-governance is still a distant dream and substantial efforts should be made by government and civil society to realise its potential. It would be pertinent here to identify the deficits of democratic decentralisation in India

Deficits in Democratic Decentralisation

Democratic decentralisation has not realised its real potential as it suffers from some deficits. Political masters, ministers and bureaucracy, have refused to devolve power to the panchayats. Various parallel bodies such as the District Rural Development Department, line departments like health, irrigation, agriculture, education, etc. have usurped most of functions, funds and functionaries and undermined the importance of the PRIs (Panchayati Raj Institutions). These institutions are always short of staff, funds and functions. State governments and State Finance Commissions have yet to work out the terms of sharing of taxable resources. Local bodies have also not yet been fully empowered to levy and collect taxes, user charges and other revenues. Lack of any financial base makes these institutions very weak.

One important hurdle is domination of PRIs by elites of society who rule by proxy. They prevent participation of representatives of women, SC and ST community in the activities of PRIs. Lack of training programmes for representatives of the PRIs is also a major constraint in effective functioning of these institutions. Without proper training, they lack the perspective and management (administrative and financial) skills to handle PRIs.

Despite these hurdles, some states like Kerala, West Bengal, Madhya Pradesh and Karnataka have made good progress in making PRIs effective self-governing institutions. Other states have begun rather slowly. But public expenditure in panchayats has increased substantially to Rs.1.2 trillion (2007) from Rs. .36 trillion (2004) through nearly 120 centrally sponsored schemes. So these institutions have a very critical role in ensuring development at grassroots level but the challenge is to make these institutions effective and robust. Government and civil society must take up this challenge, otherwise voice of poor and marginalised would never reach the policy makers in State/ central capitals and they would never be beneficiaries of development. This paper discusses only the role of civil society (NGOs, Community based organisations) in strengthening PRIs.

Role of Civil Society in strengthening Panchayati Raj System

Civil Society can take up number of activities like mobilisation, capacity building and monitoring and evaluation for strengthening Panchayati Raj system. We shall limit our discussion to successfully tested initiatives of Participatory Research in Asia (PRIA) and other community based organisations in different parts of the country. These initiatives are mainly related to mobilisation of Gram Sabha, capacity building of informal community organisations and elected representatives and promoting Right to Information and social accountability in PRIs. Let us discuss these initiatives:

Strengthening Gram Sabha

Capacity enhancement intervention at this level would entail an appreciation of collective identity of gram sabha. Community must be made aware of the importance of Gram Sabha for development planning, monitoring of programmes and its role of collective decision making for public good. One of the primary requirements of strengthening Gram Sabhas is to conduct meetings at regular intervals, to discuss and develop local development plans. In many places campaigns are organised by NGOs and CBOs to inform the local citizens before the actual Gram Sabha meetings. Informational and educational materials (like posters, handbills, leaflets, brochures, etc), folk performances (like folk songs, street plays), video films and rallies are extensively used to inform about the role of Gram Sabha in working of gram panchayat.

With perspective that well-informed electorate can only elect transparent and accountable citizens representatives, large scale ***Pre-Elections Voters Awareness Campaigns (PEVAC)*** have been organised in partnership with other voluntary organisations, State Election Commission and local bureaucracies. This includes massive educational interventions on various aspects of elections including how to cast votes, election of good candidates, making decision to vote on basis of manifestoes of candidates, etc. The campaign approach includes street plays, street meetings and distributions of posters, pamphlets as well as door-to-door educational interventions

After the election, a series of orientation meetings explaining the role of Gram Sabhas as a collective entity are organised. The other purpose of these meetings is to discuss problems and issues and to identify needs and priorities of the people. These orientation meetings also serve the purpose of initiating a dialogue between various marginalised groups and ERs.

Capacity Building of Elected Representatives

There is strong need for enhancing capacity of ERs as majority of them are first time entrants into panchayati raj system. Their capacity in terms of role and responsibilities of elected representatives, administration and financial management of Gram Panchayats, undertaking participatory micro planning and budgeting exercises, etc need to be built. Structured educational event (different durations) has been used by PRIA and other organisations for the purpose. These events are followed by exposure visits to performing panchayats, interface with elected representatives of other panchayats and officials of government departments, which have helped ERs in learning by experience. PRIA in collaboration with other voluntary organisations has organised capacity building events in a campaign mode, which was called ***Panchayati Raj Jagruka Abhiyan*** (Campaign on Awareness Building for Panchayati Raj).

Simultaneously, efforts have been made to form a network of elected representative at the block, districts and state level. The purpose of these networks is to negotiate with State for further devolution of power, functionaries and resources. The capacity building programmes are not a one time event; instead they are a long-term process for systematic learning of new knowledge, skills and attitude.

Strengthening Leadership Among Marginalised

The 1992 Act sought to correct the prolonged marginalisation of women, SC, ST by reserving seats and obligatory gram sabha meetings. However, as a result of illiteracy, social discrimination, patriarchal social practices and economic injustices most of ERs of deprived sections are not aware of their roles and responsibilities and remain silent in the meetings of gram sabha and panchayat. They are not able to articulate group specific interests or exercise their own judgment in decision making. Hence their participation in PRIs remains limited.

Capacity building programmes for marginalised community organized by PRIA and other CBOs focus on perspective building (women, dalit and tribal rights, group/collectivisation process, group dynamics, and understanding on resolving groups conflicts), awareness about functioning of PRIs, role and responsibilities of elected leaders of these institutions and skills required to handle responsibilities like gram sabha mobilisation, bottom up planning, conducting panchayat meetings, preparing panchayat budget, etc. Exclusive events are also organised for women, tribal and dalit elected representatives for sharing of experiences and peer learning. In many locations, exclusive networks of women, tribals and dalits have been promoted in order to add weight to their voice in interface with government machinery.

Panchayat Resource Centres as Agents of Change

Information has become a major source of power and control and the ordinary citizens have been systematically deprived from having access to relevant and authentic information. It is believed that those who are left out of the information revolution are apt to be left out of the benefits of development as it happens. This growing information gap has thus become one of the main reasons for the panchayats not functioning as institutions of local self-governance.

Working with the notion that knowledge is power, PRIA and its partners' interventions to strengthen Panchayati Raj Institutions have always contained a strong educational element. One such intervention has been setting up of resource centres known as Panchayat Resource Centres (PRC) at the block level. One of the main purposes of these PRCs is to proactively access information form the government departments regarding various development schemes and resources and disseminate the same to the members of Gram Sabha and Gram Panchayat. These centres provide the much-needed information at the grassroots, which enables ordinary citizens to make 'informed' choices and decisions and ask questions from ERs, which in turn will enhance accountability.

Promoting Right to Information

Right to Information Act, which came into force on 12 October 2005, is one of the most significant legislations enacted in India. It recognises that in a democracy, all information held by the government ultimately belongs to people. Making information available to citizens is a part of normal government functioning because the public has a right to know what public officials do with their money. The Act seeks to establish transparency and accountability in the functioning of government institutions. A common man by seeking information under RTI can not only ensure better public services but also make government institutions accountable to the people. The Act also mandates PRIs to disclose information about their activities voluntarily. As awareness of the Act among ERs is quite low, NGOs can help PRIs in voluntary disclosures in proper formats.

NGOs and CBOs can mobilise citizens to use this law to get information about development programmes in gram panchayat. Gram panchayats can also use the Act to collect information about development programmes from line departments and Block Development Officers and District Collector. Mahiti Shakti Abhiyan (Federation of ERs in Karnataka) has used it to get information about expenditure incurred from all departments in their gram panchayat area. Thus RTI can be used to collect and collate all information related to development programmes in villages, which hitherto has remained hidden from citizens. Such disclosures may lead to frequent questioning of government department about expenditure, which would prevent mal-practices in these departments.

Promoting Social Audit

Social Audit can be one of the important tools for promoting accountability in gram panchayats. This is a process by which, details of the resources (financial and non-financial) used by government departments in development programmes and its impact, are shared with the people, often through a public platform such as the Gram Sabha/ Social Audit Forum.

The process of audit involves the following components: 1) availability of details about development programmes, expenditure and impact; 2)organising end-users/beneficiaries; and 3) scrutiny of information by end users. Different approaches to conduct social audit have been observed across India; it can be conducted in campaign mode by NGOs / CSOs, gram panchayat can facilitate social audit, NGOs / CSOs can conduct it in selected locations and lastly, gram panchayats along with some CSOs can take it up.

Social audit has had varied experiences across India. Resistance of ERs and local officials, culture of silence and conflict of interests of dominant castes and deprived castes also hamper the process of social audit. But it certainly checks corruption as ERs and officials are afraid that any development programme can be scrutinised by community at any time. Realising the efficacy of social audit as an instrument of accountability, central government has embedded it in NREGS (National Rural Employment Guarantee Scheme) and proposes to make social audit part of all the centrally sponsored programmes in the country.

Conclusions

Democratic decentralisation in India, no doubt, suffers from some deficits but it has some achievements to its credit as well. These institutions have enhanced the political consciousness of the people, provided space to marginalised sections in governance and involved common masses in planning, implementation and monitoring of development programmes. The 73rd amendment has certainly deepened democracy in India. Some of the constraints in the functioning of local self-governance can be tackled by pro-active approach of state governments and innovative models of capacity building by civil society.

Acronyms

ERs (Elected Representatives), SC (Scheduled Castes), ST (Scheduled Tribes), PRIs (Panchayati Raj Institutions), NGOs (Non-Governmental Organisations), CBOs (Community Based Organisations)

References

Tandon, Rajesh & Bandyopadhyay, K.K., Capacity Building for Effective Democratic Local Governance: Experience from India, *Participation and Governance*, Vol. 10, Number 31, November 2004, PRIA, New Delhi.

Rai, Manoj et al, *The State of Panchayats: A Participatory Perspective*, PRIA, 2001, New Delhi.

Tandon, Rajesh, *Voluntary Action, Civil Society and the State*, 2002, Mosaic Books, New Delhi.

The State of Panchayats:2007-2008, Vol 1, IRMA, Ministry of Panchayati Raj, GOI, 2008 New Delhi.

Transnational Terrorism in the Information Space of Kazakhstan

Lessya Karatayeva

There is a set of narratives, explaining the nature of terrorism.

The elements of S. Huntington's theory of clash of civilisations are taken as the basis for one of such narratives. The other narratives rest on the idea that contemporary terrorism results from the transformation of the society from its agrarian state to the industrial and informational society. The advocates of this narrative apply the terminology that was most thoroughly developed by A. Toffler in the framework of the concept of waves. The logic explaining the nature of terrorism is the following:

Rampant development of new information and telecommunication technologies has the character of global information revolution which increasingly influences the politics, economy, government, finance, science, culture and other areas of social life within national borders and worldwide

We are witnessing today the Information Technology revolution, which designates the progression to a completely new type of society, an information society. One of its basic attributes is its global character.

On the face of it, information and telecommunication technologies, globalisation of trade flows and globalisation of security systems easily spread all over the planet.

However, the third wave has deeper layers—new global values, new motivation for politicians, new standards of everyday life, work, education, new economy with new resources, new capital and new relations between companies and their clients, between employer and employee, new means of production and new implication of surplus exchange value.

Majority of the ethnics adopt new values and new traditions that make them give up everything which had been important for previous generations. There is a definite contradiction of values here, and, therefore a consensus is actually not possible.

With power unbalance not in favour of those who resist globalisation, terrorists' methods are applied.

On the other hand, it is well known that information space has a number of features distinguishing it from the space of reality. We should pay our attention to the difference of their boundaries and limits. One of the features of information space is its infinity; there cannot be little of it. The current development of means of communication makes it actually unlimited. Nevertheless, its boundedness and openness does not exclude its localisation within a nation space as well. It has nothing to do with jamming stations and curtains specially designed by the government bodies to protect the population from negative influence on their minds from abroad. Localisation of information space reflexes the demand for certain information. In other words, by identifying ourselves with a certain community we share its discourse. The localisation of information space depends on coverage zone of the discourse. Therefore, we should remember that an information object can be specific in terms of its national localisation. Information and knowledge are becoming one of the strategic resources comparable to traditional resources.

Most of the times, the state has a great capability to form signal system of national information space, the discourse generated by the state may determine the behaviour of the population of the country.

Going onto the second part of my speech, I should make some provisos. First, it is difficult to estimate interdependence of the transnational terrorism and globalisation in the absence of precisely determined and conventional definition. Secondly, the given speech does not directly deal with terrorism; we shall speak about the threat of terrorism, proceeding from the condition, that the threat of terrorism is always constructed. Hence, the space, in which the researches were carried out, whose results are submitted in the speech, is an information space. In this case, the author offers to pay attention on the information space of the Republic of Kazakhstan, as the RK is the state, which borders on the countries that have undergone several terrorist attacks, but in whose territory a non-terrorist act has been registered officially.

The task of the given speech is to define the features of the articulation of the transnational terrorist threats in various segments of Kazakhstan's information space. For a start, we shall allocate segments of information space (IS) within the framework of which the researches were carried out:

First: official IS. Second: mass media. Third: unofficial IS.

Within the official information space, political significant speakers articulate the threat of the transnational terrorism.

All spectrums of analysed speeches can be divided into two groups: the speeches addressed to the population of the Republic of Kazakhstan and the ones addressed outwards. The analysis of speeches and TV appearances shows that, on the domestic level, the problem of terrorism is not much articulated, in contrast with the articulation of its presence for an 'external' audience. The statements of the president before the 'external' audience lead to the following conclusions:

Firstly, in his statements, N. Nazarbayev emphasises that the threat of terrorism, transnational terrorism in particular, is steadily growing. In as early as 2000, he pointed out the existence of such threats and its transborder character. Later, in 2005 he said that 'terrorism has become the most dangerous challenge to the international security system[1]. The scale of this threat has today overpassed all predictions. The number of other challenges related to terrorism has also increased'[2].

Secondly, N. Nazarbayev repeatedly stated that religious differences cannot be considered as the source of terrorism, there is no any 'clash of civilizations' leading to terrorism. The roots of terrorism are social: they are in poverty and human rights abuse. Let me give a number of quotations in order to illustrate that point. "It is generally known", Nazarbayev said, "that terrorism is flourishing in poor and unstable countries. There is such a country in our region. It is Afghanistan… most of the predictions of inevitable 'conflict of civilisation' have not been factually realised yet. However, we should be aware of the fact that religious tensions provide the social basis for transnational terrorism and religious extremism[3]. Human rights abuse, poverty and environmental degradation are the likely soil for expansion of the ideas of terrorism"[4].

"Thirdly, terrorism is not a threat which is apart from anything else. There are certain co-factors. The number of challenges related to terrorism has increased. These are, mostly, the conflicts that have resulted from nationalism, ethnic and religious tensions; these are also drug trafficking and organised crime as well as illegal arms trafficking and money laundering. Drug trafficking provides financial base for terrorism. One-third of current 'terrorist economy' is drug production and trafficking."[5]

Fourthly, unlike most experts in counter-terror, who argue that there is no threat of terrorism in Central Asia, president admits that: "terrorism and extremism present an actual problem for Kazakhstan considering the current trend to globalisation of transnational terrorism, rooted from interdependent factors of political, social and economic character in the region and worldwide.

Counter-terrorism is one of the priority tasks for Kazakhstan in maintaining its security".

Fifthly, the president always attracts the attention of international community to the transborder, transnational and global character of the threat. We can prevent it only by having a real, efficient collective counter-terror system. President N. Nazarbayev repeatedly spoke on the point: at the opening session of International Conference on Peace and Reconciliation on 13 February 2003, at the International Forum 'Eurasian Integration' in Astana on July 18–19 , 2004 and while addressing the Academy of Social Science of PRC on 21 December 2006[6].

Sixthly, counter-terror activity should not be military or politically oriented. In fact, effective counter-terrorism activity should involve further improvement and unification of counter-terror legislature on global level, working with information (including technology and psychology), ideological counter-strategy, financial and economic as well as military and political efforts.

Seventhly, it is worth mentioning that in his statements, President N. Nazarbayev emphasises the efficiency of regional and international organisations in their counter-terror activities, of the UN in the first place. This organisation defines the principles of fighting against terrorism and maintains control over multilateral counter-terror efforts of international community. He says,"UN represents today joint efforts of all states concerned with seeking compromise in order to restrain terrorism"[7].

Having analysed the annual address of the President to the people of Kazakhstan, one can notice that terrorism was not mentioned in the earliest addresses (1997–1999). The threat of terrorist acts was first mentioned by him in 1999: "military conflicts in neighbouring countries and their potential spread to Kazakhstan is the major challenge to our security in next few years. This threat can be manifested in flows of refugees, provocations aimed at involvement of Kazakhstan into a military conflict, terrorist acts in the territory of the country, aggravation of situation near the borders"[8].

In 2000 the threat of terrorism is articulated as a real one. One of the sources of this threat for Kazakhstan is Afghanistan[9]. The annual address of 2001 mentioned terrorism but did not distinguish it form the other threats: "these are the succession of economic crises, instability on our south borders, expansion of bloody conflicts, growth of terrorism, spread of drug addiction and AIDS, escalation of crime in many countries. All these dangerous phenomena can make negative impact on us"[10].

In the annual address in 2004, the President for the first time emphasised the joint efforts of all international communities in order to fight against transnational terrorism.

Considering all, we can say that the threat of terrorism is not articulated much in the annual addresses of the President of Kazakhstan,

The analysis of press and TV channels has shown the following results[11]:

Terrorism is articulated as the threat number one in the world and, therefore is undiversified, at the same time it is driven out of the territory of the Republic of Kazakhstan. There is no national localisation. There is not even regional localisation. The most frequent references are those to the 9/11, Madrid 2004, Beslan 2004. Fight against Khyzb-ut–Takhrir is a Kazakhstani particular case.

Social and financial hardship is articulated as one of the main causes of terrorism.

Terrorism is clearly linked with 'shadow' financial flows and corruption.

And, the most important finding is that mass media in Kazakhstan has not created the image of terrorism; rather it has created the image of counter-terrorism. Given that the state and its special security services are considered both on the official and unofficial level to be the main body carrying out counter-terror activities, the media in the country creates the positive image of the state, not by informing the readers and viewers on their achievements in fighting against terrorism in the country but by telling them about the recognition of such efforts by other actors of global counter-terror system.

There is no visualization of terrorism, its aftermath and its masterminders in Kazakhstani media.

Unofficial information space reflects perception of the threat of transnational terrorism by the population of RK. Concerning the results of the public opinion survey carried out by the author[12], the findings are the following: more than half of the population, sharing the government's opinion on the presence of the threat of transnational terrorism in Kazakhstan, does not feel any such threat in their daily life. The sources of terrorism are: religious intolerance and separatism for 68.9 %, religious intolerance for 42.2 %, religious separatism for 26.7 %, natural consequence of clash of civilisations and cultures for 8.4 %, social injustice for 5.6 % of the respondents. Answering the question on the terrorist organisations under the legislation of RK, the respondents most frequently mentioned Al Qaida (36.6%), Khizb-ut-Takhrir (33.8%), Hamas (15.4%), Hezbollah (9.8%). 46.4% of respondents could not answer the question. From 14 organisations criminalised under Kazakhstani legislation, the respondents named only 5. The mention of Hamas and Hezbollah can be explained by the fact that they are much spoken about by international media. Some of the respondents mentioned Al Jazira as a terrorist organisation; this shows how little they think about the issue. They are confused because they remember the name heard from the radio and TV, and, given that the name of the TV channel is most of the time mentioned because of the recent developments in the Middle East and Afghanistan or a televised address of Osama Bin Laden. In general, the population in Kazakhstan is not hesitant about the capacity of state bodies to carry out their counter-terror activity. One of the most frequently mentioned organisation which is involved in counter-terror is Shanghais Cooperation Organisation (36.6%), the UN is the most successful one. The results of the survey show that the way of thinking of the population about terrorism is highly stereotyped.

Thus it is possible to derive the following conclusions:

- On an official level, there are no efforts for constructing the threat of the transnational terrorism within Kazakhstani information space.
- On an instrumental level (mass media), terrorism is articulated as the number one problem in the world, thus, the threat is universalised, but at the same time, it is removed beyond the Republic of Kazakhstan. There is no national localisation. There is not even a regional localisation.
- The population of Kazakhstan as a whole shares the official discourse of the transnational terrorism, however, in a passive mode. The results of the public opinion survey enable to assume that the population of Kazakhstan has given the settlement of the issue to complete the government control.
- On any of these levels, globalisation is not articulated as the reason for transnational terrorism, however its global character is a condition which should be taken into account at the time of construction of the counter-terrorist system.

Notes

1. The President of the Republic of Kazakhstan Nursultan Nazarbayev's Speech to the Opening Ceremony of the International Conference of the Peace and the Concord, 13 February 2003. .
2. The UN Security Council, IV Anti-Terrorist Committee's Special Meeting, The President of the Republic of Kazakhstan Nursultan Nazarbayev's Speech, 26 January 2005.
3. The 62 Session of the UN's General Assembly, The President of the Republic of

Kazakhstan Nursultan Nazarbayev's Speech, 25 September 2007.

4. UN Security Council, IV Anti-Terrorist Committee's Special Meeting, The President of the Republic of Kazakhstan Nursultan Nazarbayev's Speech, 26 January 2005.
5. Ibid.
6. The President of the Republic of Kazakhstan Nursultan Nazarbayev's Speech to the Opening Ceremony of the International Conference of the Peace and the Concord, 13 February 2003.; The President of the Republic of Kazakhstan Nursultan Nazarbayev's Speech to the International Forum "The Eurasian Integration" Astana, 18-19 June 2004.; The President of the Republic of Kazakhstan Nursultan Nazarbayev's Speech at the Academy of Social Sciences of the People's Republic of China, 21 December 2006.
7. UN Security Council, IV Anti-Terrorist Committee's Special Meeting, The President of the Republic of Kazakhstan Nursultan Nazarbayev's Speech, 26 January 2005.
8. Address to the People of Kazakhstan by the President of the Republic of Kazakhstan Nursultan Nazarbayev, September 1999.
9. Address to the People of Kazakhstan by the President of the Republic of Kazakhstan Nursultan Nazarbayev, October 2000.
10. Address to the People of Kazakhstan by the President of the Republic of Kazakhstan Nursultan Nazarbayev, October 2001.
11. In this case the publications for the period of 2007-08 were observed. Defining the set of the research subjects it was considered the peculiarities and the level of importance of the issue for being used in the political struggle (the level found as lowest) Also key points of the Report of the Vice-minister of Culture and Information of the Republic of Kazakhstan Ye. Babakoumarov "The Information Policy and the Struggle against Terrorism". The Media with national coverage were analyzed ("Kazakhstanskaya Pravda", "Egemen Kazakhstan" "Panorama", magazines "Kontinent", "Mysl", TV Channels "Kazakhstan", "Khabar", "El Arna". ITVRC "Mir")
12. The opinion poll of September-October 2007.

Section IV

Globalistation: Security and Strategic Dimensions

Energy Geopolitics in Eurasia

Ajay Patnaik

Introduction

It is no coincidence that the eastward expansion of NATO was followed by revelations about Caspian energy reserves. Both these issues were related to the creation of a new world order in which the US primacy is an essential condition. Strategic thinkers in the US like Huntington and Brzezinski talked of the critical importance of Eurasia to fulfill this objective. If Eurasia is to be dominated, the power of Russia has to be curtailed, which meant confining Russia to its natural borders and not allowing it to have any say in the developments in its neighbourhood let alone beyond Eurasia—a neo-containment strategy. The closest American allies in the post-Cold War period—the so called New Europe or Eastern European members of NATO—even added new dimensions to containment by arguing for its expansion to former Soviet republics like Ukraine to be a buffer against Russia. According to Aurel Braun, "Poland, in particular, seems to be deeply influenced by former US national security advisor Zbigniew Brzezinski's argument that Russia suffers from imperial nostalgia, that it has alienated all its neighbours, and that the independence of Ukraine is essential in preventing Russia from becoming an empire".[1] In this thinking, which dictated much of the US policy towards Russia during the Bush administration, an enlargement of NATO to the Ukraine and Georgia would both create a buffer to segregate Russia and contain it as well.

While it was easy to attract East European states to NATO embrace, the same could not be true for the former Soviet republics outside the Baltic region. There was still a lot of dependence on Russia in economic and security spheres. To weaken that dependence without overtly confronting Russia, energy diplomacy was the tool deployed to push Russia out of the former Soviet space. In reply, Russia has also used the same tool to counter the Western moves in the region. Today, energy is the most effective tool of

Russia to woo or punish former Soviet republics depending on their position in the great power divide.

The current Washington strategy, according to Engdahl, targets many Eurasian former Soviet republics which per se have no known oil or gas reserves. What they do have, however, is strategic military or geopolitical significance for the Washington policy of dominating the future of Eurasia.

A look at the Eurasian map and at the target countries for various US-sponsored Colour Revolutions makes this unmistakeably clear, argues Engdahl. The US has troops in Pakistan, Afghanistan, Kyrgyzstan.. Uzbekistan, until the Andhijan events, had an American base and there are fresh efforts to reengage that country for military cooperation with the US.[2] These states serve as a potential US-controlled barrier or buffer zone between Russian and Iranian Caspian energy sources.[3] Georgia and Azerbaijan thus become crucial to the US strategy of creating a chain of allies around Russia's southern periphery.

Significance of Caucasus and Central Asia

Russia's soft underbelly lies across its southern frontier—in Caucasus and Central Asia. Planned NATO expansion to Ukraine and Georgia, NATO troops in Afghanistan, and US bases in Central Asia created a great sense of vulnerability for Russia. While the West tries to draw the states in Caucasus-Central Asian region by diversifying their energy transport dependence away from Russia, the latter has done everything to ensure that Russia remains the major factor in the energy sector development of the former Soviet republics.

Of course, the Eurasian states had their own fault lines which helped external powers to polarise the region. During the last years of Soviet Union, Armenia-Azerbaijan conflict took shape and later developed into a full-fledged war. In Georgia, two former autonomous areas with different nationalities rebelled after loosing their autonomy under the new nationalising leadership. To each of the conflicts, Russia was inevitably drawn. The loosing side invariably accused Russia of siding with the other party. While in Central Asia, the states could follow multi-vector foreign policy, in the Caucasus, it was zero sum. Thus, when Armenia joined the Russian-led Collective Security Treaty in May 1992, the same month Azerbaijan withdrew from the Commonwealth of Independent States (though it rejoined later). Similarly, the urge by South Ossetians and Abkhazians to join with the Russian Federation has been construed by Georgia as a ploy by Russia to divide and weaken the country. Even joint peace-keeping by an agreement with Georgia did not leave Russia unscathed. It was accused of using peace-keeping as a means to prevent integration of the two break-away regions with Georgia. The inability of Azerbaijan and Georgia to win in the conflicts created gulf between Russia and these two Caucasian states. This created a huge opportunity for the US to give shape to its strategy of containment of Russia and encircling Iran.

From the time when Washington under Clinton created a Caspian task force headed by then Deputy Secretary of State, Strobe Talbott, (with representatives from Energy and Commerce Departments, the National Security Council and the CIA) the aim was to marginalise Russia in the region.[4] Since then American moves in Central Asia and the Caucasus regions include an all-out effort to find alternative oil routes as well as explore the possibility of future NATO enlargement to these regions. Such moves are in direct contradiction to Russian, Chinese and Iranian interests. The joint NATO-PfP (NATO's Partnership for Peace programme for former Soviet republics) programme has been holding military exercises since 1997 in the region. All the Central Asian republics have also joined NATO's North American Co-operation Council (NACC). Significant in this process was the formation in December 1995 of the Central Asian Battalion, set up with the participation of troops from the above two (PfP and NACC) and Uzbekistan, under NATO auspices and US CENTCOM (Central Command) support with a mandate in peace-keeping and conflict-management.

According to Stephen Blank, Central Asia represents a new frontier policy of the United States, which now deploys all its instruments of power to establish itself as a major player in Central Asia and across the entire CIS. Since the days of the Clinton administration, US National Security Strategy has made the integration of the former Soviet republics into Western economic, political and military institutions and practices a fundamental policy objective. Blank further underlines that despite the rhetoric of geo-economic rivalry, the intensifying struggle over Caspian energy sources also reveals a much more bare-knuckled and traditional rivalry. "Notwithstanding its rhetoric about win-win outcomes, in practice the growing involvement in the Caspian region is in the highest degree strategic or even geopolitical and aims to enhance US and no other state's influence. It combines all the traditional instruments of power, superior economic potential and military prowess, and a commitment to integrating the area more fully into the West in terms of both defence and economics", he states.[5]

Energy Diplomacy

The strategy of using energy diplomacy to promote strategic goals in the CIS began with the decision to construct the Baku-Tbilisi-Ceyhan (BTC) pipeline. United States and Turkey seriously looked at the possibility of finding a route that is politically most stable and reliable route and came with the option of an expensive and long-distance Baku-Tbilisi-Ceyhan route that would bypass Russia and Iran. The BTC pipeline was originally proclaimed by BP and others as The Project of the Century. Zbigniew Brzezinski was a consultant to BP during the Clinton era, urging Washington to back the project. In fact, it was Brzezinski who went to Baku in 1995, unofficially, on behalf of President Clinton to meet the then-Azeri President Haidar Aliyev, in order to negotiate the new independent Baku pipeline routes including what became the BTC pipeline.

Brzezinski also sits on the board of an impressive, if little-known, US-Azerbaijan Chamber of Commerce (USACC). The chairman of USACC in Washington is Tim Cejka, President of ExxonMobil Exploration. Other USACC Board members include Henry Kissinger, and James Baker III, the man who in 2003 personally went to Tbilisi to tell Shevardnadze that Washington wanted him to step aside in favour of the US-trained Georgian President Mikhail Shaakashvili. Brent Scowcroft, former National Security Adviser to George H.W. Bush, also sits on the board of USACC. Dick Cheney was a former board member before he became Vice-President. A more high-powered Washington team of geopolitical fixers, underlines Engdahl, would be hard to imagine. This group of prominent individuals certainly would not give a minute of their time unless an area was of utmost geopolitical strategic importance to the United States or to certain powerful interests there.[6]

While this policy succeeded in drawing Azerbaijan and Georgia away from Russian dependence, vigorous Russian energy diplomacy in rest of the Caspian and Central Asian states resulted in denying the US the early advantage that accrued to it especially after BTC went operational in 2005 and the South Caucasus pipeline completed in 2006. Though this deprived Russia of the energy tool in relation to Azerbaijan, the latter had to pay heavy economic price for overlooking Russia. Azerbaijan and Georgia had to forego cheap Russian energy and as a result Azerbaijani exports suffered to meet internal demand and the needs of Georgia. It had to use the gas from Shah-Deniz field for this purpose rather than earn lucrative profits by exporting to Turkey.

The Caucasian geopolitical polarisation was visible when Russian ally Armenia managed to get gas at the preferential rate of 110 USD per billion cubic metres in 2006, when state-controlled Russian gas company Gazprom demanded a more than doubling of prices for gas to Azerbaijan and Georgia (from \$110 to \$235 per 1000 billion cubic metres). Azerbaijan responded by agreeing to supply gas to Georgia at subsidized price (\$120) for next five years. In return, Azerbaijan state-owned gas company SOCAR purchased significant parts of the Georgian gas distribution networks at the end of 2008.[7]

Kazakhstan remains an important country for the competing energy diplomacy that is going on in Eurasia. A significant amount of Kazakh oil would be needed to feed the BTC pipeline since reserves in Azerbaijan's Azeri-Chirag-Guneshefi field would peak in 2010. Though Kazakhstan promised in 2006 to supply 53 million barrels a year and eventually 175 million barrels a year, which is vital for Azerbaijan and BTC investors, the Trans-Caspian pipeline has not materialised and Kazakh oil is transported mainly through tankers since late 2008.[8]

On the other hand, a bilateral pact reached in May 2002 on the division of the Caspian Sea played a pivotal role in improving economic cooperation between Astana and Moscow. Kazakhstan also agreed to a 15-year deal under which Kazakhstan would commit to exporting at least 15 million tons of crude oil per year via the Baku-Novorossisk pipeline. In 2002, Kazakhstan pumped 17.5 million tons via this route which climbed to about 19 million tons in 2003. The Russian oil giant LUKoil has invested at least \$500 million in Kazakhstani energy development since 1996.[9]

Kazakhstan-Russia cooperation in the energy sector has grown enormously. Kazakhstan exported in 2007 more than 60 million tons of oil through Russian pipelines, under a long-term agreement signed in 2002. Both have signed bilateral agreements delineating their sectors in the Caspian and decided to jointly develop three oil fields in the north-west of the Sea—Kurmangazy, Tsentralnoe and Khalynskoe.[10]

The CPC pipeline from Kazakhstan's Tengiz fields to Russian port of Novorossisk has a capacity of 700,000 barrels per day and is a vital outlet for Kazakh oil. The first phase was completed in 2001 and further expansion was agreed on 17 December 2008 by the energy ministries of both countries. It is expected to be completed by 2013 that could nearly double the capacity to about 1.3 million barrels per day.[11]

The geopolitical race has intensified around the issue of construction of Trans-Caspian and South-Stream pipelines. It is in Russia's interest that the Tran-Caspian Gas Pipeline (crossing the Caspian to Azerbaijan and from there it would follow the route of the Baku-Tbilisi-Erzurum pipeline and to be extended to Europe) remains on paper. In this calculation Turkmenistan is critical to the energy diplomacy of Russia. Turkmenistan is Central Asia's largest gas exporter, due to its much smaller population.[12] The main end user for Turkmen gas is Ukraine. This gas is supplied through Russian pipelines and Russia has started paying 'market prices' for Turkmen gas since 2007. As a result, Ukraine also had to pay Russia more for the gas.

Russia's decision to pay higher prices for Central Asian gas, according to Indra Overland, can be understood partly as a measure to fend off Western competition in that region, and partly as a means of keeping Central Asian gas under its control.[13] Kazakhstan, along with its Central Asian neighbours Turkmenistan and Uzbekistan, will receive a huge increase in energy-related revenue. Ukraine, though, stands to lose the most under the new pricing framework for Central Asian natural gas.

Russia achieved a major breakthrough in the Turkmen energy sector, which apart from a limited swap deal with Iran has not been able so far to create an alternative to the northern route (through Russia) to export its gas. In April 2003, Russia signed a 25-year agreement on gas co-operation that stipulates 'gradual increase formula' for the purchase of gas from Turkmenistan. Starting in 2004, Russia began to buy under this agreement 6 billion cubic metres of gas per year at a price of $44 per thousand cubic meters, 50 percent of which would be paid in cash and the rest in kind. Allowing for the quality and pricing of bartered goods, the final aggregate value of Turkmen gas is around $33 per thousand cubic metres, compared to $100-plus that Russia gets from its West European customers. By 2009, Russia will be buying virtually all of Turkmen gas, amounting to 80 billion cubic metres by 2028, and Russia will retain the exclusive right to re-export the gas beyond Russia.[14]

In a positive for Russia's energy diplomacy, Turkmenistan, instead of showing interest for the Trans-Caspian pipeline, has continued negotiations with Russia and Kazakhstan on rebuilding the PriKaspiskiy pipeline which will reinforce Russia's control over Turkmen exports. Even the two other pipelines that exist or going to be operated soon are to Iran and China, which is fine with Russia since it makes less of Turkmen gas available in future for Trans-Caspian pipeline if and when it materialises. The 190 million dollar Korpeje-Kord-Kuy pipeline to Iran was completed in 1997 and includes a 25-year contract for 5–6 billion cubic metres m per year. The pipeline to China is nearing completion and is the longest in the world. It spans 7,000 kms with an annual capacity of 30 billion cubic metres. This project is a significant one in the post-Soviet period for Turkmenistan and would pass through Uzbekistan and Kazakhstan.[15]

Russia seems to have gained an upper hand in recent years so far as sealing gas deals with some of its CIS neighbours is concerned. Yet the situation could change in future. The latest spat in the energy geopolitics of Eurasia relates to the future of the proposed Nabucco pipeline.[16] Nabucco pipeline is a 3,300 kms project costing around $10.1 billion. Its six original partners are Austria, Bulgaria, Germany, Hungary, Romania and Turkey. The pipeline is another one after the BTC to bypass Russia and Iran. The Nabucco pipeline will link the gas fields of Azerbaijan to Western Europe without passing through either Russia or Ukraine. The first stage from Austria to Turkey is scheduled to be completed in 2013.

A rival project is the proposed Gazprom's South Stream pipeline which is also due to take gas from the Caucasus region through Bulgaria and into the EU. South Stream is due to start pumping in 2013. It seems both projects are likely to be delayed because of the current slump in demand and fall in prices in the international market. When energy markets recover again, the race will pick up. Till then, it is a game of ensuring that future delivery of gas through the pipelines is assured.

Since both pipelines would skirt Ukraine, it has activated its energy diplomacy around the Odessa-Brody pipeline. During the Ukrainian-Russian wrangling over the price of gas in 2006, Ukrainian President Viktor Yushchenko headed to Astana for talks with Kazakhstan's President Nursultan Nazarbayev. Yushchenko had hoped he could persuade Nazarbayev into an export arrangement that cuts out Russia. Instead of giving a commitment to the Odessa-Brody pipeline, which Ukraine seeks to expand, Nazarbayev stated clearly that Russia held the key to any decision. "The question of the Odessa-Brody project remains open. We have to agree with Russian oil transportation organizations to supply the necessary volumes to Ukraine", Nazarbayev told a news conference.[17]

The Odessa-Brody pipeline was intended to diversify Ukraine's energy imports and to make the country a transit corridor for supplying Caspian oil to Europe. Discussed in the 1990s, the project was finally completed in 2002. But there were no suppliers for this pipeline at a viable price and no buyers (refineries in Central and Western Europe) ready to sign import contracts committing to purchase oil through this pipeline. By July 2004, the Ukrainian government under Kuchma's presidency agreed to a Russian proposal for the reversal of the pipeline by transiting Russian oil from Brody in the north to Odessa in the south, to be shipped further to the West by tankers.[18]

After the Orange revolution, the new leadership again toyed with the idea of diversification and an agreement was reached on principle in early July 2006 with Poland, the Czech republic and Slovakia for extension of the Odessa-Brody pipeline to Plotsk in Poland.[19]

The deteriorating Russia-Ukraine relations following regime change in Ukraine resulted in a bitter row over energy prices and stoppage of gas supplies on 1 January 2006 for three days. The chances of Ukraine dealing directly from Turkmenistan were small, both due to tensions between the two countries and Moscow's growing control over Turkmenistan's gas supplies. The 4 January 2006 agreement between NAK Naftogaz Ukrainy, Gazprom and RosUkrEnergo restored gas supplies and assured continuous supplies, while the upward revision of price for Russian gas was accepted. As a result, Russia remains the sole supplier of not only Turkmen, but also Uzbek and Kazakh gas to Ukraine. According to Balmaceda, the fall out of the agreement was the end of the Nasha Ukraine's nineteen-month hold over power and strengthened those who advocated closer relations with Russia.[20]

Russian response to neo-containment strategy has been to build a strongly integrated space in the CIS in the shape of 'Common Economic Space' between Russia, Ukraine, Belarus and Kazakhstan. It was also building bridges with European states like Germany through major economic projects like Baltic Pipeline System (BPS), the Blue Stream and the Tengiz-Novorossisk pipelines. The pipeline from Tengiz field in Kazakhstan to Novorossisk port in Russia was completed and in July 2001 tankers started shipping Kazakh oil. This pipeline was to minimise the future impact of BTC pipeline.

However, the US buoyed by its military presence in Central Asia and neighbouring Afghanistan went ahead with its strategic objective of squeezing Russia out of Central Asia and Caucasus by successfully orchestrating regime change in some states and using these changes to pressurise other states. The pro-American regimes in Ukraine and Georgia were becoming strong pawns in the US strategic game.

The regimes in Azerbaijan and Kazakhstan were under increasing pressure in the run up to their presidential elections in 2005. However, Baku was reassured of American assistance during President Ilham Aliev's visit to the White House in April 2006, where the issues of democracy were not even included in the agenda. The same was the case with Kazakhstan, which agreed to visiting American Vice-President Dick Cheney's wish list. Following Cheney's Vilnius speech raising the pitch on democracy. The praise for the just elected Nazarbaev, despite West's severe criticism of the nature of elections, had the desired effect. The agreement during American Vice-President's visit was on export of Kazakh oil through BTC pipeline to make it viable beyond 2010.[21]

Russia's counter move was a trilateral summit in Turkmenistan following a visit by the Russian President to Kazakhstan in May 2007, where Kazakhstan agreed to export most of its energy through Russian pipelines by extracting a higher price for Kazakh gas to be exported to Europe.[22]

Geopolitics and Energy

The Central Asia-Caucasus region is important from energy point of view. In the Caucasus, Azerbaijan has enormous oil and gas resources. In Central Asia, three out of five countries have huge gas and oil reserves, of which Kazakhstan and Turkmenistan are Caspian states. As a result, the Central Asia-Caucasus region has been a theatre for intense American engagement.

Taking energy to Europe has been traditionally through Russian pipelines. But the neo-containment strategy, that began in the post-Cold War period with NATO decision to expand to former Soviet sphere of influence including the Baltic republics of the former USSR and intended expansion to Georgia and Ukraine, could not be effective if Russia controls the supply lines. That is why the US decided to open a new pipeline (BTC) to the Black Sea from the Caspian coastal city of Baku in Azerbaijan through Georgia. It required the very two states—Azerbaijan and Georgia—aggrieved with Russia to give shape to the new pipeline.

Taking energy to the West, by passing Russia is not only expensive but required shaping the geopolitics of the regions involved. Geographically, these land locked countries share borders with larger markets and countries which can provide access to the sea. Azerbaijan and Turkmenistan are next to Iran and can use the Gulf ports of Iran, through either pipelines or swap arrangements. Kazakhstan is on the border of Russia and China. Russia already takes away bulk of Kazakh gas. China has recently built a pipeline to Kazakhstan. The only way some of these countries could be persuaded was to draw them close to the US orbit and away from Russia. Though for a brief period Uzbekistan was wooed, but Caucasus proved to be more conducive for the US geopolitical moves, given the existing fault lines in the region and Russia's strained relations with some of the states there.

The same factor was used to create even a regional security grouping in 1999 called GUAM (which included Georgia, Ukraine, Azerbaijan and Moldova). Since the BTC pipeline is long and through a difficult terrain, the viability of the route would depend on continuous and increase supply of energy through it. Given the fact that Russia has been aggressively pursuing its energy diplomacy, the West could protect its own interests in the region by strong control of the ruling establishment. The change of regime in Georgia through the so called 'Rose Revolution' has to be understood in this back ground.

In this tug of war between two global powers— Russian and the USA— the newly independent states of Eurasia have found themselves lured or coerced to tilt to this side or the other. The game is Zero Sum. Gain by one power is perceived as a loss for the other. While Russia picks up more stakes in the region, the US is making efforts to bring these states into its sphere of influence by a more subtle method, creating non-governmental networks to effect regime change. The successful regime changes in Georgia, Ukraine and Kyrgyzstan were as much a result of internal discontent as of external manoeuvrings.

As a pro-US regime in Georgia strongly pushes for NATO membership, Russia-Georgia relations deteriorated so much that there was a war between them in August 2008. Some of the frozen conflicts have come to life again.

The involvement of external powers has complicated the inter-state as well as internal disputes making their resolution even more difficult. There is greater militarisation in Central Asian and Caucasus than there was at the time of independence. Foreign military bases and alliances have sprung up. Spending on defence and acquisition of weapons have grown, when the economies are yet to fully recover from the post-Soviet economic hardship.

Conclusion

Energy has emerged as the most important factor that is shaping the geopolitics of Eurasia. The significance of energy is not just for its value as a commodity in short supply in most parts of the world, but due to its role as an instrument to advance the strategic goals of global and regional powers in the Eurasian space. Such has been the game that those who cannot play it in strategic terms and look to the region merely as a source of oil and gas are bound to become marginal beneficiaries of the energy wealth of Eurasia. Energy is part of a larger strategic competition between the two main players— Russia and the USA—with some regional powers playing second fiddle in the process. Energy has been the legitimising factor that hides the real strategic games. The seeming gains to the energy producing and transit countries of Eurasia are a charade. These states are being used as pawns and the benefits from being on either side of the super-power divide are short-term. In reality some of the shorter routes to world markets and access to nearby large markets in South and North-East Asia have so far remained exclusive to the energy-producing states. The Eurasian region has witnessed greater militarisation and conflicts as a consequence of great power rivalry. In the quest for strategic gains, all possible instruments from energy diplomacy to regime change and deployment of troops and bases have been deployed. This has brought greater instability to the Eurasian region.

Notes

1. Aurel Braun, "Enlargement and the Perils of Containment", in Aurel Braun (ed.), *NATO-Russia Relations in the Twenty-First Century*, Routledge, London, p.63.
2. The US is reportedly wooing Uzbekistan following the decision by Kyrgyzstan to close the Manas airbase. Both countries have reached agreement on the use of Navoi airport for commercial transit of non-combatant American cargoes to Afghanistan. Alexander Shustov, "Uzbekistan: A turn to the West?, *Strategic Culture Foundation*, 15.6.2009 (Online).
3. F. William Engdahl, "Color Revolutions, Geopolitics and the Baku Pipeline" *Global Research*, June 25, 2005 http://www.globalresearch.ca/index.php?context=va&aid =518
4. R. Hrair Dekmejian and Hovan H. Simonian, *Troubled Waters: The Geopolitics of the Caspian Region*, I.B. Tauris, London, 2001, p. 134; S. Neil Macfarlane, "The United States and regionalism in Central Asia", *International Affairs*, Vol.80, No.3, May 2004, p.450
5. Stephen Blank, "The United States and Central Asia", *Journal of International Affairs*, Vol.56, No.2, Spring 2003, p.136
6. Engdahl, Ibid.
7. Heidi Kjaernet, "The Energy Dimension of Azerbaijani-Russian Relations: Maneuvering for Nagorno-Karabakh, *Russian Analytical Digest*, No. 56, 3 March 2009 (Online)
8. Ibid.
9. *RFE/RL Central Asia Report*, Vol.4, no.30, 10 August 2004
10. Heidi Kjaernet, "The energy Dimension of Azerbaijani-Russian Relations: Maneuvering for Nagorno-Karabakh, *Russian Analytical Digest*, No. 56, 3 March 2009 (Online)
11. Heidi Kjaernet, "The energy Dimension of Azerbaijani-Russian Relations: Maneuvering for Nagorno-Karabakh, *Russian Analytical Digest*, No. 56, 3 March 2009 (Online)

12. Turkmenistan produced 72 bcm in 2007. The same year Uzbekistan produced 65 bcm and Kazakhstan 13 bcm. But while Turkmenistan (5 million population, widespread poverty and lack of industrialisation) can export 75 percent of its gas, Uzbekistan (55 million population) had only 15 bcm and Kazakhstan (15 million population) 2.4 bcm for export. Indra Overland, "Natural Gas and Russia-Turkmenistan Relations", *Russian Analytical Digest*, No. 56, 3 March 2009, pp.9-21 (Online)
13. From paying Turkmenistan $65 in 2006 and $130 in 2008 per 1000 cubic mts of gas, Russia agreed to pay $350 for the same amount in 2009 during the first quarter of 2009. Indra Overland, Ibid; also, http://www.eurasianet.org/departments/news/articles/eav062609b.shtml
14. *RFE/RL Central Asia Report*, Vol.4, no.30, 10 August 2004
15. The Turkmenistan-China pipeline would cover188 km in Turkmenistan, 530 km in Uzbekistan, 1,300 km in Kazakhstan and 4,500 km in China. Indra Overland, Ibid.
16. The Nord Stream gas pipeline – or the North European Gas pipeline – was signed between Germany and Russia on 18 September 2005. This pipeline will allow Gazprom to deliver gas from Vyborg directly to Greifswald on the north-eastern coast of Germany through a 917 km line, the first trunk l ine of which is scheduled to be completed in 2010 with a capacity of 27 bcm. The gas can also be transported to France and the UK. The second phase of the line will take gas to Sweden and Russian enclave of Kaliningrad and the total amount could rise to 55 bcm. annually. Gazprom would have 51 percent stake in this project of $ 6-10 billion and the rest being shared equally between BASF Wintershall and E.On Ruhrgas of Germany. The pipeline would bypass transit countries like Balitc states and would be under the Baltic Sea.
    Kirsten Westphal, "Germany and the EU-Russia Energy Dialogue" in Pami Aalto (ed.) *The EU-Russian Energy Dialogue*, Ashgate, Aldershot, 2008, p. 107.
17. *Eurasianet.org*, 14 March 2008 (Online)
18. Margarita M. Balmaceda, *Energy dependency, politics and corruption in the former Soviet Union*, Routledge, London and New York, 2008, p. 73.
19. Ibid., p. 120.
20. Ibid. pp. 125-136, 137, 143-144.
21. Pavel K. Baev, *Russian Energy Policy and Military Power*, Routledge, London, 2008, pp. 133-137.
22. Ibid., pp. 137-138.

Belarus between the West and the East in the Context of Globalisation

Viachaslau Menkouski

The Republic of Belarus is involved today in the process of globalisation. Belarus borders Russia to the north and east, Ukraine to the south, Poland to the west and Lithuania and Latvia to the north. Following the collapse of the Soviet Union, Belarus declared independence in 1991. Since 1996, Belarus has been negotiating with Russia to merge into a state union called the Union of Russia and Belarus, but as of now Belarus is an independent state. And I hope it will continue to remain so.

Most of Belarus' population (approximately 10 million people) reside in the urban areas surrounding state's capital city of Minsk and other regional centres. Like many other European countries, Belarus has a negative population growth. More than 80 % of the population is native Belarusians, with sizable minorities of Russians, Ukrainians and Poles. Since a referendum in 1995, the country has had two official languages: Belarusian and Russian.

Belarus was a founder member of the Commonwealth of Independent States (CIS). In addition to the CIS, it has the membership in the Eurasian Economic Community (EEC) and the Collective Security Treaty Organisation (CSTO). Belarus has been a member of the International Non-Aligned Movement since 1998 and a member of the United Nations since its foundation in 1945. Belarus has been participating in the NATO Individual Partnership Programme since 1997. The official stand of Foreign Affairs Ministry is that 'activity with governments and international organisations on a multilateral ground, involvement in activity of international organisations and associations are today of major compounding exterior policies of our state'.

Russia is the largest trading partner of Belarus, accounting for nearly half of the total trade. The European Union is the next largest trading partner, with nearly a third of foreign trade. The Republic of Belarus is situated in the centre of Europe. The shortest transport communications connecting the CIS countries with the states of West Europe are laid within its territory.

Belarus between the East and the West

The geopolitical specific features of Belarus' position are connected with its location on the boundary of East Slavic and West European civilisations. The territory of Belarus was always perceived by its neighbours as well as local residents as a cultural border zone which frequently faced the different interests of the neighbouring people. For Poland, the Belarusian land was 'the Eastern Frontier', and for Russia and the Soviet Union, Belarus served as the 'Western Gate'. From here is the present definition of Belarusians by the neighbouring states, which depends of on their own geopolitical interests. They define Belarus as a nation focused on the West to rapprochement with the European Union, or as a nearest ally of present Russia to be merged into it. The Belarusians themselves do not consider the boundary position as a problem, considering it as the natural advantage for a variety of cultural and economic relations with neighbours. Belarus essentially defends the idea of good-neighbourhood and does not consider any state as a potential opponent.

It would be desirable to notice, that many modern Belarus scientists, recognising the relevancy of globalisation factors, nevertheless, consider that the internal factors make a dominating impact on the transformation of basic values of Byelorussians and their social and cultural identity. From this point of view, the key factor in post-Soviet transformation of basic values as well as social and cultural identity of Belarusian population, which defines its modern condition and prospects on the near future, is the unique Soviet social, cultural and political heritage. This heritage can be considered as the factor connected with former integration of Soviet republics which exists up to present. With a big share of probability, it is possible to assert that the Soviet stereotypes of mass consciousness, former values and life representations remain in Belarus in a large volume as compared to many others post-Soviet republics.

Arguments of Globalisation Supporters

Globalisation is a blessing, the optimum form for the further development of human civilisation. The fundamental proof of globalisation utility is the undisputable fact that trading and financial communications between various countries become stronger, the borders disappear and the migration in field of labour, technology and finances accrues. Linguistic and cultural systems for reduction of communicative difficulties are unifying. Globalisation brings the big benefit, both to small and middle business as well as to the hired workers of all countries.

If Belarus refuses globalising processes, it inevitably will appear on a roadside. The intellectual elite will be compelled to leave the country and integrate into a foreign society. Belarus will not have resources to buy modern technologies. The quality of life will be much lower than in that of developed countries.

Arguments of Globalisation Opponents

The position of globalisation opponents can be defined in the terms of 'the plot theory'. They consider that there is an arrangement of small group of superrich people, the companies and the countries which try to establish a new order in the world, to divide people into three or four 'economic grades' and strongly strengthen the exploitation mechanism. Globalisation conducts definitive stratification in developed and developing countries. It is a new form of the world war which the West, led by the USA, is conducting for an establishment of a uniform world order.

If Belarus is involved in globalising processes, the financial position of the overwhelming majority of population will sharply worsen. The rich will become even richer, and poor even poorer. Belarus will lose its independence. The international economic organisations will substitute the national government. Thus globalisation will lead to infringement upon fundamental rights and freedom of the person.

Considering the Belarusian-Russian relations, the Russian political scientist A. Dugin wrote that at the moment of wreckage of the USSR, it was accepted that the globalisation which has come instead of 'the Iron Curtain' will bring us the blessings of the Western civilisation. However, the satiation of these 'blessings' has given a boomerang effect, and there have already been talks about the Western colonisation, threat to the sovereignty. The Statement of A. Dugin 'What is globalisation and how to struggle with it?'[1] is very significant. He relates Belarus to a number of countries resisting the single-polar globalisation model.

Supporters of the Western Orientation in Belarus

At present the groups interested in European integration are small in Belarus. Supporters of European idea are basically representatives of intellectuals. The insufficient interest of wide strata of Byelorussians in orientation to the West European model is connected, first of all, with existing non-liberal economic system in which the State is the basic owner of production means as well as employer. In such conditions, people are afraid that with a change in economic model, they can lose their source of existence, which though not too rich is stable.

An interesting example for the analysis of potential «movement on the West» is the collection *The European Prospect of Belarus: Intellectual Models–Vilnius 2007*[2]. The Belarusian researchers consider that the growth in popularity of Europeanisation idea will be possible when: 1) potential advantages to citizens caused by introduction into the European Union will be perceived as exceeding potential losses; 2) the speed and the scale of transformations will promise bonuses fast enough; 3) the rules of transition will be feasible and clear to the majority of citizens; 4) the transition process itself will solve some of internal macroeconomic problems.

Of course, the situation in Belarus is in many respects dependent on the Russian influence.

Supporters of Eastern Orientation of Belarus

For the last few years, the Belarusian-Russian relations have been one of the brightest phenomena in the development of integration processes on the post-Soviet territory. Political, economic, military cooperation, rapprochement in other spheres, plans for creation of the Allied State have put forward the Belarus-Russian component on the first place in the Commonwealth of Independent States (CIS).

According to Belarus researcher A. Russakovich [3], the following factors actively influence the condition and prospects of integration association with participation of Belarus and Russia: 1) the approach of the European Union directly to borders of Belarus and Russia; 2) ability of Russia to carry out the plans providing participation of Commonwealth countries in security system led by Russia; 3) the success of economic component in integration projects.

It is necessary to notice that the CIS has undergone considerable transformation during the years of its existence. The basic impulse for its creation proceeded from leaders of Belarus, Russia and Ukraine. The basic directions of the CIS activity was: coordination of foreign policy, realisation of the uniform control over nuclear weapons, cooperation in formation and development of common economic space as well as systems of transport and communications, environment protection, coordination of immigration policy, struggle against the organised crime and interactions in other spheres. During the initial years of its existence, the CIS has executed its function for international legal registration of the USSR disintegration and has further turned into some kind of consulting club, in essence.

One aspect connected with the reflexion of the problem of modern integration processes between Russia and Belarus is public Belarusian opinion. Remarks professor V. Shadursky[4], on the basis of polls, it is possible to draw the following conclusions: 1) the majority of Belarusian citizens support the political course for close interaction with Russia; 2) according to public opinion, the course for cooperation between Belarus and Russia has its limits; 3) the majority of Belarusian citizens (more than 70 %) wish that their country stay an independent state. For a considerable part of the Russian society and its elite, this situation is a test. It is necessary to make efforts and to recognise the existence of friendly sovereign Belarus and Belarusian nation, related but nevertheless separate.

When participating in interrogations, Belarusians were given the choice to opt for 'Integration with Russia' or 'Introduction into the European Union'. Equal number of respondents opted for Russia and EU (on various interrogations). Generally the integration into EU is supported by citizens of Belarus who are younger than 40 years, having secondary special and higher education, working in private business, urban inhabitants.

It is necessary to notice that high level of liking for the western vector of integration exists among Belarusians in the condition when the official propaganda for introduction into EU is not conducted in Belarus. On the contrary, analysing the European integration, the number of mass media makes the main emphasis very frequently on existing problems and difficulties rather than on successes and advantages. Europe is attractive on a number of indicators, first of all on a high standard of living. In the choice between 'the improvement of economic situation' and 'the independence of Belarus', the first option was chosen by more than 60 % of respondents.

Position of the Belarusian State towards Globalisation

We will analyse an official state position of Belarus, first of all, on the basis of the performance of the President of Byelorussia A. Lukashenko. First of all, I will pay attention to the performance in the United Nations Assembly (September 2005)[5]. A. Lukashenko defined the following basic positions: 1) the world today is unipolar, with all the following negative consequences; 2) Belarus, according to the United Nations, belongs to the developed countries with a high level of human development; 3) Belarus wants not much from the planet: the peace and stability, the rest we'll create ourselves; 4) there are no internal conflicts in Belarus, and we do not create problems for neighbours, we do not dispute, either for their territory or for their choice of the way of development; 5) the variety of ways to progress is an eternal value of our civilisation, and the freedom in choosing the way of development is a main condition for the world democratic arrangement.

Substantive provisions of mutual relations on the post-Soviet territory can be tracked to the Presidential performance at the international forum *the Eurasian Integration: Trends of Modern Development and Globalisation Calls* (Astana, 18 June 2004)[6]. The basic theses: 1) in the modern world, the economic integration dominates all points and planet regions; 2) the stimulation of cooperation of the former Soviet Union people is dictated objectively by requirements of simple people as well as the historical traditions and coherence of our economies; 3) the union of Belarus and Russia is an example of cooperation between the two countries people's interests; 4) the major mission of Euro-Asian Economic Community (EuroAsEC) is to prepare for a occurrence in global world trading system.

As per the estimation of the West European vector in Belarusian foreign policy, the head of our state has reminded that economic relations of Belarus with the Western Europe is in the stage of development for the withdrawal of lasting trade barriers. 'And as to the policy, I am convinced that in due course Europe will realise that it cannot keep the proper life without Belarus, which is the European heart'.

Conclusion

Globalisation is an objective, a natural historical process conducted to speed up the move of society and state due to the usage of new transport, communication and information know-how; for reduction of room and time of the sectioning people. In these conditions, the civilisation is exhibited in new quality and with new capabilities for progressing.

Tendering new capabilities, globalisation at the same time has failed to resolve global problems of the mankind such as increasing poverty, economical, demographic and ecological imbalance. The efforts of all countries in the world are indispensable for the solution of these problems.

Many problems, existing in the modern world, cannot be decided by one or several countries separately from global community. For this purpose, there has to exist a multilateral mechanism for solving global problems. It will provide equal rights for all countries, without depending on their size and location.

The major features of Belarusian situation in the conditions of offensive globalisation are its integrated approach and complexity:

- Today civilisation feature can be defined as a boundary between the East Slavic and the West European models;
- In the modern Belarus society, both tendencies: the centripetal (national Revival) and the centrifugal (integration with the stronger neighbour) are present simultaneously;
- The Belarusian state, considering geopolitical as well as social and cultural realities spends the multivector foreign policy directed on an establishment of mutually advantageous relations with the West and the East;
- At the moment, the Belarusian state and society are in condition of civilisational choice which has essentially a great value for the future of Belarus.

Notes

1. Available from http://evrazia.info/modules.php?name=News&file=article&sid=392.
2. Available from http://www.ehu.lt/publishers/publications/scientific/0009025/.
3. Available from http://soyz-2004.narod.ru/rusakovich/.
4. Available from http://soyz-2004.narod.ru/shadurskiy/.
5. Available from http://worldcrisis.ru/crisis/161302.
6. Available from http://www.president.gov.by/press18723.html.

Global Stability with 'American Face': Problem or Solution for Central Asia?

Alexey S. Dundich

On September 11, 2001 American cities New York and Washington were attacked by terrorists. It was a shock for USA and for the rest of the world. After 9/11, American anti-terrorist politics was systematised in the conception of 'War on terror'. In 2002, US President George Bush issued 'The National Security Strategy of the United States of America', an annual report, to Congress. In this document, the President had showed an assertion that USA had the right for pre-emptive strike on American enemies and declared the war, together with American 'allies and friends', on all terrorist organisations, groups and persons[1]. Under the aegis of stability conception, two long-term wars have been launched by the USA: war in Iraq and war in Afghanistan. Countries belonging to Axis of Evil were defined. Anti-terror coalition, led by USA, became an instrument of new international stability order type, set instead of nuclear strategic stability of bipolar world. New threat of Islamic terrorism and danger of nuclear proliferation has kept many countries united under US leadership in the face of security issues.

US Presence in Central Asia

After the dissolution of the Soviet Union, post-Soviet Central Asia (CA) was a low priority region for US foreign policy. Senator Alan Cranston mentioned in his report to the Committee on Foreign Relations, "Central Asia is remote, economically backward and ethnically doesn't bind with America. Thus, US foreign policy in post-Soviet area should be concentrated on new democratic Russia. However, Central Asia should not be ignored due to the presence of natural resources". He also said, that US has a 'strong interest' in avoiding chaos in this area and in Kazakhstan's nuclear power conservation. Another goal of Washington in Central Asia, according to Senator Cranston, is to promote a model of American democracy as an example for the CA countries and not to promote the model of another country[2].

The global superpower, which has been having sustainable interests in the region, has gained a big influence here during 1990s and has gradually made a big part of post-Soviet 'allies vacuum'. CA gained more international attention in the middle of 1990s when 'Taliban' control over the Afghan territory was spreading. International actors like Russia, China and the EU, the USA were concerned about the challenges and threats to the stability in the post-Soviet region—Islamic extremism, interethnic conflicts, narcotic traffic and arms traffic.

Negative development of the situation in Afghanistan forced CA countries to count on American political and military support, while traditional Russian military assistance could not always be obtained on time. In the beginning of 1999 Uzbekistan dropped out of the Collective Security Treaty Organisation (CSTO), led by Russia, and became a member of the US supervised GUUAM Organisation (Georgia, Ukraine, Uzbekistan, Azerbaijan, Moldova). The Taliban activity near the Uzbekistan border compelled this country to look for reliable help. In these kind of circumstances, Uzbekistan became the main US partner in the region.

We could see the elements of US oriented security system forming during the so called Batken Events. At the time of Islamic Movement in Uzbekistan, there was large scale militants' invasion in Kyrgyzstan, the country was in a very difficult situation and used to look for international assistance from elsewhere in the world. Kyrgyzstan was forced to ask US for jeep cars, uniform, communication equipment, medical supplies, buses, military mountain equipment within the framework of US Foreign Military Financing Program (FMF)[3]. It created a good opportunity for US to do a favour to Kyrgyzstan in connection with its own interests.

Almost two decades after the collapse of the USSR, the American policy in the region has been developed irregularly. At the time of independence of regional countries, US priorities here have changed several times. Every change reflected the intensity of American participation in regional deals. The strongest impulse at increasing the presence of US in CA was exerted by anti-terrorist operations in Afghanistan, following the terrorist attacks on New York City and Washington DC in September 2001. In 2001–2002, CA region became a strategically important territory for support of Afghan operation.

In this period it was important for Washington to achieve an agreement with CA government for deployment of the anti-Taliban coalition military bases in CA. USA had negotiated with Kyrgyzstan and Uzbekistan about the deployment of airbases on their territory. 'Gansi' airbase was deployed in 'Manas' airport near the Bishkek in December 2001. It had more than 1000 military staff. In Uzbekistan, the Kharshi-Khanabad base was created, where about 1.5 thousand soldiers were deployed. During a visit of Uzbekistan's President I. Karimov to Washington DC, the Declaration on Strategic Cooperation between US and Uzbekistan was signed.

At the time of preparing and conducting the anti-Taliban operations in Afghanistan, other dimensions, which earlier and later influenced the American foreign policy in the region, were 'put on back burners' in order to organize airbases for supporting operations in Afghanistan. However, after an intermediate victory over Taliban forces in 2002-2003, Washington started to be guided by other factors. First of all, USA resumed strong critique of Uzbekistan government for undemocratic ways of country governance. In 2004, US put the responsibility for terrorist attacks in Tashkent and other Uzbek cities on Uzbek government. From Washington's point of view, it didn't give enough opportunities to opposition for an open and legal expression of their own view, forcing oppositionists to use illegal and extremist methods in struggle for power. The result of this policy was the cold US-Uzbekistan relations.

As any nation-state, USA proceeds from the requirements of national interests. In this case, these interests consist in reaching a security situation in the region and eliminating threats to security. But, strong American civil society compels American government to act according to national democracy ideals, sometime notwithstanding national interests. According to Sergei Glebov, researcher from Smith College (MA, USA), idealism on the one hand and realism on the other hand are creating a contradiction in US foreign policy[4].

The crisis happened between Washington and Tashkent because there was a difference in assessment of reasons and circumstances of Andijan unrest suppression by Uzbek government in May 2005. American administration criticised President I. Karimov for 'disproportional reaction'. In response, Tashkent and a number of other CIS countries suggested to USA to define terms of American military presence on CA bases. Then, in July 2005, Uzbekistan demanded the withdrawal of the Kharshi-Khanabad base within 6 months. At the end of 2005, American troops were withdrawn from Uzbekistan. On November 14, 2005 the Uzbekistan-Russia Ally Relations Treaty was signed.

At the end of 2000 for Washington especially CA resources were attractive for restoring Afghan economy, where situation still remains far away from stability. Role of countries which are located on the north of Afghanistan, according to American idea, consist in establishing strong trade and economic, transport, diplomatic links in the framework of 'Grand Central Asia' building, in which American specialists include Afghanistan and post-Soviet CA republics. One of the American policy ideas, according to Secretary of State Assistant in Central and South Asia R. Boucher, is to see in Afghanistan, a bridge between Central and South Asia[5]. So, Afghani neighbours must have an impact on stabilisation and economic progress in this country.

After the expiration of Tajik-Afghan border surveillance by Russian troops, the USA activated its aid to Tajikistan for border strengthening. USA also had negotiations with Turkmen government about the possibility to use aerodromes on Turkmen territory for supporting military operations in Afghanistan. These negotiations turned more active after the death of Turkmenistan's President S. Niyazov (December 2006), with his successor G. Berdymuhammedov.

NATO Activity in Central Asia

Since the appearance of New Independent States in Central Asia, NATO has become one of the American policy and American Global Stability Order tools in the region[6]. NATO security map in Central Asia was constructed on bilateral basis with states of the region; exclude such organisations like *Shanghai Cooperation Organisation* (SCO) and *Collective Security Treaty Organisation* (CSTO).

The most prospective participant of NATO programmes in the region seems to be Kazakhstan. In 1994 Kazakhstan joined 'Partnership for Peace' (PfP) and participated in training manoeuvres of Central Asian Peacekeeping Battalion (CENTRASBAT) under the aegis of NATO. In 2004 USA and Kazakhstan signed a treaty on military cooperation for 5 years. The main purpose of American-Kazakh agreement was to develop the infrastructure in the western regions of Kazakhstan and to strengthen Kazakh navy on the Caspian Sea. In return, Kazakhstan suggested the option of US air forces to use bases in Taras, Semey and Shymkent.

In January 2006 Kazakhstan and NATO signed the *Individual Partnership* Action *Plan. So, Kazakhstan became the first country which signed such a plan. It had included Kazakh military specialists' preparation by NATO specialists, guard border surveillance cooperation.*

Kyrgyzstan had no active cooperation with NATO until 2001, when the base of anti-Taliban coalition was deployed here. The lease of this base was reconsidered several times for an increase.

In 2001 Tajikistan became a participant of PfP programme. Tajikistan provided American air forces the possibility of using airdromes in Kulab (south of country), Kurgan-Tube (south of country) and Khujand (north of country). The main dimension of NATO-Tajikistan interrelation became a traffic in narcotic drugs problem.

Neutral Turkmenistan practically did not participate in NATO activities.

Energy Resources Factor

Energy resources factor was important for formulating US national interests in Central Asia. Prospects of using Central Asian oil and gas are intensively discussed by American researchers.

Thus, R. Cullen in his article 'Central Asia and the West' pays attention to such problems like the possibility of CA oil transportation to the West, using high technologies in the Caspian area and financing oil production, minimisation of Iran participation in oil transportation from Central Asia[7]. Pakistani journalist Akhmed Rashid claimed that the only goal of geopolitical game is to gain control over the oil resources[8].

According to official American position, the first priority of US contemporary interest in Central Asia is to weaken Russian energy resources control in the region. The official US task is to make their strategic ally Europe to feel more comfortable. According to M. Bryza, the US task is to diversify, diversify, diversify… [9]. At the same time, USA, getting oil from Persian Gulf states, can consider Central Asia as a reserve energy source. Stability in the region is important also because of the impact of different factors on the growth of global oil prices.

There are within CA researchers who view of the American policy in the region through a prism of energy determinism. Though, Kazakh researcher N. Aytmakhanov believes that USA appears in the different regions of the world following oil and, as a consequence, in some way is involved in all conflicts which have happened because of oil. According to his opinion, the Caspian region after the collapse of the USSR became one of the prior dimensions of American foreign policy due to energy resources reserves[10]. However, some part of American academic elite took cautious position in their way of penetration to CA. Harvard Professor Boris Rumer pointed priority relations with Russia for US as compared with CA countries and suggested that Russia should not be annoyed by the US activity in the region. As an advantage of American domination in this region, he named the achievement of short-term stability, access to energy resources and possibility to use CA Republics for supporting military actions in Afghanistan. But, he emphases attention of US government on the misuse of American domination, such as concentration of reasons of future instability in case of authoritarian regimes support. So, Rumer suggests creating a 'joint venture' with Russia, such as the 'Russian-American consortium for social economic development in Central Asia' for jointly solving the regional problems[11].

Bringing American stability to the region created some problems for regional development like:

War against terror has been going on in Afghanistan since 2001, but Afghanistan is still a source of instability. Moreover, its neighbours, Pakistan and Tajikistan have problems with militant insurgence and overwhelming narcotic drugs trafficking. CA countries are facing growing narcotic drugs trafficking and the still existing and spreading extremist Islam movement under the 'success cover'.

Coalition's military presençe in CA countries, the beginning of which was defined in Central Asia during The War in Afghanistan, had ambivalent consequences. Thus, Uzbekistan closed base in Khanabad after Andijan events, Kyrgyzstan has constant and sharp discussions inside its own civil society about 'Gansi' base and all countries are forced to keep in mind the Russian reaction to their every step towards America (negative rather than indifferent). In fact, Russia won in Russian-American collision in Uzbekistan after Andijan events; however Uzbekistan, still following its own special course, now taking steps to woo USA.

Interrelations between Afghanistan, Shanghai Cooperation Organisation (SCO) and Collective Security Treaty Organisation (CSTO), which arc lcd by China and Russia, can be strengthened. During the 'Afghanistan, SCO, Security and Geopolitics in Central Asia International Conference' (Kyrgyzstan, June 2008), participants mentioned that international command in Afghanistan practically led the operation to a dead-end. In particular, German Professor Lapins stressed on the discussion on contradictions between American command on the one hand and German and French command on the other hand.

Contemporary NATO policy in CA and US-CA countries bilateral agreements is an attempt to restrict SCO and CSTO influence in the region

Contemporary situation around the Iran nuclear programme and the US blockade of Iran's external economic relations (especially in energy sphere) can lead to unpredictable scenario as well.

One of the undisclosed priorities of Washington policy in CA can be the creation of counterbalance here between China and Russia, both in the regional and at the global scale. So US tries to keep the minimal military and diplomatic influence on border countries; a new practical realisation of H. Mackinder and N. Spikeman geopolitical theories. On the other hand, due to bases in Iraq, Afghanistan, Caucasus and CA Countries, US can be in full control of the Persian Gulf and Caspian Sea hydrocarbon resources and the possible deteriorating of Iran scenario.

The US wish to diversify energy transit through Nabucco and BTC and undermining Russia's and Iran's energy positions can create another source of instability

Kazakhstan is the most reliable partner for US and Russia and is also a gate for Russia to the region; so US led development of the infrastructure in the western regions of Kazakhstan and strengthening Kazakh navy on the Caspian Sea can be a cause of negative reaction of neighbour countries.

Central Asian and other post-Soviet countries take the anti-terror coalition, American military help with enthusiasm. On the other hand, American politics in the region threatens to make new cracks on the regional stability map.

Notes

1. The White House. George W. Bush. *The National Security Strategy of the United States of America.* http://www.whitehouse.gov/nsc/nssall.html
2. Alan Cranston, *Central Asia in Transition*, Washington: US Government Printing Office, 1992.
3. Letter to Military Attaché of US Embassy in Kyrgyz Republic Charles Squires from Kyrgyz Republic Ministry of Defense N10/109 by May 5, 1999, in Archive of Ministry of Defense of Kyrgyz Republic.

   The FMF Program is a US Government Program, which was created for ensuring America's security. It includes financing through grants or loans the acquisition of U.S. military articles, services, and training, supports U.S. regional stability goals and enables US friends and allies to improve their defense capabilities. So, FMF helps countries meet their legitimate defense needs, promotes U.S. national security interests by strengthening coalitions with friends and allies, cements cooperative bilateral military relationships, and enhances interoperability with U.S. forces. Because FMF monies are used to purchase U.S. military equipment and training, FMF contributes to a strong U.S. defense industrial base, which benefits both America's armed forces and American workers. Site of the Defense Security Cooperation Agency, www.dsca.mil/home/foreign_military_financing%20_program.htm
4. *Rice: Kazakhstan is not Russian zone of influence.*Rengo.ru News http://news.rengo.ru/russia/news8336/ 06.10.2008

5. Richard Boucher, *"US Foreign Policy Toward South Asia"*, Report in SAIS, Johns Hopkins University, Washington DC, USA, September 20, 2007.
6. According to NATO secretary general Jap de Hoop Scheffer, NATO is the "League of nations" without US. Meeting with students of American University in Central Asia (AUCA) and OSCE Academy. Bishkek, Kyrgyzstan, 2004.
7. Robert Cullen, "Central Asia and the West", in Central Asia and the World, edited by M. Mondelbaum. New York: Council on Foreign Relations Press, 1994, pp. 130-146
8. Ahmed Rashid, *Jihad. The Rise of Militant Islam in Central Asia*, New Heaven, London: Yale University Press, 2003.
9. Mathew Bryza, Lection *Russian Energy as a Foreign Policy Tool*. Report in SAIS, Johns Hopkins University. Washington DC, USA. February 6, 2008.
10. Nurlan Aitmakhanov, *The US Policy in Central Asia: Oil Security Problem,* in Politicheskaya Systema i Voprosy demokratizacii v stranah Centralnoi Asii (Political System and Questions of democratization in Central Asian Countries). Almaty, 2005. pp.124-138
11. Boris Rumer, *The Search for Stability in Central Asia*, in Central Asia: A gathering Storm?, edited by B. Rumer. New York: M.E.Sharp, 2002. pp. 61-62

Nuclear Crises in the Realm of Eurasian Security: The Iranian Crises and Future of NPT

Nurşin Ateşoğlu GÜNEY

Introduction

Though the focal point of this paper is not the Eurasian security realm, the NPT security regime is now in question as the Iranian nuclear issue has become a question of global significance. One can of course question this kind of upside-down approach but the fact remains that the link between Eurasian security and global security on the one hand and Middle Eastern security on the other has intensified. Thus, the Iranian nuclear crisis and the international community's approach in dealing with the situation is crucial as it has the potential of affecting the stability in Eurasia, including the nuclear and non-nuclear individual members of this region. Actually, we can read the attempts at building nuclear weapon-free zone in Central Asia[1] under the shadow of Iranian nuclear crisis as a positive attempt to prevent Eurasian security issues becoming a quasi-Middle Eastern crisis.

Is the Iranian Nuclear Crisis a Real Challenge in Determining the Future of the NPT Regime in the 21st Century?

The current row between the Western powers and Iran, especially after the second half of 2002, is due to the revelation, as a result of an IAEA investigation, of the existence of two secret Iranian nuclear facilities, one being a heavy-water nuclear power reactor near Arak, the other being a gas centrifuge uranium enrichment facility near Natanz[2]. Furthermore, the agency's follow up investigations in Iran made possible the discovery of a series of clandestine nuclear activities, of which some are reported to be in violation of Tehran's safeguarding agreement. Since then, the two sides have been engaged in a controversial dispute[3]over the question of whether Iran is pursuing a clandestine nuclear programme under the shadow of NPT or not. Tehran claims to be pursuing its legal right of developing nuclear energy for civilian purposes, a right that is entitled for state parties of non-nuclear power states in article 4 of the NPT treaty.[4] The issue has led to a deadlock between the two sides, a deadlock which is be due to several factors; first and foremost, it is inextricably linked to the loophole embedded in the NPT treaty itself, to what many now call the 'Article IV loophole'.[5] However the other factor is what is seen as Tehran administration's continuing reluctance to cooperate with the IAEA's call for further transparency, which of course obliges the Iranian government to answer to accusations and questions regarding its suspected nuclear weapons facilities.[6] At present, the current situation and the manner in which it is resolved will create a precedent for other (non-nuclear state) parties of the NPT. If in the near future a solution cannot be found, then the future credibility and efficiency of the NPT treaty would be negatively affected. For this reason, in this paper, I will very briefly try to explain how the current stalemate in the Iranian nuclear crisis has the capacity of negatively affecting both regional—in this case, the Eurasian[7] region—as well as global security, not mentioning the future credibility of the NPT regime itself.

The debates between the two proponents of divergent viewpoints on the issue of peaceful nuclear cooperation have been polarised since 2005.[8] In this regard, the first group—the non-proliferation group—draws attention 'to the dangers of the proliferation of uranium enrichment and plutonium reprocessing (ENR) capabilities which produce fissile material on demand for the use of nuclear weapons'.[9] In their view, ENR proliferation currently poses the most important challenge to both the NPT regime itself and to international peace and security in general as, they argue, the world presently abounds with latent and virtual nuclear weapons. Consequently, they defend the notion that the international community should give high priority to the prevention of the further spread of ENP capabilities rather than disarmament through available means of international cooperation. According to this point of view, strengthening of non-proliferation is an unavoidable choice in the face of the challenges facing the whole NPT community. As for those of the converse view, many non-nuclear state parties to the NPT believe that calls for initiatives that aim to strengthen non-proliferation under prevailing conditions are in fact an infringement of their inalienable rights—as stated under Article IV of the NPT treaty—to develop any peaceful use of nuclear technology that they wish to, even if such developments run the risk of legal entanglements with the NPT regime.[10]

These divergences related to Article IV of the NPT have lately increased in significance when the Iranian issue is compared with that of North Korea. Consequently, the international community, being aware of the reality of the loophole that is present in Article IV of the NPT, recently put forward several initiatives that they thought would be helpful in resolving such difficulties, including and perhaps especially the controversial problem of limiting uranium enrichment and plutonium reprocessing (ENR) capabilities. But, thus far, no solution has been reached that is acceptable to both nuclear and non-nuclear weapon state parties.[11] The failure of these initiatives of course is becoming more important in the aftermath of the 5+1 negotiations (where suspension of Iranian enrichment-related and re-processing activities was called for) on the Iranian nuclear issue, which also failed to yield any positive outcome. The Tehran government's negative standpoint since 2005 in this quarrel has certainly not helped refute the claims that Tehran is developing a clandestine nuclear programme in contravention to the safeguard agreement. On the contrary, it has put more pressure than ever on Tehran, which has now become the target of ever increasing accusations in the international arena.

Since its inception, the NPT has relied on the three basic pillars of non-proliferation, disarmament and the peaceful use of nuclear energy. In other words, the Treaty's past and future validity has been and will be directly dependent on how these three pillars are constructed, viewed and developed. Nevertheless, the interdependent relation between these three pillars in reality blocks any chances of progress in either individual case. For instance, the non-nuclear parties to the NPT, knowing that the nuclear powers are not meeting their commitments under Article VI of the Treaty today, are rightfully rejecting further non-proliferation initiatives, convinced that these measures would limit their peaceful uses of energy. These states' reluctance to accept further non-proliferation measures are due to what they see as the existence of double standards on issues relating to nuclear energy. For instance, in some cases non-party states to NPT are exempt from any safeguard agreements despite the fact that they are unacknowledged nuclear actors. Moreover, there are other cases in which some states are exempted from any safeguard agreements but at the same time they are also favoured when looking to purchase nuclear technology from one of the five nuclear countries.

On the way to the 2010 NPT Review Conference, certain efforts were made, either at the preparatory meetings or at certain NGO-based meetings (such as the Middle Powers initiative or FES initiatives), efforts which included published reports, meetings and so forth, at providing a platform for common understanding between nuclear and non-nuclear states on issues relating to disarmament, proliferation and the peaceful use of nuclear energy.[12] Thus far, at the end of these preparatory talks, despite (or as a result of) the existence of different groups of states' declared plans of actions, no concrete agreement has yet materialised.

However, just three years ago, Kofi Annan, at the 2005 NPT Review Conference, made a call for nuclear weapon states to meet their responsibilities by accepting 'further and irreversible reductions in non-strategic nuclear arsenals, reaffirming negative security assurances, in swift negotiating of a missile cut-off treaty, and in maintaining a moratorium on nuclear testing until the entry of the CTBT'[13]. Moreover, 'on the proliferation side, he urged a strengthening of the IAEA's verification machinery through the universal adoption of the Model Additional Protocol and the creation of incentives for states to forego uranium enrichment and plutonium separation capabilities.'[14] The IAEA was then supposed to assume responsibility of guaranteeing the supply of fissile material to civilian nuclear users at market rates. This initiative of Annan's has not been realised due to the collapse of the 2005 Review NPT Conference and the international community is now obliged to accepting the results of this failure.[15]

Due to the absence of a final statement at the end of the 2005 NPT Review Conference, the apparently increased tendency towards (further) nuclear proliferation seems to have become somewhat graver. In this regard, the international community first witnessed both Pakistan and India going nuclear in 1998 and then saw North Korea, after its break up the NPT in 2006, obtain a nuclear capacity; furthermore, the international community has for some time been aware of Israel's possession of some 200 nuclear warheads. After the second half of 2002, Iran's debatable nuclear programme has also become a new concern, not only for the West but also for the non-nuclear states which are party to the NPT. Under the current conditions, one can easily claim that the continuing deadlock in the Iranian nuclear crisis is bringing about an uncertain environment where the acquisition of nuclear weapons becomes less of a taboo for those desiring it for purposes which are uncertain.[16] For this reason, the situation has become an imminent concern on the one hand for those who support various initiatives which give priority to strengthening non-proliferation efforts and, on the other hand, to those states which are signatory to the NPT. Moreover, there are serious residual disarmament concerns related to the nuclear powers' liabilities left over from the previous NPT Review Conferences that are as of yet unfulfilled (such as those from the 1995, 2000 and 2005 Conferences) which may prove to be serious problems for the state signatories to the NPT.[17] In this regard, some of the new national military doctrines that declare the first use of nuclear weapons as well as the ongoing nuclear modernisation programmes carried out by some [18] of the five nuclear powers—including Western powers—have been regarded as further challenges to the current problems of the NPT regime[19]. Likewise, the US-Indian nuclear deal has also created similar concerns among states which are party to the NPT and which have already signed safeguard agreements. A host of further examples can be enumerated.

All in all, these examples, reflecting certain notions of 'double standards' in the implication of mechanisms for non-proliferation, disarmament and the peaceful use of nuclear energy, give rise to complaints by states party to the NPT, which is why it is no real surprise to the world community at large that the NPT today is under severe stress and, due to the existence of the above mentioned unresolved and problematic issues, is about to lose its credibility.

Conclusion

Under the current situation, among the several international efforts at finding solutions to the stalemate of the NPT Treaty, the Middle Powers Initiative (MPI) report published in 2007, entitled 'Towards 2010: Priorities for NPT Consensus',[20] is worth mentioning for its resemblances to Kofi Annan's 2005 recommendations to both nuclear and non-nuclear powers. Unless the two sides of the NPT agreement—namely the five nuclear powers and the non-nuclear states—give equal weight to the implications of the Treaty's mutually interdependent issues of non-proliferation, disarmament and the use of peaceful energy, constantly unfolding problems related to general issues of the NPT (such as the North Korean and Iranian nuclear problems) have the capacity to lead to further crisis and give rise to an erosion of the whole proliferation regime, including a questioning of the credibility of the NPT itself.

However, despite the current weaknesses of the NPT, the international community does not seem to have the luxury of avoiding the Treaty's important role in guaranteeing peace and security conditions of both regional and global security. This situation also holds true for Eurasia which has both nuclear and non-nuclear powers, not all of which are signatory to the NPT. Hence, the issues mentioned so far are, one way or another, related to the Iranian nuclear crisis; the aftermath of this issue and any outcome are likely to have a critical impact on the future security of this vast and important region.

Last but not the least, at this point it is worth mentioning some of the advised current measures which have been revealed just before the 2010 NPT Conference/or predatory talks that are (i) believed to strengthen non-proliferation constraints, and (ii) also believed to have the chance to create greater incentives in speeding up the Treaty's mandate for disarmament. For instance, the MPI in its report titled, 'Towards 2010: Priorities for the NPT Consensus', categorised these priorities as '(1) realisation of the liability of all nuclear powers concerning the verification of reduction of nuclear forces; (2) a de-alerting of the US and Russian Federation's nuclear standoff, which would bring about an end to a Cold War logic that is still seen as valid in some quarters; (3) accomplishment of the negotiation of a Fissile Materials Cut Off Treaty; (4) bringing the Comprehensive Nuclear Test Treaty into force; (5) a strengthening of negative security issues; (6) regulation of (the highly debatable issue of) nuclear production and supply, and finally; (7) good governance of the NPT through accepting stronger institutional capability'.[21]

Nevertheless, despite the existence of different kinds of initiatives which have been instigated either by nuclear or non-nuclear on the NPT, a consensus is yet to be achieved, which is why certain issues, such as Iranian nuclear crisis, become significantly more important in the absence of convergent attitudes on general issues (for example, the future of a possible fissile materials cut off treaty, ratification of the CTBT and such) of the NPT.

Notes

1. The five former Soviet republics committed themselves to never acquiring, manufacturing, possessing, or testing nuclear weapons by signing a treaty to create a Central Asian nuclear-weapon-free zone on September 8, 2006. Central Asia used to house part of the sprawling Soviet nuclear weapons complex. But now Kazakhstan, Kyrgyzstan, Tajikistan, Turkmenistan, and Uzbekistan have broken with this nuclear past by signing the free zone pact at a former Soviet nuclear testing site, Semipalatinsk, Kazakhstan. Negotiations on the agreement started in 1997. The Central Asian zone will be the fifth such arrangement. Countries in Latin America and the Caribbean (Treaty of Tlatelolco), the South Pacific (Treaty of Rarotonga), Southeast Asia (Treaty of Bangkok), and Africa (Treaty of Pelindaba) have also banded together to create nuclear-weapon-free zones. Mongolia has also outlawed nuclear weapons on its territory and all countries are prohibited from stationing nuclear weapons in Antarctica, on the seabed, and in outer space. "Arms Control Association Applauds Central Asian

States for Forswearing Nuclear Arms", *Arms Control Association*, September 8, 2006, http://www.armscontrol.org/pressroom/2006/20060906_CANWFZ, accessed in 2 November 2008.

2. After the revelations of Iran's clandestine nuclear activities, France, Germany, and the United Kingdom launched negotiations with Iran to address international concerns about the intent and scope of its nuclear program. These negotiations collapsed in 2005. Subsequently, the IAEA Board of Governors declared Iran in noncompliance with its safeguards obligations and referred the matter to the UN Security Council. The UN Security Council has adopted three resolutions calling on Iran to suspend its uranium enrichment-related and reprocessing activities. Two resolutions, 1737 and 1747, imposed targeted sanctions in response to Iran's unwillingness to comply with that demand. Still, Iran continues to expand its uranium enrichment program and has not fully disclosed the extent of its illicit nuclear-related activities. In August 2007, Iran agreed to a work plan with the IAEA to resolve a series of outstanding verification issues. See: "Arms Control and Proliferation Profile: Iran", Country Profiles, *Arms Control Association*, January 2008, http://armscontrol.org/factsheets/iranprofile, accessed in 2 November 2008.
3. In the face of this current impasse between IAEI and Iranian government, the agency is now unable to provide credible assurances regarding the Iranian (nuclear) case that there are no undeclared nuclear activities in Iran. See: Peter Crail, "ElBaradei says Iran Stalls IAEA Inquiry", *Arms Control*, Vol.38, October 2008. http://www.armscontrol.org/act/2008_10/IranIAEA, accessed in 2 November 2008.
4. At the end of the recent IAEA Board of Governors' session on Iran, Tehran's IAEA [International Atomic Energy Agency] envoy Ali Asghar Soltaniyeh has said "the meeting has no impact on Iranian nation's determination to benefit from its undeniable rights and mentioned that "they will continue their peaceful nuclear programme". Moreover, in the Soltaniyeh's words one can find "Tehran's clear political and clear message that , [the IAEI's further actions related with Iranian nuclear issue that will come into fore] in the Board of Governors [of the IAEI] or passing resolution will not have any effect on Iran's drive to use its peaceful nuclear energy right." See: Nuclear Envoy Says Iran to Continue Cooperation with UN Agency, BBC Monitoring Middle East. London: November 28, 2008.
5. Tad Daley, "The Nuclear Nonproliferation Treaty Turns 40 Today", http://www.globalsolutions.org/node/1096, accessed in 2 November 2008.
6. For instance; Grigoriy Berdennikov, member of the Board of Governors of the International Atomic Energy Agency, has said to RIA Novosti reports that it was important for "Iran to fully implement safeguards agreement". Further more, he also said that, "Re-application by Iran of the additional protocol to the safeguards

agreement and the implementation of confidence building measures the UN SC and the IAEA BG are calling for would facilitate progress in providing assurance that the declared nuclear material is not being diverted away from civilian activities and that there is no undeclared nuclear material or activity in Iran." See: Russian envoy says Iran nuclear issue could lead to "most serious consequences", *BBC Monitoring Former Soviet Union*, London: November 28, 2008. This view point is also shared by the Westerns in general and most of the international community.

7. "Eurasia" as a geographical concept is very ductile. Many analysts believe that Eurasia has no boundaries Depending on the policy makers' purposes and orientation, "Eurasia" may refer to countries located in what are considered are as being Asia, the Middle East and Europe. Russia is supposed to be in the Eurasian realm. Also, the five ex-Soviet Republics-Kazakhstan, Kyrgyzstan, Tajikistan, Turkmenistan and Uzbekistan-and the Caucasus states of Armenia, Azerbaijan and Georgia are included in Eurasia. Afghanistan and Mongolia have historical linkages with the Eurasian realm because of the commercial and cultural relations in the Soviet era. The Xingjian Province of Chinia has close cultural links with some of the Eurasian states like Kazakhstan. Iran, one of the Caspian littoral states, and Turkey one of the Black Sea region countries, are frequently referred to as part of Eurasia, not only from a cultural-political but also from an economic perspective since the end of the Cold War. See: Visne Korkmaz, "The New Power Calculations and 'Structured' Relations in the Fluctuating Security Environment of Eurasia" in *Contentious Issues of Security and the Future of Turkey*, Nursin Atesoglu Guney (ed.), London: Ashgate Publications, January 2007, p.99.
8. Christopher A. Ford, "The 2010 NPT Review Cycle So Far: A View from the United States of America", *Wilton Park,* United Kingdom, December 20, 2007, D:\NPT\The 2010 NPT Review Cycle So Far A View from the United States of America.htm, accessed in 2 November 2008.
9. Christopher A. Ford, "The 2010 NPT Review Cycle..., D:\NPT\The 2010 NPT Review Cycle So Far A View from the United States of America.htm, accessed in 2 November 2008.
10. Christopher A. Ford, "The 2010 NPT Review Cycle..., D:\NPT\The 2010 NPT Review Cycle So Far A View from the United States of America.htm, accessed in 2 November 2008
11. Peter Crail, "Iran Not Receptive to Revised Nuclear Proposal", *Arms Control*, Vol. 38, September 2008, http://www.armscontrol.org/act/2008_09/IranProposal, acessed in 2 November 2008.
12. For further information on these ıssues related to MPI and FES see: http://www.middlepowers.org and http://www.fes-globalization.org. Also, lately, civil society campaigns specifically directed at nuclear disarmament appear to be reawakening.

One, the "International Campaign to Abolish Nuclear Weapons" (I CAN), at www.icanw.org, focuses not just on the idea of abolition, but on building specific support for enacting a real Nuclear Weapons Convention. Another, the just-launched "Nuclear Free Future" campaign at www.nuclearfreefuture.org, seeks to enlighten the public -- especially young people engaged in politics for the first time by the 2008 election -- about the dangers that continue to prevail from nuclear power and nuclear weapons, and to demand that the presidential candidates make nuclear disarmament a central priority of their campaigns. See: Tad Daley, "The Nuclear Nonproliferation Treaty Turns…,", http://www.globalsolutions.org/node/1096, accessed in 2 November 2008.

13. Ramesh Thakur, Jane Boulden and Thomas G. Weiss, "Can the NPT Regime be Fixed or Should be Abondened ?" *Dialogue on Globilzation, Occasional Papers*, No. 40, NewYork, October 2008, http://library.fes.de/pdf-files/iez/global/05760.pdf, acessed in ' 2 November 2008.
14 Ramesh Thakur et al., "Can the NPT Regime be Fixed"..., http://library.fes.de/pdf-files/iez/global/05760.pdf.
15. Mitsuru Kurosawa, "The 2005 NPT Review Conference and Nuclear Disarmament", *Osaka University Law Review*, No.48, 2001, pp.1-44.
16 Christos Katsioulis and Christoph Pilger, "Nuclear Weapons in NATO's New Strategic Concept: A Chance to Take Non-Proliferation Seriously", *International Political Analysis*, Friedrich Ebert Stiftung, May 2008, http://library.fes.de/pdf-files/id/ipa/05425.pdf, acessed in 2 November 2008.
17 Christos Katsioulis and Christoph Pilger, "Nuclear Weapons in NATO's...," http://library.fes.de/pdf-files/id/ipa/05425.pdf.
18. According to view points of Daryl Kimball, "For nearly 40 years, American presidents have expressed their intention to fulfill the U.S. obligation under the 1968 Nuclear Nonproliferation Treaty (NPT) to pursue "effective measures relating to cessation of the nuclear arms race at an early date and to nuclear disarmament." See: Daryl Kimball, "Change Nuclear Weapons Policy? Yes, We Can", *Foreign Policy in Focus (FPIF)*, November 25, 2008, http://www.fpif.org/fpiftxt/5700, accessed in 2 November 2008. Still, few presidents have taken that goal seriously, and those who did missed historic opportunities to move closer toward a nuclear weapons-free world. Under the presidential administration of Barack Obama, U.S. nuclear weapons policy and nonproliferation diplomacy can and must change, or else the global effort to reduce the risk of nuclear war, curb proliferation, and prevent catastrophic terrorism will falter." In this regard, for instance; "(i) The failure of the Bush administration and other nuclear weapon states to make meaningful progress on their NPT-related disarmament commitments — including deeper, verifiable, and irreversible nuclear

reductions; ratification and implementation of the 1996 Comprehensive Test Ban Treaty; and negotiation of a global verifiable fissile material cut off— has complicated the task of strengthening the battered nuclear nonproliferation system. (ii) The Bush administration's decision to virtually abandon the bilateral, U.S.-Russian strategic nuclear arms control framework has also put Moscow on edge and worsened an already strained relationship between the two countries. In 2002, the administration withdrew from the 1972 Anti-Ballistic Missile Treaty in order to pursue a costly and rudimentary strategic missile defense system. Now, to Moscow's great dissatisfaction, Bush has proposed the deployment of a third anti-missile site in Poland.[Moreover], (iii) Presidents Bush and Putin did agree to the 2002 Moscow Treaty mandating reductions of "operationally deployed" strategic warheads to no more than 2,200 each by 2012. But the agreement expires the day it goes into effect and contains no verification provisions. An earlier agreement, the Strategic Arms Reduction Treaty (START) and its verification provisions, could expire at the end of 2009, leaving behind no meaningful legal framework for regulating U.S. and Russian strategic weapons". See: Daryl Kimball, "Change Nuclear Weapons Policy?...," http://www.fpif.org/fpiftxt/5700.

19. Tad Daley, "The Nuclear Nonproliferation Treaty Turns 40 Today", http://www.globalsolutions.org/node/1096, accessed in 2 November 2008.
20. *Middle Powers Initiative Report: Middle Powers Initiative Paper for the Preparorty Talks*, "Towards 2010 Priorities for NPT Consensus", New York, April 2007, http://www.gsinstitute.org/mpi/docs/Towards_2010.pdf, accessed in 2 November 2008.
21. *Middle Powers Initiative Report: Middle Powers Initiative Paper for the Preparorty Talks*, "Towards 2010 …," http://www.gsinstitute.org/mpi/docs/Towards_2010.pdf.

References

"Arms Control Association Applauds Central Asian States for Forswearing Nuclear Arms", *Arms Control Association*, September 8, (2006), http://www.armscontrol.org/pressroom/2006/20060906_CANWFZ.

"Arms Control and Proliferation Profile: Iran", Country Profiles, *Arms Control Association*, January (2008), http://armscontrol.org/factsheets/iranprofile.

BBC Monitoring Former Soviet Union, London: November 28, 2008.

Peter Crail, "ElBaradei says Iran Stalls IAEA Inquiry", *Arms Control*, Vol.38, October (2008), http://www.armscontrol.org/act/2008_10/IranIAEA.

———, "Iran Not Receptive to Revised Nuclear Proposal", *Arms Control*, Vol. 38, September 2008, http://www.armscontrol.org/act/2008_09/IranProposal.

Tad Daley, "The Nuclear Nonproliferation Treaty Turns 40 Today", (2008), http://www.globalsolutions.org/node/1096.

Christopher A. Ford, "The 2010 NPT Review Cycle So Far: A View from the United States of America", *Wilton Park,* United Kingdom, December 20, (2007), D:\NPT\The 2010 NPT Review Cycle So Far A View from the United States of America.htm.

"International Campaign to Abolish Nuclear Weapons" (I CAN), at www.icanw.org.

Christos Katsioulis and Christoph Pilger, "Nuclear Weapons in NATO's New Strategic Concept: A Chance to Take Non-Proliferation Seriously", *International Political Analysis*, Friedrich Ebert Stiftung, May (2008), http://library.fes.de/pdf-files/id/ipa/05425.pdf.

Daryl Kimball, "Change Nuclear Weapons Policy? Yes, We Can", *Foreign Policy in Focus (FPIF)*, November 25, (2008), http://www.fpif.org/fpiftxt/5700.

Visne Korkmaz, "The New Power Calculations and 'Structured' Relations in the Fluctuating Security Environment of Eurasia" in *Contentious Issues of Security and the Future of Turkey*, edited by Nursin Atesoglu Guney , London: Ashgate Publications, January 2007.

Mitsuru Kurosawa, "The 2005 NPT Review Conference and Nuclear Disarmament", *Osaka University Law Review*, No.48, 2001.

Middle Powers Initiative Report: Middle Powers Initiative Paper for the Preparorty Talks, "Towards 2010 Priorities for NPT Consensus", New York, April 2007, http://www.gsinstitute.org/mpi/docs/Towards_2010.pdf.

"Nuclear Envoy Says Iran to Continue Cooperation with UN Agency", *BBC Monitoring Middle East*, London: November 28, (2008).

http://www.fes-globalization.org.

http://www.middlepowers.org.

www.nuclearfreefuture.org.

Ramesh Thakur, Jane Boulden and Thomas G. Weiss, "Can the NPT Regime be Fixed or should be Abandoned?" *Dialogue on Globilzation, Occasional Papers*, No. 40, NewYork, October (2008), http://library.fes.de/pdf-files/iez/global/05760.pdf.

The Nexus of Globalisation and Regionalism within the Eurasian Security: Shanghai Cooperation Organisation (SCO)

Vişne KORKMAZ[1]

The Nexus of Globalisation and Regionalism: A Process and A Policy

Since the end of the Cold War, the contentious issue of the dual existence of globalisation (as a process) and of regionalism (as a policy) have dominated public and scholarly discussions. A number of academic works have recently been published on this phenomenon and its likely impacts on world politics but there is still no clear answer to the question of what globalisation's actual effects and contributions are, especially in terms of security.

Instead of concrete and elucidated views, there is a general recognition that globalisation refers to a concentration of activities at the global level as well as to the emergence of new actors and novel relations in global security. However, the appearance of novel elements in world politics does not mean the withering of traditional security actors, such as the state, or conventional security dynamics, such as the use of military force. That is why Peter Katzenstein in his book, 'A World of Regions', assumes that there exists another process which goes hand in hand with globalisation, namely 'internationalism'. Contrary to globalisation, internationalism implies territorially based international activities, traditionally either in the form of cooperation or in the form of power politics. According to Katzenstein, the continuous interaction between these two processes results in the emergence of new regions and new regionalisms, whether they are virtual or real.[2] The rise of these new regions/regionalisms actually and ironically highlights today's centripetal forces in security affairs, which are on the one hand a newly emerging international consensus on recognising the global threats and on the other hand unipolarity. Thus, since the end of the Cold War, security regionalism and/or regionalisation have become important trends in international relations, where global security management and the unipolar world order have become the new concepts of daily language.

From the perspective of the evaluation of the concept of security, globalisation first and foremost specifies continually occurring changes in security dynamics on a global scale. These changes, in fact, started to affect political visions in the late 1970s, when an awareness of a concept of 'one world' emerged under the umbrella of peace studies. However, up until the end of the Cold War and the announcement of the victory of democracy and capitalism by Francis Fukuyama, changes in security dynamics were limited to the division between the areas of society and state. Hence, the belief in the coming era of eternal peace and the reversal of this belief under the shadow of bloody conflicts in the 1990s deepened and broadened the meaning of security. Till then the referent object of security supposedly covered sub-national and supra-national actors beyond state and society, such as individuals, groups that act beyond borders and/or the whole of humanity. Accordingly, the term global has started to be used more and more to explain the nature of new threats, such as terrorism, illegal immigration, trans/international crime, environmental degradation and so on. These threats denote the existence of transnational networks, undefined victims from different national origins, and a global rhetoric used to define the root causes of these new threats, such as poverty and failures in integration processes. Furthermore, globalisation as a process and as a phenomenon reveals a change in the range of security practices. Of course it does not mean withering away of traditional practices of security within the boundaries of national and international systems. However, new constructive practices such as community building (witnessed in the creation of regional identities) or scale building (witnessed in the creation of regions) have also become part of the global security management.

Due to these triple change in the security understanding (new actors, new threats and new practices), new regions can be perceived as something more than a mere geographical entity or a shared identity between a group of states. Instead, regions are also related to (regional) *governance* that can be defined as identifiable patterns of behaviour.[3] Within this framework, regionalism embodies political activity related to security below the global level but above the national, whilst taking its legitimacy directly from the general logic of (the) 'international order' on the global level.[4] Without a doubt it can be asserted that it is not so different from the regional order of the Cold War years. It is true that the East-West conflict and the regional security institutions in the form of Cold War alliances indicated a kind of regional security order. However, during the Cold War years, regional systems and related institutions were under the shadow of an ideological conflict and regional security orders and their instruments did not reflect the autonomous function of socialisation as much as they have done since the end of the Cold War. This socialisation function of the new regionalism as complementary to peaceful international order was recognised by Boutros- Boutros Ghali at the beginning of the post-Cold War years.[5]

Not surprisingly, the middle-power states and newly emerged states of the post-Cold War order welcome this development and the opportunity it has brought to increase their influence and representation within the international and global security mechanisms. This new discourse of regional security orders for a healthy global order also brings a normative stand for the regional groupings. Actually, the normativeness of new regionalism is dependent on the success and sustainability of the regional orders of western security, being either NATO, which is a security community, or the EU, which is a regional actor trying to overtake the role of security provider on the global scale. In this way, being a region, being an imagined and/or imitated region in the words of Adler – [6] become, in the hands of states, a suitable instrument to strengthen stability and security either by transforming sovereignty to the regional institutions or, conversely, by fortifying statehood with the assistance of regional bodies in an era of new threats, one in which, on the one hand, has eroded the Westphalian state system whilst on the other has developed multi-layered, multi-centred and trans-border fighting mechanisms. That is why although the new regional groupings—one of them being the SCO—fall short of being alliances with defence and security tools, they may be seen as a different type of alliance, ones which legitimise the 'new sovereignty'[7] and serve 'intrastate security'.[8]

Consequently it is clear that globalisation is encouraging the regional pushback. The relationship between unipolarity and regionalism, however, is not so clear. Indeed, in this case, the debate is not so much about regionalism but about the very nature of the global order; the various debates and discussion have yet to establish whether we are living in an era of hegemony, hegemonic stability or hegemonic decline and newly emerging multipolarity. Apart from this important debate, one has to admit that the security understanding of the USA and Washington's use of force in pursuing its own security agenda has had an impact on security regionalisation in other geographies and furthers a competition of sorts between externally initiated (by the USA) and internally initiated (by the states of regions) regionalisms. Although the general objective of these different security regionalisms is ultimately mutual—stability and security in the region via the imposition of a regional order—there are lucid differences between the incentives of regional and ex-regional actors within the building regions: first of all, the USA or other ex-regional states have an interest in regionalism in order to maintain a regional stability and security which is in favour of their own security practices and policies rather than in dealing with immediate threats. Accordingly, the regional mechanisms can be suitable instruments for these ex-regional actors by providing a burden-sharing and/or bandwagoning incentive for the states of region in their adaptation process to the security agendas of the global powers. Whereas regional states are interested in forming security regionalisms in order to deal with 'the fear of abandonment' (in other words, ignorance of the ex-regional great powers in their struggle against major threats) on the one hand, on the other hand, and contrary to the fear of abandonment, security regionalism can, in the hands of regional states, be a convenient tool for avoiding the danger of domination by a super power determining regional security agendas. Therefore, regional collective action can be analysed not only as a bandwagoning act by the smaller regional powers in the face of global security agendas as set by the great powers but also as a balancing act against the intervention of the hegemonic state.[9] Hence, region building or regional organisation forming has utilised normativeness not only as an instrument of national sovereignty but also, and more importantly, as a remedy to unipolarity, which can be said to imply that regionalism represents an alternative order-bringing project in a politics which is shaped by the impact of globalisation.[10]

All in all, the dual processes-globalisation and security regionalisation, and the divergences between unipolar and multipolar world visions, have turned the new regions, in the words of Katzenstein, into porous creations. Due to this openness, regional organisations and the new regionalism (whether defined in terms of security conditions/dynamics imposed by a common geography[11], identity[12] or shared threat perception[13]) become places of balancing actions (either in the forms of balance of power, bandwagoning or balance of perceptions). These actions are actually policy instruments in the hands of regional states and external powers in order to adopt themselves to the changing security environment on both the regional and global scales.

The New Security Environment in Eurasia and Its Impact on Security Regionalism

'Eurasia' as a name of a region is not a new innovation. Over the last two centuries, the Eurasian region has been constructed using the assessments of classical geography (division of territory). Both the ex-regional ideas (such as Mackinder's heartland vision or expectations based on the so-called 'Great Game') and the regional vision (such as the classical Eurasianists dream of a new 'Steppe Empire' under the USSR, or Alekseev's symphonic personality idea) had a role in the construction of the notion of Eurasia. As a result of this construction, Eurasia turned out to be a regional area in which the security actions of Russia/Soviet Union took place. To a lesser extent, Eurasia was constructed as a region displaying an existential difference to the West,[14] which is why, before the end of the Cold War, it was difficult to talk about the regional *actorness* of a Eurasia independent of the policies and identities of the Soviet Union, although Eurasia itself did have a notional regional entity and identity of its own.

The fusion of Eurasian identity with Soviet identity did not, of course, create a negative impact on the regioness of Eurasia. This fusion, however, ended with the dissolution of the Soviet Union in 1991, and though some rhetoric derived from 19th and 20th century visions remains, Eurasia as a region, with the SCO as a regional (security) organisation, has emerged as an interesting example of the new trend regionalism.

Within the framework of new regionalism, adaptation to the new security environment appears to be the main motivation for the constructing of new regional groupings for the Eurasian states due to the drastic changes which have occurred in the region as a result of the end of the long stability of the Cold War. In this post-Cold War period, three new forms of threat—terrorism, internal unrest and drug trafficking[15]—have started to challenge the peace of the whole region, of which the focal point, from the perspective of security, is now Central Asia and Caucasus region.[16] The states of this region have thus been subject to an unstable ebb and flow brought about by nation building processes and to new security problems with significant cross-border dimensions, compelling state leaders to think about regional solutions.

In the eyes of the leaders of these new regimes, the most serious threat is the one posed by Islamist/jihadist terrorist groups. Of course, there are different takes as to what the root causes of fundamentalism may be, whether it is socio-economic, ethnic or secessionist in nature, but whatever the nature of the phenomena, religiously inspired terrorism, such as that of the Islamic

Movement of Uzbekistan (IMU) and similar bodies, has become one of the greatest trans-state threats to the region. Indeed, due to the nature of global terrorism[17], the IMU threatens not only the security interests of regional states such as China and the Russian Federation, but also the more distant actors such as the USA and Israel.[18] The impact of this transnational problem has broadened following the operation in Afghanistan.

The war in Afghanistan was a turning point in Eurasian security in terms of external powers' involvement. As a result of Operation Enduring Freedom, regional states seemed to be convinced of the need for international cooperation in the fight against extremism and terrorism. The operation also, concurrently, created a new strategic landscape that connected Eurasian security requirements with those of the Middle East and South and Southeast Asia. Therefore the issue is whether responsibility lies with the regional states or with the hegemonic power in fighting against the threats stemming from the state failure or failed states such as Afghanistan, has gained importance on this broadening regional scene, vis-à-vis newly developed, mostly bilateral, strategic ties between Washington and Central Asian capitals.[19] Furthermore, aside from the US war on terror and its policy of maintaining military bases in the region, the possibility of external actors' intervention in regional affairs has increased as a result of the expansion of the western normative area, reflected in, for example, OSCE election-monitoring missions or EU declarations against human right violations in the region's republics. All these changes in regional security seem to have increased the possibility of legitimacy crises in the regional states.

Building a regional organisation in order to manage security regionalisation and create a regional pattern of co-operative behaviour whilst preserving sovereign rights is an alternative principle of legitimisation for political and strategic actions of the states. Within this framework, the SCO, which partly covers the geographic area of the Middle East, Eurasia and South Asia security nexus, has emerged. Furthermore, it would also be a truism to remark that during the last few years, the SCO has taken important steps in the way of institutionalisation.

Shanghai Cooperation Organisation: What Does It Really Provide?

The Brief History of the SCO

The institutional development of the SCO can be summarised as having taken place in three phases.[20] The first phase was started by security negotiations between the People's Republic of China (PRC), the Russian Federation (RF), Kazakhstan, Kyrgyzstan, and Tajikistan in 1992. The principal aim of this grouping was to diminish possible border tensions. The end product of these negotiations was the 'Shanghai Five' in 1996. As name implies, it was not intended to create a strong regional identity. Rather, the forming of a healthy basis for 'good neighbourhood' ties was projected within the framework of Shanghai Five.[21] However, during the second phase, the good neighbourhood turned out to be the core of a potential 'regional order'. Accordingly, the Shanghai Five became a more formal institution with the announcement of a 'Declaration on the Establishment of the Shanghai Cooperation Organisation', which created a new organisation of regional cooperation by the member states of Shanghai Five together with Uzbekistan. If one tried to analyse the kind of regional order the SCO brought in the period between the years of 2001–2004 about, the judgment would be a 'regional security order'. Bringing regional order needs to a minimum standard for conducting on regional basis as well as a common understanding on two issues a)- what and how does security mean, and b)- which regional security problems should be dealt with by the states of the region. The declarations and the institutionalisation of the SCO, especially in 2004,[22] can be perceived as efforts to strengthen this kind of common understanding.

Though it is difficult to proclaim that the SCO has formed a common understanding regarding the meaning of security and the actual and conceptual boundaries of the region, regional identity, and regional responsibilities according to some scholars, the SCO has now passed into the a new phase which brings a more comprehensive and global security rhetoric to the Organisation, as well as a self-assertion of security actorness in the region and beyond.[23] Further institutionalisation plus an enlargement of the policy area and extending of membership is a feature of this phase. In 2004, the SCO received observer status at the United Nations (UN). Mongolia (in 2004) and Iran, India and Pakistan (in 2005) all joined as SCO observers. Again in 2005, the SCO signed the Memoranda of Understanding with the Association of the Southeast Asian Nations (ASEAN) and with the Commonwealth of Independent States (CIS). During the Astana Summit of 2005, SCO members reached an apparent accord when they rejected unilateral solutions to global problems.[24] Since then, multilateralism together with the principle of regional solutions to regional problems has been emphasised in SCO summit meetings.

Indeed, the third phase can be seen as a natural outcome of the new security regionalism that has also represented a normative stand—as mentioned before—more than as a stage of organisational evolution. Hence, to evaluate the success and failures of the SCO in terms of providing security in the region means taking the SCO as an example of security regionalism and assessing how particular a case it may be.

SCO, An Unfinished Story

It is interesting to see that the SCO, as an attempt at security regionalism, has the features of both hard and soft regionalism. Any kind of regionalism brings at least a vague understanding of the concept of region and tries to (re)construct regional identity. However, hard regionalism, based on formal structures, institutions, agenda setting and decision making, and rules and regulations, usually not only brings in minimum standard of conduct but also forms an entity representing the region by materialising and/or creating regional identity. That is why in the cases of hard regionalism, regional identity and regional actorness are not the subject of debate. Instead, discussions focus on the success and failures of the core institutions on a case-by-case basis, such as the EU, OSCE or NATO. Conversely, soft regionalism—witnessed in ASEAN—is built on informal processes such as dialogues, talks and consultation, usually between leaders without any formal agenda setting or decision-making mechanisms. Decisions are not the outcome of voting but of consensus. Therefore in the case of soft-regionalism, an independent regional identity or autonomous actorness of state groupings is always suspected.

Contrary to ASEAN and the other regional organisations of Asian security, the SCO has undertaken confidence-building measures, extending from border security to anti-terrorist activities. In accordance with the confidence-building measures undertaken by the Shanghai Five, the Declaration on the Establishment of the Shanghai Cooperation Organisation and the Shanghai Convention on the Fight against Terrorism, Separatism and Extremism brought not only a common understanding of the main threats in the region, so-called 'three evils', but also defined a SCO territory where the measures to combat such threats were to be applied. These two points were not only repeated continuously—as seen during the 2007 Bishkek Summit Meeting[25]—in the high level meetings and summits of the Organisation but also took a concrete form by the establishment of RATS (Regional Anti Terrorist Structure). Moreover, the SCO has a secretary in Beijing and regular meeting mechanisms between heads of state and ministerial and other high official levels. All these features lead to the conclusion that the SCO, rather than resemble an informal grouping of Asian states (without formal institutional rules but with a common understanding, usually defined as 'regional spirit'), is more akin to a formal (western-style) regional cooperation organisation rather than. Of course, the formalism within the SCO context is a valuable tool in the hands of the SCO, which not only includes the Central Asian states but also the two nuclear powers of the region—the PRC and the RF—and the observers required to present the SCO as an alternative Asian OSCE. Without any doubt, a possible role for the SCO in this framework will not be limited to election-monitoring missions, as was the case during the last presidential election in Uzbekistan or during parliamentary elections in the Russian Federation in 2007;[26] rather, it will be 'a mediation forum' to prevent conflicts between Central Asian states over the use of water resources, customs disputes, border conflicts and so on.[27]

Indeed, both the OSCE and the SCO have tended to consider security from a broader perspective, one which takes into account economic, ecological and human areas of security.[28] In the SCO, great significance is given to joint actions not only in military-strategic dimension matters but also in infrastructure, communications and in the balance of economic power and energy. Recent developments, such as the Russian proposal for a creation of a unified energy market which will cover all member and observer states of the SCO[29], as well as the Iranian offer of a declaration of joint natural gas prices, or the last Iranian plan for a common SCO currency[30], may be read not only as diplomatic-strategic manoeuvres but also as a reflection of this broader security understanding.

However, it is also a general tendency—especially among western scholars—to evaluate this broader security understanding of the SCO by looking at the consequences of the cooperation, which are admittedly moderate if we take into consideration the power of the region's states and the ambitious nature of the organisation's objectives. However, the main reason of the Organisation's moderate success is the SCO being an example of soft regionalism. Despite the formal institutional formation within the SCO, the main target of this multi-dimensional and broader security understanding has an internal security focus,[31] which is why agenda-setting power is in the hands of member states instead of solely in the hands of the secretariat. Thus, the main utility of the SCO is not in the acceleration of integration but in the fortification of sovereignty within a highly challenging security environment subject to the forces of globalisation amid debates of unipolarity vs. multipolarity.

Because of this internal security focus, Roy Allison sees the SCO as an example of 'protective integration'[32] which provides an alternative source of legitimacy to the regimes and states of the region not just in the face of new threats but also in the face of western criticisms over questionable methods of dealing with threats, a perceived failure of democracy, and human right violations, as seen during the Andijan events[33] and the recent Russian intervention in the Georgian-Ossetian conflict.[34] Therefore, Allison rightly points out the regime and sovereignty concerns of the SCO members and the priority given to national sovereignty over regional sovereignty. However calling the SCO cooperation scheme 'not real but virtual' ignored the informal understanding and socialisation functions of soft regionalism efforts.

Informal regionalism in the SCO was termed by Jiang Zemin in 2001 as the 'Shanghai Spirit'[35] and has matured during the last couple of years with the policies and decisions taken by the Organisation. One can explain the 'Shanghai Spirit' as a set of principles that bring a common pattern of behaviour to the governance of regional affairs. This regional governance may, eventually, bring about an autonomous regional identity and security culture, although it is too early to talk about any kind of regional identity when the SCO is still only 7 years old. The key governing principles of the Shanghai Spirit can be summarised under the term 'non-intervention'. Since the adaptation of the SCO Charter in 2002, this principle has been repeated continuously in almost all SCO summit meetings. This non-intervention principle can be read, together with the other complementary governing principles, such as 'respect to sovereign equality', 'consultation in decision-making' and 'rejection of hegemony and coercion in international affairs',[36] creating a suitable atmosphere for the small powers of region to form relations with the two great military and economic powers of the region, Russia and China. It also illustrates the limits of balancing between China and Russia within the Organisation itself.

Certainly, the Shanghai Spirit imposes some constraints on the efficiency of regional cooperation in the search for regional stability within the SCO, as demonstrated during internal crises like the Andijan incident, when member states disagreed on how the problem was to be dealt with. This kind of hesitancy to intervene can also be observed in Afghanistan: so far, the Afghan Contact Group continues to be the main body dealing with the situation in Afghanistan for the SCO, rather than the member states themselves. Apart from the internal messages related to the inviolability of national sovereignty, these Shanghai principles carry an important message for external actors. This is the rejection of domination of security values and policies of extra-regional states on the regional and global level. The support of multilateralism and multi-polarity in international security, together with SCO military cooperation, realised through military exercises, is usually perceived as the Shanghai's anti-western and anti-American stand. Such reductionism gained prominence for four reasons: Firstly, there exists a history of tense relations between Moscow, Beijing and Washington, which is why any security crisis in the region can give rise to Cold War rhetoric, reminiscent of old regional identities based on east-west divisions.[37] Secondly, the USA, Russian Federation and China all have great power status. Thus, global balancing—maybe not now but in the foreseeable future—among these states is expected. Thirdly, the SCO brings together nuclear and non-nuclear states of the region (ergo, possible nuclear technology exporters and importers) as well as the energy exporters and importers. The Shanghai Cooperation Organisation therefore has the potential to be a source of alternative legitimisation in developing civil nuclear energy and new energy (oil and gas) securities. Last but not least, there exists the possibility of a division of labour between Russia and China with respect to their hard (military) and soft (economic) power in the field of regulating regional security affairs. If this kind of burden and role sharing is realised, there is a high possibility of an emergence of a new regional identity, a 'Shanghai's Eurasia'.

However, these four reasons highlight possibilities, not, realities which is why the 'Shanghai Spirit' should perhaps not be read merely as a radical reflection of an anti-Western or anti-American ideology. Instead, the Shanghai Spirit can be seen as the materialisation of a more modest stand. As mentioned above, regional spirits indicate one of the basic principles of soft regionalism: 'regional problems, whether it has military-strategic dimensions or socio-political dimensions, are the responsibility of regional states', or, in other words, 'regional solutions for regional problems'.

Indeed, just after the call for the evacuation of US forces in Uzbekistan (which was not repeated during following summits and not followed by the Kyrgyzstan), Putin announced, as Medvedev did during the 2008 Summit meeting, that the SCO is not a military alliance or pact against another power. Instead, it represents a new type of international relations based on state-to-state cooperation and cultural relativism.[38] Therefore, the SCO seems to take its legitimacy from the normative ground of global security governance as a security dialogue forum, where the dialogue itself emerges as a confidence-building measures between great and small regional powers that have divergent and bilateral ties with each other and with extra-regional actors, the first and foremost being the USA and EU.

Although, this value-added new regionalism gives free hand to SCO members in dealing with security issues in regional and international affairs (called 'constructive interaction' by Russian sources),[39] there are still important constraints for the Organisation preventing it from being a major security provider and manager in the Eurasian security realm. First of all, the bureaucratic and military capabilities of the SCO are limited; RATS has no rapid deployment forces, which are *de rigueur* in combating new threats.[40] Moreover, it is questionable whether the new ties between the SCO and the Collective Treaty Security Organisation (CSTO)[41] will meet this shortage. The intentions of the member states are crucial for further developing the combat capacities of the Organisation; no clear clues exist for outside observers as to the actual intentions of the regional actors in this respect.[42] Secondly, there are huge differences between the capabilities and national powers of the great and small states of the region and there is still no specific mechanism within the SCO to cover the capability gap, apart from military and as of yet unrealised economic assistance.[43] Last but not least, there is no mechanism or plan for trans-regional co-operation (for example, between NATO and the SCO or between the OSCE and SCO, etc.) for the global security order. However, Trans-regional security cooperation necessarily requires a maturing and developing of an autonomous security and institutional culture within the SCO. Nevertheless, one also has to admit that the increasing unilateralism supported by bilateral security ties, a la the 'Coalition of the Willing', creates a major obstacle to trans-regional security cooperation. Nevertheless, international tendencies related to the global security order and to the regional security conditions in Eurasia constrain the future role and efficiency of the SCO as an institution of effective security regionalism.

Conclusion

It is still too early to reach a conclusion regarding the successes and/or failures of regional cooperation in Eurasia via the SCO. It may also be too early to evaluate any future direction, in terms of hard regionalism or regionalism, the SCO will take. The SCO may continue to keep both features till it develops its own independent security culture, which can be based on any number of factors, such as the range of cooperation between the Russian Federation and China. It can even be argued that the SCO is currently no more than a talk shop. However, both the solution of border conflicts in the region and the maintaining of (relative) peace, which is apparently the case at the moment, even though there are number of instability sources alive, remind us that even this kind of talk shop on relevant regional security issues is important for actors facing the difficulty of nation-building and region-building processes simultaneously. Unfortunately, the unilateralism in security policies and globalisation, which brings new threats on the scene, cannot ease the adaptation to the new security environment for either the old or new states of the region. Therefore, regional instruments, such as the SCO, become important variables which make balancing and bandwagoning possible. Besides, these organisations emerge as new norms-creators in this rough adaptation process and open the system for the voices and policies of region states, whether they be great or small powers. This is why one can reach the conclusion that the existence of an attempt at security regionalism is more important than its future direction in regions such as Eurasia, where the regional boundaries are continuously reconstructed by the security acts of both regional and extra-regional actors.

Notes

1. Dr, Yildiz Technical University, Department of Political Science and International Relations, Turkey.
2. P. Katzenstein, *The World of Regions,* Cornell Uni. Press, Ithaca, 2005, pp, 19-21.
3. K.J. Holsti, *The State, War, and the State of War,* Cambridge Uni. Press, Cambridge, 1996, pp, 142-143.
4. L. Fawcett, "Exploring Regional Domains: A comparative History of Regionalism", *International Affairs,* 80/3, 2004, pp, 436-437.
5. B. Boutros Ghali, *Agenda for Peace,* UN Pub., NY, 1992; B.B. Ghali, *Agenda for Democracy,* UN Pub., NY, 1996.
6. E. Adler, "Imagined Security Communities: Cognitive Regions in International Relations", Millennium, 26/2, 1997.
7. SCO and ASEAN are the good examples of this new mission of regioness, see f/e, Y.F. Khong- H.E.S. Nesadurai, "Hanging Together, Institutional design and Cooperation in Southeast Asia: AFTA and ARF", Crafting Cooperation, A. Acharya- A.I. Johnston (ed.), Cambridge Uni. Press, Cambridge, 2007.
8. R. E. Kelly, "Security Theory in the New Regionalism", International Studies Review, 9, 2007, p, 218.
9. Galia Press-Barnathan, "The Changing Incentives for Security Regionalization" Cooperation and Conflict, 40/3, 2005, p, 289.
10. B. Buzan- O. Waever, Regions and Powers, Cambridge Uni. Press, NY, 2003, p, 68, M. Pugh- W. Sidhu, United Nations and Regional Security: Europe and Beyond, Lynne Reinner, Boulder, 2003.
11. Ibid., p, 53.

12. F. Attina, The Building of Regional Security Partnership and the Security Culture Divide in the Mediterranean Region, Paper No: 040508, University of California, Berkeley, 2004.
13. D. Lake, "Regional Security Complexes: A System Approach", Regional Orders, Building Securityin a New World, D.Lake- P. Morgan (eds.), Pennslyvania University Press, University Park, 1997.
14. V. Korkmaz, "Avrasya Senfonisi / Simfoniya Yevrazii" (Eurasian Symphony) *DA, Dialog Eurasia,* 25, Summer 2007, pp, 12-16. (Turkish and Russian).
15. A. Matveeva- A. Giustozzi, "A Regional Organisation in Making" Working Paper 39, September 2008, pp, 2-3.
16. V. Korkmaz, "The New Power Calculations and 'Structured' Relations in the Fluctuating Security Environment of Eurasia" in *Contentious Issues of Security and the Future of Turkey*, Nursin Atesoglu Guney (ed.), Ashgate Publications, January 2007, p, 99
17. For details see, V. Korkmaz, "Global Terrorism and the Western Agendas; the Convergences- the Divergences" *Midwest Political Science Association 64th Annual Conference*, Chicago, April 20-23, 2006, http://convention2.allacademic.com/one/mpsa/mpsa06/index.php?click_key=1&PHPSESSID=6b40f31553f54d13c3a6c8ea45b6621b,mpsa06_proceeding_139131[1].pdf.
18. A. Matveeva- A. Giustozzi, *ibid.,* p, 2.
19. According to the Bush Administrations, the South Caucasus- Central Asia region is indispensible to both the successful prosecution of the war in Afghanistan and to the accomplishment of Washington's lily-path strategy in the Middle East. That is why, since 2003, the Central Asian Republics, Uzbekistan in particular, have been crucial for Washington in terms of acquiring intelligence, supporting humanitarian cooperation and granting basing rights. Following 9/11, the US has succeeded in concluding bilateral agreements with Uzbekistan and Kyrgyzstan to establish military bases in Karsi-Khanabad (K2), Kokadiy (Uzbekistan) and Manas (Kyrgyzstan). Also, in order to accommodate US transport aircraft, another facility has been acquired in the Kuliab region of Tajikistan to add to the Dushanbe air base that US forces use. Of course, Washington's basing and overflight rights in Central Asia are neither unconditional nor grated. However, the new security strategies of Washington in the region are also not limited to the bilateral relations between the USA and the Central Asian States. Simultaneous rapprochements between Delhi and Washington and Islamabad and Washington should also be taken into consideration.
20. Marcel de Haas- Frans-Paul van der Putten, *The Shanghai Cooperation Organisation: Towards a Full-grown Security Alliance,* M. de Haas (ed.), Netherlands Institute of International Relations, Clingendal, November 2007, pp, 7-11.

21. See in http://www.sectsco.org/html/00035.html.
22. Two permanent organs were established in that year: A Secretariat in Beijing and a Regional Anti-Terrorist Structure (RATS) in Tashkent, Uzbekistan.
23. For example see, M. de Haas- Franz P. van der Putten, *op.cit,* pp,8-10, M. de Haas, "The Shanghai Cooperation Organisation's Momentum Towards a Mature Security Alliance", January 2008, http://www.clingendael.nl/publications/2008/20080100_cscp_haas_art_sm.pdf, pp,1-30, Marc Lanteigne, "In Medias Res: The Development of Shanghai Cooperation Organisation as a Security Community", *Pacific Affairs,* 79/4, Winter 2006-2007, pp, 605-622, Flemming S. Hansen, "The Shanghai Cooperation Organisation", *Asian Affairs,* 39/2, July 2008, p, 218.
24. See Astana Declaration of 5 July 2005 at http://www.sectsco.org/htm/00500.html.
25. http://www.sectsco.org/news_detail.asp?id=1721&LanguagelD=2.
26. A. Matveeva- A. Giustozzi, *op.cit.,* s, 6, "SCO Mission: 'Elections Were Legitimate, Free & Transparent" 24 December 2007, http://www.uzbekistan.be/press-releases/138-2007.html#_4.
27. Mikhail Troitskiy, "A Russian Perspective on the Shanghai Cooperation Organization" *The Shanghai Cooperation Organization,* Alyson J.K. Bailes, Pal Duney, Pan Guang and Mikhail Troitsky, SIPRI Policy Paper, 17, Stockholm International Peace Research Institute, May 2007, p, 36.
28. M. de Haas- Franz P. van der Putten, "SCO and OSCE", *op.cit.,* M. de Haas (ed), November 2007, Netherland Institute of International Relations, p, 48. For the last affirmation of the emphasis on comprehensive security see the official announcements following the 2008 Dushanbe Summit of SCO, "SCO Leaders Say No Int'l Problems can be Solved by Merely Using Force" China View, 28 August 2008, http://news.xinhuanet.com/english/2008-08/28/content_9730813.htm.
29. Sergei Blagov, "Russia Urges Formation of Central Asian Energy Club", 07 November 2007, http://www.eurasianet.org/departments/insight/articles/eav110707a.shtml. On 3 July 2007 this Energy Club was established in Moscow. The main objective of the Club is bringing the energy-consumer, energy-producer and transit countries together to provide coordination in their energy strategies and increase energy security. At the SCO Bishkek Summit of 2007, Russian Foreign Minister Lavrov proposed active role and participation to the Energy Club by the observers of the SCO. "Moratorium on Admission to Shanghai Six to hold - FM Lavrov" *RIA-Novosti World,* 16.08.2007, http://en.rian.ru/world/20070816/71927153.html.
30. Artyom Matusov, "Energy Cooperation in the SCO: Club or Gathering?", *China and Eurasia Forum Quarterly,* 5/3, 2007, p, 96. "Results of the Shanghai Cooperation Organization (SCO) summit. What shall Tajikistan wait for?" Asia Plus, 4 September 2008, http://asiaplus.tj/en/articles/179/2418.html.

31. S. Nossel, "Shanghaid", The New Republic, http://www.tnr.com/doc.mhtml?i=w070423&cs=nossel043007.
32. Roy Allison, "Virtual Regionalism, Regional Structures and Regime Security in Central Asia" Central Asian Survey, 27/2, 2008.
33. Jeff Erlich, "One Year After Andijan: Uzbekistan Fights Its own Information War", 11 May 2006, http://www.eurasianet.org/departments/insight/articles/eav051106a.shtml.
34. Christian Lowe - Conor Sweeney, "Russia Hits Back at Western Bias over Georgia", 29 August 2008, http://www.eleconomista.es/empresas-finanzas/noticias/725121/08/08/Russia-hits-back-at-Western-bias-over-Georgia.html.
35. Zemin defined Shanghai Sprit as follows: "mutual trust, mutual benefit, equality, consultation, respect to different civilizations and common prosperity" see J. Zemin, "Deepening Unity and Coordination to Jointly Create a Brilliant Future" Speech at the SCO inaugural ceremony, St Petersburg, 15 June 2001, cited in Pan Guang, "A Chinese Perspective on the Shanghai Cooperation Organization", The *Shanghai Cooperation Organization,* Alyson J.K. Bailes, …, p,48.
36. See the Charter, http://www.sectsco.org/news_detail.asp?id=96&LanguageID=2.
37. Fred Weir, "Russia, China Looking to Form NATO of the East" *Christian Science Monitor*, 26 October 2005, http://www.csmonitor.com/2005/1026/p04s01-woeu.html.
38. V. Putin, " ShOS: Novaya Model Uspeshnova Mejdunarodnova Satrudnitcestva" President Russii, 14 July 2006, http://www.president.kremlin.ru/appears/2006/06/14/1202_type63382_107004.shtml. Also see especially Article 1st of "Dushanbe Declaration of Heads of SCO Member States" 27-28 August 2008, President Russia, http://www.kremlin.ru/eng/events/articles/2008/08/205865/205913.shtml.
39. K. Vnukov,"Moscow-Beijing: New Vistas of Cooperation" *International Affairs (Moscow),* 52/3, 2006, p, 45.
40. Indeed, this shortage is a direct result of the nature of the SCO as a (not-so) hard security organization. Indeed, there are no SCO documents containing reference to defense cooperation. Neither can any reference for the establishment of a multilateral military or police force be found. RATS's mandate is actually limited to the intelligence analysis and coordination among national agencies responsible for combating terrorism and drug trafficking in the SCO member countries. M. Troitskiy, *op.cit.,* pp, 37-38.
41. The development of closer ties between the SCO and the CSTO has not been a smooth process. Without doubt one of the reason for this is the fact that the CSTO has been a collective security alliance since 2003. Accordingly, on the CSTO and the security

structures of the CIS, the RF has an enormous impact. V. Korkmaz, "The Fluctuating Security Environment...", pp, 109-110, R. Allison, "Strategic Reassertion in Russia's Central Asia Policy" *International Affairs,* 80/2, 2004, p, 286. That is why firstly Uzbekistan then the PRC oppossed enhancing the link between the CSTO and the SCO, whereas, the RF was the main proponent of the signing of the Memorandum of Understanding (MoU) between the two organisations, (finalised on 5 October 2007) (see the MoU in http://www.sectsco.org/html/01786.html.) It is generally known that Moscow tends to invest more resources in strenghtening the military infrastructure of SCO, whilst the other member states look at such actions with suspicion, due to the huge military capabilities of the RF, and conspicuously do not wish to turn the SCO into a second CSTO. A. J.K. Bailes- P. Dunay, "The Shanghai Cooperation Organisation as A Regional Security Institution" in *Shanghai Cooperation Organisation..,* p,21.

42. It is a general tendency to observe the joint military exercises of the SCO since 2002 as the mirrors of the intentions of the members. It is difficult to say that these exercises are not important. Certainly, with these exercises, the member states intend to give the message that regional and global security problems such as terrorism should be handled by the security apparatus of the regional states. Emphasizing counter-terrorism and military assistance in the fight against the three evils also turned each military exercise into a test case determining the boundaries of the region. However, beyond the general principles of SCO regionalism, some observers argue that there are some divergences between the core states of SCO (the RF and the PRC) about the future direction of the operation capability of SCO. De Haas- F.P van der Putten, *op.cit.,* pp,41-45.
43. The SCO members, especially the Central Asian States drastically need military know-how and material inputs to raise their forces to internationally accepted standarts and acquire experience of security providing beyond their national borders. Although there have been some joint capacity-building programmes in the CSTO or CIS, the SCO members' interaction in exchanging defence equipment and technology are overwhelmingly bilateral and the RF has emerged as the main exporter of military technology and know-how to SCO states, including the PRC, and observer members. However, the SCO's economic dimension has been pushed from the beginning by Beijing. In late 2003, the PRC proposed the establishment of a free trade zone in the SCO that would provide free movement of products, capital, technology and services but the trade deficit between the Central Asian States and the PRC prevented the implementation of this project. Though worries related to the economic power of China in the Central Asian States exist, Beijing has granted $900 million buyer's export credit to SCO cooperative projects.

References

E. Adler, "Imagined Security Communities: Cognitive Regions in International Relations", Millennium, 26/2, (1997).

Roy Allison, "Virtual Regionalism, Regional Structures and Regime Security in Central Asia" Central Asian Survey, 27/2, (2008).

———, "Strategic Reassertion in Russia's Central Asia Policy" *International Affairs,* 80/2, (2004).

F. Attina, The Building of Regional Security Partnership and the Security Culture Divide in the Mediterranean Region, Paper No: 040508, University of California, Berkeley, (2004).

A. J.K. Bailes- P. Dunay, "The Shanghai Cooperation Organisation as A Regional Security Institution" in *The Shanghai Cooperation Organization,* Alyson J.K. Bailes, Pal Duney, Pan Guang and Mikhail Troitsky, SIPRI Policy Paper, 17, Stockholm International Peace Research Institute, May 2007.

Galia Press-Barnathan, "The Changing Incentives for Security Regionalization" Cooperation and Conflict, 40/3, (2005).

Sergei Blagov, "Russia Urges Formation of Central Asian Energy Club", 07 November 2007, http://www.eurasianet.org/departments/insight/articles/eav110707a.shtml.

B. Buzan- O. Waever, Regions and Powers, Cambridge Uni. Press, NY, 2003.L. Fawcett, "Exploring Regional Domains: A comparative History of Regionalism" *International Affairs,* 80/3, (2004).

"Dushanbe Declaration of Heads of SCO Member States" 27-28 August 2008, President Russia, http://www.kremlin.ru/eng/events/articles/2008/08/205865/205913.shtml.

Jeff Erlich, "One Year After Andijan: Uzbekistan Fights Its own Information War", 11 May 2006, http://www.eurasianet.org/departments/insight/articles/eav051106a.shtml.

B. Boutros Ghali, *Agenda for Peace,* UN Pub., NY, 1992; B.B. Ghali, *Agenda for Democracy,* UN Pub., NY,

1996.

Pan Guang, "A Chinese Perspective on the Shanghai Cooperation Organization", in *The Shanghai Cooperation Organization,* Alyson J.K. Bailes, Pal Duney, Pan Guang and Mikhail Troitsky, SIPRI Policy Paper, 17, Stockholm International Peace Research Institute, May 2007.

M. de Haas, "The Shanghai Cooperation Organisation's Momentum Towards a Mature Security Alliance", January 2008, http://www.clingendael.nl/publications/2008/20080100_cscp_haas_art_sm.pdf.

Marcel de Haas- Frans-Paul van der Putten, *The Shanghai Cooperation Organisation: Towards a Full-grown Security Alliance,* Netherlands Institute of International Relations, Clingendal, November 2007.

Flemming S. Hansen, "The Shanghai Cooperation Organisation", *Asian Affairs,* 39/2, July (2008).

K.J. Holsti, *The State, War, and the State of War,* Cambridge Uni. Press, Cambridge, 1996..

P. Katzenstein, *The World of Regions,* Cornell Uni. Press, Ithaca, 2005..

R. E. Kelly, "Security Theory in the New Regionalism", International Studies Review, 9, (2007).

Y.F. Khong- H.E.S. Nesadurai, "Hanging Together, Institutional design and Cooperation in Southeast Asia: AFTA and ARF", in *Crafting Cooperation*, edited by A. Acharya- A.I. Johnston, Cambridge Uni. Press,

Cambridge, 2007.

V. Korkmaz, "Avrasya Senfonisi / Simfoniya Yevrazii" (Eurasian Symphony) *DA, Dialog Eurasia,* 25, Summer (2007) (Turkish and Russian)

———, "The New Power Calculations and 'Structured' Relations in the Fluctuating Security Environment of Eurasia" in *Contentious Issues of Security and the Future of Turkey*, edited by Nursin Atesoglu Guney, Ashgate Publications, January 2007.

——— V. Korkmaz, "Global Terrorism and the Western Agendas; the Convergences-the Divergences" *Midwest Political Science Association 64th Annual Conference*, Chicago, April 20-23, 2006, http://convention2.allacademic.com/one/mpsa/mpsa06/index.php?click_key=1&PHPSESSID=6b40f31553f54d13c3a6c8ea45b6621b,mpsa06_proceeding_139131[1].pdf.

D. Lake, "Regional Security Complexes: A System Approach", in *Regional Orders, Building Securityin a New World,* edited by D.Lake- P. Morgan, Pennslyvania University Press, University Park, 1997.

Marc Lanteigne, "In Medias Res: The Development of Shanghai Cooperation Organisation as a Security Community", *Pacific Affairs,* 79/4, Winter (2006-2007).

Christian Lowe - Conor Sweeney, "Russia Hits Back at Western Bias over Georgia", 29 August 2008, http://www.eleconomista.es/empresas-finanzas/noticias/725121/08/08/Russia-hits-back-at-Western-bias-over-Georgia.html.

Artyom Matusov, "Energy Cooperation in the SCO: Club or Gathering?", *China and Eurasia Forum Quarterly,* 5/3, (2007).

A. Matveeva- A. Giustozzi, "A Regional Organisation in Making" Working Paper 39, September 2008.

"Moratorium on Admission to Shanghai Six to hold - FM Lavrov" *RIA-Novosti World,* 16.08.2007, http://en.rian.ru/world/20070816/71927153.html.

S. Nossel, "Shanghaid", The New Republic, http://www.tnr.com/doc.mhtml?i=w070423&cs=nossel043007.

M. Pugh- W. Sidhu, United Nations and Regional Security: Europe and Beyond, Lynne

Reinner, Boulder, 2003.

V. Putin, " ShOS: Novaya Model Uspeshnova Mejdunarodnova Satrudnitcestva" *President Russii*, 14 July 2006, http://www.president.kremlin.ru/appears/2006/06/14/1202_type63382_107004.shtml.

"Results of the Shanghai Cooperation Organization (SCO) summit. What shall Tajikistan wait for?" *Asia Plus*, 4 September 2008, http://asiaplus.tj/en/articles/179/2418.html.

"SCO Leaders Say No Int'l Problems can be Solved by Merely Using Force" China View, 28 August 2008, http://news.xinhuanet.com/english/2008-08/28/content_9730813.htm.

"SCO Mission: 'Elections Were Legitimate, Free & Transparent" 24 December 2007, http://www.uzbekistan.be/press-releases/138-2007.html#_4.

http://www.sectsco.org..

Mikhail Troitskiy, "A Russian Perspective on the Shanghai Cooperation Organization" in *The Shanghai Cooperation Organization,* Alyson J.K. Bailes, Pal Duney, Pan Guang and Mikhail Troitsky, SIPRI Policy Paper, 17, Stockholm International Peace Research Institute, May 2007.

K. Vnukov,"Moscow-Beijing: New Vistas of Cooperation" *International Affairs (Moscow),* 52/3, (2006).

Fred Weir, "Russia, China Looking to Form NATO of the East" *Christian Science Monitor*, 26 October 2005, http://www.csmonitor.com/2005/1026/p04s01-woeu.html.

Globalisation and Eurasian Geopolitical Discourses

Anita Sengupta

In the immediate post Cold War period, anti-geopolitics dominated the understanding of global politics. It had then been assumed that globalisation and a free flow of goods, money, ideas and people would make traditional geopolitical assumptions defunct.[1] Similarly, as geopolitics became defunct security would be entrusted to global organisations and humanitarian wars would deal with global violence. Air power as a strategic weapon would also bypass geopolitical realities. However, expectations that globalisation would transform international politics did not really work out. Similarly humanitarian warfare lacked support and air power could not substitute infantry. As a consequence a focus on the relationship between geopolitics, geography and strategy once again assumed significance.[2] The post Cold War resurgence of interest in geopolitics has been identified in two recent trends, one relating to real world changes which have taken place and the other to the theoretical paradigms which have been constructed as part of post modern critiques.[3] In the real world, changes in the global map, not least the collapse of the Soviet Union and the resulting political and territorial changes in Europe, left most geographers unprepared. At best they were able to focus on the hard territorial changes taking place within and between states, the problems of ethno territorial empowerment and the construction of new borders and the associated territorial reconfigurations of power. The second trend has been the use of theoretical and conceptual frameworks some of which are rooted in the post modern turn of the last two decades, and identified as critical geopolitics. As a part of this critique there has been an examination of geopolitical narratives of evolving events and the deconstruction of speeches and texts, giving new insights into the way the rest of the world understood the 'geo' in international relations.

This article examines a set of geopolitical discourses that reflect on the globalisation debate within the Eurasian space. Through a study of these discourses there is an attempt to address the debate on 'civilisational' and 'realist' readings of the geopolitics of political space within the region in a globalised era.

Globalisation and Geopolitical Discourse in Eurasia

With the disintegration of the Soviet Union and the emergence of new states in the region there was a revival of certain geopolitical concepts and models that had become largely defunct in the recent past particularly in the Eurasian context. [4] The revival of geopolitics followed by the emergence of geo-economics meant that a large part of writings on the Central Asian region once again defined it in terms of traditional geopolitical concepts. [5] The idea of a 'new' great game became a persistent one in writings that alluded to a revival of the struggle for control over the region and this revival was situated within the context of acquiring control over the 'heartland'. Since the 1990s the use of the term and concept of the 'new great game' and the 'heartland' overshadowed the analysis of events in Central Asia and the Transcaucasus.[6] While in the 1990s the metaphors were used to explain geo-economic competition, particularly for oil and gas, 9/11 added a new dimension of geo-strategy. Most of these great game writings had geopolitical references or allude to them as significant. It has been argued that much of the analysis that used these concepts however did so without any qualification. The term 'new' great game was in itself inaccurate since it refers back to events that were totally dissimilar. In particular the linking of the current situation in the region with geopolitical projections that had emphasised its significance in world politics is driven more by romanticism than any correct understanding of the concepts of geopolitics.[7] In the post 9/11 era, with the recognition of the significance of the region in any *war against terror*, 'heartland' theories once again re-emerged in a large number of writings on the region. This was as true of the post Soviet world as well as of the west.

In fact, in the state identified by Halford Mackinder as occupying the most desirable geopolitical position in terms of getting access to the 'heartland', Russia, the return of geopolitics was evident.[8] At the end of the Cold War, Russia's post communist Minister of Foreign Affairs,

Andrei Kozyrev, noted that the Russian administration had comprehended quite fast that geopolitics was taking the place of ideology.[9] Kozyrev also argued that more recently geopolitical narratives like the 'clash of civilisations' or the 'axis of evil' has become the focus of attention in foreign policy circles. This indicates that while on the one hand a realist reading of global politics in terms of a 'chessboard' re-emerged particularly in the Eurasian context, on the other hand a 'civilisational' dialogue emerged as significant in discourses of international relations and international security. Among the many attempts at charting out patterns of global politics in the post Cold war context two opposing views of political geography emerged as significant. Francis Fukuyama in his *The End of History* predicted that the end of the Cold War would also signal the end of conflicts between societies and states as has been hitherto known.[10] Arguing against this position Samuel Huntington, first in an article in the *Foreign Affairs* and then in a full length book noted that conflicts at all levels will not only continue but will become more pronounced.[11] Huntington elaborated a paradigm for understanding political relations across the globe based on a vision of humanity divided and classified in terms of respective 'civilisations' to which individuals and communities belong. The precise spectrum of inter-personal and inter-group affinities that bind a civilisation into a single unit has been defined in various ways. Huntington emphasised the importance of culture and cultural identity as the cement that holds civilisations together. Within this element he singled out religion as the principle defining character of civilisations.

Huntington's thesis elicited global response and became the centre of a global debate that involved not just political theorists and practitioners but also political geographers.[12] The importance that Huntington accorded to political geography has been critically examined by Mark Bassin.[13] Bassin argues that Huntington uses the term civilisation in two distinct ways. On the one hand, civilisation is simply a synonym for culture and since this does not possess a defined geographical-territorial dimension, civilisation in this particular sense is non-geographical. In the second sense however, a civilisation represents the agglomeration of communities as a tangible geographical entity. Here civilisation is identified as the highest geographical or spatial order of cultural affinity. Huntington identifies civilisational macro-agglomerations that have existed over the past millennium: Sinic, Japanese, Hindu, Islam, Orthodox, Western, Latin American and African. These, in Huntington's view, represent the 'traditional' and enduring global division of humanity and it is these civilisations that will define the fabric of the international order in the twenty-first century. Huntington writes:

In sum the post Cold War world is a world of seven or eight major civilisations. Cultural commonalities and differences shape the interests, antagonisms and association of states. The most important countries in the world come overwhelmingly from different civilisations. The local conflicts most likely to escalate into broader wars are those between groups and states from different civilisations. The predominant patterns of political and economic development differ from civilisation to civilisation. The key issues on the international agenda involve differences among civilisations. Power is shifting from the long predominant West to non Western civilisations. Global politics has become multipolar and multicivilisational.[14]

In terms of political geography Huntington's civilisational approach has been criticised as effacing geographical specificity and place based particularity of conflicts. However, Bassin argues while *antigeographical* in some sense, it does engage with geography in various ways.[15] In discussing how Huntington understands the role of geographical space in the political process Bassin notes:

At an early point in the *Clash of Civilizations* Huntington discusses how the factor of geography has figured in the civilisational analysis that he draws upon, and he reflects on its significance for the particular historical processes and political constellations that are the subject of his attention.[16]

Huntington acknowledges the importance of geographical factors in his analysis and references to the force of 'geopolitical' realities are scattered throughout his book. These results in what Bassin calls 'an awkwardly managed tension' between geography on the one hand and culture on the other.[17] This inconsistency emerges clearly from his treatment of the significance of geographical location. In places he accords this an autonomous significance but in others he argues that geographical proximity and location possess no meaning in and of themselves. His reaction to regionalist models of international development is negative as it offers an alternative to Huntington's own scheme of 'civilisational' affinities. He argues that cooperation within a given region can take place only to the extent that that geography coincides with culture, that is, only if there is a civilisational commonality among states.

The full ambiguity of Huntington's engagement with geography emerges from his discussion of the significance of territory. On the one hand he makes it quite clear that the struggle over territory per se does not represent a significant element in the primal antagonisms that drive the clash of civilisations. Huntington argues that conflicts today focus less on territory and involve broader inter civilisational issues, such as human rights, democratic norms, terrorism and 'western' civilisation. In fact in Huntington's vision of cultural identity attachment to a geographical space is of no consequence. However, Huntington also notes that territory does figure as an important source of conflict in the clash of civilisations. He also acknowledges a symbolic and affective element in the territorial imperative and recognition of the salience of territory as a key element in identity structures. Bassin argues that this ambiguity between a realist acknowledgement of geography as objective and an affirmation of the primacy of the subjective non geographical factors has resulted in the simultaneous recognition of and refusal to recognise the place of geography in politics.[18]

Bassin compares Huntington's position with an earlier attempt to chart out the future shape of global politics by George Kennan. He notes that Kennan's perspective was influenced by Halford Mackinder's 'heartland theory' and its reformulation by Nicholas Spykman. Bassin argues:

A comparison of the respective texts, however, is most revealing. Briefly Mackinder and Spykman offered geostrategic visions that were driven by a geographical logic inherent in the existential spatiality of the regions involved. Above all, this involved factors of location and juxtaposition, relative size, land versus sea and resource endowment. Kennan adopted their tripartite model of global political morphology and then critically animated it through the introduction and prioritisation of the factor of ideology, in the form of Marxism or Soviet Communism. For Kennan it was ultimately the geographical configuration and juxtaposition of the heartland plus its dominant ideology that made it so strategically dangerous to a free world led by the United States. Mackinder's analysis, by contrast, does not even include ideology as a category in this sense.[19]

In the post-Soviet context it was this de-ideologised Mackinderian vision that emerged as a significant alternative discourse in defining the shape of international relations particularly in the Eurasian context.[20] The attractiveness of the Mackinderian discourse stemmed both from the problems inherent in the basic premises of the civilisational discourses as well as their depiction of the region as a conflict prone zone. The need of the hour was in terms of a portrayal that would look beyond ideological contradictions and focus on a region that would prove attractive to investments. Emphasising an alternative realist vision of a resource rich region with a stress on connectivity proved to be useful in terms of defining the Eurasian space within the international arena since transportation technology for natural resources is once again at the centre of global debates. American analyst Ross H Munro, for instance, notes:

A new Silk Road of modern railroads and highways that would effectively give China a land route to the west, ultimately to Europe and to an Iranian opening on the Persian Gulf, would have enormous strategic consequences possibly comparable to the impact that the advent of the Suez and Panama canals once had.[21]

The Mackinderian prediction of the Eurasian region as the 'heartland' that because of its resources and position would determine the destiny of world politics thus proved useful both for those within the region as well as those outside for whom an emphasis on geo-economics seemed more useful than an emphasis on geo-culture and its attendant debates, the 'end of history' and the 'clash of civilisations'.[22]

On the one hand, the 'end of history' argument assumed that an ideologically divided global space would no longer be relevant in the post Cold War situation. The relevance of this argument could only be defined in terms of a reality where not just ideological but also social and economic contradictions had been resolved, a reality that was very far from that of the newly independent states in the post disintegration period. It also, therefore, predicted the emergence of a global order guided by the norms of a single hegemon, once again a situation that the 'multi-vector' stance followed by states in the post-Soviet space could not agree upon. On the other, there was emphasis on a looming specter of 'civilisational' in particular religious identities emerging as significant and resulting in a 'clash of civilisations' as a reaction to more than half a decade of atheist propaganda. In fact in the post-Soviet context, it was repeatedly argued that displaced Islamic structures of the region would now fill the 'vacuum' that the disintegration of the Soviet Union had created. As such clashes in classic 'contact zones' like Central Asia where, according to Huntington's mapping, Orthodoxy met Islamic and Buddhist civilisations was a distinct possibility. On the other hand, contact zones are also spaces where there is intense multi directional contact among civilisations and there was realisation that the Central Asian space could be more usefully defined in terms of the latter.

Within the region while a civilisational debate is occasionally referred to it is soon lost within a more realist globalisation debate where the idea that chances of conflict are reduced with the interaction among people and movement of goods and idea is questioned. A representative example is Karybek Moldobaev's critique of the 'end of history' and 'civilisational' debates in the *Journal of Turkic Civilizational Studies* Moldobaev, Professor at the Turkish Manas University at Bishkek, begins his article on 'The Conflict of Civilizations- Is it a Myth or Reality' with the argument"

As soon as the bipolar system of the global order collapsed, all of a sudden on a scene of history appeared a star called 'a phenomenon of civilisations'.[23]

This he notes was argued out in two ways. While Samuel Huntington emphasised a 'clash' of civilisations that would ensue, Francis Fukuyama spoke of an 'end of history' with the resolution of all contradictions. Moldobaev is not in agreement with either. He notes that the future would be dedicated not to a 'fight for ideas' but to a realisation of 'economic and technical problems', contradictions within which have most certainly not been resolved. Moreover, Moldobaev only refers to the civilisational debate in the first two pages of the article. The remainder is a critique of globalisation and its institutions that emphasises how globalisation failed to create 'common good' that would lead to the resolution of 'economic and technical' contradictions.

Similarly, Peter Baofu, Associate Professor at KIMEP, Almaty, dismisses the contemporary civilisational debate as falsely 'structured' in his article 'Globalisation and the Civilisational Debate'.[24] He writes:

One most important example is none other than the contemporary debate on the multiple clashes and dialogues among different civilisations. But this debate is very misguided, since the disagreement say between universal civilisationalists and their multi-civilisational counterparts is relevant only upto a certain point beyond which neither side is correct…[25]

Like Moldobaev, Baofu also emphasises that the darker side of globalisation is hegemony. He argues that while one global modern legacy of post modernity is the diffusion of Western values, the other is its instrumental character. As a result there has always been some opposition to the 'hegemonic' oppression be it in the form of anti-colonial struggles, post colonial quest for economic development and new identity and a 'post-post colonial' problematique of how to deal with globalism in the cultural sphere. These, he notes, constitute three more global modern legacies to posterity. This makes the rise of a universal civilisation (or the 'end of history' argument where the emergence of a single conflict less society is predicted) unrealistic. On the other hand he argues, conflicts are never just 'cultural' therefore a 'clash of civilisations' based on religious identities remains farfetched. He argues

...........both multi-civilisations and universal civilisation will be our human future (foreseeable for the former and distant for the latter). And even when a more universal civilisation becomes feasible in the distant future, it will not be any less hegemonic (oppressive) to its enemies. Besides, as political scientists, sociologists and economists often point out conflicts among nations and other units are not solely civilisational (cultural).[26]

The civilisational debate within the Eurasian region and particularly in Central Asia has been restricted to a search for common linkages with a Turkic civilisation where linguistic commonalities have been emphasised. The focus has been on the creation of a *Commonwealth of Turkic Speaking States* with an aim to creating an energy hub based on availability of natural oil and gas in Central Asia and Caucasus with Turkey as the point of transit of this oil and gas for the rest of the world, but particularly for the EU. A very realistic return of geopolitics is therefore evident, a return that takes notes of cultural possibilities but remains focused on strategic geopolitical ends.

Conclusions

There is a tendency to view contemporary issues pertaining to the Central Asian region within a wider framework of the global context as a microcosm of world politics. Discourses are based on the fact that an abiding feature of the modern world is its complex connectivity. This is exemplified by the networks of interconnections and interdependences that characterise every aspect of modern social life. It is this connectivity that pervades all accounts of globalisation.[27] The discourse on globalisation is replete with metaphors of global proximity of a 'shrinking world'. The creation of globalised spaces also inevitably implies the creation of a degree of cultural 'compression'. The resulting deterritorialisation is then taken to fundamentally transform the relationship between the places that one inhabits and cultural practices, experiences and identities. What remains significant is to take note of the very creative ways in which geopolitical debates have been reinterpreted in keeping with changing global dynamics. What has been attempted here is to underline this in the course of geopolitical debates from within the region.

Notes

1. For details of this argument see Harvey Sicherman, "The Revival of Geopoltics", *The Intercollegiate Review,* Spring 2002, www.fpri.org/pubs/200204.intercollegiatereview.sicherman.revivalgeopolitics.pdf.
2. See for instance Colin S. Gray and Geoffrey Sloan (eds) *Geopolitics Geography and Strategy,* London Portland OR: Frank Cass, 1999.
3. See David Newman, "An informed and Proactive Geopolitics" in a *Forum* on "Is there a politics to geopolitics?" Organizing Editor: Alexander B. Murphy, in *Progress in Human Geography,* Vol 28, No 5, 2004.
4. The term geopolitics disappeared from academic and public discourse after the Second World War because of its connection to German *Geopolitik* and the Nazi regime. It was progressively reclaimed from the 1970's by those who wished to move away from ideology and bring 'national interest' back on the agenda. For details see Virginie Mamadouh and Gertjan Dijkink, "Geopolitics, International Relations and Political Geography: The Politics of Geopolitical Discourse", *Geopolitics* Vol 11, No 3, 2006.
5. A large part of these writings emphasized strategic location and natural resources as the reason for this renewed geopolitical interest. See for instance Dashdorjiin Bayarkhuu, "Geopolitics of the New Central Asia", *World Affairs*, Vol 8 No 1, January-March 2004.
6. While the entire corpus of writings is difficult to enumerate some representative examples include Alec Rasizade, "Entering the Old Great Game in Central Asia", *Orbis* Vol 47, No 1, Winter 2003 ; Ian Cubbertson, "The new Great Game", *World Policy Journal* Vol 11, No 4, Winter 1994-95 ; Rajan Menon, "The New Great Game in Central Asia", *Survival,* Vol 45, No 2, Summer 2003; M.E. Ahrari, "The dynamics of the new Great Game in Muslim Central Asia" *Central Asian Survey* Vol 13 No 4, 1994; Kathleen A Collins and William C Wohlforth, "Central Asia: Defying Great Game Expectations", in Richard J Ellings and Aaron L Friedberg with Michael Wills (eds) *Strategic Asia 2003-04 Fragility and Crisis,* The National Bureau of Asian Research, September 2003. Similarly the metaphor of the Eurasian region as the 'chessboard' is reflected in a number of writings, see, K Gajendra Singh, "Strategic Chess Moves Across Eurasia", *World Affairs,* Vol 9 no 3, Autumn 2005.
7. For a critique see Matthew Edwards, "The New Great Game and the new great gamers: disciples of Kipling and Mackinder" *Central Asian Survey,* No 22 (1) March 2003.
8. For a detailed essay that examines this return in terms of a necessity to come to terms with a shrunken geopolitical 'space' see John Erickson, "Russia Will not be Trifled With: Geopolitical Facts and Fantacies", in Colin S. Gray and Geoffrey Sloan (eds)

Geopolitics Geography and Strategy, London Portland OR: Frank Cass, 1999.

9. Cited from Paul Reuber, "The Political Representation of Space after the Cold War and in the New Millennium", in a *Forum* on "Is there a politics to Geopolitcs?" Organizing Editor: Alexander B. Murphy, in *Progress in Human Geography,* Vol 28, No 5, 2004.
10. Francis Fukuyama, *The End of History and the Last Man,* London: Hamilton, 1992.
11. S. P. Huntington, "The Clash of Civilizations?", *Foreign Affairs,* Vol 72 No 4, 1993 and *The Clash of Civilizations and the Remaking of World Order,* (first printed by Simon and Schuster, 1996) New Delhi: Viking, 1996.
12. For a detailed note on responses to Huntington's thesis see note 3 in Mark Bassin, "Civilizations and Their Discontenets: Political Geography and Geopolitics in Huntington's Thesis', *Geopolitics* Vol 12, 2007.
13. Bassin, "Civilizations and Their Discontenets: Political Geography and Geopolitics in Huntington's Thesis'.
14. Huntington, *The Clash of Civilizations and the Remaking of World Order.*
15. Bassin, "Civilizations and Their Discontenets: Political Geography and Geopolitics in Huntington's Thesis'.
16. Bassin, "Civilizations and Their Discontenets: Political Geography and Geopolitics in Huntington's Thesis'
17. Bassin, "Civilizations and Their Discontenets: Political Geography and Geopolitics in Huntington's Thesis'.
18. Bassin, "Civilizations and Their Discontenets: Political Geography and Geopolitics in Huntington's Thesis'.
19. Bassin, "Civilizations and Their Discontenets: Political Geography and Geopolitics in Huntington's Thesis'.
20. For instance in his early writings Uzbek President Karimov emphasized this *deideologization* in the economic sphere.(See Islam Karimov, *Uzbekistan Along the Road of Deepening Economic Reform* Tashkent:"Uzbekiston", 1995)
21. Ross H Munro, "China, India and Central Asia", in Jed C Snyder (ed) *After Empire, The Emerging Geopolitics of Central Asia,* Washington: National Defence University Press, 1995.
22. See for instance Adam Smith Albion, " Tsentralnaya Aziia: 'Sredizemye' Evrazieskovo Materika", *Obshestbinnoe Mninie-Prava,* No 1 1998.
23. Karybek Moldobaev, "The Conflict of Civilizatons-Is it a Myth or Reality"? *Journal of Turkic Civilizational Studies,* No 2, 2006.
24. Peter Baofu, "Globalization and the Civilizational Debate', in *Globalization and Turkic Civilization* Proceedings of International Symposium on the Occasion of the 10th Anniversary of the Establishment of the Kyrgyz-Turkish Manas University,

Bishkek November 10-11, 2005, Kyrgyz-Turkish manas University Publication 87 and Centre for Turkic Civilizational Studies Publization 10, Bishkek 2006.

25. Baofu, "Globalization and the Civilizational Debate'
26. Baofu, "Globalization and the Civilizational Debate'.
27. For a detailed discussion see John Tomlinson, *Globalization and Culture*, Cambridge: Polity Press, 1999

Central and South Asia in the Globalised World

Bek-Ali Yerzhan

In my paper I am focusing on the issues of interaction between Central and South Asia in the globalised world. The paper begins with discussing issues of cooperation in Central Asia. It proceeds with interaction in South Asia. And it ends up with cross-regional interaction between Central and So Asia.

Before the globalisation phenomena, two regions were actually experiencing some trends of globalisation such as exchange of trade and culture. The Silk Road was functioning as a linking line between these two geographically close regions. Historical changes which took place in Central and South Asia limited/stopped this interaction. The occurrence of South Asian countries as independent in late 1940s and those of Central Asians in late 1990s pushed a process of revival of once effective interaction between two regions.

Globalisation and Central Asia

The collapse of the Soviet Union paved the way for Central Asian Republics (CARs) to become independent. While independence of CARs was largely recognised by international community, the republics remained in a shaky situation in the early nineties. Civil war erupted in Tajikistan, investors were not eager to invest in a risky region, social development was at zero level, people were discouraged by the political developments and economic hardships.

Today CARs are more or less stable countries which are undergoing the process of formation. The region represents countries with different social, economic and political development. The 70–year common Soviet history created interdependence of the countries in the region. It is unusually high as they face the reality of an inherited regionally integrated transport system, taking into account that the countries are physically isolated from the global markets and have relatively small domestic markets. Regional cooperation is critical to achieving efficient regional transport and transit systems and promoting integration into international commerce.[1]

From the outset, the regional cooperation was topical and a debatable issue among the academia and decision-making institutions. The reason for hot debates on the issue is the pressing necessities of present global trends such as globalisation, international security challenges and regionalisation.

Generally, the countries of region perceive that regional cooperation is a necessity. The following factors force regional states to necessitate cooperative activities in Central Asia:

- the countries share inherited public infrastructure that was established as a unified system and requires a regional approach to rehabilitation. The weak economic performance in the first half of the 1990s may have forced national governments to concentrate on domestic issues rather than regional. This is a changing trend since most of domestic social and economic issues are bound to be resolved through regional interaction.
- the existence of extensive structural interdependence and expansion of energy generation and distribution capacities and the water-energy nexus; Tajikistan, Kyrgyzstan have abundant hydro resources, Kazakhstan, Uzbekistan and Turkmenistan are rich with oil and gas resources. The region is unique in a way that oil and gas rich countries depend on water rich countries and vice versa. Kazakhstan, Uzbekistan and Turkmenistan have already begun exporting hydrocarbon resources to near and far abroad. Tajikistan (Nurek hydro-electric station (HES), Sangtudin HES 1 and HES 2, Rogun HES and Zeravshan HES) and Kyrgyzstan (Toktagul HES, Naryn HES, Kambaratan HES) are capable of producing enough electricity for the regional consumption as well as export them to Russian, Chinese, Indian, Afghani and Pakistani markets.[2] The Eurasian Economic Community (EEC) in this sense is working hard on reestablishing water-energy nexus in the region. For example, in 2004 a first step towards that goal was made. The drafts of Concept of Water-Energy, Food and Transport Consortiums were launched.[3]
- a need to harmonise regulatory standards and working practices in financial markets, communications and other investment services across the region to facilitate private sector growth.[4] It is the private sector and the medium and small size entrepreneurs who are building effective transborder trade and regional economic links.

- reducing barriers to intraregional trade and transit to overcome disadvantages of segmented national markets, thereby making the region more attractive for foreign and domestic investors.[5] Individually the countries have limited business appeal. The close regional cooperation would make a win-win game in business and investments.
- developing a regional transport network to minimise the location disadvantage and facilitate access to large neighbouring and global markets.[6] According to B.Karimov, Head of Intergovernmental Council on Roads, the issues of railroad and motor transportation between Tajikistan and Uzbekistan negatively affect Tajik economy by 5–6% of GDP annually and Uzbek economy by 3–4%.[7]
- regional countries face common challenges such as human and drug trafficking, extremism and intolerance of any kind. Moreover, a number of negative regional externalities can be tackled only by adopting a regional approach. These include environment degradation, of which the Aral Sea is a prime example, land degradation and desertification, which have reduced agriculture fields and availability of arable land and the spread of communicable diseases and pestilence.[8]
- historically, CARs share similar cultural, social and linguistic traditions.[9]

On the whole, there is an understanding of the need for regional cooperation. Several initiatives were launched in the region within international institutions such as Eurasia Economic Community (EEC), Shanghai Cooperation Organisation (SCO), Economic Cooperation Organisation (ECO), and Asian Development Bank, European Bank of Reconstruction and Development. The regional leaders also announced some of their proposals for regional cooperation. In early 1990s, the Uzbek President Karimov initiated Central Asian Common Market, in 2006 the Kazakh President Nazarbayev on his part proposed the establishment of Union of Central Asian countries. Today all Central Asian initiatives on cooperation are concentrated in the work of EEC.

However, the progress has been modest so far. The challenges in promoting regional cooperation include but not limited to the following:

- a perception that pay-offs from regional projects do not match the effort required to prepare them; uncertainty about distribution of gains and fears of losing out, rather than seeing regional cooperation as a win-win situation;
- leaders' reticence to recognise suprasovereign entities given the acute sensitivity to national sovereignty;

- weak political will and weak mutual trust by governments;[10]
- smaller countries' fear of their larger neighbours and a tussle for political supremacy among the larger countries within the region.[11] At the same time, there is different significance of regional cooperation for the countries. For example Tajikistan's economy needs more cooperation from the Uzbek side rather than Uzbek economy from the Tajik one;
- relatively poor government capacity for intraregional cooperation in most CARs; [12]
- weak institutional and management capacities of national governments;[13]
- growing divergence in economic policies and performance.[14] Thus, regional countries face different social and economic challenges. Consequently, national governments focus on different aspects of regional interaction and cooperation prioritising their national, social and economic challenges;
- at present, hundreds of documents and agreements on promoting Central Asian interaction have been adopted by the regional countries. However, the problem remains in implementing them and creating necessary circumstances for intraregional cooperation.

The countries of the region have to fulfill several objectives if they want to get best of regional interaction. The *first objective* is increasing trade and integration with large markets, both globally and in the region's proximity.[15] The CARs have to secure access to markets in Russia, China, South Asia, Iran and Turkey to export natural resources, goods and services. The *second objective* for regional cooperation, related to the first, is to improve full-fledged, all level economic cooperation especially small and medium size trade within the region to reduce costs of transport, communication and facilitate transit.[16] This will allow CARs to become integrated with inter-regional corridors and to use their location to their advantage. This will restore its historical role as a land bridge between some of the world's most dynamic, large and emerging economies. Furthermore, in Central Asian case an important *objective* is to create favourable political atmosphere within each and every regional state towards regional economic cooperation through political meetings, science and scholar cooperation and culture. The *fourth objective* is to improve supplies of water-energy that are required not only to sustain growth but are also basic necessities in harsh climatic conditions.[17] This requires rehabilitation and subsequent expansion of both energy generation and transmission capacities. Central Asia is an energy-surplus region. In the long term, it could export significant volumes of energy to neighbours such as Afghanistan, the PRC, South Asia and even Eastern Europe via the Russian network or/and Caucasus. Necessary conditions would be a resolution to intraregional issues in energy trade and successful rehabilitation of the regional network. The *fifth objective* of regional cooperation is to tackle negative externalities such as environmental degradation, the spread of communicable diseases like tuberculosis and HIV, narcotics trade and trafficking in humans. To sum up, regional cooperation is essential to attaining these strategic objectives.[18]

Globalisation and South Asia

In my paper I term three countries (Afghanistan, India and Pakistan) of South Asia as South Asia. This has been done taking into consideration geographic proximity, historical link and trade and business perspective.

The countries of South Asia share many equally important characteristics. For centuries before and during the British ruling, the South Asian region except Afghanistan had been, by and large, an open economic space with relatively free movement of goods, labour, capital and currency. During the British era, the commonality of the region was deepened through a shared form of administration, judiciary, military, education system, and integrated transport and communication system. However, the events leading to and following the partition of British India (which had included most of South Asia) in 1947 brought about a fracturing in the polities and economies of the major countries in the region, and left deep scars on the psyche and politics. India and Pakistan fought three wars. Tense relations between some major countries in the region made prospects for regional cooperation in South Asia difficult. Afghanistan sank into internal conflicts and wars. However the increasing trend toward globalisation and regionalisation in other parts of the world have made South Asian countries realise the need to fully participate in this process to maximise the benefits from greater economic integration.[19] Moreover, the need to face common challenges such as environment, energy deficiency and poverty has become an important regional concern, requiring close regional coordination. Relations between India and Pakistan have greatly improved and the composite dialogue between the two countries is progressing. In 2004 South Asian FTA (SAFTA) was established and is expected to be fully operational by 2016.[20] These factors have, to a large extent, contributed to the changing environment favouring regional cooperation in South Asia.[21] Land and air transport between India and Pakistan was restored after the Islamabad Summit. Nonetheless, the low level of current activity in transport of goods between the two countries often occurs via a third country, which is enormously costly. With the thawing of relations between India and Pakistan, potential opportunities exist for cooperation in the areas of road, rail, civil aviation, energy transportation and shipping. Specific projects could include upgrading border facilities at Atari Wagah (largest border point between India and Pakistan), upgrading and expanding existing bus service, improving and expanding connecting air links and building road links between the two countries.[22]

Figure 1

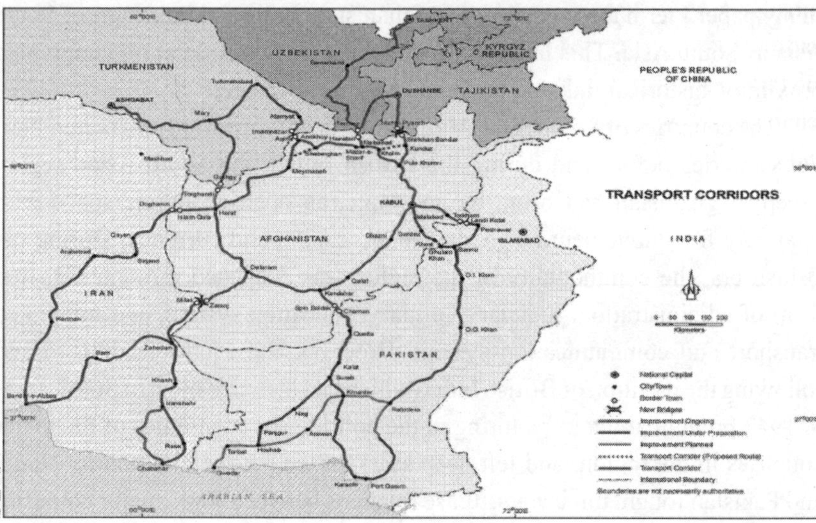

Source: Alamgir M.(2005, March 3 and 4). Report on the Economic Impact of Central-South Asian Road Corridors. *Report prepared for the Second Ministerial Conference on Transport and Trade in Central and South Asia.* Asian Development Bank. p.8

Afghanistan in spite of appalling security situation is determined to rebuild its economy and reestablish economic and transportation links with neighbouring countries. It sees itself as a critical land bridge between Central Asia and the South Asian region. Recognising this importance, Afghanistan was inducted as the eight member of SAARC at the Dhaka Summit.[23] The transit facility for gas from Central Asia to Pakistan and India through Afghanistan could generate sizeable revenues for Afghanistan, and improve the availability and reduce the cost of energy for Pakistan and northern India. [24] In May 2002, the heads of state of Afghanistan, Pakistan and Turkmenistan met in Islamabad to discuss the possibility of establishing a major gas pipeline through the three countries. The Turkmenistan-Afghanistan-Pakistan (TAP) Natural Gas Pipeline Project consists of 1,600 kilometres of gas pipeline that can transport up to 30 billion cubic metres of natural gas annually from the Dauletabad fields in southeast Turkmenistan to consumers in Afghanistan, Pakistan, and possibly India. The expected cost is about $3.3 billion. Asian Development Bank (ADB) provided technical assistance for conducting feasibility studies, assessing security-related issues and preparing the framework agreement.[25] Apart from energy, the trade arteries crossing Afghanistan would be of great value. The new corridors (North-South and East-West) provide a strategic alternative to traditional transit routes through the Russian Federation or the Caucasus for the Central Asian republics and contribute to enhancing Afghanistan's rehabilitation works as a major trade hub between Europe, the Middle East and Central Asia.[26]

Figure 2

Source: Van Z.E. (2005, December). Reconnecting Afghanistan. *Asian Development Bank Review*.p10

It is conspicuous that would-be effective regional cooperation in South Asia can help achieve economic and social development and reduce negative regional externalities. It can help eliminate physical and non-physical barriers; cross-border development of basic infrastructure, such as highways, railways, shipping and air connectivity, inland waterways, power grids and telecommunication links, can reduce physical barriers to the movement of goods and people across national boundaries, which can in turn expand regional trade and tourism, increase foreign exchange earning capability and create labour-intensive activities generating employment opportunities; quicken the pace of domestic development by widening the options available to participating countries; and expand markets for goods and services; thus promoting economies of scale and reducing transaction and transportation costs.[27] In addition, regional cooperation promoting both physical infrastructure and institutional reform, such as trade and investment facilitation, can significantly increase the region's potential attractiveness to investors, to the benefit of all participating economies. Therefore, regional cooperation can play an important role in assisting South Asian countries speed up economic growth and, more importantly, promote pro-poor growth.[28]

However, the region is not without risks. The most serious risk comes from possible unfavourable political events that result in renewed tensions between countries in the region. However, it seems that internal security challenges and turbulences within the national states of South Asia pose more tension which would echo to the regional status quo. A second risk is that national governments and political parties often use blame game in their election campaigns. This kind of attitude degrades achieved progress in regional cooperation and creates negative atmosphere for fostering cooperative relationship. A third risk relates to the possibility (and/or perception) that some participating countries will gain more than others from regional cooperation and integration in South Asia, such as a regional free trade agreement. Finally, lack of adequate funding may hold back implementation of regional cooperation projects.[29]

Cross-regional Interaction Between Central and South Asia in the Globalisation

The globalisation process is making the entire world into one small village. The process enhances intraregional and cross-regional interactions. Central and South Asia are not exceptions in this process. The history of two regions provides good ground for interaction in trade, economy and culture. The globalisation has its negative face in cross-regional interaction. The historical Silk Road has changed to drugs and arms smuggling and human trafficking road today which is destructive for the region and also the whole world.

The present day regional republics of Central Asia are in permanent search for diversified energy, trade and transport partners. While enjoying good relations with its northern, eastern and western neighbours, CARs relations with its southern neighbours remain undeveloped. The southern direction provides the shortest possible route of access to dynamic markets and world waters. And Central Asia, itself being land bridge, can be transit route for Pakistan and India to Europe, Southern Russia and upper China. Pakistan's Karachi, Gwadar, Port Qasim port are comparatively cheaper and shorter outlet for Central Asian natural energy resources and its trade to the outside world. Afghanistan, India and Pakistan serving as transit routes can themselves be abundant market for CARs. No one doubts consumption rate increase in India as its economy grows. Pricewaterhouse Coopers reviews predict that India will be number one in growth rate by 2050.[30] In globalisation, India can no longer afford a self-reliance policy. It has to reap benefits of globalisation and integrate itself into regional and cross-regional interactions.

Being part of globalisation, international development institutions such as Asian Development Bank (ADB) are concerned in fostering cooperation between Central and South Asia. ADB has supported various regional and sub-regional cooperation programmes namely the South Asia Sub-regional Economic Cooperation (SASEC) Programme, the Central Asia Regional Economic Cooperation (CAREC) Programme, the Sub-regional Economic Cooperation in South and Central Asia (SECSCA) Programme.[31]

The ADB launched the Central and South Asia Transport and Trade Forum. The Forum emphasised on two major corridors: the North-South Corridor and the East-West Corridor. The corridors are supposed to create linkage in the whole transcontinental transportation system. Studying the potential benefits of North-South corridors, the ADB found that overall trade can increase by as much as 15%, or $12 billion, for the regions as a whole if transportation and trade facilitation are improved.[32] The ADB organised the first ministerial conference on transport and trade in Central and South Asia held in Manila in 2003. The participants were ministers from Afghanistan, Pakistan, Tajikistan, Uzbekistan and Iran (as an observer). They agreed to promote regional trade and economic cooperation by improving the transport corridors. The ministers endorsed the establishment of the Central and South Asia Transport and Trade Forum (CSATTF) as an instrument for such cooperation.[33] In 2005 China, India, Kazakhstan and Kyrgyzstan joined the Forum. That year the Corridor Development Plan was endorsed by the Forum participants. The Plan programmes are prepared for infrastructure improvement, transit facilitation, knowledge sharing, and capacity development.[34] The CASATTF pointed to importance of two corridors: (1) the North-South Corridor (connecting Tajikistan, Turkmenistan and Uzbekistan through Afghanistan to the ports of Karachi, Gwadar and Port Qasim in Pakistan) totalling about 2,800 kilometres; and (2) the East-West Corridor (connecting the same countries, through Afghanistan to the ports of Bandar-e-Abbas and Chabahar in Iran) totalling about 2,900 kilometres. Road links along the two corridors have been improved steadily during the last 2 years. In 2002, about 40% of the total length of each transport corridor was considered in good condition with adequate maintenance, while the remaining 60% was identified as in need of rehabilitation and/or upgrading. Presently, about 40% of the total length of each corridor (about 1,100 kilometres) has been improved or is being improved with external assistance, leaving about 20% for rehabilitation and upgrading. The government of Iran has upgraded the road from Bandar-e-Abbas to Dogharun to a two-lane asphalt-pavement standard as well as the link from the newly developed Chabahar port to the Milak-Zaranj border. A bypass route to the Chabahar-Iranshahr link in Iran is currently under construction. In Turkmenistan, the government is improving the road link between Atamurat and Imamnazar (the adjacent border to Afghanistan). In Uzbekistan, the road section between Tashkent and Termez (745 kilometres) has been improved. European Union (EU), Islamic Development Bank, World Bank, and bilateral partners such as the governments of India, Iran, Japan, Kuwait, Saudi Arabia, Pakistan and United States have provided funding to improve the other part of the Afghanistan ring road and access roads to the neighbouring countries located along the CSATTF(Central and South Asia Transport an Trade Forum) corridors. The World Bank has assisted Afghanistan in reconstructing the Hairatan border and, in cooperation with EU, the Torkham border. The border facilities at Islam Qala, Shir Khan Bandar, Torghundi and Zaranj in Afghanistan have also been upgraded with assistance from the governments of Iran, Germany and United States.

Transport and trade along the CSATTF corridors are presently constrained at the transport nodes where transshipment often takes place, different modes of transport meet and infrastructure facilities, mostly border facilities, need further development or improvement. Under CSATTF, the following eight major border crossings have been identified along the two corridors.

- Hairatan-Ayritom/Termez (Afghanistan-Uzbekistan border)
- Shir Khan Bandar-Nizhniy Pyandzh (Afghanistan-Tajikistan border)
- Torkham-Torkham/Landi Kotal (Afghanistan-Pakistan border)
- Waish/Spin Boldak-Chamman (Afghanistan-Pakistan border)
- Zaranj-Milak (Afghanistan-Iran border)
- Islam Qala-Dogharun (Afghanistan-Iran border)
- Torghundi-Gushgy (Afghanistan-Turkmenistan border)
- Aqin-Imamnazar (Afghanistan-Turkmenistan border) [35]

In 1995, China, Pakistan, Kazakhstan and Kyrgyzstan signed an agreement for the construction of the Almaty-Karachi roads, connecting Central Asia with the Arabian Sea. In addition to the north-south route via Iran, a new road link via the Chinese region of Xinjiang and the Pakistani Karakoram Highway was proposed. A rail and road network, connecting Almaty, Bishkek and Kashgar to Islamabad and the Pakistani seaports of Karachi and Gwadar, offered a relatively viable alternative to other routes.[36] Kazakhstan, Uzbekistan, Afghanistan and Pakistan signed an agreement on railroad from Termez to Mazare-Sharif and Kabul and Peshawar, Islamabad. All Central Asian countries have closely integrated transportation communication. So once this road is active, it links all CARs to Pakistan and can be prolonged to India.[37]

The above mentioned measures include customs related issues. To address customs-related issues, CSATTF has identified the following five major areas: (1) simplify and harmonise customs procedures and documentation, (2) develop modern border concepts such as joint border processing and one-stop service, (3) share information and communications technology-based data for customs operations, (4) introduce modern customs techniques such as risk management and post-entry audit, and (5) build capacity of local and national customs administration officials. [38]

In addition to the physical improvement of the transport corridors, developing an efficient transit system is crucial to the goals of CSATTF. A number of constraints have been identified in transit facilitation of the region, including transshipment, unofficial checks and fees, domestic transport sector protectionism, and lack of national mechanism for transport, transit and trade facilitation. To overcome those constraints, CSATTF has adopted two approaches:

(1) *accession to the relevant international conventions* (These international conventions are (a) Convention on Road Traffic, (b) Convention on Road Signs and Signals, (c) International Convention on the Harmonisation of Frontier Control of Goods, (d) Convention on the Contract for the International Carrying of Goods by Road, (f) Conventions Pertaining to Perishable Goods, (g) Customs Convention on the International Transport of Goods under Cover of the Transports Internationaux Routiers (TIR) Carnets, (h) Customs Convention) and (2) *development of efficient corridor transit*. To support the development of efficient transit arrangements, CSATTF has identified the need for: (1) modernisation of existing bilateral agreements, (2) development of transit strategy based on bilateral and/or multilateral agreements, (3) introduction of TIR in the region, and (4) examination of potential for other transit systems.[39]

The today's cross-regional interaction lacks regional approach. Mainly individual CARs and individual South Asian countries are building relations on the bilateral level. The preference of low level bilateral interaction between countries rather than intraregional and cross-regional is due to the challenges which include but not limited to (1) poor infrastructure facilities; (2) inadequate regional transport network, particularly missing links, and lack of connections to state capitals, production centres, markets, and land access to ports; (3) modernisation, increasing capacity and removing bottlenecks; underdeveloped transport logistics services (4) weak corporate governance (5) restrictive trade policies (6) different customs laws and procedures; (7) limited coordination of infrastructure investments; (8) low level of private sector participation; (9) capacity constraints in both public and private sectors; (10)security concerns involving drugs and human trafficking.

Opportunities of cross-regional interaction coexist with its challenges. The opportunities include the following:

Energy: Central Asia has huge proved and estimated hydrocarbons and natural resources. South Asia can serve as transit rout for transportation as well as market for the export of hydrocarbons.

The Asian Development Bank supported a feasibility study to establish the Turkmenistan-Afghanistan-Pakistan-India (TAPI) pipeline. In May 2002, the heads of state of Afghanistan, Pakistan, and Turkmenistan met in Islamabad to restart the Natural Gas Pipeline Project.

The project aims to construct natural gas transmission pipeline of 1,700 kilometres to transport 30 billion cubic metres of gas per year from

Turkmenistan's Dauletabad gas fields to Afghanistan, Pakistan and possibly to India. The route proposed is from Dauletabad to the Afghan cities of Herat and Khandahar and then to Multan in Pakistan. The ADB estimates the cost of the project to be $3.3 billion and projects that its implementation will take five years. The TAPI project, if constructed as planned, will enable Afghanistan to reclaim its status as the land bridge between Central and South Asia.

The Termez-Kabul-Peshawar-India route (TKPI) pipeline would connect the southernmost city in Uzbekistan, Termez, to Kabul via the Mazar-i-Sharif and then would run from Kabul to Islamabad. Termez is 300 kilometres from Kabul and Kabul is 200 kilometres from Peshawar, which in turn is about 250 kilometres from Islamabad. Extending this route to India would only require about 250 kilometres via Lahore, the major economic centre of Lahore-Amritsar. The distance of the TKPI route is only half of TAPI, 1,700 kilometres. It will take the pipeline through much more populated areas but still reach the same destinations in Pakistan and India. Notably, it will also go through Kabul, brining additional benefits to Afghanistan's energy starved capital. The construction of the gas pipelines could create substantial revenues for Afghanistan. It is estimated that if the pipeline to Pakistan existed today, and if Afghanistan charged world prices for transport of gas through its country, it would be earning about $1 billion to $1.5 billion in annual revenues from the gas pipeline tax alone. The Afghan Government could reap another $0.5 billion in revenues on the transport of oil from Central Asia to South Asia.[40] Pakistan would benefit too because it is not able to sustain the current demand in its domestic market and because it is transporting gas and oil thousand of kilometres inland from its ports. Further, India would find an additional source of energy and would diversify its ability to bargain for its growing needs.[41]

Figure 3

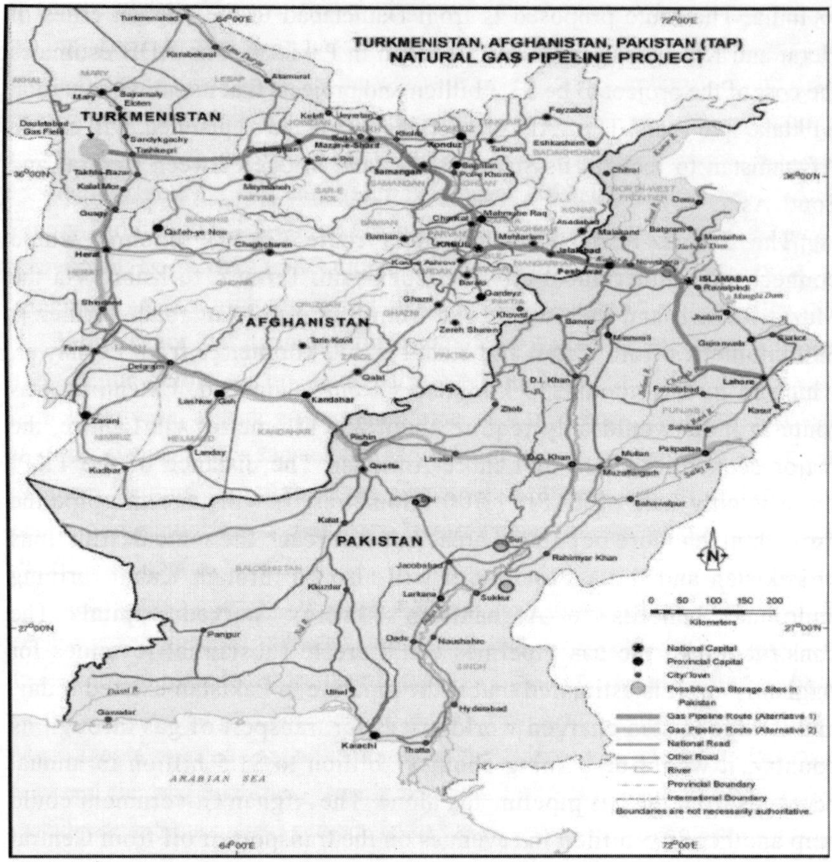

Source: Chander IS. (2002, December).Technical Assistance for the Feasibility Studies of the

Turkmenistan-Afghanistan-Pakistan Natural Gas Pipeline Project. *Asian Development Bank*.p.3.

The proposed pipelines will also bring significant indirect economic benefits. They would create jobs, promote the construction of new and improved infrastructure, and increase the availability of electricity, gas and oil to regional industries. Households along the length of the energy corridor from the Uzbek border to Pakistan would see their incomes rise. The pipelines represent an opportunity to have locally owned small private community power stations which can act as small energy generators providing the local populations not only with jobs but with cheap energy.[42]

Rebuilding Afghanistan: CARs are ready to work closely with Pakistan and India in rebuilding Afghanistan which remains a common concern. It is in the hands of Afghan people and their neighbours to make it a place of transit and a place of contact and not an obstacle to cooperation between Central Asia and South Asia.

Geographical location (land bridge): Central Asia is situated in crossroads of China, Russia, Caucasus and Europe. It can serve as transit route for Pakistani and Indian goods to above mentioned directions. Being a land locked country, Kazakhstan is developing land ports. It is constructing 'Khorgos' land port on the border with China. In the framework of this project, Kazakhstan is constructing Khorgos-Saryozek railroad which is intended to link transchinese rail road with Central Asian transport and industrial corridor. Central Asian corridor on its part is connected with Russian railroads which are close to Europe. Moreover, it is constructing Taskala-Ozenki, land port on the border with Russia, and Caspian sea port in Aktau. These three ports (Khorgos, Taskala-Ozenki and Aktau) have to link Kazakhstan to international transport corridors.[43]

Railway: Kazakhstan, Turkmenistan and Iran are building new railway (Uzen-Kyzylkaya-Bereket- Etrek-Horgan). In October2007, Kazakhstan, Turkmenistan and Iran signed memorandum on this new railway. The railway length is 670 kms (Kazakhstan-120 kms, Turkmenistan-470 kms, Iran-70 kms). The construction estimates are $620 million.[44] Taking into account good and constructive Indo-Iranian relations, India has all opportunities to benefit from the project.

Medium and small sized manufacture: All CARs strive to build economy based mainly on medium and small sized manufactures. So, there is opportunity for Pakistani and Indian medium and small sized manufactures to establish joint ventures with their Central Asian counterparts in various fields of common concern such as petrochemicals, tourism, machinery building, food processing, textiles, transport logistics, metallurgy and construction materials. The location of Central Asia makes it easier to export their products to Chinese, Russian, Caucasian and European markets.

Cotton: South Kazakhstan and neighbouring Uzbekistan produce cotton of high quality. Pakistan and India can look for opportunities to set totally integrated textile plants in Kazakhstan and Uzbekistan.

Tea: Notwithstanding the popularity of Indian tea, it does not have full-fledged tea blending and packing factory in Kazakhstan. The per capita consumption of tea in Kazakhstan is 1.5 kilograms. This is amongst the highest in the world. So India can set a factory and take advantage of Kazakhstan's geographic location.

Medicine: CARs can cooperate with South Asia in medical field. It is not only pharmaceuticals, India is known for its cheap and qualitative medical facilities such as Appollo, Fortis and Maxx.

Education: Central Asian youth are flooding abroad to study. Indian institutes of technology and management, and Pakistanis institutes of technology and management could be popular destinations for the youth and engineers provided that information on these institutes is available in annual education fairs and in the respective embassies. Academic cooperation in social sciences and humanities between Central Asian universities, think-tanks and their South Asian counterparts is at a low level. This causes a lot of misperception and misunderstandings for Central Asian scholars of South Asia and vice versa.

Human resources: Former head of Sustainable Development Fund of Kazakhstan Mr.Kelimbetov acknowledged that to keep today's economic development and grow further, Kazakhstan will require up to one million highly and medium skilled personnel.[45] Pakistan and India have cheap, qualified and huge human resources in this regard.

Tourism: Tourism from South Asia to Central Asia and vice versa is too low. Central Asia is blessed with beautiful nature and climate and is an ideal destination for tourists. Two-way tourism can be a massive growth area between Central and South Asian tour companies

Military: The newly adopted Kazakh military doctrine puts emphasis on peace-keeping operations by Kazakh army. In this regard, Pakistan and India owe great experience in the field and can share it through exchange of military institutions and officers. India has two of the finest defence training institutions—the National Defence Academy in Khadakvasla (Pune) and the Indian Military Academy in Dehradun; the same can be said for Pakistani military academies and institutions in Rawalpindi. These military institutions along with Russian, American, Turkish and European institutions, where Central Asians are getting trained, can be destinations for Central Asia military officers.

Conclusion

Finally, present day interaction between two neighbouring regions is characterised by uneasy situation in Afghanistan, Indo-Pakistan relations and insufficient regional cooperation and conflicts within Central and South Asia.

These factors hamper enhancement of interdependence and cooperation in all spheres of energy, trade, transport and culture.

There are huge opportunities for mutual cooperation in the globalisation between Central and South Asia. Here two important lessons have to be learned. The most important lesson learned in advancing regional and cross-regional cooperation in the globalised world is that strong political commitment by the participating countries is a critical factor. Another important lesson learned from ongoing cooperation initiatives is the need to ensure the right balance between improving hard and soft infrastructure. Improving regional and cross-regional physical (or 'hard') infrastructure, such as roads and bridges, and physical customs facilities, is important to facilitate cross-border movements of goods and people. However, policy and procedural reforms of 'soft' infrastructure, such as harmonisation of standards, liberalisation of transit barriers and streamlining of customs procedures, are just as important if benefits of regional and cross-regional cooperation are to be realised. Therefore, interaction and the building of synergies between 'hard' and 'soft' infrastructure need to be enhanced in regional and cross-regional cooperation activities in the globalised world.

Notes

1. Asian Development Bank. Regional Cooperation Strategy and Program for Central Asia Regional Economic Cooperation (CAREC) member countries (Azerbaijan, Kazakhstan, Kyrgyz Republic , Mongolia, People's Republic of China, Tajikistan , Uzbekistan) 2005–2007 , Manila: Asian Development Bank. July, 2007. http://www.adb.org/Documents/CSPs/CAREC/2004/CSP-CAREC-2004.pdf
2. Vinokurov.E. Voda, *Energia i kapitaly. Budushee vneshne ekonomicheskogo kompleksa Tsentralnoi Azii* (Energy and capital. Future external economic complex of Central Asia).Bishkek: October, 2007. Retrieved July, 2008, from http://www.analitika.org/
3. Ibid.
4. Asian Development Bank. Regional Cooperation Strategy and Program for Central Asia Regional Economic Cooperation (CAREC) member countries (Azerbaijan, Kazakhstan, Kyrgyz Republic , Mongolia, People's Republic of China, Tajikistan , Uzbekistan) 2005–2007 , Manila: Asian Development Bank. July, 2007. http://www.adb.org/Documents/CSPs/CAREC/2004/CSP-CAREC-2004.pdf
5. Ibid.
6. Ibid.
7. Razumov Y, "Ministry transporta EvrAzES vyskazalis' protiv proekta tranzitnoi dorogi iz Kitaya" (in Russian) (Transport ministers of EurAsEC expressed their

objection against transit routes from China). *Panorama*, no 43, 9 November 2007, p. 11.

8. Asian Development Bank. *Regional Cooperation Strategy and Program for Central Asia Regional Economic Cooperation (CAREC) member countries (Azerbaijan, Kazakhstan, Kyrgyz Republic , Mongolia, People's Republic of China, Tajikistan , Uzbekistan) 2005–2007* , Manila: Asian Development Bank. July, 2007. http://www.adb.org/Documents/CSPs/CAREC/2004/CSP-CAREC-2004.pdf
9. Ibid.
10. Ibid.
11. Ibid.
12. Ibid.
13. Ibid.
14. Ibid.
15. Ibid.
16. Asian Development Bank. *Regional Cooperation Strategy and Program South Asia (2006-2008*). Manila: Asian Development Bank.2005. http://www.adb.org/Documents/CSPs/South-Asia/2006/CSP-SA-2006.pdf
17. Asian Development Bank. *Regional cooperation and integration Strategy*. Manila: Asian Development Bank. July 2006. p40.
18. Asian Development Bank. *Regional Cooperation Strategy and Program South Asia (2006-2008*), Manila: Asian Development Bank. 2005. http://www.adb.org/Documents/CSPs/South-Asia/2006/CSP-SA-2006.pdf
19. Ibid.
20. Ibid.
21. Ibid.
22. Ibid.
23. Ibid.
24. Ibid.
25. Lunev I. "Indiskii marsh" (Indian march) (in Russian). *Rossiya v globalnoi politike*. October 2007. pp 13-18
26. Asian Development Bank. (2006, July), *Regional Cooperation and Iintegration Strategy*, p. 31.
27. Byrd, W. , "Prospects for Regional Development and Economic Cooperation in the Wider Central Asia Region", Paper prepared for the Kabul Conference on Regional Economic Cooperation, World Bank.Washington D.C. 2005. p.55.
28. Asian Development Bank. *Regional Cooperation Strategy and Program South Asia (2006-2008*), Manila: Asian Development Bank. 2005. http://www.adb.org/Documents/CSPs/South-Asia/2006/CSP-SA-2006.pdf

29. Ibid.

30. Asian Development Bank. *Regional Cooperation Strategy and Program South Asia (2006-2008*), Manila: Asian Development Bank. 2005. http://www.adb.org/Documents/CSPs/South-Asia/2006/CSP-SA-2006.pdf

31. Asma Shakir Khawaja. Pakistan and the 'New Great Game. *IPRI Paper, 5*. April, 2003. Retrived March 10,2008, from http://ipripak.org/papers/pakandnewgame.shtml

32. Chichkin, A. Brosok cherez Gindukush. Vozobnovlena rabota nad proektom evroaziatskoi jeleznoi dorogi Uzbekistan –Afghanistan – Pakistan –India. (Leap through Hindukush. The railway Uzbekistan- Afghanistan –Pakistan –India is renewed) (in Russian) *"RG"–economy,* May 15, 2007. p10.

33. Asian Development Bank. *Regional Cooperation Strategy and Program South Asia (2006-2008*), Manila: Asian Development Bank. 2005. http://www.adb.org/Documents/CSPs/South-Asia/2006/CSP-SA-2006.pdf

34. Ibid.

35. Ibid.

36. Ibid.

37. Ibid.

38. Ibid.

39. Ibid.

40. Kaufmann, K. and Feizlmayr, A.H. "Analysis pegs pipeline ahead of LNG for Caspian area to China" *.Oil and Gas Journal*, April 2003. 102(10).p. 58.

41. Masood A. "Afghanistan". Paper presented at First Kabul Conference on Partnership, Trade and Development in Greater Central Asia. April 2006.p12

42. Byrd, W. Prospects for Regional Development and Economic Cooperation in the Wider Central Asia Region. Paper prepared for the Kabul Conference on Regional Economic Cooperation, 2005. , January 2006. World Bank.Washington D.C. p.55

43. Balgin R.Interview with Z.Sultanbekova, general director of "ASME". *Delovaya Nedelya*, May 11, 2007. pp 2- 9

44. Gilt N. Iz "Kazakhstana v Iran – po novoi doroge" (Kazakhstan to Iran through new road) (in Russian). *Izvestia –Kazakhstan,* Dec.5, 2007. p12

45. Razumov Y. "Instituty razvitiya stali svyzuyushim mehanizmom mejdu morvoi I kazakhstanskoi ekonomikoi" (Development institutes have become mechanism between global and Kazakh economy) (in Russian). *Panorama.* May 25, 2007. p11.

India's Energy Diplomacy in the CIS Region

Nalin Kumar Mohapatra

Introduction

Contrary to the expectation from diverse quarters, the CIS states of erstwhile Soviet Union are playing a catalytic role in shaping the contours of global geopolitics. What heightened their importance in the global arena is that now they are emerging as a major destination for both state and non-state actors who are trying to reap the benefits of natural resources like oil and gas. In this sphere, the Caspian states, Russia, Kazakhstan, Turkmenistan and Azerbaijan, and Central Asian states like Uzbekistan, having significant gas resources, are the emerging players in the CIS states. Since world economy is moving at a fast pace and there is a great demand for energy, these five post-Soviet states emerged as the catalyst forces for supplying global energy.[1] As per an estimate of International Monetary Fund, today around half of the energy produced in this region is exported across the globe from a mere 22 percent in 1992. Due to energy, these states are involved in a complex 'energy game', aimed at ensuring some sort of 'energy equilibrium between demand and supply'. Another important aspect of this 'energy game' is that though some CIS states are not involved in this and are not producing any oil or gas resources, but they are emerging as strategically vital in the sense that they act as transient countries. In this regard, one can give the example of Georgia, Armenia, Ukraine, etc. The complex 'energy game' has also been called as the 'inter-dependency game' in this vast Eurasian space. For instance, Baltic countries and Ukraine are accruing major profits by acting as transient countries.[2] The present paper is an attempt to portray complexities involved in the energy politics. India, which is emerging as a major economic force in Asia, is also actively pursuing this policy of securing energy from various sources. The present paper will examine some of the trajectories associated with 'energy security' in the CIS and the Indian policy of securing the same.

Energy Profile of CIS States

Before embarking on India's oil diplomacy in the CIS states, one has to look at the exact energy figures of these countries. Different studies give different figures about the exact position of oil and gas in this region. In this article, the author is using the energy figures given by British Petroleum.

Table-1: Proven Caspian Oil and Gas Reserves
(At the end of 2006)

Name of CIS States	Oil (in thousand Million barrels)	Gas (in Trillion Cubic Meters)
Azerbaijan	7.0	1.26
Kazakhstan	39.8	1.90
Russian Federation	79.3	44.60
Turkmenistan	0.6	2.67
Uzbekistan	0.6	1.74

Source: BP Statistical Review of World Energy, June 2008.p.6 and 22. http://www.bp.com/productlanding.do?categoryId=6929&contentId=7044622

India's Energy Requirement

The presence of vast oil and gas in this region provided an opportunity to India to initiate an active foreign policy in this region. India used its traditional historico-cultural relationship with this region as a leitmotif in pursuing its goal of securing energy from this part of the world since India is also an 'energy deficit' country. According to the Draft Report of the Expert Committee on Integrated Energy Policy, set up by the Planning Commission, the demand for imported energy will increase in future. The report further says that "our dependence on imported energy has increased from a level of 17.85 percent of Total Primary Commercial Energy Supply (TPCES). The report adds that "oil import constituted 72 percent of our total oil consumption".[3] Similarly, the recent Energy Information Administration in its official country report gives a glaring picture about India's energy need. As per the EIA report in 2007, India was the fifth largest consumer of oil and consumed around 2.8 million barrels of oil which then increased to 3 million barrels.[4] Like the oil sector, the EIA predicts that India will have to meet its rising demand for natural gas by importing it from various countries. India has a deficit for gas resources because of their bourgeoning demand from fertiliser and power sectors. The EIA report adds that India consumed around 1.5 Trillion Cubic Feet (TCF) in 2007 and the demand will more than double by 2030.[5] According to a conservative estimate, India will overtake both Japan and Russia by 2030 in terms of energy consumption and will stand behind the United States and China.[6] If this assessment proves to be correct, than India will have a major energy crunch in future. At present, as per the EIA 2007 report, India is importing a major chunk of its oil from West Asian states like Saudi Arabia and Iran. While from Saudi Arabia it is importing around 23 percent, from Iran the percentage is around 17.[7] This shows the excessive dependence on the oil and gas sectors of the West Asian countries by India. In this regard, the policy makers of India are emphasising the need to diversify the energy sources to meet the future needs and successfully using India's foreign policy as part of oil diplomacy in a broader framework.[8]

India's search for energy resources in the Caspian and Central Asian states is a part of India's overall diplomacy in this region. The Indian policy makers are trying to use the traditional goodwill and warmth as a means to get leverage in the oil and gas sectors of this region. India's active energy diplomacy in the CIS and Central Asian states is gaining momentum though there is still a lot to do.[9]

India's Energy Odyssey and the CIS Region

To meet these requirements, Indian oil companies are interested in acquiring their base in Central Asia. After a long overture, India in recent years has been making some inroads in the oil and gas sectors of Kazakhstan. For instance, Oil and Natural Gas Commission Videsh Limited (OVL) finalised an agreement with KazMunaiGAz (KMG). Both OVL and KMG decided to develop two blocs of the Caspian part of Satpayev and Makhambet. In the preliminary round of discussion, the Kazakh side gave consent to offer 50 percent of stake in the Satpayev bloc on nomination basis (later it was reported that it is offering a minor stake). The Indian side is also expressing its keenness to use their technical skills in laying pipeline routes in Central Asia.[10] India's energy giant OVL is also interested in securing a share in the government owned Kazakh Company MangistauMunaiGas, reportedly holding a total oil reserve of 812 million tonnes and a recoverable reserve of 194 million tonnes.[11] Recently, OVL has been planning to acquire the US Company Transmeridian

Exploration Inc which has a significant presence in Kazakhstan. Similarly in Turkmenistan also, the Indian oil giant OVL is interested in acquiring 33 percent stake in two oil fields at a cost of Rs. 1.5-2 billion. In this regard, OVL signed a deal with Denmark's Maersk Oil and German Oil and Gas Firm Wintershall, which hold significant stakes in these two blocs.[12] India's energy diplomacy in the CIS states received a big boost when the Kazakh President visited India in the month of January 2009. During his visit, Mittal Energy Limited (MEL), Oil and Natural Gas Corporation (ONGC), OMEL, KazMunaiGaz (KMG) and National Oil Company of Kazakhstan signed an agreement on exploring the highly lucrative Satpayev bloc.[13]

India is not far behind Uzbekistan. Gas Authority of India Limited (GAIL), the public sector industrial giant from India, in collaboration with UzbekiNeftGaz, a state owned enterprise of Uzbekistan, plans to establish two gas plants with a capacity of 0.1 million tonnes per annum. As per an estimate, the total cost of these two plants will be around $50–60 million. The deal in this regard was signed when Indian Prime Minister Manmohan Singh visited Tashkent in April 2006.[15]

Both public and private sector companies of India are also interested in securing their presence in Russia. In this way, they are giving tough competition to western oil companies. Indian oil giant OVL has invested about $1 billion in the Shakhalin-1 project. The visit of India's Petroleum and Gas Minister Shri Murli Deora marked a significant step in the direction of energy cooperation between the two countries. During his visit, India expressed its keenness to participate in Shakhalin-3 project. India has also showed its keenness for joint projects with Russian companies. For instance, it has been reported that OVL and Rosneft are planning a joint exploration and development project in East Siberia. It has been reported that the Siberian bloc contains large amount of oil and gas. For instance, as per an estimate, a bloc of Siberia named as Veninsky contains 169.4 million tonnes of oil and 258 billion cubic metres of gas. The other three blocs in this region are likely to contain more than 600 million tonnes of oil, 770 billion cubic metres of gas. One may recall here the fact that there was a plan for Gazprom-GAIL joint partnership, which also included the building up of the Iran-Pakistan-India Gas pipeline routes.[16] Recently OVL bought the London based The Imperial Energy, which has a significant stake in Russian and Kazakh oil fields, by paying around £1.4billion. This is a major achievement in India's oil diplomacy in this region since The Imperial Energy has a significant stake in Caspian oil fields.[17] India has also been making inroads into the Azeri oil and gas sectors. In April 2007, during the visit of India's Commerce Minister Jairam Ramesh to Baku, Azeri President Ilham Aliyev showed his intention to develop energy ties with India. In this regard the Azeri state oil company SOCCAR is also showing keen interest in entering into joint production agreement. [18]

Another problem that hinders India's energy diplomacy in this region is the development of viable trade route that can connect India with the Caspian states of CIS. The Iran-Pakistan-India and Turkmenistan-Afghanistan-Pakistan- India (TAPI) pipeline projects are in doldrums and nobody knows when these routes will be opened.[19] So the alternative is the development of pipeline routes that can accrue benefits to both India and CIS states. For instance, Russia is developing the ports of Makhachakhla, Lagan and Olya situated in the Caspian Sea. Similarly, Bandar Abbas is emerging as a major route for transportation of oil and gas. Apart from the Bandar Abbas Route, the North-South Transport Corridor Project, in which India is a founding member, is also going to play an important role in delivering oil and gas to India. Last month, in the joint meeting of Iran-India Joint Working Group, it was suggested that Iran's Sahid Rajaei Port, Russia's Astrakhan port and India's Jawaharlal Nehru Port will coordinate with one another for strengthening transport linkages. The meeting also decided on the establishment of a line from India's Astrakhan port through Sahid Rajaei port. [20]

Apart from the existing routes, there is another route that can be converted into oil pipeline route, the historical Chen-Chenmore Route. There is an existing rail line route, of around 1,760 kilometres, connecting Urumchi with Lasha. So the oil and gas grids of Central Asia and Caspian states can be connected with Xinjiang and a new pipeline route can be laid down that can connect the Caspian states along the rail route. From Ladakh, laying down of this pipeline can connect India.[21] Though many criticise this route as highly utopian, only time will tell its feasibility.

Conclusion

A closer survey of India's energy diplomacy in the CIS region shows that India is taking active interest in exploiting the hydrocarbon resources of this region. However, India is far behind other powers like the European Union and America in exploiting the region. In this regard, New Delhi should use its traditional relationship with this region as a stepping stone to build partnership in terms of securing oil and gas. India's economic growth rate and technical capabilities will certainly add to its strength in pursuing vigorous energy diplomacy in the region.

Notes

1. See for instance, Shirin Akiner, (ed.), *The Caspian : Politics, Energy and Security,* Routledge Curzon, London, 2004; Hooshang Amirabmadi (ed.), *The Caspian Region at a Crossroad*, Basingstorke, McMillan,2000.
2. See for details in Paul Mathieu and Clinton R.Sheils, "The Commonwealth of Independent States' Troubled Energy Sector" in IMF, Vol.39, No.3, September 2002,p.1 www.imf.org/external/pubs/ft/fandd/2002/09/mathieu.htm - 28k -; Marcus Svedberg, "Energy in Eurasia: The Dependency Game" in *Transition Studies Review,* Vol.14, No.1, 2007,pp.195-197
3. Draft Report of the Expert Committee on the Integrated Energy Policy, Planning Commission, Government of India, 2005, p.57. Planning Commission.nic.in/reports/genrep/intengpol.htm
4. Energy Information Administration, http://www.eia.doe.gov/emeu/cabs/India/Oil.html
5. Ibid., Natural Gas, http://www.eia.doe.gov/cabs/India/NaturalGas.html
6. Tanvi Madan, *The Brookings Foreign Policy Studies Energy Security Series: India,* November 2006, p.14, http://www.brookings.edu/fp/research/energy/2006india.pdf.
7. http://www.eia.doe.gov/cabs/India/Full.html
8. Sudha Mahalingam, "In Pursuit of Energy Security", 1 February 2005.
9. Devendra Kaushik, "India and Central Asia: Renewing a Traditional Relationship", *South Asian Survey* op.cit.
10. Richa Mishra, "Kazakh Co. OVL to finalise deal on Satpayev Bloc", *The Hindu Business Line,* 8 October 2007.
11. "ONGC Eying Kazakh Oil Assets", www.reuters.com/article/rbssEnergyNews/idUSL864432720081008 - 82k -;http://www.expressindia.com/latest-news/ONGC-eyeing-Kazakh-oil-asset-Source/370899/
12. *The Hindu Business Line,* 24 July 2007; *Tribune,* 6 January 2007.
13. ONGC Website, http://www.ongcvidesh.com/NewsContent.aspx?ID=163
14. *The Hindu Business Line,* 24 July 2007; *Tribune,* 6 January 2007.
15. Richa Mishra, "GAIL to Set-Up LPG Plants in Uzbekistan", *The Hindu Business Line,* 2 May 2006.
16. Sascha Muller Kraenner, *China and India's Emerging Energy Foreign Policy,* German Development Institute, 2008,p.12; "Petroleum Minister Returns from a Successful Visit of Russia :Strategic Ties Of Cooperation Between India and Russia Emphasised", http://pib.nic.in/release/release.asp?relid=44620; " Igor Tomberg, " Russia-India Energy Dialogue: Traditions and Prospects", *Ria-Novosti,* ;. 7 February 2007, www.ria-novosti.org.; John Helmer, "India Plays at Russian Imperial Roultte", www.atimes.com/atimes/South_Asia/JJ30Df07.html - 46k

17. "India's ONGC agrees £1.4bn takeover of Imperial Energy", www.atimes.com/atimes/South_Asia/JJ30Df07.html - 46k http://www.telegraph.co.uk/money/main.jhtml?view=DETAILS&grid=&xml=/money/2008/08/26/bcnimps126.xml
18. "India's quest for role in Azerbaijan oil sector bearing fruit", *The Hind, Business Line,* 14 April 2007. http://www.thehindubusinessline.com/2007/04/14/stories/2007041404051000.htm
19. Sascha Muller Kraenner, *China's and India's Emerging Energy Policy,* op.cit; Tanvi Madan, The Brookings Foreign Policy Studies Energy Security Series, op.cit.
20. Atul Aneja, "The Politics of Trade Routes", *The Hindu, 30 April 2007;* "Iran-India Port, Shipping Cooperation", ttp://www.instc.org/News/NewsE/Item.asp?SubID=749&RowNo=2&CurPage=1&NewsID=810&qsFromSearch=
21. See for details Devendra Kaushik, "India and Central Asia: Renewing a Traditional Relationship", *South Asian Survey* Vol. 5, 1998, pp. 231-244.

The Importance of Central Asia for the International Powers: A Case Study of Iran-Central Asia Relations

Dr Enayatollah Yazdani

Introduction

The collapse of the Union of Soviet Socialist Republics (USSR) in 1991 made salient the geopolitical, economic and cultural importance of the five former Soviet Central Asian republics of Kazakhstan, Kyrgyzstan, Tajikistan, Turkmenistan and Uzbekistan. As a result, Central Asia, a closed and hard-to-reach region of Eurasia, once again achieved a significant position on Eurasia's map, with increased geopolitical and strategic weight. As a region that during the Cold War remained in the background of international politics, Central Asia has attracted the attention of the global and regional powers. It started to gain prominence in the strategic objectives and politico-economic ambitions of many global and regional powers. On the other hand, the region's geopolitics, its strategic location and enormous natural resources made it an area where powers such as the Russian Federation, the United States, China, Turkey, Iran, Pakistan, India, Saudi Arabia, Japan, Israel, and the European Union (EU) vie for influence.

This paper while focusing on the region's importance and growing position in international arena, examines Iran's policy towards Central Asia. The paper argues that with the opening up of Central Asia the Islamic Republic of Iran has become engaged in the region for different combinations of geopolitical, economic and security reasons.

Geopolitics of Central Asia: Preliminary Observations

Central Asia was part of the 'Heartland' and its pivotal geographical position allowed it to play a central role in relations among nations of Eurasia in the Middle Ages, as the bridge between China and Europe. In the modern world, its importance grew as the great powers of the time sought power and influence along its borders. The Bolshevik revolution of 1917 and subsequent 70 years of Soviet rule closed the region to influences from the outside world, but with the Soviet Union's demise it again rose to prominence in geopolitical and strategic calculations. Indeed, in the post-Cold War era Central Asia's geostrategic importance and natural resource potential have made it a focus of attention in Eurasian geopolitics.[1] Any consideration of its republics' international politics has to be based on geopolitical, religious, economic and regional realities.

In fact, the emergence of independent states in Central Asia has both literally and figuratively changed the map of Asia and affected the world, particularly the surrounding regions, notably the Middle East, South and West Asia. The region borders Russia in the north, Iran and Afghanistan in the south, China in the east and the Caspian Sea in the west. This geographical location has made it strategically important. Furthermore, it is located at the centre of Eurasia, connecting Eurasia not only from East to West, but also from South to North. More importantly, it is surrounded by four major world civilisations: Christian, Confucian, Islamic and Hindu, and Asian powers, Russia, China and India. In addition, the region lies at the strategic juncture between four nuclear powers, Russia, China, India and Pakistan. In the meantime, another aspect of the region's geopolitical importance should not be overlooked: the rise of political and commercial competition over the energy resources, namely oil and gas, and particularly the routes for export pipelines.[2]

Such a geopolitical position, in fact, is a significant factor that has not only made the region attractive to the outside world but also placed it at global challenge, especially after the events of 11 September 2001.

Central Asia: A New Frontier in International Arena

During the Soviet era, the Central Asian republics never gained the status of independent actors in international relations. Foreign relations were directed by the central government, and the central leadership determined foreign policy goals and priorities. After the collapse of the USSR, when these independent countries set out to outline a new framework of relationships with the outside world, this situation changed.[3]

The independence of the republics and Russia's partial withdrawal from Central Asia changed the geopolitics of the region from a closed area to one opening up to other interested foreign actors. Under the new circumstances, the countries found themselves in the interest zone of many regional and global powers, attracting widespread attention because they have emerged at a point where the political, economic and security interests of various powers converge.

Independence brought the formal establishment of foreign embassies along with rapid development of communication between the republics and the Middle East, South Asia, East Asia, Western Europe and the United States. Rivalry between various forces in the region added to friction and historical grievances within the Commonwealth of Independent States (CIS).[4]

The Central Asian republics' orientation to the outside world would greatly affect the power and national security planning of neighbouring and other interested states, principally the United States, Russia, China, Iran, Turkey, India, Saudi Arabia and Pakistan. How these actors have acted in Central Asia can influence geopolitical alignments in the region. It is also important to grasp how these states, and others whose interest is acute though less direct (for example, the EU, Japan, and Israel), position Central Asia into their strategic thinking. In fact, the initial power vacuum created by the collapse of the Soviet Union has pulled regional states and some international actors into an intensive competition for power and influence in the area. Obviously, each has specific objectives and the competition has economic, political, ideological and religious dimensions.

Furthermore, the events of 11 September 2001, the subsequent anti-terrorist campaign in Afghanistan and US military deployment in Central Asia, have given a new strategic importance to the region.

The Islamic World and Central Asia

When the Central Asian republics became independent, it was widely expected that their isolation from the Islamic world would end, and they would rapidly develop relations.[5] But it soon appeared that, although the region's states have sought to expand relations with some Islamic countries, they have not tried to play the 'Islam card' in their foreign relations.[6]

Some have argued that Central Asia's leaders ignored the religious factor as an instrument for developing relations with the Muslim world. A. Hyman, for example, has pointed out that 'none of them desired their shared Muslim religion to intrude as a factor in their relations with neighbours'.[7] Central Asian policy toward Palestine is a vivid example of playing down the religious element. As mentioned earlier, no state in the region has followed the ideological line of Iran or Saudi Arabia, on the Palestine issue, by restricting relations with Israel. B. Shaffer echoed this view, arguing that the foreign policy that emerged in the Central Asian republics '[did] not support the culturalist explanation of foreign policy'.[8] She added: '...culture seems to give us little explanation or predictive power in understanding the foreign policies of these states'.[9] Instead, the republics have striven to enhance their politico-economic ties with Israel.

The Muslim world's interests in Central Asia can be divided into three categories: political, ideological and economic.[10] The motivations of Muslim countries in exploring the potential for new relations with the Central Asian republics are mainly political, though Central Asia's potential as a market and its resources of oil and gas have also played a part. Some Islamic states have attempted to deal with the region through their own ideological model; and there has been a kind of ideological competition between their political establishments, Turkey emphasising its secular model, Saudi Arabia supporting strict *Wahhabism* and Iran showing little interest in political Islam.[11]

The leading Muslim countries vying to maximise their influence in the region are Iran and Turkey, and to a lesser extent, Pakistan, Saudi Arabia and Afghanistan.

Iran's Policy towards Central Asia

The emergence of the independent Central Asian republics onto the international stage presented a new frontier for Iran's policymakers. Iran has a long history of relations with, and cultural influence over, Central Asia, which was essentially part of the sphere of Iranian civilisation in its various manifestations. Iran's national and cultural renaissance after the Arab invasion occurred in Central Asia, especially in Samarkand, Bukhara and parts of present-day Afghanistan.[12] The demise of the USSR and the emergence of independent states in the region once again have created opportunities and security threats for Iran.[13] Tehran established official relations with the region's states in November 1991. Given the importance of the region, senior Iranian figures, including Presidents Rafsanjani, Khatami, and Ahmadinejad visited the region.[14] Iran, relying on its location as a bridge between Central Asia and the Persian Gulf, has sought an important role in the region's politics and economics. At the 11th International Seminar on Central Asia and the Caucasus on 8–9 December 2003, Iranian former Foreign Minister Kamal Kharrazi maintained that the new conditions following independence in 1991 created a good opportunity for pursuing Iran's and the republics' common interests.[15] He said: 'To stabilise this region we needed first to establish political relations with the countries of the region, second to develop economic cooperation…third to play an instrumental role in the region's security, and finally, Iran wishes that foreign competition in the region be replaced by regional cooperation'.[16]

Tehran has pursued two sets of policies, the first political and security, the second economic and cultural. At the political and security levels, conflict in Tajikistan and developing instability in the region became of great concern for Iran's policymakers who, according to some analysts, feared it might invite foreign intervention and a new influx of refugees into Iran.[17] In the cultural sphere, historical relations between Iran and Central Asia in linguistics, customs and religion could play a role. Iran has viewed the region as an opportunity to develop its economic ties, and some of these landlocked states see Iran as a natural link and gateway to the high seas.[18]

In particular, Iran's relations with Kazakhstan and Turkmenistan are based on mutual interests in the energy and transportation sectors.[19] Iran could help these countries to develop their oil and gas industries and pipelines. In this connection, the Kazak President said, '…our investors who work on oil consider that the most beneficial route is through Iran to the Persian Gulf'.[20] According to an *Interfax* report of 9 March 2004, the contract for building a reservoir park in Turkmenistan, with a capacity of 3,000 tonnes, to be completed in August 2005, has gone to an Iranian company, Pars Energy.[21] Iran's relations with Turkmenistan have been the best of all with the post-Soviet republics. Niyazov, former president of Turkmenistan, and Khatami described Ashghabat-Tehran relations as a pattern for the rest of the region: 'An example of fraternal good-neighbourly relations'.[22] This is partly because of the absence of any major security problems, the political stability in Turkmenistan and the possibility for developing economic ties.[23] Completion of the 295 kms Mashhad-Sarakhs-Tajan Railway has linked Turkmenistan's railways to those of Iran, and given Iran an opportunity to use Turkmenistan's rail networks to transport goods to other regional countries, particularly Uzbekistan.[24] Nevertheless, obviously, some events have affected relations between these neighbours. In 2003 the Turkmen government awarded a contract for rebuilding its refinery at Seyidi to the Israeli company Merhav, and on 8 September 2003 President Niyazov expressed the hope that Merhav would continue to participate in Turkmenistan's economic development.[25] The company is also developing software for a database that Turkmenistan intends to use for tracking the arrivals and departures of all foreign and Turkmen citizens.[26]

Iran has a common culture and language with Tajikistan, and was the first country to establish diplomatic relations with it. It played a significant role in ending the Tajik civil war, beginning with a ceasefire agreement signed in Tehran in 1994.[27] In August 1995, Iran hosted a peace summit attended by Tajik president Imomali Rahmanov and Abdollah Nouri, leader of Tajikistan's Islamic Movement, at which both sides agreed to extend the ceasefire and form a joint deliberative council to narrow their differences. Tehran maintained amicable relations with both sides and never supported the Tajik Islamists' aim to create an Islamic government, even though Tajik opposition leaders were in Iran from 1993 to 1998.[28] Coordinating policy with Moscow, in 1997 Tehran participated in preparing the General Agreement on Establishment of Peace and National Accord and Protocol on Mutual Understanding, signed by the Rahmanov and Nouri. Iran hosted the second, sixth and eighth rounds of peace negotiations, one consultative conference, and two meetings between the Tajik president and the opposition leader.[29]

Iran's relations with Uzbekistan, however, have been more difficult. Uzbekistan was the last Central Asian country in which Iran established an embassy. Comparatively, even though Uzbekistan has a pivotal position in the region, it 'has not been as attractive to Iran as the other republics', partly due to the Uzbek government's suspicions of Iran's intentions.[30] For example, in October 1993 an Iranian presidential visit to Tashkent did not go very well, partly because Karimov refused to let an Iranian cultural centre open in Samarkand.[31] Uzbekistan was also the only Central Asian republic to support the 1995 US-proposed trade embargo against Tehran, in part prompted by Iran's purchase of Russian nuclear reactors.[32]

In general, Iran's leaders are convinced that economic presence is the key to increased influence in the region, and Iran has had good trade relations with it, particularly Turkmenistan, though its investments there are not comparable with Turkey's, as discussed below.[33] Iran also facilitated the Central Asian states' admission to the ECO.[34] On this, former Foreign Minister Ali Akbar Velayati articulated: 'The Islamic Republic of Iran is convinced that regional cooperation is the only guarantor of regional peace, security, and stability. It is in this light that bilateral and multilateral relations are being forged with the countries of Central Asia and the Caucasus'.[35] He also said: 'The ECO pursues objectives like trade among member-states, and the encouragement of sustained development and active participation in international trade'.[36]

While Iran's role in economic and political developments should not be exaggerated, it is nevertheless fair to say that it has contributed to the economic development and political stability of the region, and is likely to continue to do so.[37] One of the important dimensions of Tehran's policy towards this area is security. Of course, this is not a new consideration for Iran, indeed, as Abbas Maleki, former Deputy Foreign Minister of Iran, has written: 'For the past two centuries, the greatest threat to Iran's security and territorial integrity was posed by the Russian empire and its successor the Soviet Union'.[38] For Iranian foreign and national security, maintenance of stability and peace in Central Asia has become a significant security objective since 1991. Velayati stated that 'the Islamic Republic could not have remained passive in the face of the deteriorating security conditions on its northern border after the collapse of the Soviet System'.[39] Therefore, one can argue that Tehran has given priority to maintaining stability in the region and securing its borders as much as possible. Khatami said in Ashghabat in 1998: 'Stability here is our task—we should not create excuses for aliens to penetrate into our region'.[40] During his visit to Bishkek on 5 September 2001, Kharrazi affirmed that Iran's relations with Central Asia were designed to overcome such threats to stability as drug trafficking, organised crime and the Afghan conflict.[41] Iran played an effective role in conflict resolution in Tajikistan. Iran feels threatened by NATO's eastward expansion, especially by the enthusiasm with which Central Asian leaders embraced Programme for Peace (PfP). During his visit to Moscow in March 2001, Khatami asserted that 'any foreign presence in the Central Asian region can upset the balance of peace and stability there'.[42] More importantly, in the aftermath of 11 September 2001, a US military presence in the region poses a further potential threat.

Although Iran has sought to strengthen ties with Central Asia, it has been careful not to jeopardise its good relations with Moscow, which are important to its national and security interests.[43] In 1996 Velayati claimed that Iranian-Russian relations were 'at their highest level in contemporary history'.[44] Thus one can argue that, for Tehran close multi-dimensional relations with Moscow are more important than ties with the region's states.

In other words, for Iran, relations with Russia as a strategic balancer, regionally and globally, as a source of trade and arms, and as a partner in political and economic regional patterns are significant. In this connection, Iran's regional policy in regard to Tajikistan's civil war (and the conflict in Chechnya) had become increasingly 'Russiacentric'.[45] Iran's former Defence Minister, Ali Shamkhani, had confirmed that closer defence relations between Teheran and Moscow are both necessary and inevitable, not least because both perceive a US-led NATO presence in Central Asia as a potential threat and feel that NATO's eastward enlargement will escalate regional tensions and crises.[46] The US-led invasion of Iraq in 2003 alarmed Iran to such extent that friendly relations with Moscow are now crucial for its national security.[47]

In attempting to develop its influence in Central Asia, Iran has faced some political, economic and religious limitations and challenges.[48] Economically, due to 8 years of war with Iraq (1980–1988), Iran has faced financial dilemmas, and has been unable to invest considerably in the region.[49] Furthermore, Iran represents Shiite Islam, while about 85 percent of Central Asians are Sunni Muslims.[50] Although Iran has not emphasised its Shiism in policy towards this area, its reputation as Shiite and as a would-be exporter of revolutionary Islam has caused the West and some of the region's states to challenge its influence, whereas the opportunities for influence provided to other Muslim countries such as Turkey and Saudi Arabia by the majority Sunni population have gone largely unremarked.[51] B. Rumer, for example, argued that 'Tajikistan in particular has been a prime target of attempts [by Iran] to export the Islamic revolution'.[52] R. Burnashev, a Kazak scholar, has also claimed that one element of Iran's regional policy has been 'the attempt to strengthen the role of Islam in Central Asia'.[53]

Islam as such has not in fact been a major dimension of Tehran's policy towards this region; instead it has been motivated more by political, economic and strategic variables. Arguably, Iran has not attempted to disseminate political Islam in the region, or to export its revolution there, but what some Central Asian states, particularly, Uzbekistan, view as an Islamic threat has engendered a very cautious attitude toward Tehran. Some of the region's analysts, such as K. Syroezhkin, of the journal *Kontinent* in Almaty, have argued that the Iranian government 'took a pragmatic position toward Central Asia. Aware that the rapid dissemination of Islamic idea in Central Asia was impossible, Iran concentrated on three tasks: economic cooperation, creation of joint transportation routes, and then resolution of issues involving the Caspian Sea'.[54]

Externally, two issues have challenged Tehran's policy in Central Asia. First, the United States has been seeking to isolate Iran, particularly in respect of energy resources and pipelines. This has been Washington's policy since 1991. In 1992 Secretary of State, James A. Baker 3d, emphasised that: 'Washington planned to move quickly to open embassies in the Central Asian republics of the former Soviet Union to counter expanding Iranian influence in these newly independent Muslim states'.[55] In contrast Iran has also both frequently voiced opposition to the US position in the region and tries to cooperate with Russia and China in the framework of Shanghai Cooperation Organisation (SCO) against Washington's interests there.[56] Second, as mentioned earlier, some of the region's states, especially Uzbekistan, are reluctant to develop closer relations with Tehran.[57] Many in and outside the region, particularly in the United States, feared that Iran would try to export its Islamic revolution to the newly independent states, and suspicion of Iran's intentions has limited its influence at the state level.

Conclusion

This paper demonstrated that the Soviet Union's disintegration provided the Central Asian republics with opportunities to establish their own foreign relations. It argued that, due to the need for nation-state building, international legitimacy, technical and economic assistance and security, the states have been attempting to join the international community through establishing relationships with a broad spectrum of countries and joining international and regional organisations.

In addition the growing international attention to the area shows that it has gained considerably in geostrategic importance following the collapse of the Soviet Union. This paper also explored how the region's geopolitical importance, energy resources, economic and political problems have caused the outside world to pay attention to it and rush to establish relations with the newly independent republics. As a result, Central Asia has become a field of geopolitical competition for regional and international powers.

The paper confirmed that although Iran as a regional power has tried to play a role in Central Asia, Islam as such has not in fact been a major dimension in Tehran's policy towards the republics, instead it has been motivated more by politico-economic and strategic variables.

Notes

1. For a detailed discussion see G.E. Fuller, 'Central Asia's geopolitical future', *Post Soviet Prospects*, Vol. II, No. 8, October 1994, pp. 56-60.
2. For a comprehensive discussion see C. Arvanitopoulos, 'The Geopolitics of Oil in Central Asia', *Thesis*, Vol. 1, No. 4, Winter 1997/1998, pp. 18-27, and K. Tokaev, 'The major Geopolitical Challenges of Central Asia Today', Palais d'Egmont, Brussels, 30 October 2003.
3. For a brief description of changes in Central Asia's international situation see B. Rumer and S. Zhukov, eds., *Central Asia : The Challenges of Independence*, Armonk: M E Sharpe, 1998, pp. 98-102, L.A. Stone, *The International Politics of Central Eurasia*, Orem: Central Eurasian Publications, 2001, pp. 55-67.
4. See 'Russia, China share positions on CIS relations', *BBC Monitoring Former Soviet*

Union, London, 23 March 2007. p. 1, Gladkyy Oleksandr 'American Foreign Policy and US Relations with Russia and China after 11 September:[1]', *World Affairs*, Vol. 166, No. 1, Washington, Summer 2006, pp. 3-24, R Menon, 'The new great game in Central Asia', *Survival*, Vol. 45, No. 2, London, 1 June 2003, pp. 187-210, S. Blank, 'India's rising profile in Central Asia' and D. Khidirbekughli, 'US geostrategy in Central Asia: A Kazak perspective', *Comparative Strategy*, Vol. 22, No. 2, New York, April/June 2003, pp. 139-158 and pp. 159-169, S.T. Hunter, 'Iran's pragmatic regional policy', *Journal of International Affairs*, Vol. 56, No. 2, New York, Spring 2003, pp. 133-147.

5. For more information see J.O. Voll, 'Central Asia as a Part of the Modern Islamic World', in B.F. Manz, ed., *Central Asia in Historical Perspective*, Boulder: Westview Press, 1994, pp. 62-81, Robins, op. cit., pp. 36-54, and E. Abdullaev, 'The Central Asian nexus: Islam and politics', in Rumer, ed., *Central Asia: A Gathering Storm*, pp. 245-298.
6. Lounev and Shirokov, op. cit., pp.351-374, S. Akiner, 'Islam in the Newly Independent Central Asian States in the 1990s', *Harvard International Review*, Spring 2006, pp.62-65.
7. Hyman, op. cit., pp. 75-94. See also G. Tazmini, 'The Islamic revival in Central Asia: A potent force or a misconception?', *Central Asian Survey*, Vol. 20, No. 1, March 2001, pp. 63-85, 'The history of Islam in Central Asia', 23 July 2002, at WWW.khurasaan.com [accessed 12/4/2008], and M. Haghayeghi and F. R. von der Mehden, 'Islam and energy security', in Y. Kalyuzhnova, A.M. Jaffe, D. Lynch and R. Sickles, eds., *Energy in the Caspian region: Present and Future,* New York: Palgrave, 2002, pp. 86-105.
8. B. Shaffer, ed., T*he Limits of Culture: Islam, Foreign Policy and the Caspian*, Cambridge: MIT Press, 2003, pp. 21-29.
9. Ibid, also for more discussion see Hyman, op. cit., pp. 75-94.
10. For more information see Robins, op., cit., pp. 36-54.
11. Ibid.
12. Hunter, *Central Asia Since Independence,* p. 7. Khorasan is now a province in northeast Iran. Iran's location, ethno-demographic situation and cultural and civilizational impact have at all times made it an integrating factor in the geopolitical expanse that includes Central Asia. Most countries or territories of the present-day region were in the past parts of Iran or tied to it with all sorts of bonds –some of them are even conquered parts of Iranian territory. All have been exposed to Iranian cultural influence, including the culture of economic development. Iran was mainly responsible for disseminating Islam as a unifying religious constant. However, the specificity of state formation in the 19th and 20th centuries, and inclusion of Central

Asia and Caucasus in the Russian Empire, then the Soviet Union, decreased Iranian influence. H.A. Shirazi, *Melliyathaye Asiaie Miane*, Tehran: Amir Kabir, 1999, pp. 120-143, N. Mamedova, 'Political and economic situation in Iran: Its impact on the relationships with Central Asia and the Caucasus', *Central Asia and the Caucasus*, Vol. 20, No. 2, 2007, pp. 98-114.

13. See E. Herzig, 'Regionalism, Iran and Central Asia', *International Affairs*, Vol. 80, No. 3, May 2004, pp. 503-517.
14. Former Iranian President Rafsanjani, visited Central Asia in October 1993, Spring 1994 and April 1997, and current president Khatami visited it in April 2002, September 2004.
15. Iran's Foreign Minister, Kamal Kharrazi's speech on the importance of Central Asia and the Caucasus in Iran's foreign policy, '11th International Seminar on Central Asia and the Caucasus', December 8-9 2003, Tehran, Iran, Iranian Students' New Agency (ISNA), 9 December 2003.
16. Ibid.
17. See Rumer, ed., *Central Asia: A Gathering Storm*, pp. 3-68, M.J. Omidwarnia, 'Amniat dar Asiai Markazi va Qafqaz dar gharn 21', *Asiai Markazi va Qafqaz*, No. 34, Tehran, Summer 2001, pp. 45-62, S. K. Sajjadpour, 'Iran, the Caucasus and Central Asia', in Banuazizi and Weiner, op. cit., pp. 197-215.
18. Rumer, ed., *Central Asia: A Gathering Storm*, pp. 3-68.
19. Dekmejian and Simonian, op. cit., pp. 74-95, and B. Khajehpour-Khouei, 'Survey of Iran's economic interests in the Caspian, in H. Amirahmadi, ed., *The Caspian Region at a Crossroad: Challenge of New Frontier of Energy and Development,* New York: St. Martin's Press, 2000, pp. 75-86, A. Bigdeli, 'The transit position of Islamic Republic of Iran and the Central Asian states', *Amu Darya: The Iranian Journal of Central Asian Studies*, Vol. 6, No. 12, Tehran, Summer 2002, pp. 181-206.
20. Cited by E. Patricke, 'Tyler, Kazakstan leader urges Iran pipeline route', *The New York Times*, 10 December 2001, p. A12. See also N. Ghorban, 'By way of Iran: Caspian's oil and gas outlet', in Amirahmadi, op. cit., pp. 147-154.
21. 'Iran to build gas export terminal in Turkmenistan', *Interfax*, Ashgabat, 9 March 2004. For more see N. Entessar, 'Iran: Geopolitical challenges and the Caspian region', in M.P. Croissant and B. Aras, eds. *Oil and Geopolitics in the Caspian Sea Region*, Westport: Praeger, 1999, pp. 154-180 and N. Ghorban, 'Iran's potential role in the development and utilisation of oil and gas of the Caspian region', *The Iranian Journal of International Affairs*, Vol. XII, No. 2, Tehran, Summer 2006, pp. 264-284.
22. Quoted from *Neitral'niy Turkmenistan*, 9 February 2001, in V. Mesamed, 'Iran: Ten years in post-Soviet Central Asia', *Central Asia and the Caucasus* (online), Vol. 13, No. 1, 2002, at http://www.ca-c.org/journal/eng-01-2002/04.mesprimen.shtml

[accessed 16/10/2007].

23. S.K. Sajjadpour, 'Iran, the Caucasus and Central Asia', p. 208. Iran is fourth among 63 trading partners of Turkmenistan, it has already contributed to dozens of large projects, and there are about 150 treaties and agreements between them. See Mesamed, op. cit.
24. The project was inaugurated in 13 May 1996 by Presidnet Rafsanjani of Iran in the presence of leaders and dignitaries of about 50 countries and International organisations. *Ettelaat*, Iran's Daily Newspaper, 13 May 1996, p. 6. However, the opportunity is limited by difference in gauge; the Iranian gauge is 1435mm, the former Soviet system 1524 mm so goods have to be transshipped or wheelsets changed. This railway would connect all five Central Asian countries and Russia to the Iranian network and Persian Gulf, but the problem of gauge difference will remain. It is not, however, insuperable; similar gauge-changing facilities exist between standard-gauge (1435 mm) European systems and those of Spain and of the former USSR, and at standard-gauge China's borders with Kazakstan and Russia, and gauge-changing takes a matter of a few hours rather than days.
25. 'Israeli company to rebuild Turkmen oil refinery', *Weekly News Brief on Turkmenistan*, 5/11 September 2003, p. 7. See also Economist Intelligence Unit, Country Profile, Turkmenistan, 2nd Quarter 1996, p.30.
26. 'Israeli company to rebuild Turkmen oil refinery', p. 7.
27. For a good account of relations between Iran and Tajikistan see M. Mesbahi, 'Tajikistan, Iran and the International Politics of the 'Islamic Factor'', *Central Asian Survey*, Vol.16, No.2, 1997, pp.141-158.
28. A. Tarock, 'Iran's Policy in Central Asia,' *Central Asia Survey*, Vol. 16, No. 2, 1997, PP. 185-200, and K. Abdullaev and C. Barnes, *Politics of Compromise: The Tajikistan Peace Process*, London: Conciliation Resources, 2000.
29. K.L. Afrasiabi and A. Maleki, 'Iran's foreign policy after September 11', *The Brown Journal of World Affairs*, Vol. IX, No. 2, 2003, pp. 255-265.
30. Sajjadpour, op. cit., p. 210.
31. O. Roy, 'The Iranian foreign policy toward Central Asia', at http://www.eurasianet.org/resource/regional/royoniran.html [accessed 26/3/2008].
32. K. Alimov, 'Uzbekistan's foreign policy: In search of strategy', The Eisenhower Institute, at http://www.eisenhowerinstitute.org/programs/globalpartnerships/securityandterrorism/coalition/regionalrelations/ConflictBook/Alimov.htm [accessed 12/2/2008], and S.F. Starr, 'Making Eurasia Stable', *Foreign Affairs,* Vol. 75, No. 1, January/February 1996, pp. 80-92.
33. It seems total investments barely reached $0.6 to 0.8 billion. In 1995/1996 the trade turnover with Central Asia and Transcaucasus (without Georgia) was $803.3m; in

1996/1997, $1,053.6m; in 1997/1998, $876.5m; in 1998/1999, $604.2m. For detailed information see 'Foreign Trade', *Salname-ye Amarie Keshwar (*Iran's Annual National Statistics), Tehran/Iran, 2000/2001, and *Hambastegi,* Tehran, 14 March 2001, p. 13.

34. ECO was established in 1985 by Iran, Pakistan and Turkey, to promote economic, technical and cultural cooperation among its members.
35. A.A. Velayati, 'The Constructive Role of the Islamic Republic of Iran in Maintaining Regional Security', *Amu Darya: The Iranian Journal of Central Asian Studies*, Vol. 1, No. 2, Tehran, 1996, pp. 183-191.
36. Ibid.
37. A. Maleki, 'Iran and Turan: Apropos of Iran's relations with Central Asia and the Caucasian republics', *Central Asia and the Caucasus* (online), Vol. 11, No. 5, 2007, at http://www.ca-c.org/journal/eng-05-2001/11.malprimen.shtml [accessed 22/12/2007].
38. Ibid., Sajjadpour, op. cit., p. 213. For a comprehensive discussion see P.M. Goudarzi, 'Tahdidat aminiati dar Asiai Markazi: Moured Kyrgyzstan', *Asiai Markazi va Qafqaz*, No. 34, Tehran, Summer 2001, pp. 129-140 and N. Sonboli, 'Iran va Amniat Asiai markazi dar doran pas az 9/11', *Asiai Markazi va Qafqaz*, No. 37, Tehran, Spring 2004, pp. 103-119.
39. A.A. Velayati, 'The Islamic republic of Iran, Central Asia and the Caucasus', Address at the Crans Montana Forum, Switzerland, 20/23 June 1996, *Keyhan,* Iran, 24 June 1996. For detailed discussion on security see H. Peimani, *Regional Security and the Future of Central Asia: The Competition of Iran, Turkey, and Russia,* London: Praeger, 1998.
40. *Resalat, Tehran's daily Newspaper,* 19 June 1998, p. 11.
41. Kabar (News*),* Kyrgyzstan, 5 September 2001, p. 3.
42. Islamic Republic News Agency (IRNA), Tehran/Iran, 16 March 2001.
43. S. Blank, 'Russia and Iran in a new Middle East', *Mediterranean Quarterly*, Vol. III, No. 4, Fall 1992, pp. 108-128, Freedman, 'Russian-Iranian relations in the 1990s', pp. 65-80, B. Shaffer, 'Partners in Need: The Strategic Relationship of Russia and Iran', *Policy Paper*, No. 57, Washington Institute for Near East Policy, 2001, pp. 4-12, S.T. Hunter, 'Iran's pragmatic regional policy', *Journal of International Affairs*, Vol. 56, No. 2, New York, Spring 2003, pp. 133-147.
44. IRNA, Teheran/Iran, 7 March 1996, p. 2.
45. M. Mesbahi, 'Iran', *Conference Report* (Central Asia and the South Caucasus: Reorientations, Internal Transitions, and Strategic Dynamics), the National Intelligence Council, Washington, April 2000, pp. 31-33.
46. E. Eefgil, and L.A. Stone, 'Iran and Turkey in Central Asia: Opportunities for rapprochement in the post-cold war era', *Journal of Third World Studies*, Vol. 20, No.

1, Spring 2003, pp. 34-58.

47. However, some observers think the US invasion of Iraq will have some positive results for Iran, such as possible future Shiite ascendancy in Iraq. But, apart from the end of Saddam's regime, Iranian officials view the invasion as a threat to Iran's security. More importantly, it is unlikely that Shia could gain a dominant role in a future Iraqi regime. For more on this see Iranian Newspapers News and Agencies *Ettelaat, Kyhan, Hamshahri,* IRNA, and ISNA, March/September 2003, A. Maleki, 'Iran and Russia: Neighbours without Common Borders', in G. Chufrin,ed., *Russia and Asia: The Emerging Security Agenda*, Oxford: Oxford University Press, 1999, pp. 230-265, Shaffer, 'Partners in Need: The Strategic Relationship of Russia and Iran', pp. 4-12 and D.L. Smith, op. cit., pp. 23-38.
48. Mamedova, op. cit., Mesamed, op. cit. and M.E. Ahrari 'The Dynamics of the New Great Game in Muslim Central Asia', *Central Asian Survey*, Vol. 13, No. 4, 1994, pp. 525-539.
49. M. Field, 'Tehran's overtures to Central Asia fall on deaf ears', *The Financial Times*, 15 April 1992, p. 5, Mamedova, op. cit., and Maleki, 'Iran and Turan: Apropos of Iran's relations with Central Asia and the Caucasian republics'. Several Iranian private-sector companies are involved in joint ventures in Central Asia, but the amounts invested are not significant. In addition, private companies and businessmen in Iran have had little experience of investing abroad. Interestingly, cultural and linguistic affinities have played only a minor role in determining the pattern of Iran's economic relations, as illustrated by its low level of economic engagement in Tajikistan. According to Iran Radio, the Tajik President said in Parliament 'Iranian-Tajik economic cooperation was at a very low level', 'Trade with Iran to improve after Tajik head's speech in parliament', *Voice of the Islamic Republic of Iran*, Mashhad, 30 April 2006, at http://www.eurasianet.org/resource/tajikistan/hypermail/200005/0000.html [accessed 10/1/2008], and Tarock, op. cit., pp. 185-200.
50. M.E. Ahrari, 'The Dynamics of the New Great Game in Muslim Central Asia', pp. 525-539, A. Black, *The History of Islamic Political Thought: From the Prophet to the Present*, New York: Routledge, 2001, pp. 33-37.
51. Ahrari, op. cit., pp. 525-539, see also D.L. Smith, op. cit., pp. 30-41, Entessar, op. cit., pp. 154-180, and Mamedova, op. cit.
52. Rumer, ed., *Central Asia: A Gathering Storm*, p. 36.
53. Burnashev, op. cit., pp. 114-165.
54. K. Syroezhkin, 'Central Asia between the gravitational poles of Russia and China', in Rumer, ed., *Central Asia: A Gathering Storm*, pp. 169-207.
55. *New York Times,* 6 February 1992.
56. For more information on this issue see S. Blank, 'The post-Soviet States and the post-

Saddam Middle East', *MERIA*, Vol. 10, No. 2, June 2007, pp. 123-158.

57. Turkmenistan is an exception; Turkmen-Iranian relations are developing well. See Hunter, 'Iran's pragmatic regional policy', pp. 133-147, Rumer, ed., *Central Asia: A Gathering Storm*, pp. 3-68, Robins, op. cit., pp. 36-54 and D.L. Smith, op. cit., pp. 41-49.

The Turkic Brotherhood Policy and Its Effects on the Globalisation Process in Central Asia

Selcuk COLAKOGLU

Introduction

The end of the Cold War has become a historical turning point not only for international system, but also for Central Asia and Turkey. The collapse of the Soviet Union has created fifteen newly independent states and five of them have common cultural, ethnic and religious links with Turkey. Therefore, declaring independence of Azerbaijan, Kazakhstan, Kyrgyzstan, Uzbekistan and Turkmenistan in 1991 was also an emotional development for Turkey and Turkic Republics. Newly emerging Turkic states, which have great deal of economic and strategic potentials, were offering new opportunities for Turkey's foreign policy. On the other hand, Turkey had played a facilitator role in integratating the Turkic Republics to the international community.

In general, Central Asia and the Caucasus were important for all regional as well as global actors. The region is located in the centre of Eurasia and has important neighbouring countries such as China, India, Iran, Pakistan, Turkey and Russia. Especially China, Russia and India are major powers, important for regional as well as global politics, owing nuclear capabilities, huge military power and economic and demographic potentials. The most important and influential players have been the Western countries, particularly the US, and multilateral financial and security organisations dominated by the West, notably the World Bank, the IMF, the OSCE and NATO. Turkey, as a NATO member and an aspirant for EU membership, was certainly a beneficiary of the post-Soviet systemic changes.[1]

Besides, a number of soft security threats for both regional and global powers such as drug trafficking, terrorism and religious fundamentalism emanate from Central Asia and neighbouring regions. The region has also a great potential of conflict due to the ethnic and religious mixture. The Soviet republican borders were not depending on its ethnic and linguistic borders. Soviet authorities, following an imperial policy of divide and rule, made sure that different ethnic groups were placed within various republics. Central Asia and Caucasus are rich in energy resources as well. Apart from strategic importance of the region, newly discovered oil and gas resources in Central Asia and Caspian Sea basin are enough to make the region still important for the global economy.

The main purpose of this paper is to clarify Turkey's facilitator role towards Turkic republics to integrate them to international community. It will also be analysed whether the 'Turkish Model' was helpful to the Central Asian and Caucasian states in the process of globalisation.

Early Period of Relations (1990–94) and the 'Turkish Model'

During the Cold War, Turkey was afraid that reconciled relations between East and West would erode its strategic importance for the Western allies and lead the US to reduce its military and economic assistance to Turkey. Turkey was well aware that as long as the Soviet Union remained intact, there would be a limit to acceptable Turkish presence in Central Asia and Caucasus, and Russia would remain the main player. Independence of Turkic republics in the fall of 1991 caused tremendous excitement in Turkey. The collapse of the Soviet Union led Turkey to believe that it could become the political leader of the newly independent Central Asian and Caucasian republics.[2]

Turkey warmly welcomed the creation of six new Muslim republics in the region. Five of them—Azerbaijan, Kazakhstan, Kyrgyzstan, Turkmenistan and Uzbekistan are usually called as 'Turkic Republics'. Turkey's warm welcome to the newly born republics was strongly affected by the fact that Turkish people and the population of the Turkic Republics are of the same ethnic and linguistic origins. Thus, Turkish politicians, intellectuals, the media and public warmly welcomed the newly independent Turkic republics. Turkish people started to believe that a community of Turkic states would be established. Many analysts considered that Turkey possessed certain characteristics that might appeal to the leaders of the new Turkic societies. These characteristics included a relatively dynamic free market economy, secular government, a respect for Islamic traditions and a democratic system.[3] The Turkish Model was eagerly welcomed by all three parts: Turkey, the West, and Turkic Republics.

The West, including the US and Western European countries, supported and promoted the Turkish Model to the Turkic Republics, which made Turkey extremely satisfied. After a meeting with the Turkish Prime Minister Suleyman Demirel in Washington on 13 February 1992, President George Bush signed Turkey 'as the model of a democratic, secular state which could be emulated by Central Asia'.[4]

In the early period of dissolution of the Soviet Union, the Western world, especially the US, eagerly supported the Turkish Model because of several reasons. First, it was assumed that with the end of the Soviet Union, a power vacuum had been created in Central Asia, as it was believed that Russia was not able to control the former Soviet territory. The candidates to fill this power vacuum in Central Asia were Iran and Turkey. Many Western analysts saw the competition as between the secular, progressive model represented by Turkey and extremist, reactionary model represented by Iran.[5] Iran represented an anti-Western and radical regime; on the other hand, Turkey represented democracy, secularism, the free market economy and pro-Western stance. The Turkish Model was accepted as an important instrument by the West to fill the power vacuum in the Caucasus and Central Asia. Therefore, the Western world feared that the Muslim Republics could adopt the Iranian model and hence they strongly supported the Turkish Model.

Besides, the West favoured the Turkish Model because it was assumed that there was positive public opinion in Turkic Republics towards culturally similar Turkey. Thus, the most attractive alternatives models for Central Asia would be either Iran or Turkey, but not Western democracies.[6]

At the economic pace, the ex-communist Turkic Republics needed to reform their centrally controlled economies, but they had no experience of free trade and the requirements of a market economy did not exist in the republics. Therefore, Turkey represented a fresh and helpful example for their transformation. Turkey's success in economic transformation was another factor which encouraged the West to support the Turkish Model.[7]

On the other hand, the leaders of the newly independent states of the Turkic world also appeared to be interested in developing links with Turkey. There were also several reasons for Turkic leaders to pay attention to the Turkish Model. First of all, the Turkish experience had made a transition to a more market-oriented economy from an economy in which the state was the major actor. Second, the Turkish experience differed from Islamic formulas that were being proposed by Iran and Saudi Arabia. Third, Turkey was thought to have better connections with the Western world.[8] Especially in the early 1990s, Turkish model, seen as a bridge between Islamic world and Western world, was considered as an ideal way for Turkic Republics.

Uzbek President Islam Kerimov also declared 'I announce to the whole world that my country will go forward by the Turkish route…'. Mohammed Salih, the leader of Uzbek opposition Erk Party, said similar positive words about the Turkish model.[9]

The Western proposal of the Turkish Model affected Turkish politicians and encouraged them to make such enthusiastic statements about Turkic world. President Turgut Özal frequently stressed on the idea that the twenty-first century would be a 'Turkic century', while Prime Minister Süleyman Demirel pointed out the Turkic world that extended from the 'Chinese Wall to the Adriatic Sea'.[10]

President Özal clearly stated Turkey's position toward Turkic Republics "Fantasies of pan-Turkism are totally out of the question, especially in today's world. These republics are all separate states. They are equal and brotherly states. We can form a community with them. For example, we can work as a group at the United Nations and we are together in ECO (Economic Cooperation Organisation). In time, we can become a community of Turkish states, just like the Arabs, but we must regard all of them as independent states. Let no one even think of a big brother role".[11]

In the early 1990s, Turkey had some great diplomatic problems with the Western world such as Turkey's refusal by the EU, isolation on crucial issues like Cyprus, the PKK-led Kurdish separatism and terrorism, and the water conflict with Syria and Iraq over the rivers Fırat (Euphrates) and Dicle (Tigris). Turkey considered the Turkic Republics as natural allies who could support the Turkish claims on international issues.[12]

The declarations by Central Asian leaders that they wanted to follow the Turkish Model and a number of political groups and parties in Central Asia and the Caucasus with pro-Turkish and even pan-Turkish tendencies in early 1990s, also seemed to warrant Turkish optimism.[13]

Within a year, all parties gradually became aware of the limitations and constraints of Turkey. Central Asian countries had gained experience in conducting their own foreign policies and had become integrated into international arena. Turkic leaders had travelled throughout the world and discovered various models of socio-economic development, especially of East Asia. These alternative connections made them realise that there were other choices available to them besides the Turkish or Iranian models. Additionally, the political and economic problems Turkey were evident during this period.[14]

Although the Turkic Republics initially regarded the Turkish Model as a social and economic miracle, however when they visited Turkey, they found a country with huge structural economic and social problems. The Turkic Republics understood that the Turkish living standard could not be a long-term final goal as the Turkish Model was not a social and economic miracle. They had become aware of the fact that Turkey had not enough fund to subsidise Turkic Republics. Turkic Republics also realised Turkey's serious domestic political problems, including the Kurdish problem and PKK-led terrorism that raged throughout the 1990s and the destabilised political environment.[15]

The most important was the unwillingness of the newly born states to submerge their recently acquired independence within a broader organisation. Moreover, some of these states had ambitions of becoming the leaders in Central Asia. Another factor was Russia's continued dominance and its opposition to the creation of a Turkic group. Especially after 1993, Russia clearly declared its intention of regaining control over the former Soviet territory known as the 'near abroad doctrine'. There were economic reasons for the former Soviet economies dependent on the other republics. The high degree of regional specialisation that had been achieved during the Soviet era had resulted in a high level of intra-regional trade.[16]

In the security fields, Russia did not want to see a rival power settled in the former Soviet territory. Each of the Turkic Republics has different security concerns and, therefore, had different ideas about how it should conduct its relations with Russia. About 25 million ethnic Russians living in the Caucasian and Central Asian states also encouraged Russia to control the former Soviet territory in order to guarantee their civil rights.[17]

The most important cause of Turkey's setbacks was the fall of Ebulfezl Elcibey's pro-Turkish government in Azerbaijan in June 1993. Haydar Aliyev succeeded his position and at that time it was widely believed that he was backed by Moscow. Turkey interpreted this event as part of the Russian strategy of reasserting its ex-colonies. Aliyev's initial statements to the effect that he wanted to restore a balance in Azerbaijan's foreign relations by improving ties with Iran and Russia seemed to feed these concerns. In initial pace, the Turkish government continued to support Elcibey and refused to recognise the new government.[18] Thus, Turkey's initial positive image as a sister strong state was badly undermined after the fall of Elchibey. So then, the Turkic

Republics did not want to have a new big brother after just getting rid of the old one. Uzbekistan called most of the students who were sent to Turkey for education back to Uzbekistan in the mid-1990s, as Uzbek leadership believed that these students were recruited by the Uzbek opposition led by Mohammed Salih in Turkey.[19]

After the first year of independence, Western knowledge of the region and its economic, cultural, social and strategic issues increased, and Western support for the Turkish Model declined too. There were also other important reasons behind the decline in Western support for the Turkish Model.

Firstly, after some time, the West realised that although Iran had some geo-strategic advantages in the region, it had significant limitations as well. Iran was an Islamic state; however, the effect of Iran in the Turkic Republics was very limited because of sectarian difference. Iran was a Shiite state; on the other hand, the majority of the population of the Turkic states was Sunni, except for Azerbaijan. Iran's influence even over the Azeri population was very limited as Azeri people were Turkic and their nationalistic feelings were stronger than their religious motivation. Also, Iran had an ethnic Azeri minority living in the northern part of the country. Mostly because of these shortcomings, Iran began to pursue a more pragmatic policy toward Muslim republics.[20] The danger of the Iranian model in the Turkic Republics was the main reason which led the West to promote the Turkish Model to the region as a counter-ideology. Therefore, because of Iran's shortcomings in the region, the main reason behind Western support for the Turkish Model diminished. Besides, all the Turkic Republics already welcomed the main characteristics of the Turkish Model within a year after the independence. Therefore, promotion of the Turkish Model did its role successfully by attracting the interests of the Turkic Republics towards the West instead of the radical Middle East, especially Iran.

Since the Turkish Model had played its part, there was no longer any need for further support to it. Besides, there was a danger of revival of pan-Turkism for the West, Russia and China.[21] Further support for the Turkish Model might have encouraged this trend and therefore support for it suddenly declined.

Turkic Republics assumed that Turkey was powerful enough, economically and politically, and was ready to help them establish their new states. All of them welcomed the aspects of the Turkish Model related to secularism, the market economy and closeness and cooperation with the West, but the democratic aspect of the Turkish Model was not warmly welcomed. In this case, almost all former Soviet republics wanted to establish close relations with the West, because they realised that the developed states of the West, as well as the Pacific, were in a better position than Turkey to give economic assistance. After realising this, Turkic Republics stopped talking about the Turkish Model. The West also realised that they did not need a third party like Turkey.[22] After the initial emotional welcome for Turkey and the Turkish Model, the Turkic Republics then became more realistic, although they did not abandon the Turkish Model.

Realisation of Policies (Since 1995)

By early 1995, Turkey had already begun to regain lost ground in the Caucasus and in the following years it further consolidated its position. Turkey avoided direct involvement in any issue such as Chechnya, South Ossetia and Abkhazia. Beyond regional conflicts, Turkey's desire to become a regional hub for Caspian energy resources came true.[23]

The fear of Turkey generated by Aliyev's coming to power proved unfounded. Aliyev discovered that Russia was neither willing nor able to force the withdrawal of Armenian troops from the occupied Azerbaijani territory and return Karabakh region to Azerbaijani control. Moreover, Aliyev soon understood that Azerbaijan's economic future, and especially the development of its energy resources, depended on its maintaining good relations with the West. This had led the new leadership to resume a policy of close relations with Turkey in all areas of activity. Turkey signed a Declaration on Deepened Strategic Cooperation with Azerbaijan in 1997. Turkey trained Azeri military personnel, Turkish military advisors were active in Azerbaijan and there were a number of Azeri military personnel serving in the peacekeeping force in Kosovo as part of the Turkish contingent.[24]

Georgia's foreign policy also became closer in a pro-Western direction to the point that President Shevardnadze expressed his country's desire to one day become a member of NATO. This shift in Georgia's foreign policy has had a positive impact on relations with Turkey. Finally, Turkey signed military assistance and cooperation agreements with Georgia in 1999.[25]

However, Turkey found itself in a strong competition with Russia in Central Asia. Although the Central Asian countries' relations with Turkey improved, Kazakhstan, Kyrgyzstan and Tajikistan developed closer ties with Russia. The principal reasons for this development were Russia's proximity, the presence of large Russian minorities in these countries, especially in Kazakhstan, and their security needs. Uzbekistan was the only country in Central Asia to adopt a more pro-Western and anti-Russian stance. Uzbekistan joined a pro-Western grouping of members of the Commonwealth of Independent States (CIS) that included Georgia, Azerbaijan, Ukraine and Moldova (GUUAM).[26]

Meanwhile Turkish-Uzbek relations never achieved the degree of closeness of Turkey's ties with Azerbaijan or Georgia. This situation had been partly due to Uzbekistan's ambition to become a regional power in Central Asia and an important partner of the West. Turkey and Uzbekistan have had tense relations since 1999 following the incursion of Uzbek Islamists into Kyrgyzstan. According to Uzbek officials, the Uzbek nationalist and pan-Turkish leader Muhammad Salih was also involved in this incursion. After this incident, the Uzbek government ordered the closure of a number of Turkish schools and relations between the two countries strained considerably.[27]

It was also visible that Turkey-Turkic Republics relations reached a degree of equilibrium in the middle of 1990s. Turkey did not emerge as the main influence in Caucasus and Central Asia, either politically, economically or even culturally. But, neither did the pessimistic view of Turkey become irrelevant. Turkey succeeded in establishing extensive political, military, economic and cultural relations with Central Asian and Caucasian countries. Turkey was particularly influential in Azerbaijan and Georgia and had a considerable presence in Turkmenistan, Kyrgyzstan and Kazakhstan. Turkey became an important player in both regions.[28]

Turkish Model was used as a facilitator following the end of Soviet Union for Muslim republics to attract their attention to the West rather to Iran or Saudi Arabia. After achieving this, the West ended its support to the Turkish Model. However, radical religious movements around the world and ongoing conflicts, especially in the Middle East, Caucasus and Balkans, encouraged people to talk about Turkey again as a balance of regional conflicts.[29] During his trip to Turkey in November 1999, US president Bill Clinton stressed that Turkey had a significant role to play in the volatile regions. Clinton paid his attention to the need of a facilitator between Europe and the Islamic world and implied that Turkey was a bridge between the Christian and Islamic cultures. The US began to regard Turkey as a strategic ally to tackle the problems in a region from Balkans to Central Asia and Middle East. Besides, the West still had some doubts whether Russia had given up its historic ambitions of penetrating south.[30]

The countries of Caucasus and Central Asia are rich in oil and gas and they want to transport their energy resources to the world markets. Because of Turkey's geo-strategic position in the region, the US wants to cooperate with Turkey. For the global war against terrorism in the post 9/11 era, Turkish Model seems to be important and the current developments may possibly bring Turkish Model to the political ground to see whether it can be used as an instrument in international relations. Turkey can be an important instrument to play a unique role within EU as well as within the Eurasia.

Turkey's Contribution in Diplomatic and Political Sphere

Turkey was the first state to extend diplomatic recognition to Uzbekistan, Kazakhstan, Kyrgyzstan, Turkmenistan and Azerbaijan. Shortly afterward, all the presidents of the Turkic Republics paid visits to Ankara: Nursultan Nazarbayev of Kazakhstan in September 1991, Saparmurad Turkmenbasi of Turkmenistan, Islam Kerimov of Uzbekistan and Askar Akayev of Kyrgyzstan stopped in Ankara in December, while Ayaz Muttalibov of Azerbaijan came in January 1992.[31]

Ankara soon became aware that some institutional capability was needed to promote multidimensional relations between Turkey and the Turkic states. One of the important instruments was the introduction of regular Turkic summits. The first Turkic Summit, the Ankara Summit, was held in the Turkish capital in October 1992.[32]

The newly born states did not have well-developed diplomatic services and they did not have the corps of diplomats trained under the Soviet era. Therefore, Turkey's offers of diplomatic guidance and support were welcomed. Turkey had served as a guide in promoting the participation of Central Asian and Caucasian states in international forums such as the Organisation on Security and Cooperation in Europe (OSCE), the United Nations (UN), and the Organisation of the Islamic Conference (OIC). Through Turkish efforts, Azerbaijan joined the Black See Economic Cooperation (BSEC) which came into existence in 1992. Similarly, Turkey helped getting the five Turkic states join the Economic Cooperation Organisation (ECO), which was originally established to promote political, economic, and cultural cooperation between Turkey, Iran and Pakistan in 1985 as the successor organisation of Regional Cooperation for Development (RCD) that remained in existence from 1964 to 1979. Turkey also helped the Central Asian Turkic republics in joining the TACIS Committee of the European Union, the European Bank of Reconstruction and Development (EBRD) and the United Nations Development Program (UNDP).[33]

Table-1: Memberships to the International & Regional Organisations[34]

Countries	COE	EU	OSCE	NATO	WTO	BSEC	OCAC	CIS	OCST	ECO	EURASEC	CASCO	GUAM	SCO
Azerbaijan	x	!	X	!	!	x	!	x	0	x	0	x	x	0
Kazakhstan	0	!	x	!	!	0	x	x	x	x	x	x	0	x
Kyrgyzstan	0	!	x	!	x	0	x	x	x	x	x	0	0	x
Turkmenistan	0	!	x	!	0	0	0	A	0	x	0	x	0	0
Uzbekistan	0	!	x	!	!	0	x	x	0	x	x	0	0	x
Turkey	x	A	x	x	x	x	!	0	0	x	0	0	0	0

Abbreviations

COE	Council of Europe
EU	European Union
OSCE	Organisation on Security and Cooperation in Europe
NATO	North Atlantic Treaty Organisation
WTO	World Trade Organisation
BSEC	Black Sea Economic Cooperation
OCAC	Organisation of Central Asian Cooperation
CIS	Commonwealth Independent States
OCST	*Organisation of Collective Security Treaty*
ECO	Economic Cooperation Organisation
EURASEC	*Eurasian Economic Community*
CASCO	*Caspian Cooperation Organisation*
GUAM	The GUAM *Organisation* for Democracy and *Economic Development*
SCO	*Shanghai Cooperation Organisation*
X	*Member*
!	Observer Member
0	Non-member
A	Associate Member

Economic and Trade Relations between Turkey and Turkic Republics

In the field of economy between Turkey and the Turkic Republics, there is currently an intense activity. Initially, Turkey overestimated its ability to extend assistance to the new sister republics and also misjudged the ability of the republics to bring about the necessary changes in their administration and politics so as to become integrated to the world system. Some economic and commercial agreements were signed with Azerbaijan (1992), Kazakhstan (1991), Kyrgyzstan (1991), Turkmenistan (1995), and Uzbekistan (1995).[35]

Entry to the markets of the Turkic Republics seems to have followed an identifiable pattern in the first years of their independence. The Turkic states have also had a great difficulty in paying for their trade with Turkey. To overcome these difficulties, Turkey founded Turkish International Cooperation Agency (TICA). TICA helped promote the Turkish private sector in doing business in the former Soviet republics. In addition to TICA and Turkish Eximbank, foundation of a non-governmental bilateral business council, the Foreign Economic Relations Board (DEİK), has promoted economic and cultural relations with the Turkic states.[36]

Turkey also played a pivotal role to improve communication and transportation facilities of Turkic Republics. Turkey donated digital telecommunication exchanges to each of the five Turkic Republics. When Turkic Republics became independent, there was no way to reach them by air except through Moscow. The Turkish Airlines initiated direct flights to Baku, Tashkent, Almaty, Ashgabat and Bishkek in 1992. Even today, some of the most convenient and reliable connections to the Caucasian and Central Asian are served by the Turkish Airlines. As these states have developed their own national air carriers, all have started to offer frequent flights to Istanbul.[37]

Land transport, in contrast to air transport, could not be improved easily. Turkey first opened a border crossing at Sarp into the Ajaristan region of Georgia. This made it possible for trucks to go through Georgia into Azerbaijan, where they would then take the truck ferry from Baku to Turkmenbashi port in Turkmenistan. From there, all cities in Central Asian could be reached.[38]

Turkey also helped Turkic Republics develop human resources. Well-trained individuals in the fields of economics, banking, management, accounting, diplomacy and other similar fields were needed in the newly born countries in order to develop a reliable public service system.[39]

Turkey tried to get the Turkic Republics to make a commitment to support the construction of a pipeline that would carry Caspian oil to the Mediterranean. Most importantly in 1998, the presidents of Turkey, Azerbaijan, Georgia and Kazakhstan signed the Ankara Declaration, confirming the Baku-Tbilisi-Ceyhan (BTC) pipeline as the main pipeline project.[40] The pipeline construction began in early 2002 and was completed in 2005. Another parallel project between Turkey, Azerbaijan and Georgia was the South Caucasus Pipeline (SCP) project to bring natural gas from the Shah Deniz (Azerbaijan) through Georgia into Turkey.[41] Construction of SCP project started in 2003 and finished in 2006. Completion and starting of operations of BTC and SCP have made Turkey an energy terminal for Caspian basin energy resources.

Cultural Cooperation between Turkey and Turkic Republics

Another important instrument was the expansion of Turkish language and culture. Turkey also opened schools in each of the republics, a commitment that has already been achieved. These schools, in addition to teaching students standard Turkish which would enable them connect with Turkey, teaches English which constitutes the critical instrument through which these countries can relate to the world.[42] These public or private Turkish schools are aiming at native countries to constitute Turkish speaking elite that can replace the Russian-speaking elite. These schools have been welcomed by the Turkic Republics since they offered education above regional standards. It is expected that Turkish will become the *lingua franca* of the Turkic world.[43]

Turkey initiated a programme in which a total of 10 000 students, 2 000 from each of the five republics, were provided scholarships to study at Turkish universities. By 1997, 7545 students from Turkic states had enrolled at Turkish universities and colleges. Turkish Police Academy and War Academy have also invited students from Turkic Republics.[44]

In early 1990s, two public Turkish universities: the Ahmet Yesevi University, a Turkish-Kazakh university in the city of Turkistan, and Manas Univesity in Bishkek, a Turkish-Kyrgyz university, were founded. Turkish businessmen have also founded four private universities in Kazakhstan (Suleyman Demirel University), Kyrgyzstan (Ataturk-Alatoo University), Turkmenistan (Turkmen-Turk University) and Azerbaijan (Qafqas University).[45]

The possibility of developing a standard alphabet for Turkic languages was one of the important purposes of Turkey. A meeting for common alphabet was organised by the Turkish Ministries of Culture and Education in 1992 and the Ministry of Foreign Affairs in 1993. So far, all Turkic Republics except Kazakhstan and Kyrgyzstan have adopted the Latin alphabet. The presence of large Russian population appears to have kept Kazakhstan away from considering changing their alphabets at this time.[46] However, there are some difficulties reaching at a common Turkic language because there are enough differences among Turkic languages. For example, a Turk and an Azeri cannot understand a Kyrgyz or a Kazakh. Russian still remains the principal language of ex-Soviet zone.[47]

In a different arena of cultural interaction, Turkey has started television broadcasts to the Turkic Republics via satellite since 1992. The programmes, which reflect the life and society in Turkey, would also be designed to convey a sense of community among the Turkic people. However, Turkish state channel, TRT, did not perform successfully. On the other hand, Turkish private TV channels, Samanyolu, TGRT, Star TV and Show TV, started to broadcast in the region and have gained an audience in the region and are widely watched.[48]

The Turkish Ministry of Foreign Affairs established The Turkish Culture and Arts Joint Administration (TÜRKSOY) in 1994 to serve officials from the Turkic Republics and representatives from Turkic-populated areas of the Russian Federation. The main goal of TÜRKSOY organisation is to promote cultural interactions among the Turkic Republics.[49]

Turkish help was also important in the field of religion as Turkey wanted to export its model of moderate Islam. The Turkish Presidency of Religious Affairs (TPRA) sent books and religious servicemen, *Imams*, to the Turkic Republics. First of all in Ramadan 1990, the TPRA sent four *Imams* to the USSR. Besides, students from the Turkic world also came to Turkey for religious education. Turkic Muslims needed books on religion and mosques in the region needed repairing. Turkish businessmen have also supported construction of mosques and provided books on religion and Turkish culture. Although their aims were different, Turkey, Iran and Saudi Arabia began to send Holy Korans and other religious books to the Republics, and experts were sent to teach Islam.[50]

With the initiative of TPRA, Eurasian Islamic Council was established and it meets periodically to discuss cultural and religious problems of former communist states. TPRA helped to open Theology Faculties in Azerbaijan, Kyrgyzstan, Turkmenistan, Romania and Bulgaria.[51]

Conclusion

In the early period of dissolution of the Soviet Union, Turkey considered the Turkic Republics as natural allies who could support the Turkish claims on international issues because of Turkey's cultural, historical and ethnic ties with the Caucasus and Central Asia. Therefore, it was expected that Turkey had become one of the main players in Caucasia and Central Asia, as an alternative of Russia, Iran and China. However, Turkey's own economic and political shortcomings and domestic problems in 1990s prevented it from playing the leading role which it aspired.

By mid-1990s, Turkey realised its regional policy and began to regain its lost ground in the following years, especially in the Caucasus. During the process, Turkey avoided direct involvement in any issue such as Chechnya, South Ossetia and Abkhazia. Turkey mainly concentrated on common projects with regional countries such as pipelines projects for Caspian energy resources. In the new process, Russia, Iran and China transformed from rivals to partners in Central Asia for Turkey. New Turkish foreign policy is now focusing on 'soft power identity' in general and paying much more attention to 'win-win policy' rather than the'zero-sum game' for all actors in the Caucasus and Central Asia. This policy makes Turkey an important player in Eurasia.

Notes

1. Richard Weitz, "Averting a New Great Game in Central Asia", *The Washington Quarterly* 29, no.3, (2006), p.155
2. Shireen Hunter, "Turkey, Central Asia, and the Caucasus: Ten Years after Independence", *Southeast European and Black Sea Studies* 1, no.2, (May 2001), p.11.
3. Cengiz Candar and Graham E. Fuller, "Grand Geopolitics for a New Turkey", *Mediterranean Quarterly*, (Winter 2001), p.34.
4.. Idris Bal, "Turkish Model as a Foreign Policy Instrument in Post Cold War Era: The Cases of Turkic Republics and the Post September 11th Era", In *Turkish Foreign policy in Post Cold War Era*, edited by Idris Bal. Boca Raton: Brown Walker Press, 2004, p.330.
5. Shireen Hunter, "Turkey, Central Asia, and the Caucasus: Ten Years after Independence", *Southeast European and Black Sea Studies* 1, no.2, (May 2001), p.3.
6. Idris Bal, "Turkish Model as a Foreign Policy Instrument in Post Cold War Era: The Cases of Turkic Republics and the Post September 11th Era", In *Turkish Foreign policy in Post Cold War Era*, edited by Idris Bal. Boca Raton: Brown Walker Press, 2004, p.335.
7. Cengiz Candar and Graham E. Fuller, "Grand Geopolitics for a New Turkey", *Mediterranean Quarterly*, (Winter 2001), p.33.
8. Gul Turan, Ilter Turan and Idris Bal, "Turkey's Relations with Turkic Republics", In *Turkish Foreign policy in Post Cold War Era*, edited by Idris Bal. Boca Raton: Brown Walker Press, 2004, p.307.
9. Idris Bal, "Turkish Model as a Foreign Policy Instrument in Post Cold War Era: The Cases of Turkic Republics and the Post September 11th Era", In *Turkish Foreign policy in Post Cold War Era*, edited by Idris Bal. Boca Raton: Brown Walker Press, 2004, p.331.

10. Alexander Murinson, "The Strategic Depth Doctrine of Turkish Foreign Policy", *Middle Eastern Studies* 42, no.6, (2006), p.946.
11. Shireen Hunter, "Turkey, Central Asia, and the Caucasus: Ten Years after Independence", *Southeast European and Black Sea Studies* 1, no.2, (May 2001), p.9.
12. Idris Bal, "Turkish Model as a Foreign Policy Instrument in Post Cold War Era: The Cases of Turkic Republics and the Post September 11th Era", In *Turkish Foreign policy in Post Cold War Era*, edited by Idris Bal. Boca Raton: Brown Walker Press, 2004, p.334.
13. Shireen Hunter, "Turkey, Central Asia, and the Caucasus: Ten Years after Independence", *Southeast European and Black Sea Studies* 1, no.2, (May 2001), p.11.
14. _____, "Turkey, Central Asia, and the Caucasus: Ten Years after Independence", *Southeast European and Black Sea Studies* 1, no.2, (May 2001), p.13.
15. Tarik Oguzlu, "Soft Power in Turkish Foreign Policy", *Australian Journal of International Affairs* 61, no.1, (2007), p.88.
16. Lerna K. Yanik, "Allies or Partners: An Appraisal of Turkey's Ties to Russia, 1991-2007", *East European Quarterly*, (September 2007), p.351.
17. Idil Tuncer, "The Security Policies of the Russian Federation: The 'Near Abroad' and Turkey", *Turkish Studies* 1, no.2, (Autumn 2000), p.97.
18. Sener Akturk, "Turkish-Russian Relations after the Cold war (1992-2002)", *Turkish Studies* 7, no.3, (2006), p.343.
19. Idris Bal, "Turkish Model as a Foreign Policy Instrument in Post Cold War Era: The Cases of Turkic Republics and the Post September 11th Era", In *Turkish Foreign policy in Post Cold War Era*, edited by Idris Bal. Boca Raton: Brown Walker Press, 2004, p.339.
20. _____, "Turkish Model as a Foreign Policy Instrument in Post Cold War Era: The Cases of Turkic Republics and the Post September 11th Era", In *Turkish Foreign policy in Post Cold War Era*, edited by Idris Bal. Boca Raton: Brown Walker Press, 2004, p.335.
21. Selcuk Colakoglu, "Soğuk Savaş Sonrası Türk Dış Politikası (in Turkish; Turkish Foreign Policy in the post-Cold War Era)", In *Yakın Dönem Türk Politik Tarihi*, Süleyman İnan & Ercan Haytoğlu. Ankara: Anı Yayıncılık, 2007, p.339.
22. Mustafa Aydin, Foucault's Pendulum: turkey in Central Asia and the Caucasus", *Turkish Studies* 5, no.2, (Summer 2004), p.7.
23. Suat Kiniklioğlu and Valery Morkva, "An Anatomy of Turkish-Russian Relations", *Southeast European and Black Sea Studies* 7, no.4, (December 2007), p.542.
24. Nasuh Uslu, "The Russian, Caucasian and Central Asian Aspects of Turkish Foreign Policy in the Post Cold War Period", *Alternative: Turkish Journal of International*

Relations 2, no.3-4, (Fall-Winter 2003), p.172.

25. _____, "The Russian, Caucasian and Central Asian Aspects of Turkish Foreign Policy in the Post Cold War Period", *Alternative: Turkish Journal of International Relations* 2, no.3-4, (Fall-Winter 2003), p.172.
26. Idil Tuncer, "The Security Policies of the Russian Federation: The 'Near Abroad' and Turkey", *Turkish Studies* 1, no.2, (Autumn 2000), pp.105-106.
27. Shireen Hunter, "Turkey, Central Asia, and the Caucasus: Ten Years after Independence", *Southeast European and Black Sea Studies* 1, no.2, (May 2001), p.14.
28. Fiona Hill, "Seismic Shifts in Eurasia: The Changing Relationship between Turkey and Russia and Its Implications for the South Caucasus", *Southeast European and Black Sea Studies* 3, no.3, (September 2003), pp.62-63.
29. Mohammad Karim, "Globalization and Post-Soviet Revival of Islam in Central Asia and the Caucasus", *Journal of Muslim Minority Affairs* 25, no.3, (December 2005), s.445.
30. Idris Bal, "Turkish Model as a Foreign Policy Instrument in Post Cold War Era: The Cases of Turkic Republics and the Post September 11th Era", In *Turkish Foreign policy in Post Cold War Era*, edited by Idris Bal. Boca Raton: Brown Walker Press, 2004, p.341.
31. Gul Turan, Ilter Turan and Idris Bal, "Turkey's Relations with Turkic Republics", In *Turkish Foreign policy in Post Cold War Era*, edited by Idris Bal. Boca Raton: Brown Walker Press, 2004, p.298.
32. Shireen Hunter, "Turkey, Central Asia, and the Caucasus: Ten Years after Independence", *Southeast European and Black Sea Studies* 1, no.2, (May 2001), p.9.
33. Gul Turan, Ilter Turan and Idris Bal, "Turkey's Relations with Turkic Republics", In *Turkish Foreign policy in Post Cold War Era*, edited by Idris Bal. Boca Raton: Brown Walker Press, 2004, p.325.
34. Adapted form Esra Hatipoglu, "Güney Kafkasya veOrta Asya'da 'Büyük Güçler' Arasındaki Oyun: Bölgesel Örgüt ve Oluşumların Rolü (in Turkish; Game among 'Great Powers' in South Caucasus and Central Asia: The Roles of Regional Organisations and Initiatives)", In *Orta Asya & Kafkasya Güç Politikası*, edited by M. Turgut Demirtepe. Ankara: USAK Yayınları, 2008, p.21.
35. Tuncay Babali, *Caspian Energy Diplomacy: Since the End of the Cold War*, Ankara: Turkish Foreign Policy Institute, 2006, pp.126-127.
36. Shireen Hunter, "Turkey, Central Asia, and the Caucasus: Ten Years after Independence", *Southeast European and Black Sea Studies* 1, no.2, (May 2001), p.11.
37. Gul Turan, Ilter Turan and Idris Bal, "Turkey's Relations with Turkic Republics", In

Turkish Foreign policy in Post Cold War Era, edited by Idris Bal. Boca Raton: Brown Walker Press, 2004, p.300.

38. _____, "Turkey's Relations with Turkic Republics", In *Turkish Foreign policy in Post Cold War Era*, edited by Idris Bal. Boca Raton: Brown Walker Press, 2004, p.300.
39. Tuncay Babali, *Caspian Energy Diplomacy: Since the End of the Cold War*, Ankara: Turkish Foreign Policy Institute, 2006, pp.126-127.
40. Nasuh Uslu, "The Russian, Caucasian and Central Asian Aspects of Turkish Foreign Policy in the Post Cold War Period", *Alternative: Turkish Journal of International Relations* 2, no.3-4, (Fall-Winter 2003), pp.172-173.
41. Mustafa Aydin, Foucault's Pendulum: turkey in Central Asia and the Caucasus", *Turkish Studies* 5, no.2, (Summer 2004), p.16.
42. Mehmet Kutalmis, Turkish outside Turkey: The role of Turkish in Turkey's International Relations", *Journal of Academic Studies*, No.25, (2005), p.135.
43. Shireen Hunter, "Turkey, Central Asia, and the Caucasus: Ten Years after Independence", *Southeast European and Black Sea Studies* 1, no.2, (May 2001), p.9.
44. Bulent Aras, "Turkey's Policy in the Former Soviet South: Assets and Options", *Turkish Studies* 1, no.1, (Spring 2000), p.45.
45. Berrak Kurtulus, "Cooperation in the Fields of Education and Science between Turkey and Turkish Republics", *Eurasian Studies*, (Spring-Summer 2000), p.43.
46. Gul Turan, Ilter Turan and Idris Bal, "Turkey's Relations with Turkic Republics", In *Turkish Foreign policy in Post Cold War Era*, edited by Idris Bal. Boca Raton: Brown Walker Press, 2004, p.305.
47. Shireen Hunter, "Turkey, Central Asia, and the Caucasus: Ten Years after Independence", *Southeast European and Black Sea Studies* 1, no.2, (May 2001), p.10.
48. Gul Turan, Ilter Turan and Idris Bal, "Turkey's Relations with Turkic Republics", In *Turkish Foreign policy in Post Cold War Era*, edited by Idris Bal. Boca Raton: Brown Walker Press, 2004, p.306.
49. Bulent Aras, "Turkey's Policy in the Former Soviet South: Assets and Options", *Turkish Studies* 1, no.1, (Spring 2000), p.45.
50. Idris Bal, "Turkish Model as a Foreign Policy Instrument in Post Cold War Era: The Cases of Turkic Republics and the Post September 11th Era", In *Turkish Foreign policy in Post Cold War Era*, edited by Idris Bal. Boca Raton: Brown Walker Press, 2004, p.337.
51. Bulent Aras, "Turkey's Policy in the Former Soviet South: Assets and Options", *Turkish Studies* 1, no.1, (Spring 2000), p.46.

Chinese Policy in Central Asia

Adil Kaukenov

The Chinese policy in Central Asia is a part of the global foreign policy strategy of the People's Republic of China. As the basic priorities and problems of global foreign policy strategy of the People's Republic of China which have the direct bearing on its in Central Asia, it is possible to underline the following:

- Maintenance of a favourable international situation for development and modernization of the People's Republic of China.
- Prevention of attempts of restraining power growth of the People's Republic of China.
- Diversification of China's access to energy resources.
- To assure the world community that economic growth and military modernisation of the People's Republic of China does not represent threat to the interests of other countries.
- Maintenance of isolation of Taiwan on international scene (to a lesser degree).

The second group is represented by the factors determining the importance of region for China:

- ***The factor of maintenance of stability of the western provinces of the People's Republic of China.***
- The People's Republic of China aspires by means of distribution of the influence in Central Asia to secure 'rears' due to the western limits, having provided with the safety and development of Xinjiang and other western provinces. In a view of recent events in Tibet from March 10–14, the given problem gets special importance.
- Also geopolitical prevalence of the People's Republic of China in Central Asia is obviously necessary for the country in context of counteraction of the US policy on restraint of its further growth and oppositions to unipolar system, and a leading position of the USA at economic, political and military levels.

- ***An economic factor.*** An intensification of trade and economic relations of the People's Republic of China with the countries of Central Asia allows Beijing to use economic and resource potential with a view of development of the western territories. The markets of the countries of Central Asia are an ideal vector for the external economic activity as remoteness from world sea communications complicates their output on the basic markets of the world for manufacturers of the western areas of China. As a result, today over 80 percent of the general commodity circulation of China with the Central Asia is made through Xinjiang.
- ***The energy factor.*** Energy resources of the Central Asia represent greater importance for China. An arrangement of Central Asia in immediate proximity to China enables to transport hydrocarbonic resources through ground pipelines. The importance of power cooperation of China with the countries of Central Asia is staticized even more in view of prospect of expansion of the Central Asian highways up to Northern Iran.
- ***Transit potential of region.*** Central Asia is important for Beijing as the important transport corridor in the long term can provide China an overland output to Iran and further to the Europe. Occurrence of an opportunity of a lining of overland highways through the territory of the countries of Central Asia is important for Beijing in context of diversification of overland routes to Europe, and also reduction of terms of delivery of Chinese production.

In connection with this, the basic purpose of foreign policy of China today is preservation of an external world to concentrate all forces to own internal development. The key concepts of the Chinese policy of steel are firstly, *'peace development'* and secondly, *'the harmonious world'*. Also in this case it is necessary to mention five key principles of realisation of the international relations in the Chinese policy:

- *mutual respect of the sovereignty and territorial integrity,*
- *non-aggression,*
- *non-interference to interiors of each other,*
- *equality and mutual benefit,*
- *peaceful coexistence.*

Modern Chinese policy in the Central Asia is notable for its pragmatism and constant underlining of the fact that priorities for China lay exclusively in the sphere of development of good neighbourhood and in realisation of economic interests.

It is necessary to note that Central Asia became the so-called range for many diplomatic initiatives of China, for implementation of some new diplomatic methods and the mechanisms not applied anywhere by China earlier.; certainly, creation and the subsequent development of the Shanghai Cooperation Organisation which became one of the basic conductors of the Chinese diplomacy in region is pertinent here.

The fact that China has suggested for the first time to adhere to 'the Shanghai spirit' logically follows from the first initiative, based on 'mutual trust, mutual benefit, equality, meeting, respect for variety of civilisations, aspiration to joint development'.

It was offered here for the first time to build so-called 'harmonious region'. The leader of China Hu Jintao in a speech at SCO summit in June 2006 suggested the construction of a 'harmonious region on the basis of the long-term world and joint prosperity' in Central Asia.

It is necessary to mention that the policy of China **in relation to the adjacent states** lays also on a basis of the Chinese diplomacy in the Central Asian region. The key idea of the Chinese policy here has two basic formulations, namely 'good neighbourhood and partnership', including terms like 'friendliness, safety, enrichment'.

The term 'friendliness' touches the sphere of political connections with the neighbouring states; the sense of the given concept consists in development of good-neighbourhood connections with all adjacent countries.

'Safety' mentions relations in sphere of safety; the sense of this part of the concept consists in that the adjacent countries should have a feeling of safety and rest in relation with China as its neighbour.

'Enrichment' touches the sphere of economic policy; the given term declares that China during fast economic development should render more help to the neighbouring states and do it in such a way that they also could benefit by fast economic growth in China. Proceeding from the given concept, China allocates soft loans to the countries of region for realisation of large projects in such spheres as natural resources development, construction of the infrastructure of transport and communication, water-power engineering, etc. But it is necessary to note that financial and economic resources are given on favourable terms with a condition of use of the Chinese techniques and equipment, and also attraction of experts from China. For example, two individual extra agreements about 'delivery of the equipment from the People's Republic of China for hydro power plant-2 at the Andizhan water basin' and about 'delivery of the equipment from the People's Republic of China for hydro plant MGES at Aharagan water basin' have been signed in March 2007 between National Bank of Foreign Trade Activities of the Republic of Uzbekistan and Export-Import bank of China. The total sum of the credit for the first project is 10.03 million dollars and for the second, it is 5.9 million dollars. On the credit conditions, given for a period of 15 years, including 5 years grace period under the interest rate of 3 percent, delivery of the Chinese technologies and services is provided. Erection of two electric lines 'South-north' and 'Lolazor-Hulton' in Tajikistan has been done because of China and the participation of the Chinese company TBEA. For their realisation, China Exim Bank allocated long-term credit of $300 million to Tajikistan with the annual rate of 2.2 percent for a period of 25 years, 7 out of which are a grace period. Also the State bank of Development of China has allocated to Kazakhstan, a credit for the sum of $200 million for the construction of Moinak Hydroelectric Power Station; the supplier of works on designing and construction of station 'on a turn-key basis' is the Chinese International Corporation for water management and power.

But, in view of a real foreign policy and external economic rate of China, such concepts are represented, at the least, too optimistically. Nevertheless, they also serve as tools within the limits of the Chinese diplomacy.

The key basis of this diplomacy is more often named as the use of so-called strategy **of *soft power***. Transformation of this concept, borrowed from the American political science, into a component of official party policy occurred at the Seventeenth Congress of Communist Party of China when the appeal 'to increase cultural soft power of the state' was mentioned in report of Hu Jintao.

It is known, the theory of 'soft power' means the use of 'non-material imperous resources' **of culture and political ideals** in the interests of influence on behaviour of people in other countries—unlike influence by means of 'rigid force' of weapon or money.

For China it is especially important, as at the moment it cannot use the military and political potential for influencing neighbours, including Central Asia. Economic pressure in view of power and prospects of China in this area is represented more really, though now it is presented in the form of primary appeal of financial and investment opportunities of China within the limits of cooperation with the states of region.

Thus, in view of this, cultural influence of China in the Central Asia is hard to distribute, **China makes accent on strengthening of 'strategic reputation' which underlies trust of other states in it.**

Besides these concepts which are called to create peace and friendly environment as much as possible around of the People's Republic of China, it is necessary to mention the concrete diplomatic mechanisms used by China in the Central Asia.

They are caused by the following key interests of China in region:

First of all, the basic strategic purpose of China in the Central Asia is maintenance of its own safety. Here enters both maintenance of regional safety and aspiration to protect China from the possible sources of instability proceeding from territory of the states of region. The basic diplomatic mechanism in this case is participation in work of SCO. China, being as a matter of fact, the initiator for creation of SCO and its subsequent development into a new format, tries not to loose the status of the main motive—power of the given organisation. SCO allows the People's Republic of China to achieve the purposes and to distribute its own influence in region, not restraining interests of Central Asian states and not causing their protest (*no less than not causing the protest of Russia*). Within the limits of the given conference, there is no sense in stopping the value of SCO for the promotion of interests of the People's Republic of China in the region. Nevertheless, it is necessary to mention, the SCO is a tool by means of which China can carry out expulsion of the USA from the region, and reach parity and try to surpass Russia in participation in regional questions.

China brings essential dividends from official **refusal of intervention in internal affairs of the state.** For many Central Asian states, it serves as serious advantage when comparing of China with other possible political partners.

An important aspect of the Chinese policy in the Central Asia is the complexity of actions directed towards maintenance of interests **of power safety of the People's Republic of China.** Diversification of energy sources, and also aspiration to provide own western provinces power resources and the enterprises on their processing and the further transportation have great influence on the policy of China in the region. It is reached by the signing of contracts at a level of heads of the states, in particular, about creation of joint projects in the sphere of power. This important tool becomes **activity of the Chinese companies.**

Other group of interests of China in the Central Asia include **maintenance of its own economic interests.** It also is a priority of the Chinese diplomacy in region.

In view of essential backlog from Russia in military and cultural connections with the countries of the region and in distribution of ideas, rather 'the Chinese threat', China makes the rate on economic penetration into region as a means of achievement of its own interests.

Thus it is necessary to note that decisions of strategically important problems and also practical realisation of tasks according to China's strategy are carried out within the limits of a bilateral format, as realisation of many projects within the limits of SCO restrains interstate contradictions in the Central Asia, and also because of the presence of Russia at the organisation. So the arrangement on a construction of a gas pipeline China-Turkmenistan, passing through Turkmenistan, Uzbekistan and Kazakhstan, has been achieved at a bilaterial level. Another example is the soft loan of 900 million US dollars given by China to the countries of SCO for stimulation of the Chinese export. Concrete discussion of projects and transactions on which the credit would be allocated was carried out on a bilateral basis. Besides, financing was carried out not within the limits of SCO but by means of Inter-Bank association of SCO on a bilateral basis.

The whole given complexity of actions is directed on strengthening the position of the People's Republic of China in the region. Strong presence of China and the Chinese capital at the foreign trade balance and in strategically important sectors of economy of the countries of the region, the presence of the transport and communication infrastructure connecting the Central Asia with China create conditions which, at any state of affairs (change the country leaders, hit of the country in sphere of influence of other power), no country can ignore. Also the economic component of strategy of China concerning the Central Asia is called to limit domination of Russia in foreign economic relations of the countries of Central Asia.

As basic elements of the given policy, it is possible to allocate the following:

- **Expansion of the People's Republic of China trading contacts to the countries of region**. On the basis of results of 2006, **the share of the People's Republic of China in cumulative commodity circulation of the Central Asian countries has been 12.68 percent** (10.8 billion US dollars). Within 1992–2006, volume of trade of the countries of region with China has increased by 25.6 times. In January–September 2007, the volume of commodity circulation of China with the countries of Central Asia was about 13.5 billion US dollars.

- **Providing access to power resources of the countries of the region by means of a construction of pipeline system connecting the region with China.** Today, the countries of Central Asia are considered by China as potential suppliers of hydrocarbonic raw material. At present, their share in the Chinese import of oil and gas is insignificant. In this connection, the construction of the oil pipeline, opening access to deposits of the Caspian region (oil pipeline Kenkiyak-Kumkol), and also construction of the gas pipeline, connecting large gas deposits of Turkmenistan with China (a gas pipeline Turkmenistan-China) will allow China 'to adhere region to itself' strategically in the long term.
- **Occurrence of the People's Republic of China in strategically important sectors of economy in the countries of the region**. Today, the Chinese companies participate not only in the development of oil, gas and natural resources of the countries of the region, but also in such spheres as water-power engineering, telecommunications, transport sector, etc.
- **The Construction of transport and communication system between the region and China.** Expansion of railway and automobile highways connecting region with the western areas of China will promote further intensification of trade and economic relations between the sides. So in March 2008, the agreement between the People's Republic of China and Kazakhstan was reached on opening seven new direct autoroutes (4 cargo lines: Urumchi-Karaganda through check points Horgos, Zimunai, Baketu and Alashankou; 3 passenger highways Urumchi-Karaganda through check points Zimunai, Baketu and Alashankou). In March 2007, Kyrgyzstan signed the contract with the Chinese company on rehabilitation of motorway Osh-Sarytash-Irkeshtam. The importance of the given project is that except Kyrgyzstan, the neighbouring Uzbekistan and Tajikistan will be in a zone of influence of this corridor.
- **Rendering financial and economic help by the People's Republic of China to the countries of the region.**

As a whole it is possible to note that the foreign policy of the People's Republic of China is closely connected with the priorities of internal development because priorities of the foreign policy are considered in Beijing through a prism of internal priorities, such as necessity to support steady economic growth and internal political stability, and also association of China. In many respects, this moment defines the character of foreign policy of China, its goals and approaches.